CAMBRIDGE STUDIES IN EARLY MODERN HISTORY

Editors

J. H. ELLIOTT   H. G. KOENIGSBERGER

FRANCE AND THE ESTATES GENERAL OF 1614

CAMBRIDGE STUDIES IN EARLY MODERN HISTORY

Edited by Professor J. H. Elliott, Princeton University, and
Professor H. G. Koenigsberger, King's College, University of London

The idea of an 'early modern' period of European history from the fifteenth to the late eighteenth century is now widely accepted among historians. The purpose of the Cambridge Studies in Early Modern History is to publish monographs and studies which will illuminate the character of the period as a whole, and in particular focus attention on a dominant theme within it, the interplay of continuity and change as they are represented by the continuity of medieval ideas, political and social organization, and by the impact of new ideas, new methods and new demands on the traditional structure.

FRANCE AND THE
ESTATES GENERAL OF
1614

J. MICHAEL HAYDEN

Department of History, University of Saskatchewan

CAMBRIDGE UNIVERSITY PRESS

Published by the Syndics of the Cambridge University Press
Bentley House, 200 Euston Road, London NW1 2DB
American Branch: 32 East 57th Street, New York, N.Y. 10022

© Cambridge University Press 1974

Library of Congress Catalogue Card Number: 73–82456

ISBN: 0 521 20325 2

First published 1974

Photoset and printed in Malta by St Paul's Press Ltd

TO MY FATHER AND MOTHER

CONTENTS

ILLUSTRATIONS AND TABLES

GRAPHS

MAP

TABLES

PREFACE

In the years since I began this book many people have been both professionally and personally kind to me. I must first thank Professor Edmund Kearney who pointed me toward the subject and Professor Edward Gargan who pushed me forward. Professors Victor-Lucien Tapié and René Rémond helped me in France, as did many librarians and archivists, especially the departmental archivists. In the United States and Canada the librarians of the Cleveland Public Library, Newberry Library, the University of Detroit and the University of Saskatchewan were very helpful. Professors Paul Lietz, William Trimble, Raymond Schmandt and the late John Kemp, S.J., all then at Loyola University, Chicago, provided valuable criticism of an earlier version of the middle chapters of this book as did Orest Ranum and Lloyd Moote. A Fulbright fellowship financed the start of my work in 1960 and generous research grants from the University of Detroit and the University of Saskatchewan have helped me in the intervening years. A small part of Chapter 1 and much of Chapter 3 appeared in my article, 'Continuity in the France of Henry IV and Louis XIII: French Foreign Policy, 1598–1615', *Journal of Modern History*, XLV (1973), 1–23. My former colleagues, N. J. Gossman and Hilda Neatby, and my present colleagues I. N. Lambi, S. F. Gradish and H. C. Johnson have provided encouragement and advice. Mrs Margaret MacVean labored nobly with my impossible script through several versions and many miserable months. Mrs Mildred Mair patiently read the final typescript and checked the calculations in the appendices. Michael, Aileen and Tommy were patient throughout.

Finally there is Joan who saved my sanity and repaired my prose. Without her there would have been no book.

November 1973   J. M. H.

INTRODUCTORY NOTE

One of the problems in writing about the early seventeenth century is the orthography. Not only is the spelling different from modern usage, but it was a matter in which much freedom was exercised. In all quotations, whether in French or English, the original spelling with all its eccentricities has been maintained, except that accents have been added. In translations from the French, modern English has been used since it would be meaningless to try to reproduce seventeenth-century English. Names and terms are spelled according to the usage of present-day historians. In the footnotes and bibliography the original spelling is used, but accents have been added and where applicable v's have been changed to u's and i's to j's. This was done in accord with standard French practice.

In the absence of any accepted short-title list for French works, the long titles of some books and pamphlets have been shortened in such a way that meaning would not be lost, yet the footnotes and bibliography would not be overburdened. In all cases where there was a shortening this is noted with ellipses.

ABBREVIATIONS

A.A.E. – Archives des Affaires Etrangères
A.C. – Archives Communales
A.D. – Archives Départementales
A.Mun. – Archives Municipales
A.N. – Archives Nationales
A.S.F. – Archivo di Stato, Florence
   Arch. Med. – Archivio Medicei
   Carte Strozz. – Carte Strozziano
A.S.V. – Archivio Segreto Vaticano
   Fond. Borgh. – Fondo Borghese
   Nunz. fr. – Nunziatura di Francia
B.M. – British Museum
   Stowe MS – Stowe Manuscript
B.Mun. – Bibliothèque Municipale
B.N. – Bibliothèque Nationale
   Cinq Cents – Cinq Cents de Colbert
   Clairambault – Collection Clairambault
   Dupuy – Collection Dupuy
   Moreau – Collection Moreau
   MS fr. – Manuscrit français
   MS fr. n.a. – Manuscrit français nouvelle acquisition
   MS ital. – Manuscrit italien
Bibl. Ars. – Bibliothèque de l'Arsenal
Cal. St. P. – Calendar of State Papers, Domestic Series of the Reign of James I,
   Mary Green, ed., Vols. VIII–IX, London, 1858.
LMHIV – Lettres Missives de Henri IV, Berger de Xivery, ed., 9 vols., Paris,
   1843–1876.
Reg. délib. Paris – Registre des délibérations du Bureau de la ville de Paris, Paul
   Guérin and Jean le Grand, eds., Vols. XIV–XVI, Paris, 1921–1927.

INTRODUCTION

If history is what one remembers then the meeting of the Estates General of France in 1614 is history. To the reader with even a casual knowledge of the events of early modern Europe the date 1614 means the last meeting of an Estates General in France until 1789. But other events did occur in 1614. There were the meetings of the Addled Parliament in England, the Riksdag in Sweden and the Estates in Lorraine, Artois and Hesse. Delegates from the Estates of all the Austrian Habsburg lands except the Tyrol met at Linz to plan resistance to the growth of Habsburg central government. The discoverer Pedro Paez found the source of the Blue Nile. Sir Walter Raleigh published his *History of the World*. Rubens completed his 'Deposition from the Cross'. William Harvey was preparing his first lecture on the circulation of the blood. But it is the meeting of the Estates General in France that is remembered by historians when the year 1614 is recalled.

One reason for this memory is that the next meeting of the Estates General, which came a precise and easy-to-remember 175 years later, was so important for the history of Europe. For those interested in French history the traditionally accepted failure of the Estates General in 1614 conveniently marks the beginning of absolutism; especially since the future Cardinal Richelieu made his political debut as a deputy of the First Estate.

On a more sophisticated level 1614 plays a part in the overall pattern of French history. It lies midway between the lowest ebb of the fortunes of the French monarchy during the Hundred Years' War and its destruction during the French Revolution. The strength of the monarchy and France had increased from the end of the Hundred Years' War until the death of Henry II in 1559. Then followed the thirty years of chaos that were the Wars of Religion. The reign of Henry IV marked a revival in the fortunes of France and the monarchy. But his assassination in 1610 ushered in another period of decline that lasted until Cardinal Richelieu began to reorganize France after 1624. 1614, then, marks a secondary low point in the development of absolutism between the fifteenth and the end of the seventeenth centuries.

In the work of another group of historians 1614 is used as the terminal point in the history of the Renaissance monarchy. They see the character of the French monarchy in the fifteenth and sixteenth centuries as consultative in that, partly from conviction, partly from weakness, it continually convoked more or less representative assemblies of various types to gain the support of the people. In this view absolutism came to France only after 1614 when the kings became strong enough and ruthless enough to rule without consultation.

As a result of my own research I prefer to look at 1614 in another context.

1

After a period of growing royal power France, from the mid sixteenth century through the 1620s, was faced with civil war or the threat of civil war caused by the growth of royal power, political rivalries, religious reform and economic dislocation. During these years after the 1550s when more often than not French rulers were weak, the fortunes of the country were in the hands of a small group of professionally trained and experienced men whose main interest was to serve the crown. These men devised methods, usually not very heroic ones, to deal with continually recurring crises. Their overall aim was to preserve the monarchy until better days. Henry IV's reign and the early years of Richelieu's ascendancy were essentially part of this era. Connecting those two periods was the regency of Marie de Médicis. From 1610 until 1616, when her grip on the government began to weaken, she ruled the country with the aid of three of her late husband's most trusted advisers: Nicholas de Neufville, *seigneur* of Villeroy, the Secretary of State for Foreign Affairs; Pierre Jeannin, Controller General of Finances; and Nicholas Brûlart, *sieur* of Sillery, the Chancellor. These men found themselves, between 1610 and 1616, in the same type of situation as they had been personally involved in since the mid sixteenth century. The same men used the same policies to meet the same conditions. And they had the same success – the monarchy was preserved. Under Henry IV, after 1598, the monarchy had been in a strong position, as it would begin to be again under Richelieu near the end of the 1620s. But to the leaders of government in 1614 the years of Henry IV were exceptional. They were too good to be true. Their job in 1614 was what it had been for most of their professional lives – to hang on until better days.[1]

It is not the purpose of this book to trace the history of France from the Wars of Religion to the Thirty Years' War nor to offer a comprehensive study of the reigns of Henry IV and his widow. Not even a full history of the regency of Marie de Médicis is intended. In view of the present state of scholarship any of these tasks is far too ambitious. The purpose of this book is to study the Estates General of 1614 in the context of the policy of the Regency government to meet a continuing crisis and in itself as an expression of the desires of the groups and individuals who made up France at the beginning of the seventeenth century.

During the years 1610 to 1616 nobles conspired, Huguenots were restless,

---

[1] Two books that point in a limited way toward a similar conclusion are A. D. Lublinskaya, *Frantsiya v nachale XVII veka 1610–1620* (Leningrad, 1959) and S. Mastellone, *La Reggenza di Maria de' Medici* (Florence, 1962). Neither book, however, considers the economic and diplomatic evidence to be discussed in chapters two and three. Of distinct help from the other direction, through the perspective of the sixteenth century, are N. M. Sutherland, *The French Secretaries of State* (London, 1962) and especially Raymond Kierstead, *Pomponne de Bellièvre* (Evanston, 1968).

2

royal officials enriched themselves, Rome demanded concessions, Spain threatened France's territory but Marie de Médicis and her advisers held on. If they had openly opposed any one of these forces France would have been torn apart. If they had been less skillful in their policy of vacillation, compromise, promise and feint, France would have fallen apart. This is the context in which the Estates General of 1614 has to be seen. The Estates General was called not to reform France but as part of a complex and hidden but definable policy designed to meet a series of long-term problems that had been worsened by the assassination of Henry IV and by the minority of Louis XIII.[2]

But once an Estates General met it had a life of its own. The meeting in 1614 provided within the bonds of ritualized performance a means of expression for the diverse elements that comprised French society in the early seventeenth century. The debates of the First Estate reveal the dependence of the majority of the clergy on privilege and the drive of a small group for reform. The *cahiers* of the Second Estate express the desire of most of the nobility for the revitalization of feudalism and the realization of a few of the power of capitalism. The Third Estate continually voiced conflicting concern for local privilege and royal power. This most diverse of estates retained a loyalty to old ways, strove for absolutism and uttered many of the same grievances that their descendants would in 1789 – all at the same time.

In spite of the importance of present problems and the grievances of the deputies, tradition and ritual played a distinct role in 1614. Elections, opening and closing ceremonies and the form of the meetings were traditional and followed a pattern. Even the grievances of the deputies tended to remain the same over the years. The deputies in 1614 understood the problems of the past, not those of the future. They understood the France of Francis I and Henry II, not the France of Louis XIV. The nature of the past that influenced the Estates General of 1614 has been discussed for almost two centuries. However, the debate was blurred for a long time by a misunderstanding of the fate of the institution and by the political allegiances of those conducting the inquiry. The Estates General did not die in 1614; it was a potential governmental institution until the personal reign of Louis XIV. After 1661, though, it became identified with a period that the now dominant France wished to forget. Only Fénelon among major writers of the Age of Louis XIV favored the revival of the institution. For men like Colbert and Bossuet the Estates

---

[2] Recent interpretations of the Estates General of 1614, which differ from the one adopted in this book, include George Rothrock, 'The French Crown and the Estates General of 1614' (unpublished doctoral dissertation, University of Minnesota, 1958); Rothrock, 'The French Crown and the Estates General of 1614'. *French Historical Studies*, I (1960), 295–318; Claude Alzon, 'Quelque observations sur les Etats Généraux de 1614', *Journées Internationales Paris, 1957* (Louvain, 1959), pp. 35–42; A. D. Lublinskaya, 'Les Etats Généraux de 1614–1615 en France', *Album Helen Maude Cam* (Louvain, 1960), I, 229–245.

General was interesting only as a lesson from the past. In the mid eighteenth century the Encyclopedists devoted a few pages to the subject. But it was not until the announcement of a new meeting of the Estates General in 1788 that the interest of Frenchmen was excited once again. In 1788 and 1789 numerous works dealing with all of the Estates General but concentrating particularly on the meeting in 1614 were produced; some of these were published; others remained in manuscript. During the first half of the nineteenth century the Estates General were studied by men eager to support their political position for or against the revolution or the monarchy. Competitions established by the *Academie des Sciences morales et politiques* resulted in several books but it was only in the last quarter of the nineteenth century that the Estates General began to be studied by independent scholars not primarily interested in political justification. The lines were soon drawn between legal theorists, most connected with the *Faculté de Droit* of the University of Paris and political historians. This division has been maintained down to the present, though interest has spread beyond France and both social and institutional historians have also entered the discussion.[3]

The origins of the French Estates General have long been a subject for debate. Whether one goes back to the *Concilium Trium Galliarum* or the *Placitum Generale* of Pre-Capetian France or chooses to emphasize either the feudal duties of aid and counsel or the Roman Law theories of *Plena Potestas* and *Quod omnes tanget*; whether one finds a new departure in 1302 or chooses to say that the Estates General did not take its completed form until 1484, the fact remains that by the late fifteenth century the French kings had permitted the development of an institution that allowed the representatives

---

[3] For Colbert see B. N. Mélanges de Colbert 83 fols. 74r–106r; for Bossuet, B. N. Collection Clairambault 364; for Fénelon, Françoise Gallouedec-Genuys, 'Fénelon et les Etats', *Album Helen Maude Cam*, I, 277–290. *Encyclopédie, ou dictionnaire raisonné des sciences, des arts et des métiers* (Paris, 1751–1765), VI, 20b–27a, XIV, 143a–143b, 146b, XVI, 918a, XVII, 880b. An example of the range of interest of the scholars of 1788–1789 in what happened in 1614 can be seen from *Catalogue Raisonné des ouvrages qui parurent en 1614 et 1615 à l'occasion des Etats* (n.p., 1789). An example of unpublished material can be found in B. N. Collection Moreau 307. For the use of the Estates General as a buttress for differing political opinions see Henrion de Pansey, *Des Assemblées Nationales en France depuis l'établissement de la monarchie jusqu'en 1614* (Paris, 1829) and Augustin Thierry, ed., *Recueil des monuments inédits de l'histoire du tiers état* (Paris, 1856), III. For a further indication of the interest of both Thierry and François Guizot see *Extrait du Journal de l'instruction publique*, no. 2 (January 5, 1850). The competition established by the Academie in 1840 is described by Joseph Meyniel, *Le Président Savaron, ses théories, ses ouvrages* (Paris, 1906), pp. 32–33. At least three books published between 1843 and 1845 resulted from this competition. Auguste Boullée, *Histoire complète des Etats généraux et autres assemblées représentatives de la France depuis 1302 jusqu'en 1626*, 2 vols. (Paris, 1845); E. J. B. Rathery, *Histoire des Etats généraux de France* (Paris, 1845); Antoine C. Thibaudeau, *Histoire des Etats-généraux et des institutions représentatives en France depuis l'origine de la monarchie jusqu'à 1789*, 2 vols (Paris, 1843).

of certain groups to present their complaints to the king in return for their support of royal policy or the collection of new taxes. It is also apparent that by the late fifteenth century the French kings were worried that the Estates General might establish a claim to redress of grievances before the granting of the monarchy's wishes as was beginning to happen elsewhere in Europe. As a result the French monarchy began to substitute for it the meetings of regional or restricted assemblies to maintain occasional contact with important segments of society and to gain support for crucial decisions. A full Estates General was not called again until 1560.[4]

The next three meetings of the Estates General in 1560, 1576 and 1588 were all called in response to the chaos of the Wars of Religion. In the confusion of civil war the Estates General might have had an opportunity to develop its power if the three Estates could have agreed on a common program. They could not, and French opinion, spurred on by the actions of the illegally convoked Estates General of 1593, turned against the Estates General and in favor of the policies of the new King Henry IV. This description of what happened in the second half of the sixteenth century is incomplete. It does seem to fit the facts if the meetings are studied from the point of view of legal theory or through local records. However it ignores the royal government without which any of the Estates General could not have existed. The assemblies of the late sixteenth century need more study, but based on what is known of the men who advised the successive Valois kings and who were still in office in 1614 it can be argued that for them the calling of the Estates General was a calculated risk in the face of desperate conditions. They sought to win for the royal government both popular support and time to solve the problems connected with the Wars of Religion. These men knew that the deputies would be divided and counted on this fact. The policy worked until 1614. The unity of the three estates in that year may have contributed to the decision never to call them together again.

It is beyond question that by the end of the sixteenth century the French Estates General can best be described by its failures. The deputies had failed

---

[4] The most valuable sources for tracing the development of the Estates General are Jacques Cadart, *Le régime electoral des Etats généraux de 1789 et ses origines* (Paris, 1952); Jean-Paul Charnay, 'Naissance et développement de la vérification des pouvoirs dans les anciennes assemblées françaises', *Revue historique du droit français et étranger*, ser. 4, XL, no. 4 (1962), 556–589; XLI, no. 1 (1963), 20–56; G. Griffiths, *Representative Government in Western Europe in the Sixteenth Century* (Oxford, 1968); Ferdinand Lot and Robert Fawtier, *Histoire des institutions françaises au moyen âge*, 2 vols. (Paris, 1957–1958); Emile Lousse, *La société de l'Ancien Régime* (Louvain, 1943); J. Russell Major, *Representative Institutions in Renaissance France, 1421–1559* (Madison, 1960); Antonio Marongiu, *Medieval Parliaments: a Comparative Study*, trans. S. J. Woolf (London, 1968); François Olivier-Martin, *Histoire du droit français des origines à la révolution*, 2nd ed. (Paris, 1951); Georges Picot, *Histoire des Etats généraux considérés au point de leur influence sur le gouvernement de la France de 1355 à 1614*, 5 vols., 2nd ed. (Paris, 1888).

to obtain the right to meet regularly, to consent to taxation, or even the uncontested right to verify their own elections. Above all they had not gained the right to redress of grievances before supply. Rather they had to fight continually to get some vague answer to their grievances before dismissal by the king.

Some perspective on the situation of the Estates General of 1614 can be gained from a comparison with the other representative and parliamentary bodies in early seventeenth century Europe. To the northwest the English parliament was in the process of establishing its control over taxation and becoming a permanent fixture in the English constitution. The troubles of the monarchy, the Reformation, the size of the country, the method of representation, and the lack of competition from an institution like the *Parlement* in France were fashioning a different role for Parliament.

In the Spanish Netherlands the Estates served as a means for tax collection with power of gaining redress though it did not meet between 1600 and 1632. In the United Provinces the States General was the government. In the Duchy of Lorraine all important affairs were submitted to the Estates General for consideration. In Sweden the *Riksdag* was well on its way to becoming part of the normal machinery of the state as a result of the conscious effort of Gustavus Adolphus.

In much of the Holy Roman Empire the Estates of the individual principalities still had a definite role to play. These Estates had developed out of feudalism, the rulers' need for money, and succession crises in the fourteenth and fifteenth centuries. In so far as these problems continued, so did the role of the Estates, though the Thirty Years' War, and later wars and the influence of Louis XIV would significantly modify the situation. The *Diet* of the Holy Roman Empire was collapsing as the concept of the union of the *Kaiser* and the *Reich* lost its practical validity. The Estates of the Habsburg lands were losing their struggle with the newly vigorous central government for control of local affairs. To the East the Polish *Sejm* used its power to prevent government though it rarely used its power to further government.

Bit by bit during the late sixteenth and the seventeenth centuries the parliaments of Italy ceased to exist and by the opening of the eighteenth century of the three that remained only that of Sicily had any real power. Nevertheless as long as they did exist, and there were eight at the beginning of the seventeenth century, they met fairly frequently and played a role in financial affairs. In Spain the *Cortes* of Castile had been brought under control by Philip II though it continued to meet fairly frequently. In Aragon the *Cortes* still had financial power.

In all of this diversity two kinds of representative bodies can be distinguished, those few which had managed to win a place in government and those which through atrophy or the growing power of the rulers were disappearing after a period of relative power. At first glance it would seem that the French Estates General fits neatly into the second category. This is not so. It may share a common origin with the Estates and Diets that were disappearing, but the French kings had prevented their Estates General from ever gaining significant power over any aspect of government and had prevented any regularity of meetings and thus the possibility of ever achieving a permanent place in French life. The valid comparison is between the French provincial estates and the second group of European representative bodies. The disappearance of the French Estates General came not from the changing socio-economic life of France or from a new political theory, but as the logical result of a constant policy of the French monarchs. This policy was determined at least as early as 1484 and after that date the Estates General existed only when a group of administrators chose to use it as an instrument to handle specific problems and to preserve the monarchy between 1560 and 1614. When these adminstrators died shortly after 1614 their instrument died with them.

I

MAY 14, 1610

In the middle of the afternoon of Wednesday May 14, 1610 Henry IV sought relief from the round of official functions that had started the preceding day with the coronation of his wife Marie de Médicis and which gave no sign of ending until Sunday. He and a group of friends set out for a coach ride through the streets of Paris. But the Right Bank was crowded and their progress was slow. At about four o'clock as Henry's driver was trying to extricate himself from the heavy traffic in the rue de la Ferronnerie a figure leapt out of the crowd wielding a dagger. Henry IV was assassinated by a madman. François Ravaillac had earned his footnote in history, and France had lost its fifth king in fifty years, the third to die suddenly and violently in that time, and the second to be assassinated within twenty years.

The coach returned to the Louvre at top speed, but the occupants knew that it was already too late. They had seen far too much death to be mistaken. They also knew that Henry IV's death came at a crucial point in the history of France. The king who had ended the Wars of Religion and had restored unity and prosperity to his country had been killed on the eve of his departure for a military campaign that would have enabled France to resume the battle against Habsburg domination that it had been forced to abandon in 1559.

One of the men who had been in the coach was the Duke of Epernon, colonel general of the infantry. He immediately stationed troops in the streets to prevent the possibility of trouble as the news of the attack spread. The people of Paris who heard the rumors and saw the troops were no more prepared for Henry IV's death than their fathers or grandfathers had been when Henry II had been killed in a tournament in their city in 1559. For those with a penchant for historical parallels there were too many similarities to be found between 1559 and 1610. Henry's son Louis XIII was only eight years old and was said to be as sickly as the young Francis II had been. Once again the Queen Mother was not only a foreigner but a Medici. Once again there was the possibility of widespread civil disturbance.

Three of Henry's advisers were aware that the similarities were misleading. These three, *les Barbons*, the Greybeards, all nearly seventy, had been around in 1559 and had been active in government ever since. Nicholas Brûlart, *sieur* of Sillery, the Chancellor, Nicholas de Neufville, *seigneur* of Villeroy, Secretary of State and virtual Minister of Foreign Affairs, and

Pierre Jeannin, diplomat and jurist, immediately allied themselves with Marie de Médicis. They persuaded her to obtain the *Parlement*'s immediate confirmation of her appointment as Regent. Marie had been proclaimed temporary Regent during Henry's absence only the day before, but the *Parlement*'s official approval was needed to strengthen her position now that Henry was dead. Within three hours of the assassination this had been accomplished.

Villeroy, Sillery and Jeannin knew that Henry had left behind him a royal government that worked and that had the sincere allegiance of the majority of the people. Moreover, through the efforts of their younger colleague the Duke of Sully, this government had saved enough money to buy the loyalty of the minority that was certain to cause trouble.[1]

In 1610 France was not divided into two implacably hostile religious groups as it had been when Henry III was assassinated in 1589. The Huguenots were assured of a place in French society, and the Catholics had accepted this, if with bad grace. The nobles were not organized into three armed camps as they had been in 1559. There was only one man, the First Prince of the Blood, Henri de Bourbon, Prince of Condé, who had both the position and the inclination to threaten Marie's position as Regent and he was out of the country. Most important the people of France were in no mood to support another civil war. The thirty-five years that had followed the death of Henry II were still too real to be romantic.

Marie de Médicis had her supporters and was officially declared Regent before anyone could recover from the shock of Henry's death. By the time that Condé had returned to court in July the government had organized itself

---

[1] Maximilien de Bethune, Duke of Sully (1560–1641) joined the court of Henry of Navarre in 1571, rising in power from 1596 onwards. He resigned his post of Superintendent of finances in early 1611 though he kept a number of his lucrative offices. Nicolas de Neufville, *seigneur* of Villeroy (1543?–1617), served as a secretary of state under Charles IX, Henry III, Henry IV and Louis XIII; from 1610 to 1617 he controlled foreign affairs. Pierre Jeannin (1540–1622), formerly a member of the *Parlement* of Dijon and a supporter of the Duke of Mayenne from 1578, became one of the principal councilors of Henry IV and controller general of finances under Louis XIII. He like Sillery served as a diplomat on a number of occasions. Nicolas Brûlart, *sieur* of Sillery (1544–1624) who, like Villeroy, was descended from Parisian municipal officials who had entered royal service, began his career in the *Parlement* of Paris, remained loyal to the crown throughout the Wars of Religion, became chancellor in 1607, was disgraced in 1616, regained first place in the Council but not the Seals in 1617, regained the Seals in 1623. Villeroy's royal service began the earliest, in 1559. Several books that show these men in action are Sutherland, *The French Secretaries of State*, Kierstead, *Bellièvre*, David Buisseret, *Sully and the Growth of Centralized Government in France 1598–1610* (London, 1968); J. Nouaillac, *Villeroy, Sécretaire d'état et ministre de Charles IX, Henri III et Henri IV* (Paris, 1909); Edmund H. Dickerman, 'The King's Men: the Ministers of Henry III and Henry IV, 1574–1610' (unpublished dissertation, Brown University, 1965). Edmund H. Dickerman, *Bellièvre and Villeroy: Power in France under Henry III and Henry IV* (Providence, R. I., 1971).

9

and had taken effective measures to solidify its position. It had saved face by fulfilling Henry's commitment to send an army to the Rhine to join English, Dutch, and German troops in the capture of Cleves-Jülich. It had sought to appease the nobles through increased pensions and gifts and the people through the revocation of edicts that empowered obnoxious royal officials to check on back taxes. And it had lowered the price of salt.[2]

All this had been very difficult to accomplish in the face of the personal rivalries, struggle for influence, general chaos and confusion that characterized the months after Henry's death. Sully was one of the first victims of the situation. His hesitation in coming to court after the assassination and his haughty manner and bad temper when he arrived marked him for removal from the government, especially since he opposed the cautious policies adopted by the three advisers whose experience in government so far outdated his and who remembered all too well the days before Henry IV. Sully could not forget either the boldness of Henry's last days or his favor with that monarch. Those around him had never particularly liked him and were not loath to begin to push him aside.[3]

Sully's retirement in early 1611 did not bring an end to the internal problems of the new government. The struggle for influence continued throughout the Regency period. Alliances and counter alliances followed each other. Villeroy became the dominant member of the government. He was supported by Sillery and Jeannin even though Sillery's office as Chancellor should have made him paramount. As Concino Concini, the husband of Marie's closest friend, began to gain personal influence over her and as the great nobles continually switched sides in the background, Sillery detached himself from

---

[2] B.N. MS fr. n.a. 23369, pp. 178–179 (Antoine de Loménie to the Marquis of La Force, July 24, 1610). *Lettres patentes du roi . . . portant révocation de plusiers édicts et commissions extraordinaires . . .* (Paris, 1610), pp. 3–24. See also *Mercure François*, 1, 132a–132b, 504b–510a. The French of the early seventeenth century did not have a word to describe the king and his close advisers working as a group because they were not regarded as a single entity. Rather the king ruled with the advice, if he wished to listen, of certain men whom he had chosen. No office, not even that of Chancellor which was theoretically a lifetime position at the head of the bureaucracy, carried any guarantee of access to the king's ear. During the years 1610–1615 Marie de Médicis chose to listen to three men, and for the sake of convenience when referring to Marie and one or more of these men acting in concert the words Regency, Regency government or government will be used. These words, especially when used interchangeably, are far less loaded than words such as administration or ministry, both of which are completely foreign to the early seventeenth century. Since the three men shared no common titles, when they are referred to as a group separate from Marie they will be called advisers rather than the anachronistic 'ministers'.

[3] Abel Desjardins, *Négociations diplomatiques de la France avec la Toscane pendant le XVIe siècle* (Paris, 1886), v, 638 (Matteo Botti to Grand Duke of Tuscany, June 19, 1610). B.N. MS fr. n.a. 23369, p. 174 (Loménie to La Force, July 8, 1610).

10

the triumvirate and aligned himself with Concini, who previously had allied himself with Villeroy. This happened near the end of 1613. Villeroy managed to maintain his position until the spring of 1615 and then bit by bit had to give ground. Through it all Jeannin went about his business. Most importantly, through it all Marie de Médicis remained in control.[4]

Beyond the Louvre the Regency government had to worry especially about those groups who had the greatest potential to cause unrest, the nobles, the Huguenots and the royal officials. Each group had numerical strength, grievances and a history of disloyalty. Each had many opportunities to capitalize on the possibilities offered by a Regency period.

The group with the longest history of troublemaking during a Regency was the nobility. The excuse that they were fighting not against the minor king but in order to save him from his corrupt advisers was a firmly established part of their heritage. But in this case those who were inclined to be troublesome were too divided and disorganized to act without leadership. The solution found by the Regency government was simple, if expensive – to buy the loyalty of the great nobles. Money was available and it was used. The temptation for *les grands* to lead a rebellion was effectively diminished.

The Regency acted swiftly to forestall the threat posed by the Huguenots. The Edict of Nantes was renewed eight days after Henry's death. Continual reassurances of this renewal followed: three times in 1612, once in 1614, twice in 1615. The Huguenots were a definite threat at the time of their assembly at Saumur in 1611 but the government managed to defuse this crisis by granting some of their requests and then stalling with the rest. It was no secret that Marie de Médicis had little love for the adherents of what was officially known as *la religion prétendue réformée*. But it became clear to more and more Huguenots that they were safe enough to be able to complain about all sorts of minor matters. Their existence as such was assured.[5]

[4] For the beginning of the noble division see B.N. MS fr. n.a. 23369, pp. 176–179 (Loménie to La Force, July 18 and 24, 1610). The diplomatic correspondence between 1610 and 1615 is filled with details of the intrigues and counter intrigues in the French court. A reflection of the confusion can be found in Berthold Zeller's three books: *La minorité de Louis XIII, Marie de Médicis et Sully* (Paris, 1892); *La minorité de Louis XIII, Marie de Médicis et Villeroy* (Paris, 1897); *Louis XIII, Marie de Médicis chef du conseil* (Paris, 1898). There were too many charges and counter charges and above all too many rumors to make it feasible to discuss the situation succinctly. The contemporary who came closest to describing the overall pattern is Richelieu in *Mémoires du Cardinal de Richelieu* (Paris, 1907), I, 102–104.

[5] B.N. F 25926 (confirmations of the Edict of Nantes). A.N. K 109, no. 12 (request of Huguenots of Foix for protection); *Archives historiques de la Gironde*, X (1868), 550–551 (complaints of the Huguenots of Bordeaux). For general developments see J. Viénot, *Histoire de la Réforme française* (Paris, 1934), II, *passim*. To pacify the Catholic clergy the government allowed them to use part of their annual 'gift' to the government to buy back their alienated domains. Louis Serbat, *Les assemblées du clergé de France* (Paris, 1906), pp. 139–144; Pierre Blet, S. J., *Le clergé de France et la monarchie* (Rome, 1959), I, 137–153.

As it turned out the royal officials never were a serious problem. When the chance came in 1614 for them to take matters into their own hands, they did not. All contemporary references to Condé's followers in that year speak of *Messieurs les princes et officiers de la couronne*. But these officers are never named and no significant group of royal officials of any rank whether from the bureaucracy or the king's household openly supported Condé's revolt. When the elections for the Estates General were held, the point at which royal officials could have assured Condé's control of the Estates General, they did just the opposite. They were the men who came to Paris to give explicit support to the policies of the Regency government.

The loyalty of these bureaucrats is partly explained by the effectiveness of the *paulette*. Devised by Sully in 1604 as a means of producing revenue and renewed in 1612, the *paulette* had another dimension, one that does not seem to have been thought of by its inventor.[6] By insuring, for a yearly payment, the right of passing an office on to one's heirs, the *droit annuel* freed office holders from the influence of the nobility who in the past had been the procurers of offices for their clients. Thus the potential for disloyalty was reduced.

There was another means available to keep the royal officials in line. The Regency government began its career by abolishing a whole series of new offices and instituting official investigations of tax evasion in an effort to gain popular support. Henry IV had done this in the past for the same reason. It was a way of counterbalancing popular discontent with taxes.[7] In both cases before long the discontinued offices were recreated to raise money.[8] The temptation is to dismiss this as simply typical of the Old Regime. To some extent this is true. On the other hand from the point of view of the office-holder a tremendous insecurity was created. The office-holder, now free of the influence of the nobles, had to depend on the king not to abolish his office or to create so many similar ones that the monetary value and prestige of his office became negligible. Conspicuous loyalty to the government was one means of staving off this disaster.

---

[6] Despite J. R. Major, 'Henry IV and Guyenne: A Study concerning the Origin of Royal Absolutism', *French Historical Studies* IV (1966), 363–383, the preponderance of evidence still indicates that revenue was the major purpose of the *paulette* for Sully, not an attempt to win control over the bureaucracy. See Roland Mousnier, *La Vénalité des offices sous Henri IV et Louis XIII* (Rouen, n.d.), pp. 560–566; A. D. Lublinskaya, *French Absolutism: the Crucial Phase, 1620–1629*, trans. B. Pierce (Cambridge, 1968), pp. 234–236; Buisseret, *Sully*, pp. 72–73.

[7] Compare *Mercure François*, I, 359b–360a with *ibid.*, 505b–509a.

[8] Any number of examples could be cited beyond those listed in E. Maugis, *Histoire du Parlement de Paris* (Paris, 1916), II, 266–269. For example, *Edict du Roy pour la levée des droicts d'entrée modérez* (Paris, 1597); *Lettres patentes du Roy . . . pour la révente en heredité de tous les offices de commissaires à faire les rooles des tailles . . .* (Paris, 1631); *Déclaration du roy sur l'édict de création & restablissement des officiers de finance triannaux* (n.p., 1616). The *Mercure François* reports many occurrences too, for example, I, 362a–362b.

12

All this seems a very uncertain way of governing, but it was the best that could be done with an uncertain system. It was all that anyone had ever been able to do. France was too vast and too bound by past privilege and abuse for anything short of revolution to bring fundamental change.[9] But beyond the myriad of local officials with conflicting loyalties, beyond the self-important lieutenants-general striving toward noble rank and the complacent noble *baillis* and seneschals, beyond the pension-collecting nonentities who were the royal governors, there came the bureaucrats in Paris. Paris was full of time-servers, but at the core of the government there was an efficient group of old-line, well trained bureaucrats.

General lines of policy were handled on an informal basis by Marie de Médicis through discussion with Villeroy, Jeannin and Sillery in the *Conseil des affaires*. The legend of a secret council composed of Concini, his wife Leonora Galigai, the papal nuncio Cardinal Ubaldini, the Spanish ambassador Inigo de Cardenas, the Jesuit royal confessor Pierre Coton, Villeroy, Jeannin, Sillery and his son Pierre Brûlart, Isaac Arnauld and Louis Dolé seems to have originated with Sully. He describes this council in the part of his memoirs relating to 1610 when he was being pushed out of the government and was reacting angrily. No other contemporary sources mention this council and there is not only no evidence that it ever existed; there is, in the cases of Ubaldini and Cardenas, proof that they were not part of such a council.[10]

Villeroy concentrated on foreign affairs assisted by Sillery's son Pierre Brûlart, viscount of Puisieux, who had the right of succession to Villeroy's position as Secretary of State. Antoine de Lomenie, count of Brienne, Louis Potier, *seigneur* of Gesvres and Paul Phelypeaux, *seigneur* of Pontchartrain, the other secretaries of State, handled internal affairs though Villeroy sometimes interested himself in these as well. Jeannin was assisted in the management of financial matters by Arnauld, Dolé and Giles de Maupeou. These men, with the exception of Dolé, either had long experience in government or came from families long connected with royal service. The individual influence of Villeroy's and Jeannin's assistants is difficult to determine but the work of another group, those who assisted Sillery in the *Conseil d'Etat et des Finances* and in the *Conseil privé* is more apparent. There were all sorts of people who were theoretically members of either the first council which was in charge of general administration of the kingdom or the second which handled special

---

[9] Examples of the imperfections of the system can be found in the records of the *Parlement*, for example A.N. Xla 8647, fols. 508v–510r; Xla 8648, fols. 13r–14r, 144v–145v, 151r–152r, 167v–169v. These citations concern only exceptions to the reform of waters and forests granted in the years 1613–1615; examples regarding taxation, naturalization, etc., could also be cited.

[10] Sully, *Economies Royales* in Michaud and Poujoulat (eds.), *Nouvelle Collection des Mémoires* (Paris, 1854), XVII, 386. For Ubaldini and Cardenas see Chapter 3 below.

13

appeals, but most never or rarely showed up to perform their duties.[11] Among those who did there was a small group who were consistently present; about ten for each council. A smaller group was almost always present at the meetings of both. In 1614–1615 this select group was made up of five men: Jean de Thumery, Louis Lefebvre, Jean Bochart, Michel de Marillac and Merry de Vic. These men could be called the core of the second rank of the administrative bureaucracy. Like Villeroy, Jeannin and Sillery they had served the royal government for a long time and like them they served as a bridge between the France of Henry II and the France of Richelieu.[12]

The judicial system was headed by the coherently organized *Parlement* of Paris. Despite its quirks and its passions it got its work done. There were all sorts of ways in which conflict could arise between the king and his council on the one hand and the *Parlement* of Paris on the other. But usually it did not. It was news when there were difficulties. There was no real way in which the *Parlement* of Paris could lead the other *Parlements* of France. But usually it did. Marie added to this harmony between the Crown and the *Parlement* of Paris and between the *Parlement* of Paris and the other *Parlements* whenever she could. But she showed firmness often enough to keep the members of the *Parlements* under control. The policy of Henry IV was continued, a policy of healthy respect and overall direction.[13]

---

[11] The best sources for the royal council are R. Mousnier, 'Le conseil du roi de la mort de Henri IV au gouvernement personnel de Louis XIV', *Etudes publiés par la Société d'histoire moderne* I (1947), 29–67 (republished in Mousnier, *La Plume, la faucille et le marteau* (Paris, 1970), pp. 141–178) and R. Mousnier 'Les règlements du conseil du roi sous Louis XIII', *Annuaire-Bulletin de la Société de l'histoire de France* (1946), pp. 92–211. Some background material can be gained from R. Mousnier *et al.*, *Le conseil du roi de Louis XII à la Révolution* (Paris, 1970). See also Georges Pagès, *Les institutions monarchiques sous Louis XIII et Louis XIV* (Paris, 1933).

[12] The names of the men most active in the royal council were established through the records of the *Conseil d'Etat* and *Conseil privé* in A. N. Series E and V6. The careers of the five men who, in addition to Sillery, regularly attended both councils in 1614–1615, illustrate the comments made above. *Jean de Thumery, sieur* of Boissise (1549–1625), councilor in the *Parlement* of Paris (1573), ambassador to England (1598–1602), to Germany (1609), involved in negotiation with Condé in 1614 and ambassador to Holland (161?); *Louis Lefebvre, sieur* of Caumartin and of Boissy-en-Brie (died 1623), councilor in the *Parlement* of Paris (1579), master of requests (1585), president of the Grand Council, ambassador to Switzerland (1605–1607), guardian of the Seals (1622–1623); *Jean Bochart, seigneur* of Champigny (died 1630), son of a councilor of State, master of requests (1585–1607), ambassador to Venice under Henry IV, intendant of justice in Poitou, controller-general of finances, superintendent of finances (1624–1626), First President of the *Parlement* of Paris (1628–1630); *Michel de Marillac, sieur* of Fayet (1563–1632), councilor in *Parlement* (1586), master of requests (1595), superintendent of finances (1624–1626), Guardian of the Seals (1626–1630); *Merry de Vic, sieur* of Ermenonville (died 1622), councilor in the *Parlement* of Paris, master of requests, ambassador to Switzerland, intendant of justice in Guyenne, Guardian of the Seals (1621–1622).

[13] Maugis, *Parlement*, II, 266.

Strangely enough, despite all the legends, the financial system worked. Jeannin gave a clear description of the system to the Estates General in 1614, though the figures he used as illustrations did not correspond with those of any single year.[14] The problem was not the system itself but the fact that most of the money raised by indirect taxation was already committed before it was ever collected. Again past abuse intruded. Collection expenses, the costs of local government, the payments to various individuals as interest on loans or as bribes for their support were all deducted by local officials from the taxes collected. All of this left the government with little room to maneuver.[15]

Not only was tax revenue difficult to find but Sully had saved at the most only fifteen million *livres* and a substantial part of that sum had to be spent for coronation, burial and war expenses in May and June 1610. More went for the first bribes given to the nobles. France also owed a substantial sum to foreign countries. If France were to continue to survive more had to be found without enraging the taxpayers. And then there was the rest of Europe. France's neighbors could be counted on to try to capitalize on her potential weakness during a Regency. Legend has it that the French government was weak during the Regency of Marie de Médicis and that France capitulated to its age-old enemies. Yet there was no invasion. France lost no territories, no rights, no prestige. There was no declaration of bankruptcy. As a matter of fact life went on as usual.

There are many legends connected with the Regency. For three hundred years it had been said that Marie de Médicis herself was a fat, brainless, priest-ridden Italian harridan, descended from money-lenders, under the influence of a sorceress, Leonora Galigai, and her husband the effeminate, ruthless, greedy Concino Concini. It is no wonder (in this view) that the stalwart, dashing, independent-minded Frenchman, Henry IV, had no use for her while he lived and that after his death, in which she may have been implicated, France was almost destroyed by her.

If Henry IV had not been assassinated, if Marie de Médicis had had better propagandists, if her reputation had not been in the hands of the French, the traditional picture might have been different: Marie de Médicis, a handsome woman descended from a long line of Emperors, Kings of Spain, Dukes of Burgundy and Renaissance Princes, was sold to an unprincipled, rapacious adventurer who cruelly mistreated her and abandoned her time after time for low-born mistresses, despite the fact that she bore him the children he desperately needed both to secure the throne for his family and to form alliances with the more established houses of Europe.

---

[14] *Traicté du revenu et despense des Finances* in Florimond Rapine, *Recueil très-exact et curieux ... assemblées des Estats ... 1614 ...* (Paris, 1651), pp. 525–550.

[15] A graphic example of the percentage of tax income already tied up can be found in Sully's own files: A.N. 120 AP 28, fols. 57r–126r.

15

The truth lies somewhere in between the two extreme statements. The purpose of what follows is to cut through some of the myths that have grown up around the reigns of Henry IV and Marie de Médicis to illustrate that there was no sharp break in French history in 1610. This is necessary so that the Estates General of 1614 can be seen in its proper context. The financial and foreign policies of the two rulers will be the center of attention for three reasons: the Regency has been criticized most in those areas, the Estates General was vitally concerned with these two issues, and finally these were the major concerns of the French government during the period.

There is much evidence that could be used to make the Regency of Marie de Médicis the turning point in French history. A singular number of influential people died during the years 1610 to 1617 opening the way for a new generation. There were changes in literature wrought by Malherbe, Voiture and Balzac which prepared the way for classicism. There were changes in the genre of ballet and set design which heralded the Baroque. Mores and morality were altered by religious reform, the revival of skepticism, the development of the Parisian salons, and the publication of L'Astrée and brought corresponding changes in social consciousness.

It would be easy to single out 1614 as the key year in all the change. After all, five hundred important men from throughout the whole of France had a chance to participate in the political and cultural life of the capital, get a close look at the royal government, and discover the views of other classes and other regions, most for the first and only time in their lives. But this would be playing games. The same sort of game that Richelieu played in his *Mémoires* when he tried to make 1616, the year he first held a government post, seem far more important than it was. Just as Richelieu's foreboding introduction to the year 1616 has helped to obscure the basic similarity of his policies to those of his immediate predecessors so isolation of the Regency of Marie de Médicis hides its basic continuity with the reign of Henry IV.

2
FRENCH FINANCIAL POLICY
1600–1615

The area in which the Regency government has been most heavily criticized and about which the deputies of the Estates General of 1614 asked the most persistent questions is that of financial policy. In order to understand this policy it is necessary to consider the general economic and political conditions of the first third of the seventeenth century.

The great nobles were the major source of potential trouble for the Regency government. The same noble leaders or their now grown up sons who had caused so much havoc from the 1560s through the reign of Henry IV were ready to seize the new opportunity created by the assassination. The problem facing the Regency, then, was to keep the great nobles happy and to lessen their influence over other groups in society who could cause serious unrest. As Henry IV had found, only gifts, preferment, or threats could control *les grands*. Such means cost money, thus money was the overriding internal concern of the government. At the same time the government found it expedient to lower a number of taxes in order to please the mass of the people. It was necessary to increase expenditures at a time when traditional revenues were decreasing.[1]

The methods used to collect money were similar to those Sully had used in the first decade of the century, squeezing every possible *sou* from the collecting of indirect taxes and from extraordinary sources of government income. There were no radical programs, no radical changes. Villeroy, Jeannin, and Sillery did for Marie what they had done for the last Valois and the first Bourbon. If Sully had forgotten what it was like before 1605 they had not.

Jeannin explained the difficulties the Regency faced when he addressed the deputies of the Estates General in December 1614:

---

[1] There was much free advice available about the state of affairs in France and what should be done. Two examples are [Nicolas Pasquier] *Remonstrances à la Royne mère* ... (Paris, 1610), especially pp. 14–18, 23–29, 52–58 and Charles Bernard, *Discours sur l'Estat des Finances du Roy* (Paris, 1614), esp. pp. 33–90. For general background of many issues discussed in this chapter see Martin Wolfe, *The Fiscal System of Renaissance France* (New Haven, 1972).

If the critics had more thoroughly considered the reasons which led the Queen to pay more attention to the dispositions and whims of those who could help keep the peace and prevent the disturbances which could come to the kingdom than to the purse and finances, they would understand that the evil which comes from the loss of money can be repaired. On the contrary, war and disturbances among us, which come only too often during minorities, not only cost a great deal and are not capable of being regulated but are ordinarily followed by such dangerous situations that the authority of the king and the grandeur of the kingdom remain weakened forever.[2]

Sillery put it more succinctly in his address to the same body in October, 1614. The Queen spent money 'par bon mesnage polier et obliger plusiers à le devoir'. He went on to claim that Marie de Médicis had brought 'peace, justice and abundance which are the certain marks of a happy and well governed state'.[3]

Villeroy said that a king will be more praised if he spills money rather than the blood of his relatives and principal officers. He added that any group which might cause trouble had to be kept under observation. 'Negligence and slackness had been the cause of Henry III's doom; the vigilance of Henry IV was the reason for his preservation.'[4]

No one doubts that the Regency government spent a great deal of money. All the critics from Sully to the present have made this point. The only questions are how much and how well. 'How much' can be answered by a comparative study of royal tax collection and expenditure during the Regency and the preceding and following years. Any attempt to be accurate is impossible because the records are incomplete and because the men involved, including Sully, simply were not interested in exact accounting.[5] The effect of this attitude, which was only to change with Colbert, was emphasized by the archaic number system built upon twenty as a base instead of ten and expressed in semi-Roman style. It was difficult not to make an error. The final complication was that at various times all the men involved felt called upon to make themselves look good. These justifications have attracted more attention than any of the other records and the period has been judged by them. Since Sully was

---

[2] B. N. MS fr. n.a. 7262, fols. 113r–113v.
[3] A. A. E. France 769, fol. 211r.
[4] 'Advis de Monsieur de Villeroy donné à la Royne en 1611' in Mastelleone, La Reggenza, pp. 229–234.
[5] For an example of the haphazard way Sully dealt with figures see A.N. 120 AP 28, fols. 45r–46v.

the most famous adviser of Henry IV he must have been more or less right even though he exaggerated. Since Jeannin was connected with the Regency any errors or vagueness in his accounts must have been the result of his attempt to cover up evil. In fact both men cooked the books to cover up bad years, Sully especially in 1610, Jeannin in 1611 and 1616.[6]

In such a situation the only thing to do is to try to correlate every scrap of information that can be found. If this is done it will be found that the figures for governmental income and expense gathered by Roland Mallet from the now destroyed records of the *Chambre des Comptes* are basically accurate, though there are some distinct misprints and occasional miscalculations. These figures can be used for long-term comparisons with some readjustment of method.[7]

Graph 1 indicates that revenue from direct taxation (*recettes générales*) fell from 1606 to 1611, rose until 1616, then basically declined through 1627, after which it began to rise again. Sully made up for the decline with a strong increase in *gabelle* revenue, whether by tax increase or by better administration. The *gabelles* remained the prop of royal finances until 1619 when revenue from it became particularly erratic and began to drop off. At this point other indirect taxes were used to take up the slack but the income from the selling of offices and the *paulette* or annual office tax, which had really benefited its creator Sully only in 1608, became the great producer of revenue.[8] There was a rise in the income from all indirect taxes taken together from 1601 to 1610 with temporary declines every three years. Between 1610 and 1615 there was a general rise. Between 1616 and 1630 the pattern of indirect tax revenue was confused.

[6] Sully, *Economies Royales*, XVII, 375–378; Jeannin to the Estates General in B.N. M.S. fr. n.a. 7262, fols. 108r–114r. By comparison Jeannin falsified less than Sully: Jeannin elided; Sully greatly exaggerated.

[7] Jean Mallet, *Comptes rendues de l'administration de finances* ... (London and Paris, 1789), pp. 184–203, 206–211, 218–223. The major sources used to check Mallet were A.N. 120 AP 28, Sully's records, often in his hand, for 1610–1611; A.A.E. France 768–770 which include what are evidently official statements of income and expense of the government for the years 1611–1616; B.N. Dupuy 824–827, expense records of the Treasury 1611–1615. It must be noted that despite his statement to the contrary, Buisseret at times uses different figures from Mallet's for 1600–1610, especially in his record of expenses. See Buisseret, *Sully*, pp. 74–81. Sometimes this is the result of error; sometimes he used the sums taken from Sully's papers. An example of what must be a misprint in Mallet is his figure for the *recettes générales* in the *généralité* of Amiens for 1614 (p. 200). The figure given in A.A.E. France 769, fol. 306r fits much better. The figures used in what follows are set out in Appendix 1. The categories listed there are different from those in both Mallet and Buisseret and have been chosen to illustrate significant changes.

[8] Mousnier compares the ratio of the revenues from *parties casuelles* to total income for the years 1600–1643 but makes a series of transcription errors which distort the pattern, *Venalité*, pp. 391–392.

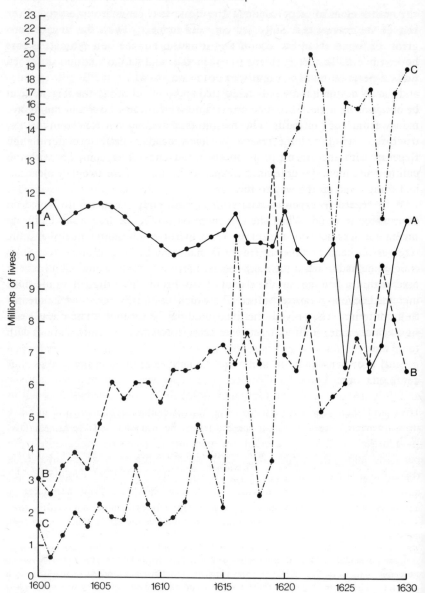

Graph 1. Ordinary royal income 1600–1630. A, Recettes générales. B, Total of indirect taxes. C, Parties casuelles.

Another element of governmental revenue that must be considered is the fate of the money that Sully had on hand in 1610. There has always been great confusion about the size of this treasure, but the best estimate is that he had five million *livres* stored in the Bastille and had in addition about ten million *livres* on hand. A vague idea of the way in which the Bastille treasure and the money on hand was accumulated and its fate during the Regency can be obtained by noting the trend of extraordinary income.[9] Sully began to save money from 1605 onwards. The Bastille treasure was not touched until the troubles of 1614, but the reserve on hand steadily diminished during the Regency with the biggest drops in 1611 and 1615. This coincides with the political situation. Trouble meant expense. Between these two dates Jeannin had things well on the way to recovery.

With regard to expenses it is evident from Graph 2 that Sully saved on everything he could. When the campaign on the Rhine that Sully had been saving for was actually fought in 1610 expenses rose dramatically and the reserves on hand dropped. If Henry IV had launched the full scale war Sully claimed he had in mind the reserves and Bastille treasure would all have been used within a few months. The debt of the French government would have increased beyond measure. Sully could save money only when he kept expenses to a minimum. The only alternative would have been to increase direct taxes significantly since indirect taxes were already being raised. Sully did not dare to do this.

Sully's own account of the extraordinary expenses for war shows that 3,524,924 *livres* beyond his projected estimate was spent between January and July 1610.[10] After the campaign at Jülich in 1610 war expenses fell in 1611 and then rose through 1617 as the internal threat from the nobility was thwarted. The next jump came during the wars against the Huguenots. In addition to the war account the two other categories of expense were pensions and gifts, which never declined for more than a year at a time throughout the period 1600–1630, and the royal household. Comparing the amounts spent by Marie de Médicis on her household and those spent later by Louis XIII's wife, it is obvious that a queen was expensive, something that

---

[9] See Appendix 1 Table III. Buisseret, *Sully*, p. 77, A.A.E. France 768, fols. 188r–235r; 769, fols. 94r, 315r; 770, fols. 79r, 208r. Mallet, *Comptes rendues*, pp. 191, 194–195, 209, 218–223. The figures for extraordinary income and expense and therefore for total income and total expense are very misleading because of the accounting system used. Sums in hand and paid to the Bastille were included on both sides of the budget under extraordinary income and expenses. Also all sorts of tricks were used to make total expense less than total income. It is much better to consider only ordinary income and expense.

[10] A.N. 120 AP 28, fols. 43r–43v.

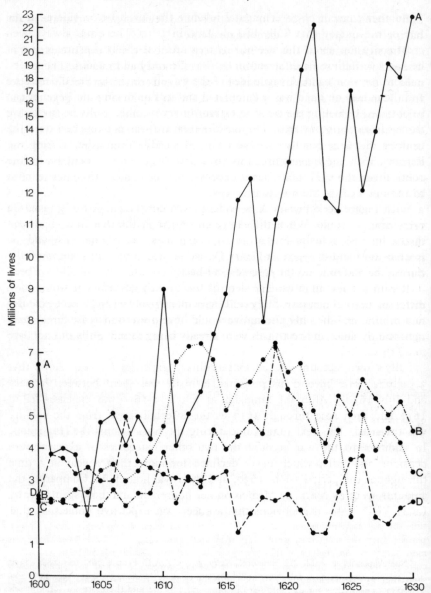

Graph 2. Ordinary royal expenses 1600–1630. A, War. B. Household. C, Pensions and Gifts. D, Other (see Appendix 1, Table II, note C).

Sully found out in 1606. On the other hand Jeannin was fortunate in not having to pay Henry IV's gambling expenses.[11]

The significance of this general pattern of income and expense cannot be assessed without some information on prices, money and salaries. There is no need to get involved in questions of secular trends or the shorter-term cycles from Kondratieff's to those of Kitchen.[12] The only question is the year-to-year price changes during the period under consideration in this chapter. Because of the peculiar nature of the economic situation in France in the late sixteenth century the price graphs have been pushed back to 1590 even though consistent data on governmental income and revenue is not available before 1600. From the viewpoint of economic history the choice of the period 1600 to 1615 or 1590 to 1630 is an arbitrary one. To discuss cycles or secular trends a much longer period would have to be considered. The question of causes of price changes is complex and there is no agreed answer. There is no need to discuss this here. In effect the only question which is relevant to this study is what were wages, prices and taxes like during the period which people alive during the Regency would remember clearly.

Recent studies, all of which pass quickly over the early seventeenth century, differ in their conclusions. There is agreement that Europe as a whole was nearing the end of a long inflationary period and was on the brink of a long deflationary one. Beyond this there are disagreements, though there is definite

---

[11] Marie used some of the money allotted for her personal use for gifts and pensions to maintain loyalties. These gifts averaged about forty-one a year, ranging from the fifty-four given in 1612 to the thirty given in 1614. Most of the recipients were government officials or members of the lower nobility. B.N. Cinq Cents 91, fols. 1r–146r; 92, fols. 1r–215r. There is no doubt though, that Marie arranged for a lot of money to be spent on herself. See for example the inventory of her jewels in A.A.E. France 769, fols. 66r–83r (the inventory includes five jewels won by Henry IV while gambling). See also Louis Battifol, *Marie de Médicis and Her Court*, trans. Mary King (London, 1908), pp. 256–260, 291–294. To balance this unfavorable account, an analysis of the information in E. Griselle, *Etat de la maison du roi Louis XIII de celle de sa mère, Marie de Médicis* (Paris, 1912), pp. 57–88, shows that the years in which Marie spent the most on her retinue were 1601–1605 and 1626–1630 – at the time she was establishing her household and at the end when she no longer cared. The two periods when she spent least were 1611–1615 and 1616–1620 – the times when saving was most necessary. An analysis of the varying number of household officials of Louis XIII shows correspondingly that there was a distinct reduction between 1611 and 1615, and then a slow climb to 1620, followed by a reduction in 1621–24, then a continuing climb. *Ibid*, pp. 1–48.

[12] For an idea of the secular trends and cycles intersecting in this period see F. P. Braudel and F. Spooner, 'Princes in Europe from 1450 to 1750', *Cambridge Economic History*, IV, ed. E. E. Rich and C. H. Wilson (Cambridge, 1967), 378–486; René Baehrel, *Une croissance: La Basse Provence rurale* (Paris, 1961), p. 573; Pierre Goubert, *Beauvais et le Beauvaisis de 1600 à 1730* (Paris, 1958), p. 386, Michel Morineau, 'D'Amsterdam à Séville: de quelle réalité l'histoire des prix est-elle le miroir', *Annales*, XXIII (1968), 178–205; Denis Richet, 'Croissance et blocages en France du XVe au XVIIIe siècle', *Ibid.*, XXIII (1968), 759–787.

support for the thesis that money was declining in real value though not as quickly as it was soon to do or had done in the past. Some support can also be found for the theory that prices and wages in France held fairly steady during the period 1600 to 1620. The weather seems to have been fairly propitious despite the fact that the world was on the brink of a 'little ice age'[13].

The basic problem in making an accurate assessment of conditions is that existing studies are based on either the analysis of secular trends, cycles or ten-year averages of a large area of Europe or year-by-year graphs of one or more commodities in one market. The graph used here unites a large amount of year-by-year data for a number of commodities from markets throughout France. This method does smooth out temporary local problems and ignores areas from which price data are not available. Thus, for example, the problems of the farmers of the Auvergne are not taken into account. Nevertheless, a fairly clear picture of France as a whole during the years 1590 to 1630 can be sketched. Until now emphasis has been placed on the long-term European inflation through the sixteenth century until about 1630–1650. Graph 3, however, shows that for the short time that Henry IV and Marie de Médicis ruled France there was actually a lull in inflation in France.[14]

The raw material for the analysis of prices is given in Appendix 2. In preparing the appendix all prices were converted to *livres tournois* and decimal fractions of *livres*, and all measures were converted to the Paris measures (in the case of wine and oil the measures of Béziers were used). In the case of each individual commodity the numbers in the appendix represent a real sum (so many *livres* per *setier*, *muid*, etc.). In the case of averages of more than one commodity the numbers are fictitious, representing magnitude only, since

[13] Pierre Deyon, *Amiens, capitale provinciale* (Paris, 1967), pp. 46, 170; Frank Spooner, *L'Economie mondiale et les frappes monetaires en France, 1493–1680* (Paris, 1956), pp. 110, 295; Gaston Roupnel, *La ville et la campagne au XVIIe siècle* (Paris, 1955), p. 4; E. Le Roy Ladurie, *Les paysans de Languedoc* (Paris, 1966), I, 404, 419–428, 431–452, 469, 474–475; Goubert, *Beauvais*, pp. 459–460; Baehrel, *Croissance*, p. 515; E. Le Roy Ladurie, *Histoire du climat depuis l'an mil* (Paris, 1967), pp. 48–55, 210–211.

[14] It is tempting to try to apply this method beyond France but the difficulties caused by differing currencies, weights and measures, not all of which have been calibrated, and the varying rates of deflation during this period make the project too difficult for the limited results that can be obtained, especially since the necessary discussion of the economic and social life of these other countries lies outside the scope of this book. Preliminary investigation shows that Spanish grain prices, wheat prices in Leyden and Utrecht and rye prices in Amsterdam contradict each other in trends and do not consistently follow the French price variations after the 1602 low. Earl Hamilton, *American Treasure and the Price Revolution in Spain, 1501–1650* (Cambridge, Mass., 1934), pp. 391–392; N. W. Posthumus, *Inquiry into the History of Prices in Holland* (Leiden, 1946, 1964), I, 573, II, 247–248, 451–453. For England see Jean Meuvret, 'Les oscillations des prix des céréales aux XVIIe et XVIIIe siècles en Angleterre et dans les pays du Bassin Parisien', *Revue d'histoire moderne et contemporaine*, XVI (1969), 540–554.

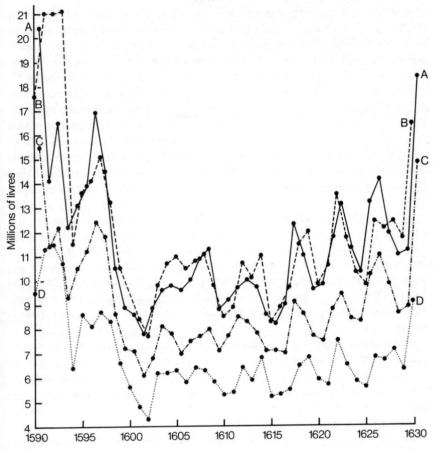

Graph 3. Prices 1590–1630. A, Wheat, année récolte. B, Wheat, année civile. C, Wheat-oats, année récolte. D, Average of all prices, année civile.

different types of measures are combined. The resulting curves are so definite in their direction that some certainty can be obtained, especially since the basic Paris–Aix–Toulouse triangle used gives prices from three separate geographical and climatic regions.

The year 1602 marked the end of a long downward slide in prices. From 1603 to 1617 prices in France were basically stable, then through 1630 the trend was upwards, with progressively greater fluctuations in the characteristic M pattern. The lowest points after 1601–1602 were 1610–1611 and 1615–1616; the next lowest were 1606, 1620–1621 and 1624–1625. The same pattern of four-to-five-year intervals results if the price averages of wheat,

25

rye, oats and wine, or barley, oil and millet are placed on a graph. The basic pattern is reinforced by the *année récolte* averages, though those tend to emphasize falling prices during the Regency.

If the average of all prices for the six-year periods 1605–1610, 1610–1615, and 1615–1620 are compared (5.95, 5.82, 5.88) they are found to be stable, with the level of the Regency prices slightly lower. The price average for the period 1600–1605 (5.55) was the lowest. These averages appear particularly favorable for the consumer when compared with those of the periods on either side (1595–1600: 7.73; 1590–1595: 9.67; 1620–1625: 6.14; 1625–1630: 7.02). If the average of all prices for the whole Regency period, 1610–1617 (5.72) is compared with that of the reign of Henry IV from 1595 onward (6.48), the more favorable economic conditions of the Regency are even more evident.[15]

The differences between the high average and low average of all prices between 1610 and 1617 was only 1.53, whereas between 1590 and 1610 the difference was 7.20. For the period 1617 to 1630 the difference was 3.40. If the average of all prices from 1603 to 1605 (6.20) is used as the mean then the greatest variation up or down between 1610 and 1617 was only 17% and that was downward. The greatest upward swing was only 9%. Comparison of wheat prices, perhaps the single most important commodity, shows similar results.

There are two more variables that have to be added to the equation – salaries and tax rates. The material available for an analysis of salaries is meager. The conclusion that can be drawn from what is known is that French workers were more or less holding their own during the Regency period. This conclusion is reinforced by the fact that in France the real value of money remained basically stable during this period.[16]

No one has ever attempted to make a detailed study of the variations in the rate of taxation in France as distinguished from the variations in the actual amount of tax revenue. Those who have done the most thorough work to date on the national and provincial levels have found indications that there was a slight readjustment downward in the rate of the *taille* during the time of Sully and the reverse during the Regency. The number and rates of indirect taxes are said to have distinctly increased during Sully's time. During the Regency

[15] The use of the Spearman correlation test confirms the above statements concerning the average of all prices (1600–1610 $r_s = 0.29$; 1610–1617 $r_s = -0.10$; 1617–1630 $r_s = 0.44$).

[16] For salaries see Baehrel, *Croissance*, pp. 604–606; Ladurie, *Paysans*, I, 470–471, II, 1008–1019; Deyon, *Amiens*, p. 516. Beatrice Veyrassat-Herren and E. Le Roy Ladurie, 'La rente foncière autour de Paris au XVIIᵉ siècle', *Annales*, XXIII (1968), 541–555; Richet, 'Croissance et blocages', pp. 766–768. Micheline Baulant, 'Le salaire des ouvriers du batiment à Paris de 1400 à 1726', *Annales* XXVI (1971), 463–483. For money value see M. Baulant and J. Meuvret, *Prix des céréales extraits de la mercuriale de Paris, 1520–1698* (Paris, 1962), I, 249.

the rates and number were decreased, though the income from these taxes continued to rise. The really severe increases did not come, though, until the time of Richelieu.[17] All this seems to be confirmed by Graph I but the lines on the graph are there for both other and more reasons than have been discovered until now.

Graph I indicates that direct tax revenue fell from 1606 to 1611, then rose through 1616, though never to the 1601, 1604–1606 levels. These levels would not be reached again until 1633. From 1617 through 1627 direct tax revenue declined in a progressively erratic fashion, perhaps connected with the wider swings in the cost of living illustrated in Graph 3. This erratic characteristic also becomes increasingly apparent in revenue from indirect taxes after 1615. Despite this, indirect tax returns continued to rise until 1619 with the exception of the *gabelle*. However, this rise less and less made up for the decline in direct tax revenue.

The predicament of the governments becomes more apparent when total revenue is considered. This revenue increased from sixteen to thirty-seven million *livres*, more than 100%, between 1600 and 1630. However, if revenue from the sale of offices, taxes on those offices and extraordinary income are excluded and only regular direct and indirect taxes are considered, the rise in revenue, from fourteen to eighteen million *livres*, is just under 30%. This parallels the rise in prices from the 1600–1604 average of 5.42 to the 1626–1630 average of 7.31, a 35% increase. But ordinary expenses alone rose by 140%, because of foreign and domestic war. The governments were not able to increase their regular revenues enough to meet even the rise in the cost of living, let alone war expenses. A progressively greater share of government revenue had to come from extraordinary sources.

To understand completely what was happening definite information on taxation rates would be necessary. The tax records that remain indicate only how much the governments managed to collect, not how much they hoped or planned to collect.[18] However, if what is known is combined with the information illustrated in Graph 4 a clearer picture emerges.

To gain support for Henry IV, Sully decreased the rate of the major direct tax, the *taille*, and either increased the more easily disguised indirect taxes or collected them more efficiently,[19] a process aided by the lower cost of living.

---

[17] For taxation rate see Buisseret, *Sully*, pp. 76–78; J. J. Clamageran, *Histoire de l'impôt en France* (Paris, 1867–1876), II, 360–363, 380–391, 404–413; Ladurie, *Paysans*, I, 481–485, II, 942. See also Isambert, *Recueil*, XV, 226–228 (edict of March 1600 on *tailles*) and XVI, 47–51 (edict of June 1614 on *tailles*); *Mercure françois* II, 132a–132b; *Arrest du conseil d'estat . . . tailles* (Paris, 1613).

[18] For the years 1610–1611 we have Sully's figures for the amount of direct and indirect taxes the government failed to collect. See A.N. 120 A.P. 28, fols. 49r–55v.

[19] Buisseret, *Sully*, pp. 76–78.

27

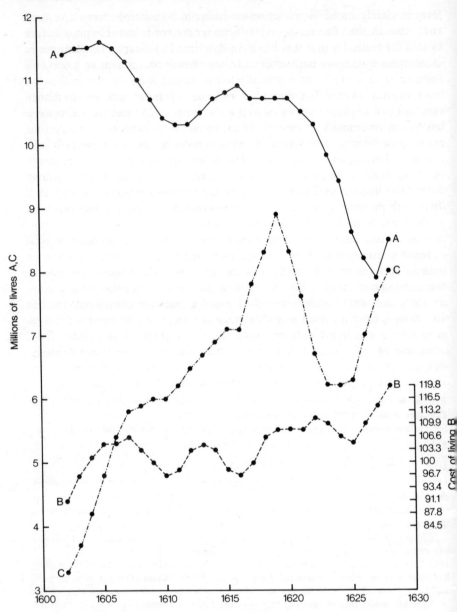

Graph 4. Five-year weighted moving averages; prices; direct and indirect taxes 1600–1630. A, Recettes générales. B, Prices (1600= 100). C, Total indirect taxes.

Jeannin clearly stated his policy on a number of occasions between 1614 and 1617, though what he said has either been ignored or branded as false. In fact he told the truth. He said that when Sully retired in January 1611 there were, in addition to the five million *livres* in the Bastille, 3,500,000 to 3,600,000 *livres* in reserve. This latter sum is what remained from the ten million on hand in May 1610.[20] Between 1611 and 1613, Jeannin said, extraordinary expenses had increased by six million *livres* for pensions and army expenses, but this increase had been covered by using money on hand and by collecting extra money from forced loans from office holders at no expense to the people.[21] The money stored in the Bastille was not touched until the revolt of 1614, when it was spent to save the state. Finally, Jeannin claimed that during the Regency ordinary yearly expenses increased by about four million *livres* over previous years because of the necessity of granting large pensions to the great nobles. Yet, he said, the government had managed to reduce the rate of indirect taxes by the equivalent of two million *livres* per year.[22]

Jeannin managed to maintain as consistent an increase in the amount of indirect revenue as Sully had, even though during the Regency period the rates of indirect taxes, especially that of Sully's favorite, the *gabelle*, were reduced, and others such as the *douane* of Vienne were eliminated. Part of the reason was that the amounts that the tax farmers had to pay the government were not reduced when the rates they could charge were reduced. The other part of the reason must have been that times were even better between

---

[20] The exact amount on hand, unlike the amount in the Bastille, cannot be determined. Reasonable estimates run from seven and a half to fourteen and a half million *livres*. See Clamageran, *Impôt*, II, 388–389, 408–409; Buisseret, *Sully*, p. 80. Sully wildly exaggerated. See *Economies royales*, XVII, 375–378. The higher figure probably includes the Bastille treasure which would bring the total to either $7\frac{1}{2}$ or $9\frac{1}{2}$ million, depending on whether the calculations were made before or after Henry IV withdrew 2,000,000 *livres* from the Bastille in April or May 1610. (Louis Battifol, 'Le trésor de la Bastille de 1605 à 1611', *Revue Henri IV*, III [1909], 203–205). It is known that between January and June 1610 there were extraordinary expenses of 4,447,636 *livres* for war, Henry IV's funeral and Marie de Médicis' coronation. (A.N. 120 AP 28, fols. 43r–44r). There seems, therefore, to be no reason to doubt Jeannin's figure for money on hand at the time of Sully's retirement.

[21] Mousnier, *Venalité*, pp. 374–375, indicates some of the means used to make royal officials pay extra sums to the government. Jeannin also managed to increase ordinary revenues in 1611. These were enough to overcome the low estimate of expenses for that year that Sully had made in the previous summer. Compare A.N. 120 AP 28, fols. 2r–14v, 17r–21v, 32r–40v and A.A.E. France 768, fols. 188r–192v.

[22] Jeannin made this claim to the Estates General in 1614, to Bouillon in 1615, and to the Assembly of Notables in 1617. The most authentic copy of Jeannin's speech to the Estates General is B.N. MS fr. n.a. 7262, fols. 108r–114r; all the printed versions are inaccurate. For 1615 and 1617 see Jeannin, *Négociations*, in Michaud and Poujoulat, *Nouvelle Collection*, XVIII, 680–681, 685–686.

1610 and 1617 than during Sully's years and thus consumption and trade increased.

A generality-by-generality analysis of the *taille* revenue shows that Sully was forcing progressively more money from the *pays d'état* though the amount collected from the whole country decreased.[23] The pattern reverses while Jeannin was in charge. Perhaps this happened because Jeannin wished to lessen the possibility of resistance in the *pays d'état*, the area of France most hostile to the central government. In any case, the overall *taille* revenue increased during the Regency after the first few years. The reason seems to have been the even better economic climate since not even Jeannin's most hostile critics accused him of raising the *taille* rate.

The amount of money a government could collect by ordinary means seems to have been related in general to the rise and fall of the cost of living as seen in Graph 4, unless the government purposely lowered a tax as Sully did with the *taille*, or took the risk of greatly increasing rates as Sully did with the *gabelle* or as was done with all indirect taxes in the period after 1625. Jeannin could afford this risk even less than Sully because of the political situation. Sully was lucky that economic conditions favored him and that he had Henry IV to back him up. Richelieu suffered the consequences in the form of popular revolts. Jeannin did not have Henry IV and could not risk increasing the rebellion potential already existing. Yet Jeannin found the money he needed. Despite good times, tax increases, and expense reduction Sully needed more revenue. He got it through extraordinary income in the form of reprisals against financiers accused of peculation and through forced gifts from the clergy, together with other undisclosed means. Jeannin by 1612 had hit upon the safer method of selling more offices and forcing loans from these officials – a policy that Richelieu would imitate.

The result of all these comparisons and conjectures can only be that, despite the historical legends that even the economic historians have been unable to escape,[24] the Regency government found ways of collecting money to meet expenses as successfully as Sully had and with as little protest from the people as Sully had produced.

The difference was that as far as Sully was concerned his role was to save money eventually to fight a war. The Regency government had in effect no choice, or rather no other wise choice than the one it took. Money had to be

[23] Mallet, *Comptes rendues*, pp. 186–189, 200–203, 206–207.

[24] See for example Clamageran, *Impôt*, II, 408, who admits that the Regency government did not do too badly with tax policy but then immediately goes on to condemn the government for spending too much money without pausing to consider why this was so. The Regency government was reputed to have been corrupt, therefore it must have been so. Clamageran also makes mistakes in the figures he uses for royal income and expense, see, for example, II, 411–413.

spent to fight the war that Sully had saved for. Then the country had to be protected from external enemies during the Regency. Finally money had to be spent to hold the powerful subjects in line.[25]

The real question then is expense. How well did the Regency government spend the money it collected? This question presents an immediate difficulty since in one sense it can be said that no one knows how much was spent. This statement is true for the whole of the first third and more of the seventeenth century. This is because a significant proportion of the budget was under the exclusive control of the king and his close advisers. Mallet did not analyze this portion of the budget, simply including it under extraordinary expense. For the period 1611 through 1615 the accounts in the Archives d'Affaires Etrangères and the Collection Dupuy of the Bibliothèque Nationale can be combined to give an adequate picture; the picture is that the funds in the control of the king were spread over the same type of expenses that are to be found in the ordinary accounts – war, household, foreign debts, and so on. Unfortunately, until someone carefully studies all the accounts over a lengthy period, nothing definite can be said except that it seems that an accurate general picture can be gained by studying the expenses revealed in the main part of the budget. There are no great secret payments hidden away in the part of the budget the king completely controlled. But there may well be important trends that some future historian will find.

To return to Graph 2 it can be seen that pensions and gifts were on the rise from 1600 through 1613. There was a jump in 1610, but this is matched by a similar rise in the years 1616 to 1619, another time of unrest. The only significant increases in the expenses of the royal household were in 1610 and 1614 when the costs of the coronation and the Estates General had to be paid. The non-essential expenses summarized as 'other' on the graph were kept down throughout the Regency. It should be noted though that through 1615 expenditures on roads and bridges were kept at a level comparable to the sums spent during Henry IV's reign. Jeannin knew as well as Sully that this was a necessary expense to maintain royal authority. What is most clear is that Henry IV's strength made it possible for Sully to curtail expenses while the Regency government could not do this because of its weak position, the commitments

---

[25] Buisseret has given some indication of the size of the foreign debt (*Sully*, pp. 82–85) but there was much more that Sully did not admit to. The Regency, as part of its foreign policy, paid much of this. A.A.E. Autriche 10, fols. 160r–160v (payment to ⸲⸱⸲ Count Palatine of the Rhine in 1614 for Henry's debt of 858,404 *livres*). For Henry's German debts see Léonce Anquez, *Henri IV et l'Allemagne d'après les mémoires et la correspondance de Jacques Bongars* (Paris, 1887), pp. 52–67. For repayment of this debt in the years 1611–1616, see A.A.E. France, 767–770, *passim*; B.M. Stowe MS 174, fol. 24r. The entire English debt was paid by 1613, see Robert Ashton, 'Deficit Finance in the Reign of James I', *Economic History Review*, 2nd series, x(1957), 15–29. See also Clamageran, *Impôt*, II, 352–355 and Laffleur de Kermaingant, 'Sommes dues par Henri IV à l'Angleterre', *Revue Henri IV*, I, 2nd ed. (1912), pp. 66–68.

abroad formed by Henry IV and because of the internal problems which could not be controlled except by the means used by Sully and his predecessors – an increase in gifts and pensions.

Much of the extra amount spent on pensions between 1610 and 1615 is recorded in two documents in the Archives d'Affaires Etrangères.[26] The people to whom these pensions were paid are not surprising – the Princes of the Blood and the powerful nobles. Again it is no surprise that Condé got the lion's share. As first Prince of the Blood his fealty was necessary; only he had a claim to power. The one name missing from all the accounts both of the *Trésorier de l'Epargne* and of Marie de Médicis' personal accounts is Concini. How much is hidden away and not mentioned can never be known. But it seems that his rewards were in the form of land and power rather than money.[27] The legend of vast sums going to the Concinis seems to be unfounded.

There is no other conclusion to this consideration of the financial policies of Sully and Jeannin than that the Regency continued the policy of Henry IV in different circumstances. Most other governments in Europe, in the first quarter of the seventeenth century, were in financial difficulty and partly as a result of this they were unable to function as effectively as they wished. But France was governed by men who had the ability to steer a consistent course and who were able to find enough money to finance their policies.[28]

How well did the Regency government spend the money it raised? The monarchy was saved. Without the expenditures, France would have faced continual civil war; not a civil war with a purpose, a goal; just endemic, interminable, inconclusive war. Any doubts on this point will be settled when Condé's rebellion of 1614 is considered. If the great nobles had not been bribed

[26] A.A.E. France 770, fols. 91r–103r, 104r–118r. Sully was among those who received gifts and pensions. On his retirement in 1611 he received a gift of 300,000 *livres* a year (Clamageran, *Impôt*, II, 404); this was more than the Duke of Mayenne received and almost as much as the Duke of Bouillon got.

[27] On one occasion, however, Concini did get some cash. This was when Marie de Médicis turned over to him the right to arrears on some *rentes* originally granted to her by Henry IV. *Reg. Délib. Paris* XV, 210–213. In addition to the offices and lands Concini and his wife received themselves, their relations also obtained similar rewards. For example, Sébastien Dori Galigai, Concini's brother-in-law, was made Abbot of Marmoutiers in 1610 and Archbishop of Tours at the end of 1616. He resigned this position and fled to Florence just before Concini was assassinated in 1617. Richelieu, *Mémoires*, I, 258–259.

[28] For the financial difficulties of European nations in the first quarter of the seventeenth century see Spooner, *Frappes*, pp. 7, 173–183, 295–328; Robert Ashton, *The Crown and the Money Market, 1603–1640* (Oxford, 1960), pp. 37–38; Frederick Dietz, *English Public Finance, 1415–1641*, 2nd ed. (London, 1964), II, 101–115, 141, 146–147, 157–161, 183–184; Heinz Dollinger, *Studien zur Finanzreform Maximilians I von Bayern in den Jahren 1598–1618* (Göttingen, 1968), pp. 194–196; Ernst Baasch, *Hollandische wirtshaftsgeschichte* (Jena, 1927), pp. 174–192; J. H. Elliott, *Imperial Spain, 1469–1716* (N.Y., 1964), pp. 279–303; John Lynch, *Spain under the Habsburgs* (Oxford, 1969), II, 30–39.

they would have rebelled earlier. Chaos would have resulted if they had rebelled before the foreign policy of the Regency government was settled, before the loyalty of the majority of the Huguenots was assured, before the government was sure of its own officials. When Condé did rebel the only chaos was within his own ranks.

3
FRENCH FOREIGN POLICY
1598–1615

The other area in which Marie de Médicis and her advisers were most heavily criticized is that of foreign policy. Villeroy, Jeannin and Sillery assured the deputies of the Estates General that they had simply continued the foreign policy of Henry IV after his assassination in order to preserve the throne for his son. Henry unfortunately left no statement of his plans. The only means available of gaining some idea of his intentions is a step-by-step analysis of his actions and achievements in the field of foreign policy. This is a necessary preliminary to any assessment of the foreign policy of the Regency and the reactions to it of the Estates General of 1614.

The basic thrust of French foreign policy during the years 1598 to 1615 was toward European peace. The reason for this policy during the reign of Henry IV was the need to provide time for France to rebuild after thirty-five years of civil and foreign war. During the Regency the purpose was to enable the government to maintain the level of recovery attained by Henry IV against the threat posed by the expected revolt of *les grands*.

During both periods the rulers of France realized the danger that the Habsburgs, especially the Spanish Habsburgs, posed. The ultimate aim of foreign policy during the whole period was in line with the tradition that dominated France from the early sixteenth through the seventeenth century – to destroy the Habsburg threat. But for the time being France had to temporize. The major effort of foreign policy had to be to prevent further Habsburg gains in Europe. This was to be achieved through threats and limited force, if necessary and if allies could be found, but preferably through the means of a marriage alliance with Spain.

Numerous legends have grown up around the figures of this period. Those surrounding Sully have produced the picture of a financial genius. Yet his achievements, though significant, were not extraordinary. The stories that surround Henry IV's life – the Grand Design, *le vert galant*, Paris is worth a Mass, a chicken in every pot – have resulted in a vague sketch of a legendary hero. He was something else, a political realist of the highest order.

For the last seventy-five years historians have attacked the story fabricated by Sully that just before his assassination in 1610 Henry was planning a vast enterprise designed to bring about the destruction of Habsburg power, the

34

political reorganization of Europe, and peace for evermore.[1] An alternative theory that appeals to some is that Henry IV was working against the Habsburgs to unite the 'stati liberi', the line of small, independent states stretching from the Baltic down the Rhine and across the Alps to the Adriatic.[2] Most historians believe that Henry was adamantly opposed to both the Spanish and Austrian Habsburgs and that when he died he was on the verge of using the question of the succession to the territory of the Duke of Cleves as a means of attacking the Habsburgs on the Rhine, an alliance with the Duke of Savoy as a pretext for conquering Milan, and perhaps was even going to invade Spain, thus starting a new campaign against the Habsburgs on all the borders of France. Another possibility occasionally mentioned is that Henry kept his options open to the end.[3] All historians agree that Henry's death changed French history.

It is necessary to consider what Henry IV did. After securing his claim to the throne against internal enemies in the early 1590s, he mounted an attack to drive the Spanish from France. In 1598, after four years' effort, he was successful. The Peace of Vervins signed in 1598 and the Edict of Nantes of the same year freed Henry from immediate worries. But France needed rebuilding and that would take time, time that could not be spent in war. From 1598 until 1609 Henry worked to bring peace to Europe.

Even before 1598 Henry IV had established his policy in Italy by siding with the Pope against the Duke of Ferrara in 1597. That the reason for this was more than just to ensure continued papal support against his internal enemies is evident in the quarrels of 1598–1601 with the Duke of Savoy. In 1588 Charles Emmanuel had gained the territory of Saluzzo from France

---

[1] Sully describes the Grand Design in *Economies royales*, XVII, 330–338, 372–379. A new edition of this work, of which the first volume appeared in 1970, is being prepared by Bernard Barbiche and David Buisseret.

[2] This thesis was first proposed in E. Rott, *Henri IV, les suisses et la haute Italie* (Paris, 1882), *passim*. Roland Mousnier has given his support in *L'Assassinat de Henri IV* (Paris, 1966), pp. 104–122, especially 106–107. For a bibliography of studies of diplomacy in the early seventeenth century see J. Michael Hayden, 'Continuity in the France of Henry IV and Louis XIII: French Foreign Policy, 1598–1615', *Journal of Modern History*, XLV (1973), 1–2. Much of this chapter and a small part of Chapter 1 appeared originally in this article.

[3] The two French works that lend support to the last theory are G. Pagès and V. L. Tapié, *Naissance du grand siècle, la France de Henri IV à Louis XIV, 1598–1661* (Paris, 1948), pp. 77–81 and J. H. Mariéjol, *Henri IV et Louis XIII*, Vol. VI, pt 2 of *Histoire de France*, ed. E. Lavisse (Paris, 1905), 107–125. It is interesting to note that the strongest support for the thesis that Henry IV kept his options open has come from a Czech and a Polish historian who wrote in their native languages in the late nineteenth and early twentieth century, but whose works have been largely ignored in western Europe. See V. L. Tapié, *Politique étrangère de la France et le début de la Guerre de Trente Ans, 1616–1621* (Paris, 1934), pp. 14–15, and Alexandre Schürr, 'La politique de Henri IV en Suède et en Pologne, 1602–1610', *Revue Henri IV*, II (1908), 25–33.

France in 1614

and in spite of promises to the contrary he was determined at all costs to keep it. Exasperated by the Duke's stalling, Henry fought a quick victorious war against Savoy. When the peace treaty was signed Henry chose not Saluzzo, which would have given France an entry into Italy, but the four small bits of territory, Bresse, Bugey, Gex and Valromey, which rounded out France's boundaries along the Rhône and left only one passage in that area open to the Habsburgs. This Henry could easily control from his new territory. In spite of French tradition and in spite of strong support for a policy of Italian expansion among his followers, he gave up any pretensions to Italy in favor of a means of controlling the Habsburgs. Henry's policy became clearer as he renewed alliances with the Swiss in 1602, providing another means of keeping the Spanish Habsburgs out of the north. He mediated peace in the political–religious battle between the Pope and Venice in 1606–1607 and then played an important role in arranging the truce between Philip III of Spain and the United Provinces in 1609. At this point the *stati liberi* thesis begins to look very tempting, especially when it becomes clear that after gaining the submission of the Duke of Bouillon in 1606 Henry IV worked for an alliance with the Protestant Princes of Germany. The thesis seems less tenable when it is remembered that the reason for Henry's intervention in the Venetian affair was to prevent the Spanish from siding with the Pope in a war; that Venice, a number of Swiss cantons and most of the German Princes had little sympathy for Henry IV; that Henry signed commercial treaties with England, Spain and Holland; and most importantly when it is remembered that in 1608 Henry became actively and seriously involved in marriage negotiations with Spain. The fact is that until 1609 Henry's foreign policy was primarily directed toward reducing tension in Europe and finding a basis for peace.[4]

It is true that Henry IV never trusted the Spanish and that it was to his advantage to keep them apart from their Austrian relations. Until 1606 he was worried about Spanish involvement in the attempt of Biron and Auvergne to foment civil war in France and tried to counter this by involving himself with the Spanish Moriscos.[5] But basically Henry wanted peace. Spain too was

[4] For Venice see A.A.E. Venise 42, fols. 3r–11r; A.A.E. Rome 23, fols. 149r–162r, 181r–195r, 259r–262r. See also Gaetano Cozzi, *Il Doge Nicolo Contarini* (Venice, 1958), pp. 93–147. For the Dutch treaty see *Mercure François*, I, 317a–322a and Henri Lonchay and Joseph Cuvelier, eds., *Correspondance de la cour d'Espagne sur les affaires des Pays-Bas au XVII siècle* (Brussels, 1923), I, 318–322, 331. For negotations leading to it see Jacques Bernard, *Recueils de Traitéz* (Amsterdam, 1700), III, 7b–8a, 39a–41a, and Antione Le Fèvre, *Sieur de la Boderie, Ambassades de Monsieur de la Boderie en Angleterre ... depuis les années 1606 jusqu'en 1611* (n.p., 1750), I–IV, *passim*. For the Swiss treaty, Bernard, *Traitéz*, III, 4b–7b, 21a–26a. For the commercial treaties, *ibid.*, 18a–19a, 30b–33a.
[5] See the letter of Henry IV to the Landgrave of Hesse, November 3, 1604, *LMHIV*, VI, 324–325. Henry was looking for Spain's weak points; see the reports on Spanish colonies and Spanish finance in A.A.E. Espagne 12, fols. 19r–20r, 131r–313v. For the Morisco involvement see Duc de la Force, *Mémoires authentiques*, ed. Marquis de la Grange, (Paris, 1843), I, xix–xx, 156 and the letters of Henry IV to La Force and La Force to Henry IV, September 1602–August 1605, in *ibid.*, I, 339–341, 348, 349, 365–366, 375–377, 378–379, 380, 397–398, 407–408. For Spain's complaints and Henry's reply in September 1605, see G. Groen van Prinsterer, *Archives ou correspondance inédite de la maison d'Orange-Nassau*, 2nd series (Utrecht, 1858), II, 361–366.

37

working for peace: with England, hesitantly with Holland, and within the Empire. In Europe as a whole the period 1598 to 1609 can best be described as a period of negotiation for a limited peace. All of the treaties turned out to be very temporary since in effect they returned Europe to the situation of the mid sixteenth century. The nations of Europe were worn out and not in the mood for an all-out attempt to solve the century-old problems that faced them. Europe was too exhausted to begin the Thirty Years' War.[6]

Then in 1609 there was a change: Henry IV became aggressive; the army was rebuilt and deployed for attack; preparations were made for the King's departure for war; his Queen was finally crowned and declared Regent in his absence. All was ready: the English, the Dutch and the German princes were on the march to help in an attack on the Rhine. The Duke of Savoy, with whom a marriage alliance had just been signed, could hardly wait for French troops to join him in an attack against Milan. There were French troops under the command of the Marquis of La Force on the Spanish border. Then, before anything could happen, Henry was assassinated on May 14, 1610. He died without having told anyone when he would march, what his goals were or why he had changed his policy. The suspicion in Europe at the time was that it had all happened because a fifty-five-year-old lecher wanted a new mistress — sixteen-year-old Charlotte de Montmorency, the wife of the Prince of Condé. In November 1609 Condé had fled with his reluctant wife to the Spanish Netherlands. Possibly Sully's original reason for concocting the story of the Grand Design was to cover up for Henry. The sheer scope of the Design did that, at least in France, though the story of his sexual prowess lived on as in the song:

> Vive Henri Quatre, vive ce roy vaillant,
> Ce diable à quatre a le triple talent
> De boire et de battre et d'être un vert galant.[7]

The facts are hard to determine. The memoirs indicate a state of confusion. Richelieu, who had no personal contact with the government in 1610 but who later knew many of the people involved, emphasized the importance of the Italian campaign; the attack against the Habsburgs on the Rhine was treated simply as the result of Henry's infatuation for Condé's wife. A similar

---

[6] For Spain's foreign policy during the years 1598–1610 see Bhodan Chudoba, *Spain and the Empire, 1519–1643* (Chicago, 1952), pp. 174–199; Rott, *Henri IV*, pp. 3–4; Rott, *Histoire de la représentation de la France auprès des cantons suisses...* (Berne, 1902), II, 538–539, 623.

[7] Quoted in Pierre Barbier and France Vermillet, eds., *Histoire de France par les chansons* (Paris, 1956), I, 130.

version is found in Bassompierre's memoirs when he could tear himself away from his own career. Pierre de l'Estoile was sure that Charlotte was the cause and talked only of an attack on Flanders. Paul Phelypeaux de Pontchartrain, who had just become a Secretary of State, briefly mentioned that Henry planned to fight on the Rhine and in Milan. Fontenay-Mareuil, who was too young at the time to know anything for certain, talked vaguely of a grand design, but found its origin in Charlotte, and saw it as a three-pronged attack on the Rhine, Milan and across the Pyrenees. François d'Estrées vaguely referred to Henry IV's plans and the necessity to change them after his death. The Marquis of La Force talked specifically of a Grand Design, which for him meant mostly an attack on Spain led by himself. But his letters of the time directly contradict his dreams of later years.[8]

What emerges from all these memoirs is that Henry was definitely planning something in late 1609, but that no one was sure what. He was planning to fight, but who, for what reasons, and on what terms no one knew. No one except perhaps his closest advisers. There were four men who had daily contact with Henry IV and who continually discussed strategy with him in late 1609 and early 1610. Sully had disqualified himself as a trustworthy witness.[9] Villeroy, Jeannin and Sillery all found occasion later to refer to the plans of 1609–1610.[10] Each time they mention only Henry's plan to attack on the Rhine and give no indication of any further design.[11] Since the Regency

[8] Richelieu, *Mémoires*, I, 23–26. He seems to have been influenced by a desire to set a precedent for himself. F. de Bassompierre, *Journal de ma vie*, ed. M. de Chanterac (Paris, 1870), I, 215–270. The fact that he had originally been the intended husband of Charlotte may have influenced his treatment of the situation. For Bassompierre and court life see M. Bondois, *Le Maréchal de Bassompierre (1579–1646)* (Paris, 1925). Pontchartrain, *Mémoires*, in Michaud and Poujoulat, *Nouvelle Collection*, XIX, 297. Fontenay-Mareuil, *Mémoires*, in Michaud and Poujoulat, *Nouvelle Collection*, XIX, 5–15. Estrées, *Mémoires du Maréchal d'-Estrées* ..., ed. Paul Bonnefon, (Paris, 1910), pp. 1–2. La Force, *Mémoires*, I, 216–222. Compare this with his letters to his wife from March 2 to May 12, 1610 in *ibid.*, II, 258–268. La Force mainly wanted to stop wasting his money at court and go home. L'Estoile, *Mémoires Journaux*, ed. G. Brunet *et al.*, (Paris, 1889), X, 46, 155, 212–213.

[9] For one example of Sully's lack of objectivity see *Economies royales*, XVII, 357.

[10] The major statements of the Regency policy were Sillery's speech to the Estates General of 1614 in A.A.E. France 769, fols. 207r–213v, Jeannin's letter to the Duke of Bouillon of June 26, 1615, B.N. MS fr. n.a. 7262, fols. 118r–127v, and his speech to the Estates General, *ibid.*, fols. 108r–114r, and Villeroy's 'Avis de Monsieur de Villeroy donne à la Royne en 1611', quoted in Mastelleone, *La Reggenza*, pp. 229–234.

[11] Marie de Médicis and Villeroy each mentioned once that Henry IV's plan had been to proceed toward Italy after success in Jülich; Boderie, *Ambassades*, V, 259, 423–424 (letters to Boderie of May 20 and September 24, 1610); however all other letters and statements contradict this. These two isolated remarks must have been meant to impress James I in the difficult days of reorganization just after the death of Henry IV.

government sent troops only to the Rhine perhaps the three were only covering up. On the other hand they were quite accurate in all of their other statements about Henry IV's reign even when this meant acknowledging the mistakes of the Regency.

The letters of Henry IV do not neglect the romantic element. In early March 1609 Henry was overworking his ambassador in Rome to obtain dispensations for the immediate marriage of the Prince of Condé and Charlotte de Montmorency. These were not easy to secure quickly because of the blood relationship and because marriages were not normally permitted during Lent.[12] The reason for the rush was fairly well known; if the girl were married to the honorable but weak First Prince of the Blood she would then be in permanent residence at court and Henry would have few problems in acquiring his new mistress. The marriage took place finally on May 17 but, after Henry had been decent enough to permit a honeymoon before moving in, Condé betrayed him by leaving court with his wife and then at the end of November fled north to the Spanish Netherlands. The effect of this on Henry was immediate; he let all Europe know what an ingrate Condé had been. He had done so much for the lad and besides Princes of the Blood were supposed to live at court. For no reason at all Condé had fled. Henry was hurt. And unless the ruler of the Spanish Netherlands, Archduke Albert, or his brother-in-law, Philip III of Spain, made sure that Condé returned to France there would be trouble.[13]

All this makes an excellent story but there were other things stirring in Europe. Most important was the involved question of who should inherit the lands of the Duke of Cleves who had died on March 25, 1609. As with Charles II of Spain a century later Europe had been waiting a long time for the death of the childless and mentally deranged Duke.[14] No one had a clear claim to his lands but many had some claim. His territories, principally Cleves, Jülich, Berg and Mark, were not large but they were densely populated, wealthy and strategically located. At stake were the borders of the Spanish Netherlands and the United Provinces, a significant stretch of the Rhine, the fate of the developing Counter Reformation in Cologne and Westphalia and

---

[12] *LMHIV*, VIII, 681, 682–683 (Henry IV to François Savary, *seigneur* of Brèves, March 3, 5, 1609). The marriage contract is in A.N. K 539, no. 21.

[13] *LMHIV*, VII, 807–811 (Henry IV to his Spanish ambassador André de Cochefilet, baron of Vaucelas, December 5, 1609); 812–813 (Henry IV to Brèves, December 9, 1609). The Spanish indecision about what to do with Condé when he first arrived and their eventual decision to protect him so that he would be an ally if war should come can be seen in Lonchay and Cuvelier, *Correspondance*, I, 343–349 (letters between Spinola and Philip III, December 29, 1609 to February 22, 1610).

[14] *LMHIV*, VI, 325 (Henry IV to the Landgrave of Hesse, November 3, 1604).

an important link in the Spanish and Austrian supply lines. The question of succession was a lawyer's dream but a politician's nightmare.[15] Henry IV could not ignore the crisis. First there was the possibility that the importance of the territory for both the Dutch and the Spanish might ruin the peace negotiations which Henry had done so much to further. Then there was the threat of the Emperor to sequester the lands himself. If Henry was ever to succeed in gaining an alliance with the League of Protestant Princes, a long-term goal, he had to do something to help them meet this threat.[16] Finally, Rome was interested because the Counter Reformation was meeting success in the Duke's lands while the two chief claimants, the Elector of Brandenburg and the Count Palatine of Neuburg, were Protestants.

Henry decided in late 1609, after the Dutch–Spanish truce had been signed, to support the Protestant claimants, who had agreed to hold the territories in common possession until their claims could be settled. At the same time he tried to convince the Pope that he was working for the peace of Christendom while the Habsburgs were interested only in their own political gain.[17] The same message went to the rest of Europe. France did not want war but it would stand firm on the Cleves question and would fight if necessary.[18]

Henry was moving carefully. He did not want to push Spain too far. But he had proof of prior Spanish hostility. Before all the trouble began he had been seriously interested in forming a marriage alliance with the Spanish. This idea had been first advanced by Pope Clement VIII in 1601 soon after Louis XIII and Anne of Austria were born in the same month. After Clement's

[15] A.A.E. Autriche 10, fols. 82r–86v; A.A.E. Allemagne 5, fols. 27r–113r; *Mercure François*, I, 387a–404b. This last would seem to be the account that Richelieu or his secretaries miscopied in *Mémoires*, I, 23–27. The best description of the development of the crisis is in L. P. Smith, *The Life and Letters of Sir Henry Wotton* (Oxford, 1907), I, 135. Some additional information is available in Maurice Lee Jr., *James I and Henri IV* (Urbana, Ill., 1970), pp. 142–167.

[16] *LMHIV*, VII, 50–53, 130–131, 146–149, 335–337, 513–514, 541–542, 648–650, 672–676 (attempts from 1606 to 1609 of Henry IV to unite and ally with the German Protestant princes). See B.N. MS fr. 4112, fols. 1r–9r. See also G. Labouchère, 'Guillaume Ancel envoyé résident en Allemagne (1576–1613) d'après sa correspondance', *Revue d'histoire diplomatique*, XXVII (1923), 160–188, 348–367.

[17] The discussion is traced in letters from Lomenie to La Force (August 23, September 7, October 18, 1609) in B.N. MS fr. n.a. 23369, pp. 143, 146–148, 154–156. See also A.A.E. Allemagne 5, fols. 27r–113r and Anquez, *Allemagne*, pp. 156–190. Henry IV's attempt to convince the Pope about Spain can be seen in *LMHIV*, VII, 760–765, 827–830 (Henry IV to Brèves, August 31, 1609, January 21, 1610); for Austria, *ibid.*, 840 (Henry IV to Boderie, his English ambassador in London, February 22, 1610).

[18] A.A.E. Autriche 10, fols. 86r–86v (Henry IV to Emperor Rudolph, October 15, 1609). *LMHIV*, VII, 784–785 (Henry IV to the German Electors, October 15, 1609).

41

death, negotiations began again early in 1608 through papal nuncios, ambassadors and the Duke of Tuscany.[19] Henry gave indications that he was interested, until the Spanish began to drag their feet and to provoke a series of incidents along the border between Basse Navarre, Béarn and Spain, beginning in September 1608 and developing through 1609 and 1610.[20]

With the decision to support Brandenburg and Neuburg in the Cleves–Jülich dispute, the protection given Condé by the Spanish provided additional reasons either openly to resist Habsburg threats or to try to frighten them. At first Henry seemed unable to decide which. In any case he needed allies. From England to Venice he searched, but help was forthcoming only from England, Holland, the Protestant Union and Savoy, and of these only his old and very untrustworthy ally Charles Emmanuel of Savoy was at all willing to throw himself into a real fight. As Henry said to the Duke of Bouillon about the German princes, 'que tout se terminera par diètes en vente, et qu'il ne s'y fera rien'.[21] This realization, and the final collapse of marriage negotiations with Spain, which he had tried to keep open in spite of everything, led Henry bit by bit from April 1609 to April 1610 to negotiate first a marriage alliance with Savoy and then a military alliance. Until the end Henry dragged his feet and the final alliance with Savoy only promised French aid after the northern part of the campaign was well under way.[22]

Henry worked out this policy with his advisers, who were pushing and pulling him in different directions, Sully toward war and towards Flanders, Villeroy away from war if possible and in the direction of Italy if necessary.

---

[19] Abel Desjardins, *Négociations*, V, 569–577, 577–580, 580–586, 689; *Mercure François*, I, 253b–254b. See also *LMHIV*, 579–587 (Henry IV to Brèves, July 23, 1608). At that time Henry IV was definitely willing to negotiate a Spanish marriage and probably was ready as early as January or February. Francisco Sihula de le Viellueze, *Matrimonios de España y Francia en 1615* (Madrid, 1901), pp. 14–15 (Philip III to Marquis of Aytona, April 6, 1608).

[20] La Force, *Mémoires*, I, 212–215; B.N. MS fr. n.a. 23369, pp. 107–110, 117–118, 120–122, 126, 128–129, 135–142, 146, 154–156 (Lomenie to La Force, June 2, 1609 to August, 18, 1609). La Force, *Mémoires*, I, 481; II, 222–223, 225–226, 227, 231–233, 233–234, 236, 237–238, 238–239, 239–240, 240–241 (Henry IV to La Force, October 22, 1608 to October 18, 1609). *LMHIV*, VII, 775 (Henry IV to Sully, September 27, 1609). La Force, *Mémoires*, II, 223–225, 228–229, 230–231 (La Force to Henry IV, June 12–July 23, 1609). La Force left for Paris in September or October, 1609 to serve his regular quarter as Captain of the Guard. See his letter to his wife of November 16, 1609, *ibid.*, II, 291–292.

[21] *LMHIV*, VII, 541–542 (letter of May 2, 1608). In 1607 Pierre Brûlart, Viscount of Puisieux, described the English as follows, 'leur timidité, augmentée par le pauvre état auquel se trouvent leurs affaires, surpasse encore leur faiblesse', Boderie, *Ambassades*, II, 500.

[22] Bernard, *Traitéz*, III, 64a–65b. The treaty of Hall with the German Princes can be found in A.A.E. Allemagne 5, fols. 83r–100v.

42

At the same time he also had to be concerned about the border with Spain. The Marquis of La Force was given instructions to be firm in the face of Spanish provocation but to remain on the defensive and to make an occasional reprisal if everything else failed.[23]

All this had its effect, especially as Henry collected his army and signed treaties with the German princes in February 1610 and with Savoy in April. Europe was now convinced that Henry meant business. England agreed to send troops to Cleves–Jülich. The Pope began to put pressure on Spain. Archduke Albert tried to mollify Henry and to explain why he was honor-bound to give refuge to Condé. Henry kept postponing the departure of his troops. He formally requested permission from the Archduke to let his troops pass through his lands on the way to Cleves. He set up an elaborate series of public functions in Paris. He even listened to the Florentine diplomat, Matteo Botti, who had a new plan for a French–Spanish marriage.[24]

Then Henry IV was murdered on May 14. The usual statement is that everything fell apart at this point. France, on the verge of glory, was doomed to wait until Richelieu came. But what actually fell apart? At the very most it was a plan for a limited attack on two fronts with a distinct possibility that there was to be only one front. The diplomatic instructions of 1609–1610 leave the impression that the Milan front was at most a diversion; the real target was the imperial position at Cleves but there had to be protection against Spain in the rear.[25] And the enemy was yielding ground. Archduke Albert agreed to allow the French troops to pass through the Spanish Netherlands. Archduke Leopold, the Imperial Administrator in Cleves–Jülich, fled

---

[23] La Force was proudest of his great rustling feat. He claimed that he rounded up 12,000 sheep and 700–800 cows in one raid. For Villeroy and Sully see E. H. Dickerman, 'The King's Men', III, 222–226, 232–234.

[24] For England, *LMHIV*, VII, 839–847, 847–851, 864–876, 889–894 (Henry IV to Boderie, February 22, 27, March 20, April 28, 1610); 895–896 (Henry IV to Archduke Albert, May 8, 1610). The frantic efforts of Cardinal Ubaldini, the papal nuncio in Paris, can be seen in B.N. MS ital. 1334, pp. 95–117. The last minute marriage negotiations are in Desjardins, *Négociations*, V, 604–610, 612–615, 616–617 (Botti to the Grand Duke, March 30, May 1, May 11, 1610). Throughout April and May the Spanish kept contact with Henry IV, trying to prevent war. Henry continued to listen. See the letters of the Spanish Ambassador in France, Don Inigo de Cardenas, to Philip III in M. Salva and P. Lainez de Barada, eds., *Coleccion de Documentos ineditos para la historia de España* (Madrid, 1844), V, 137–152. The financial accounts preserved among Sully's papers show that war preparations did not begin until April, 1610. War expenses for the January quarter of that year were 500,308 *livres*; in the April quarter they jumped to 3,024,544 *livres*, A.N. 120 AP 28, fols. 43r–43v.

[25] B.N. MS fr. 4112, fols. 1r–9r, 16r–22r, 31r–33r, 34r–38r, 57r–66v (Diplomatic instructions for ambassadors to Germany, England, Spain and Savoy in 1609–1610). See also *LMHIV*, VII, 873 (Henry IV to Boderie, March 20, 1610).

from the main fortress of Jülich and after a perfunctory siege an Anglo-Dutch army took control of the whole territory. And so for the time being the Habsburgs were out of Cleves–Jülich. As a result of the quick decision made by Marie de Médicis and the advisers she inherited from Henry IV, a French force of about 8,500 men was on hand for the campaign.[26]

There is no proof that Henry wanted to do more in 1610 than stop the recent Spanish pressures, keep the Habsburgs from the Rhine and build up a system of alliances. Villeroy wrote to La Force on June 3, 1610, 'But if our good master was not dead he would not have had to bother to cross the Seine; the keys of Jülich would have been brought to him. All of Italy would have trembled and begun to rise in his favor.'[27] Henry IV's exact plan will probably never be known, for the simple reason that he never said what it was. Perhaps he was ready to abandon his twelve-year policy of peace. It seems most probable, though, that having taught the Habsburgs a lesson on the Rhine, he would have been happy to settle for a marriage alliance with Spain as a means of protection and wait for future developments.

The Regency government did not maintain the same silence as Henry IV. Threatened by many forces and often on the defensive, the advisers of Marie de Médicis explained on several occasions in 1614–1617 just what they had been up to. When their claims are checked against the diplomatic correspondence and the treaties, it is found that they were telling the truth. And their basic message was that they changed the policy of Henry IV as little as possible, modifying it only when the facts of life of the Regency made it necessary.

Oddly enough, Villeroy, who was the most active and influential of the advisers, had the least to say in public about government policy. But his correspondence reveals that he was doing what Jeannin and Sillery described. He was doing it so well that he managed to keep the Spanish, English and Dutch informed or misinformed as he chose and on a number of occasions had the governments of these three nations all waiting for his decision.

[26] B.N. MS fr. n.a. 23369, p. 81. E. Griselle, ed., *Documents d'histoire*, III, 229–230, 242–248 (Jean de Thumery, *sieur* of Boissise to Villeroy in May and October 1610). A.A.E. Allemagne 5, fols. 116r–143r. Anquez, *Allemagne*, pp. 191–198. Estrées, *Mémoires*, pp. 7–9. Rott, *Histoire*, II, 624. For information on the varying size of the French army in the early seventeenth century see Hayden, 'Continuity', p. 11.

[27] La Force, *Mémoires*, II, 278–279. Further support for the thesis that Henry's major concern was the northeast can be found in his conversations with the Duke of Lesdiguières in October 1608, Richelieu, *Mémoires*, I, 34–45, 420–431.

Villeroy, perhaps, was the most influential diplomat of his time.[28] The most complete exposition of the foreign policy of the Regency government of Marie de Médicis was delivered by Chancellor Sillery at the opening session of the Estates General in October 1614. It is interesting to note that almost everyone who reported the event made just a curt reference to the fact that the Chancellor spoke for an hour on the policies of the government. Fortunately, one witness decided to make a copy of the speech. He was the deputy of the First Estate from Poitou, the Bishop of Luçon–Richelieu.[29]

In his speech Sillery said that the first resolution of the government had been to preserve peace within the kingdom and with neighboring states in so far as the dignity of the King and France would permit. Existing treaties had been renewed with Scotland, England and the United Provinces, as well as with the Pope, the King of Spain, the Venetians and other Catholic states and Princes. Peace with all was desired. At the same time Henry IV's promise to help the true heirs of the Duke of Cleves was honored despite the legitimate excuse provided by Henry's death. After the success at Jülich the Regency maintained good relations with both the Protestant and Catholic princes of

---

[28] Examples of Villeroy's involvement can be found throughout the volumes of correspondence addressed to him, for example, B.N. MS fr. 15581, fols. 5r–6r, 7r, 9r–10r, 20r–20v, 49r–50r, 51r–52r, 53r–54r, 60r. These letters from January to December of 1612 show Villeroy's connection with the problems of Mantuan and Imperial succession, the vacillations of the Protestant Union, the position of Venice and Switzerland, affairs in southwest France and French trading in the Near East. Examples of his contact with affairs in Italy in 1613 can be seen, *ibid.*, fols. 134r–135r, 138r–141r, 144r–145r, 148r, 153r–154r. The English and Spanish marriage negotiations are the best examples of Villeroy's power in Europe. His ability to misinform can best be seen by looking at the varying attitudes of the ambassadors in France toward the Huguenots. They were seen as a great menace only by the Spanish and Venetian ambassadors, who both saw them behind every tree. This was part of Villeroy's plan to keep Spain in line; he had convinced the Spanish that France was in danger of becoming completely Huguenot unless the Spanish did what they were told. The Venetian ambassadors picked this up, as they picked up most other things, from the Spanish because they did not have the money or influence to secure good sources of information. The Tuscans knew better but only Luca degli Asini, the representative of the Dowager Grand Duchess, had reliable contacts. The reports of the English ambassador, Thomas Edmondes, which have never before been used with any thoroughness are valuable because he had excellent contacts through the Huguenots great and small. His is often the only ambassadorial account that throws significant light on events within France.

[29] AAE. France 769, fols. 207r–213r. The best example of the treatment by a hostile witness is to be found in Rapine, *Recueil*, pp. 38–49. His statement was that the Third Estate with its poor seats could only hear the last part of the speech when the Chancellor promised that he would give the *cahiers* a favorable response. Even there Rapine heard only what he wanted because in fact the Chancellor said the *cahiers* would get a favorable *hearing*. Sillery promised a response in the first part of the speech.

Germany. When Savoy was threatened by the King of Spain, France promised help and worked for a settlement. On the other hand, when the Duke of Savoy threatened Berne and Geneva the Regency mobilized an army and warned both Savoy and Spain that France had a treaty with Berne and that for reasons of state (*par raison d'estat*) would also protect Geneva. As a result the independence of Savoy, Berne and Geneva had been preserved. In 1613 and 1614 the Regency worked to mediate the long-standing difference between Savoy and Mantua over the possession of Montferrat. France was also negotiating the dispute between the King of Spain and the Archduke of Flanders on one side and the heirs of the Duke of Cleves and the United Provinces on the other. Finally, the government had resisted Spanish pressure in Basse Navarre. The Marquis of La Force had been ordered to take revenge for Spanish mistreatment of the King's subjects and negotiations with the Spanish on the border question were now in progress. The conclusion of Sillery's exposition of foreign policy was that all of this had been done in such a way that the dignity of France had been preserved and that there had been no diminution of or prejudice to the prestige of the King or the Crown.[30]

The other important public defense of the Regency's foreign policy was Jeannin's response to Bouillon's open letter of June 9, 1615. As usual, Jeannin concentrated on finances but he also emphasized that Marie de Médicis wanted peace at home and abroad because if war were to come the present and future interests of all princes and states would involve all of Europe in the conflict. In this situation the only sensible policy was to be firm and neutral. The purpose of the Spanish marriage alliance was not to make Spain strong but to further this policy, which would be completed through a marriage alliance with England.[31]

These statements by Jeannin and Sillery can be compared with the instructions given to ambassadors. In 1611–1612, after immediate problems had been taken care of and the basic policy of a marriage alliance with Spain had been decided, ambassadors were sent to England, Germany, Spain and Savoy with new instructions.[32]

The message given to Europe was that the Spanish–French marriage alliance was necessary to guarantee peace for Europe and that Henry IV had been involved in such negotiations until the time of his death. On the other hand

---

[30] AAE. France 769, fols. 208v–210r.

[31] Jeannin to Bouillon, June 26, 1615 in B.N. MS fr. n.a. 7262, fols. 118r–127v. See the letter of Puisieux to Léon, August 7, 1619, cited in Lublinskaya, *French Absolutism*, p. 177. For Villeroy's assessment of the favorable position France held in Europe in 1612 see Nouillac, *Villeroy*, pp. 551–553.

[32] B.N. MS fr. 4112, fols. 23r–30v, 75v–88r, 39r–43v, 51r–57r. These are copies but seem to be accurate. The German instructions are exactly the same as the copy Jeannin preserved among his papers (B.N. MS fr. n.a. 7261, fols. 283v–308r). Rott used the instructions to the Swiss ambassador in B.N. MS fr. 4112 and accepted them as genuine.

the proposed marriage between the House of Savoy and the French royal family had been cancelled because the Duke of Savoy had tried to use blackmail to obtain more territory from France after Henry died. France would continue to protect Savoy from Spain, but at the same time would prevent any attempt by the Duke to invade Berne or Geneva. Marriage negotiations with England would be welcome though the English had been rather cold on this subject so far. 'German liberty' and the claims of Brandenburg and Neuburg to Cleves–Jülich would be maintained. At the same time the French would support Mathias, King of Hungary, as candidate for Emperor.

The 1612 instructions can be compared with those that Henry IV gave to his ambassadors in late 1609, early 1610.[33] They turn out to be quite similar. In January 1610 Henry IV was more openly aggressive in addressing himself to the Protestant Union though whether he would have gone beyond his one definite proposal to fight at Jülich to his vague idea of keeping the Habsburgs from the imperial throne and fighting Spain and Austria is very doubtful. He told the princes that they would have to work the first out for themselves and said nothing more about the second.

With Savoy Marie de Médicis was hardly straightforward, and she used all available excuses to get out of agreements. In April 1610 Henry, who never doubted that the Duke was a scoundrel, was still holding back as much as possible. Henry had needed an ally if he was successfully to threaten the Habsburgs and he had to take Charles Emmanuel. But even in the treaty of Brussol there was still room for France to avoid full scale war with Italy. Henry and Marie both treated the Duke as shabbily as he had often treated them.

Henry IV in 1609–1610 did everything he could to persuade the English to fight beside him, even going so far as to recognize some of the debt that James I claimed was owed him by France. With regard to a marriage alliance with England Henry and Marie both stated that France would consider favorably the opening of negotiations.

In August 1609 Henry IV told his Ambassador in Spain, the Baron of Vaucelas, that he would be willing to talk about a Spanish marriage as long as Spain started the negotiations. By 1612 Marie had committed herself to the Spanish marriage but her instructions to the Viscount of Puisieux in July 1612 were that France was not satisfied with the wording of the marriage contract. This would continue to be her strategy until late 1615, as the marriage was postponed time and again.

It is one thing to have a foreign policy; quite another to carry it out. There is no escaping that other nations will not always do what one wants them to

---

[33] B.N. MS fr. 4112, fols. 1r–9v, 61r–66v, 16r–22r, 34r–38r. For the English instructions see also Boderie, *Ambassades*, V, 1–29.

do. Henry IV had been fortunate during the years 1598 to 1609 because the basic mood in Europe favored peace. At the same time, as Jeannin said, there were many unsettled issues in which so many nations were involved that if Henry IV had challenged more than one Habsburg army Europe might have been in real trouble. Marie de Médicis' problem, as she knew it or as her advisers made it clear to her, was to pacify Europe without losing face or starting a war. During a Regency major attention always had to be focused on the trouble that was bound to come from dissidents within the country. Yet the great temptation of other rulers to intervene under the pretext of religious or other reasons had to be forestalled. One of these was James I, who saw himself as the protector of Protestants everywhere and especially in France. His efforts to settle the theological and political quarrels of the Huguenots centering around the Duke of Bouillon and Du Plessis–Mornay were only a step away from direct intervention in French affairs and, as the Regency government found out, James sometimes took that step, as when he interfered in the government's negotiations with the rebel nobles in 1614.[34]

James had an organized group to work with, the Huguenots, and was a threat. He was handled by holding out the possibility of a marriage between the Prince of Wales and the second oldest daughter of Marie de Médicis. The possibility was held out but the reality did not come. The correspondence of the English ambassador, Thomas Edmondes, is full of his and James's plans and the French maneuvers to stay uncommitted and yet involved.[35] At the same time as the French were 'handling' James he was involved in his own plans throughout Europe. He married his daughter to the Elector Palatine

[34] For examples of English involvement in French religious affairs see *Cal. St. P.*, LXVII, 107 (letter to Sir Thomas Edmondes of December 19, 1611), *ibid.*, LVIII, 69, 73; LXVIII, 35 (English concern with the works of Bellarmine in 1610 and religious controversy in 1612). B.M. Stowe MS 173, fols. 1r–2r, 5r (James I to Edmondes, July 3, 20, 1612), Stowe MS 174, fols. 12r, 23r (letters of James I of April 9, 24, 1612). *Cal. St. P.*, LXX, 33 (Archbishop Abbott to James I, August 10, 1612). The question of marriage alliance was another area in which James I stepped across the line trying to get the Duke of Bouillon to break the Spanish marriage: one example of this is in B.M. Stowe MS 173, fol. 10r (Edmondes to James I, July 21, 31, 1612). See also Prince Henry to his father, James I, on July 24, 1612 in *Calendar of the Manuscripts of the Marquis of Bath* (Dublin, 1907), II, 60–61. England and France were also continually involved in negotiations to protect their merchants trading in each other's country: *Cal. St. P.*, LXV, 54. B.N. MS fr. 15581, fol. 75r (Edmondes to Villeroy, February 13, 1613); A.N. E 48A (council meeting of January 8, 1615); A.A.E. Angleterre 26, fols. 68r–69r (complaints of France of September 26, 1616). Edmondes's correspondence is full of these negotiations. Similar negotiations were carried on between England and Spain. *Cal, St. P.*, LXVIII, 67, 97 (February, April, 1612).

[35] The death of James's eldest son Henry in November 1612 and his replacement as Prince of Wales by Charles had no basic effect on the negotiation. Nor did the arrival of Gondomar, the new Spanish ambassador to England in 1613.

at the end of 1612 after two years of negotiation and then signed an alliance with the Protestant Union. He tried to get France to join him in the alliance but Marie drew back from any deep involvement. The defense of Jülich served well to ensure that the Dutch and German princes remained friendly to France. The Dutch were further pacified by the support given them by French troops and were sufficiently distracted by their problems in the Baltic and by negotiations in 1613 and 1615 with the English over colonial rights in Asia. The German princes' disunity was guarantee enough of their inability to cause harm. The French pleased James I by working with him in negotiations in Northern Europe to maintain peace, but no commitments were made to him or to anyone else.[36]

James also had connections in southern Europe, being involved at various times in marriage negotiations with the Duke of Savoy and the Grand Duke of Tuscany, but any real trouble in this area could only come from Spain.[37] However, Spain was no real threat. The Spanish wanted the marriage alliance

---

[36] For James I, the Elector Palatine and the United Provinces see A.A.E. Angleterre 26, fols. 3r–14v, Cal. St. P., LXV, 32, 53, 87; LXVII, 35; LXVIII, 78, 102, 104; LXIX, 10; also G. N. Clark and W. van Eysinga, The Colonial Conference between England and the Netherlands, 1613–1615 (Leyden, 1940–1951), passim. For French–Dutch relations and Dutch concerns in general 1609–1614 see A.A.E. Hollande 7 passim. The Dutch were so interested in French support that not even the Spanish–French marriage alliance ruffled them. See A.A.E. Hollande 7, fol. 224r (States General to Marie de Médicis, February 18, 1612). See also B.N. MS fr. 4112, fols. 115r–118v (instructions to the French Ambassador to Holland, August 1614). The Dutch even replaced their ambassador to Paris under French pressure because of his involvement with the Huguenot leaders; see Henri Ouvré, Aubéry du Maurier, étude sur l'histoire de la France et de la Hollande, 1566–1636 (Paris, 1853), pp. 205–213. For joint French–English negotiations in Germany see A.A.E. Angleterre 26, fols. 34r, 35r, 38r, 40r–41r, 47r, 48r, 49r, 50r, 52r, 53r, 55r, 56r, 57r (letters to the French resident in Germany, Jean Hotman, seigneur of Villiers-Saint Georges, August 1612–February 1613). For France and the Rhineland see AAE. Allemagne 5, fols. 116r–143r, 144r–210v. See Ancel to his envoy the sieur of Sainte Catharine (early 1613) in Labouchère, 'Guillaume Ancel', pp. 364–366, also pp. 358–359, and Anquez, Allemagne, pp. 148–152.

[37] For James I and Tuscany in 1611–1612: Desjardins, Negociations, V, 631–632; J. D. Macki, Negotiations between James VI and I and Ferdinand I Grand Duke of Tuscany (London, 1927), pp. 75–104. For the English–Savoy marriage negotiations in 1612–1613 see Cal. St. P., LXX, 80–81; LXXI, 12, 24, 41, 51; LXXIV, 1, 22, 50. See also B.M. Stowe MS 174, fols. 146r–147v. Sporadically Spain continued to tempt England with marriage and threaten it with armadas. All this accomplished was to keep James I interested in trying to convince the French firmly to agree on a marriage alliance. Cal. St. P., LXV, 85, 87; LXVII, 82; LXXIV, 89. For the 1613 armada scare, ibid., LXXII, 7, 20, 72. For Spanish attempts to pull the French away from an English alliance see B.N. MS fr. 16116, fols. 89r, 92r, 95v (Vaucelas to Marie de Médicis, April 28 and May 6, 1614). On the whole subject see Narrative of the Spanish Marriage Treaty, ed. S. R. Gardiner, (London, 1869), passim.

with France which Marie was willing to grant as long as the oldest daughter and the oldest son of the Spanish king were the children involved and as long as the Spanish would meet her various requirements about dowries, living accommodation and suites. Marie made the Spanish wait two years before she signed the treaty on August 25, 1612 and then spent two more years discussing modifications. In addition she demanded that the trouble along the Spanish–Navarre border should be settled honorably. All of this kept the Spanish quite busy; especially since they had to be concerned about the English–French negotiations, the confused moves of the Duke of Savoy, and commitments on the Rhine, not to mention their colonies.[38]

In the south there was also the Duke of Savoy; he might cause momentary upsets as at the time when he began marriage negotiations with the English, and the French had temporarily to step up the pace of their own negotiations with England. But on the whole the Duke was so worried by the varied threats to his territory from Spain and France and so bemused by his various schemes of conquest in Italy and Switzerland that he was only an irritant. His one great fling was the attempt to take over Montferrat in 1613. The Duke of Mantua had died on December 22, 1612, leaving no male heirs. According to the custom of Mantua the successor was his brother, the nearest male heir. Charles Emmanuel claimed the territory in the name of the late Duke's daughter under the Regency of her mother, who was his daughter. When this

---

[38] For French–Spanish negotiations on marriage and Navarre see B.N. MS fr. 16116, *passim* for the French viewpoint; A.N. K 1429, 1453, 1454, 1459, 1610, 1611 for the Spanish viewpoint. It would be fruitless to list folio numbers; almost every sheet is taken up with one of these questions. For proof that the French were willing to use force to get their way with Spain see Vaucelas's letter to Villeroy, August 2, 1613 in B.N. MS fr. 15581, fols. 137r–137v. For an illustration of the continuity of French policy on the question of Navarre see the letters to La Force from Henry IV in La Force, *Mémoires*, II, 239–250, 240–241 (September 27, October 18, 1609), the letters of Marie de Médicis, to La Force, May 16, 1610 and June 6, 1610 in B.N. MS fr. n.a. 23369, pp. 156–158, 161–163. The Spanish immediately tried to capitalize on Henry IV's murder by re-opening the Navarre quarrel. But from the beginning Marie de Médicis held firm while at the same time smoothing things by letting the Moriscos continue leaving Spain through France. La Force, *Mémoires*, II, 8–12 (Letters of Villeroy and Marie de Médicis to La Force, May 23, 1610), B.N. MS fr. n.a. 23369, pp. 169–180 (Lomenie to La Force, June 28, July 8, 9, 29, 1610). Spain's original of the marriage treaty between France and Spain is in A.N. K 1634, nos. 4–5. France's original of the treaty is A.N. K 109, no. 21. Other agreements connected with the marriage can be found in A.A.E. Espagne 12, fols. 343v–362v and A.N. K 1635, nos. 9, 12, 14. At the same time as the Navarre border was being negotiated the Burgundian frontier was also under discussion; see Griselle, ed., *Documents d'Histoire*, III (1912), 248–254. The *Pax Hispanica* described in H. R. Trevor-Roper, 'Spain and Europe, 1598–1621', *New Cambridge Modern History*, IV, 260–282 was more a *Pax Gallica* than anything else during the years 1598–1615.

did not work he claimed the territory in the name of the male child his daughter just might be pregnant with, and finally he simply invaded the part of the Mantuan territory that he wanted, the isolated marquisat of Montferrat. France's answer to this was to hire 4,000 Swiss troops and plan the mustering of 2,500 French troops in Burgundy and Provence in June. This convinced Charles Emmanuel that he should agree to negotiations and, though it took more than a year and two treaties to solve the dispute, there was no real danger of war.[39]

Then there was Rome. The papal nuncio, Cardinal Ubaldini, is often said to have been part of the inner council of Marie de Médicis. But his correspondence does not give that impression. He had to arrange for meetings with Marie de Médicis and Louis XIII just as the other ambassadors did, and when he got these meetings, sometimes after hard work, he was not always successful. Ubaldini was not only the most experienced of the papal nuncios, but he had been in Paris since 1610, longer than any other diplomat. He was competent, but many of the things he wanted – no aid for Protestant princes, no marriage negotiations with England, a quick marriage with Spain – were in opposition to the policy of the Regency government and he had no success in obtaining them. The Regency did not mind fighting the *Parlement* over a bookburning or two to please Ubaldini. It was to its advantage as it had been to Henry IV's to stay on the good side of Rome for the sake of Italian affairs and

---

[39] For the reaction to Savoy–English negotiations see B.N. MS fr. 15986, fols. 4r–5r, B.N. MS fr. 15982, fols. 117r–119v. For the Duke of Savoy's position see A.A.E. Sardaigne 3, fols. 2r–15r, 62r–68v. For the Emperor's role in the dispute, as overlord of Mantua, see A.A.E. Autriche 10, fols. 174r–175r; for the Duke of Savoy's position in this matter, *ibid.*, fols. 175r–187v; for the hiring of Swiss troops see Rott, *Histoire*, III, 89–90. For the mustering of French troops see B.N. MS fr. 15581, fols. 180r–181r (Villeroy's copy of the orders for assembly). Nevers's attempts to get some of these troops can be seen in Griselle, ed., *Documents d'Histoire*, II (1901), pp. 3–10. For the peace treaties of Verceil of November 17, 1614 and Ast of December 1, 1614 see B.N. MS fr. 3711, fols. 35r–39v, 41r–44v. These two treaties were reached through the intervention of the French ambassador and the papal nuncio. On June 21, 1615 as a result of the work of the French, the English and the Venetians, a peace treaty was signed between Spain and Savoy, B.N. MS fr. 3711, fols. 46r–52r. For the progress of the negotiations see B.N. MS fr. 18009–18010 (letters of the French ambassadors in Rome, Brèves and Tresnel). Of the ambassadors in France, Thomas Edmondes had the best information on what was happening concerning Mantua, but he overestimated the size of the French force and thought that the invasion was called off for lack of money. This may have been what Marie de Médicis told Lesdiguières, the governor of Provence, who had been eager for an Italian adventure since 1610. B.M. Stowe MS 174, fols. 53r, 71r, 74v, 94r, 144v (letters of Edmondes, May 24, June 7, 18, July 29, 1613). See Chapter 4 below.

just in case anyone got ideas about challenging the sincerity of Henry IV's conversion or the validity of his marriage to Marie de Médicis. But when it came to weakening the power of the king over the French Church by officially accepting the decrees of the Council of Trent the Regency government was even more firm than Henry had been.[40]

Except for some cursory interest in events in Sweden, Denmark, Russia and the Ottoman Empire as well as a vague concern for the fate of the new colonies in Canada and Brazil, the one other foreign policy concern of the Regency was the Holy Roman Empire. The first question of importance was who should succeed Emperor Rudolph II. Henry had made some noises about keeping the Habsburgs from the throne. From the outset the Regency government supported Mathias, but did nothing directly to help or harm him, though it kept a close eye on the situation.[41] The other major problem in the Empire brings the discussion of the Regency foreign policy full circle. The two occupants of the Cleves–Jülich territory could not get along with each other. In the involved negotiations the claimants changed religions and sought outside allies. The result was the threat of war in 1614 by the allies, the Dutch for Brandenburg and the Spanish for Neuburg. These two states however had no desire to break the truce of 1609 and, after some feinting, negotiations opened which were assisted by England and France. The resulting treaty of Xanten was signed on November 12, 1614 with Jülich and Berg going to Wolfgang William of Neuburg while Elector John Sigismund got Cleves, Mark and Ravensburg. The Spanish army under Spinola refused to give up

---

[40] An example of Ubaldini's work in the early years of Marie de Médicis was the case of Edmund Richer's book in support of Gallicanism published in 1611. After a long fight Ubaldini got satisfaction: B.N. MS ital. 1334, pp. 177–179, 275–287, 288–293, 328–329 (Letters of Ubaldini of March 1611–September 1612). In the case of England he got nowhere; *ibid.*, pp. 271–272 (Ubaldini to Cardinal Borghese, January 19, 1612). For an example of Marie de Médicis' firmness with Rome, see the diplomatic instructions to the Marquis of Tresnel of April 25, 1614 (B.N. MS fr. 4112, fols. 110v–114v). For further information see Hayden, 'Continuity', pp. 21–22.

[41] Indications of the breadth of interest are to be found in A.A.E. Autriche 10, fols. 141r–151v, B.N. MS fr. 7095, fols. 11r–63v (French mission to Constantinople 1611). See also L. Horniker 'Anglo-French Rivalry in the Levant from 1583 to 1612', *Journal of Modern History*, XVIII (1946), 289–305. For the Black Sea area see Germaine Lebel, *La France et les Principautés Danubiennes du XVIᵉ siècle à la chute de Napoléon* (Paris, 1955), pp. 14–36. For Brazil see G. de la Roncière, *Histoire de la marine française* (Paris, 1923), IV, 349–359 and Antonio Ballesteros Beretta, ed., *Documentos ineditos para la historia de España* (Madrid, 1936–1944), III, 179–181, 181–183. For Canada see Roncière, *Histoire*, IV, 322–323 and Reuben Thwaites, ed., *Jesuit Relations and Allied Documents* (Cleveland, 1896), II, 155–161, 296. For the question of Imperial Succession see Chudoba, *Spain and the Empire*, pp. 189–206. For some of the Emperor's other concerns see B.N. MS fr. 6557, fols. 70r–86r (negotiations with Poland of 1613–1615) and *Mercure François* 11, 228b–242a (trouble at Aix in 1612).

the key fortress of Wesel and further negotiations were necessary, but in the end a shaky peace was maintained.[42]

In 1614–1615 Europe was emerging from the period of temporary peace, which had begun in 1598; each clash brought it closer to the Thirty Years War. Though the Regency government had some notion of the danger that Europe was in, and though it strove to maintain peace, it was not primarily interested in a campaign to save Europe from itself. Rather the primary concern of the Regency was to keep peace in Europe so that its domestic problems could be settled more easily. Marie de Médicis and Villeroy were not the dominant figures in Europe; no one occupied that position between 1610 and 1615. Consequently the Regency government could not dictate terms to all of Europe, but it did use France's strategic location, her size and wealth to keep the two most likely troublemakers under control, England off balance and Spain locked in its grip.

[42] For the Imperial side of the Cleves–Jülich question in 1614–1615, see A.A.E. Autriche 10, fols. 169r–173r; for the Protestant Union, A.A.E. Allemagne 5, fols. 211r–240r; for Neuburg, B.N. MS fr. 15581, fols. 261r–265r. For England, *ibid.*, fols. 240v–243v and A.A.E. Angleterre 26, fols. 60r–60v, 63r–63v, 66r. Also see the dispatches of the English envoy to the peace conference in Smith, *Wotton*, II, 41–84. For the Dutch involvement see A.A.E. Hollande 7, fols. 393r–396r, 401r–401v, 403r–403v, 412r, 413r–416r, 419r–420r, 421r–421v, 433r and Prinsterer, *Archives*, II, 433–440 (letters to and from Count William-Louis of Orange, August–December, 1614). The treaty of Xanten can be found in A.N. K 1469, no. 162. See also Smith, *Wotton*, I, 136–143, and Ouvré, *Maurier*, pp. 223–238.

4

THE REVOLT OF THE PRINCES:
JANUARY TO OCTOBER 1614

The meeting of the Estates General of 1614 was preceded by, and to some extent precipitated by, a rebellion led by the high French nobility. A number of the major nobles including the Prince of Condé, the Dukes of Bouillon, Nevers, Longueville, Mayenne and Vendôme, held fortresses, assembled troops and attempted to rouse the country to a state of major rebellion. The failure of this effort during the winter and spring of 1614 can be attributed both to disunity and lack of leadership among the nobles and to the measures adopted by the Regency government to contain the rebellion. A discussion of the rebellion is relevant to this study since the peace treaty signed at Ste-Ménehould in May 1614 called for the meeting of an Estates General to review conditions in the country before the King attained his majority in October 1614. During the summer and fall of 1614 action was taken by both the Regency government and the rebels to insure control of the Estates General when it finally did meet. A description of the events of 1614 derived from existing sources follows.

The difficulties faced by the Regency did not show any sign of lessening in 1613. There were three major problems in foreign affairs to be dealt with in that year: the timing of the Spanish marriages which the Spanish were trying to hurry up, the English marriage negotiations which the French were trying to slow down, and the Duke of Savoy's invasion of Montferrat. The Huguenots opposed the Spanish marriages and through their leaders Du Plessis–Mornay, the Duke of Rohan, and the Duke of Bouillon, they advocated a marriage alliance with England. The Huguenots, however, were split by the political and doctrinal differences between Rohan and Bouillon which stemmed from the Assembly of Saumur of 1611 during which Bouillon had sided with the Regency. James I was actively trying to patch up this quarrel not only for the sake of religious unity but to aid his marriage negotiations with France. James had been warned by his ambassador that *les grands* could not be trusted, that any action which they took would probably be for their own benefit, but he pushed on.[1]

---

[1] The best information on the Huguenots can be gained from the letters of Thomas Edmondes and James I in B. M. Stowe MSS 173–174. Two warnings of future trouble by Edmondes are to be found in 173, fol. 20r (July 21/31, 1612) and 174, fol. 74v (June 7/17, 1613). See also J. H. Clarke, *Huguenot Warrior: The Life and Times of Henri de Rohan, 1579*–

The great danger was that while Bouillon had lost influence with the Huguenots after 1611 he felt that he had not received a compensating reward from the Regency government. In search of a means to regain his authority, he began to encourage Condé, who felt isolated since the death of his uncle the Count of Soissons late in 1612, to assert his right to a role in government. However, Condé, who lacked education and talent, could not be pushed in any consistent direction and was susceptible to the pacifying measures of Marie de Médicis and Villeroy, as well as to the temptations offered by the Guise family, which was trying to establish a paramount role for itself. Further complications were added by the maneuvering of Concini to establish a secure place for his family in French life and the efforts of the four dukes, Nevers, Mayenne, Longueville and Epernon to further their own causes.[2]

Bouillon, encouraged by James I's attentions and Condé's pliability, made an issue of the Savoyard invasion of Montferrat. He evidently hoped that a French invasion of Savoy would so anger Spain that the marriage negotiations would be broken off. The Regency government was willing to put pressure on Charles Emmanuel to withdraw from Montferrat as part of its policy of maintaining peace. In addition, a little trouble with Spain would both please the Huguenots and help push the Spaniards toward a settlement of the Navarre problem. But there is no evidence that the Regency wanted to take open action. In the summer of 1613 orders were given to mobilize troops. Condé was won over by promising him a voice in the Council. As anti-

---

1638 (The Hague, 1966), pp. 35–47. James I promised Bouillon that he would keep secret any private dealing he had with him. B. M. Stowe MS 173, fol. 2r (James I to Edmontes, July 3/13, 1612). The Ambassador of the States General, Aerssen, also worked with Bouillon, trying to reconcile the Huguenot leaders but the French government succeeded in getting him recalled in 1613. Ouvré, *Du Maurier*, pp. 206–213.

[2] For Henri de la Tour d'Auvergne, comte de Turenne, duc de Bouillon (1555–1623) see Clarke, *Huguenot Warrior*, pp. 31–34; Auguste Laugel, *Henry de Rohan, son rôle politique et militaire sous Louis XIII* (Paris, 1889), pp. 44–45. For Condé (1588–1646) see Henri duc d'Aumale, *Histoire des Princes de Condé pendant les XVIᵉ et XVIIᵉ siècles* (Paris, 1885), II, 246, 253–254, III, 20–39; René de Cumont, *sieur* de Fiefbrun, *Véritable discours de la naissance et vie de Monseigneur le Prince de Condé jusqu'à présent*, ed. E. Halphen, (Paris, 1861), pp. xvi-xxviii, 50–51. Condé's penmanship, when compared with that of the other nobles and officials, reveals his lack of education. For Concini (1575–1617) see Fernand Hayem, *Le maréchal d'Ancre et Leonora Galigai* (Paris, 1910), pp. 1–186; also Ferdinand Pouy, *Concini, Maréchal d'Ancre, son gouvernement en Picardie* (Amiens, 1885). Despite all the discussion of their careers no satisfactory biography of Concini or his wife has yet been written. For Nevers, see Emile Baudson, *Charles de Gonzaque, duc de Nevers de Rethel et de Mantoue, 1580–1637* (Paris, 1888). For Jean-Louis de Nogaret de La Valette, Duke of Epernon (1554–1642) see L. Mouton, *Le Duc et le Roi* (Paris, 1924).

cipated Charles Emmanuel agreed to negotiate. The troops were no longer necessary, but to keep the Huguenots happy the blame for disbanding them was placed on the shoulders of the *Parlement* of Paris which had refused to register edicts for the sale of offices to support the war effort.[3]

All seemed to be going well by the end of 1613, although some murmuring was heard from Condé, Nevers and Mayenne. Savoy was willing to negotiate, Spain was conciliatory and James I was once again busy with plans for new marriage proposals. The rulers of Tuscany and the United Provinces felt that a natural interlude had come and used the opportunity to change ambassadors to France. What no one counted on was Bouillon. He was determined to get something for all his trouble.

It would have been easy for Marie and her advisers to feel optimistic during the first days of 1614. In spite of stirrings in Jülich and Northern Italy, Europe was at peace, *les grands* seemed to have been forestalled once more, and the economic situation was favorable. On the other hand, though there were many willing to praise the Queen and her government in print, there were manuscript copies of attacks on the Regency circulating. A typical example of the quality of the criticism was a poem of twenty-one quatrains that ended:

> This troop with joyfulness
> Scorning good favor
> Will serve their great princess
> Without recompense and without honor.
>
> You see then how we are,
> To serve our King forbidden
> Are the worthy men in our quarter
> Where the law is given by women.[4]

Then too at the end of 1613 an astrologer, Noël Jean Morgard, who had been foretelling assorted dire events since 1600, published an almanac that

---

[3] The best account of these developments is to be found in B. M. Stowe MS 174, fols. 9r–9v, 25r–27r, 53r–53v, 72v–74v, 94r–144v, 167r, 168r–169v, 174r–175v, 189v. See also Chapter 3 above. Edmondes believed that the *Parlement*'s refusal to register the edicts played a decisive role in the collapse of the invasion plans. That this was not true can be seen from the way in which the Regency government could find money when they really wanted it. For the Montferrat negotiations see Baudson, *Charles de Gonzaque*, pp. 84–98.

[4] B.N. MS fr. 9225, fol. 93r. The reference to women included not only Marie but all the members of the government, whom the poet had described with feminine nouns. For support of Marie's rule see among others D'Autreville, *Estat général des affaires de France* (Paris, 1617); *Mercure François* I, 504b, II, aij; *Le reveil du soldat français au Roy* (Paris, 1614), pp. 1–7. Many other examples published in the course of 1614 will be mentioned below.

predicted in part:

Janvier verra l'émotion
Que Février tost reperera
Mars les armes allumera
En Avril grand'sédition.[5]

Each month was provided with its own vaguely worded disaster. Morgard had not been prosecuted for similar pamphlets in previous years despite the edicts against such publications. But because he was a known associate of Condé and because his predictions for 1614 were popularly interpreted as foretelling the death of Louis XIII in August, he was imprisoned on January 8 and quickly sentenced to serve on board the galleys.[6] Printed refutations of Morgard's predictions, probably sponsored by the court, followed. Such prompt action indicated that in spite of the lull the government realized that all was not well.[7]

This feeling of concern was concealed for about a month as attempts were made to ascertain the seriousness of the situation. The first hint that something was amiss was given by Guillaume Ancel, the French ambassador to the Holy Roman Empire, residing in Orléans at the time, who wrote to his representative in Germany on January 11 that there was definite dis-

---

[5] Noël Jean Morgard, *Prédiction de Morgard pour la présente année MDCXIV avec les centuries pour le mesme année* (n.p., n.d.), p. 6.

[6] *Mercure François* III, 303–305; P. Boitel, *Histoire des choses plus memorables ... depuis ... 1610 ... jusques à ... 1617 ...* (Rouen, 1618) pp. 189–190. Pontchartrain, *Mémoires*, p. 328. [Claude Malingre] *Remarques d'histoire... depuis l'an 1600 ...* (Paris, 1632), pp. 218–219. In the 1616 edition Malingre had said Morgard was condemned to life on the galleys. In the 1632 edition he amends this to nine years. In fact Morgard once again published an almanac in 1619 in which he said he had served in the galleys for five years. The recently liberated Morgard had nothing but good to say about Louis XIII; *Le Manifeste de Noël Morgard ...* (Paris, 1619). At least two editions of both this work and that of 1614 were published. L'Estoile talks of Morgard's almanacs in 1609 and 1610, *Mémoires-Journaux*, X, 89; XI, 34. The earliest predictions of Morgard are those of 1600, *Prophéties de maistre Noël Jean Morgard ... en l'an 1600 ...* (n.p., n.d.). The printer of Morgard's 1614 pamphlet was also prosecuted. A.N. AD III 20, no. 65.

[7] *L'anti-Morgard, sur ses prédictions ...* (Paris, 1614), pp. 3–5; *L'anti-Mauregard ou le fantosme du bien public* (n.p., 1614), p. 3. This was one of the few contemporary works to place the major blame for the troubles of 1614 on Bouillon, pp. 4–7. *Le resveil de Maistre Guillaume aux bruits de ce temps* (n.p., 1614), pp. 1–33. The fullest condemnation of astrology in 1614 was François de Cauvigny, *Réfutation de l'astrologie judiciare* (Paris, 1614). Though Cauvigny was a professional writer it took him until May to finish his work of 67 pages. Its publication at that time shows that Morgard's predictions still attracted attention. See also the confused pamphlet by Pierre Beaunis de Chanterain, *Prédiction du soleil memorable ...* (n.p., n.d.). See B. M. Stowe MS 174, fols. 197v–198r, 199r, 203v for events in late 1613 that presaged trouble.

content in court though he was not able to discover the cause.[8] Two days later Condé left Paris, soon to be joined by other nobles. Of the foreign ambassadors resident in France, Cardinal Ubaldini was the first to begin to realize the gravity of the situation as his report of January 18 shows, though it was not until January 28 that he indicated serious worry. Thomas Edmondes left Paris near the end of January for England without realizing what was coming. Inigo de Cardenas did not report anything to Philip III about the situation until February 5, while Matteo Bartolini had nothing to report to Florence about Condé until February 10.[9]

Condé left court on January 13. He tried to mask his actions by letters to various dignitaries. The other nobles who left court all traveled in different directions, ostensibly on separate errands. However as early as January 15 Marie de Médicis wrote to Cardinal de Sourdis that she was beginning to discover how many malcontents there were. The Queen hastily began to take counter-action. The Duke of Epernon was summoned to court and the brother

---

[8] B.N. MS fr. 4116, fols. 17r–17v. The French Ambassador in Spain, Vaucelas, was primarily concerned with the health of the Infanta who had smallpox, the Navarre border question, Italian affairs, Cleves-Jülich, and Spanish attempts to hurry up the marriages, which on orders from Paris he kept pushing back from spring 1614 to the King's majority in October, to the spring of 1615, to the end of the meeting of the Estates General, B.N. MS fr. 16116, fols. 1r–259v, dispatches of January 2, 1614 to January 9, 1615. No hint of the troubles in France appear until the dispatches of March 21, 1614, *ibid.*, fol. 58r (the second of two 58r's in the volume). Several ambassadors said that Marie wanted the marriages held quickly but that Villeroy and Jeannin held back negotiations. See B. M. Stowe MS 174, fol. 277r (Beaulieu to Edmondes, February 26/March 8, 1614), AN. K 1428, no. 40 (Spanish Council of State April 19, 1614), B.N. MS ital. 1767, pp. 48–49 (Venetian Ambassador, April 14, 1614): Villeroy denied this in late 1614, B. M. Stowe MS 175, fols. 153r–154v (Edmondes to Somerset, December 30, 1614/January 9, 1615). The Navarre question was settled in November 1614, AN. K 1634, nos. 11–12, 15–16. Brèves in Rome was busy with the Mantua negotiations and a dispensation because of relationship and age for the French–Spanish marriages. He seems to have received his first information on Condé about February 17 (sent to him on January 28), B.N. MS fr. 18009, fols. 1r–44r (Brèves's dispatch of January 5–February 17, 1614). See also B.N. MS fr. 3654, the register of letters received by Brèves, fols. 57r–58v, 52r–64v.

[9] A.S.V. Fond. Borgh. Series II, No. 242, fols. 2r–5v; B.N. MS ital. 38, fols. 133r–134v; *Ibid.*, fol. 137v; *Cal. St. P* LXVII, 11; B.M. Stowe MS 174, fol. 222r. AN. K 1469, nos. 2–9, 14, K 1428, no. 36, K 1610, no. 9. A.S.F. Arch. Med. 4629, no. 2. Edmondes seems to have left Paris on his own initiative for three reasons: to try to get the money his government owed him; in hopes of being appointed a Secretary of State; and to help with the English–French marriage negotiations. He failed in all of these, though he staved off the attempt of Henry Wotton to get his position as ambassador. Edmondes left London to return to France on July 12, 1614. While he was away detailed reports were sent to him by his French secretary Jean Beaulieu. He continued to complain about his lack of money but eventually got the royal preferment he desired. *Cal. St. P.* LXXII, 6; LXXVI, 18, 34, 52; LXVII, 11, 47, 53; LXXX, 10; LXXXII, 125; LXXXIX, 39, 87; XC, 1; XCII, 15. Smith, *Wotton*, I, 134, II, 44–45; B. M. Stowe MS 174, fol. 144r. *Third Report of the Royal Commission on Historical Manuscripts* (London, 1872), p. 292b.

of the Duke of Guise was given the governorship of Provence. The Duke of Ventadour and Jean de Thumery, *sieur* of Boissise were sent after Condé who was moving south towards Orléans, to entreat him to return and receive the honors due him. Condé refused to wait for these envoys and began to move eastward toward Champagne. A letter to him from Marie on February 7 did not arrest his progress.[10]

The Duke of Longueville left court on February 10 in spite of the entreaties of Marie. Soon after this date Condé, joined by the Dukes of Longueville, Mayenne, Luxembourg, and Bouillon and their followers, met with Nevers who had left Paris on January 8, at the fortress of Mézières. This fortress was situated on the border of France in Nevers's government of Champagne. For a time they used Mézières as their headquarters, despite its commander's attempts at resistance. From this time until the signing of the treaty of Sainte-Ménehould in May the princes, as they were called, their followers, and their troops moved from place to place in the sparsely settled, rolling hills of Champagne.[11]

The Duke of Vendôme, who had been held captive at the Louvre to prevent his departure, escaped through a kitchen door just before supper on February 19. Vendôme, an illegitimate son of Henry IV, did not join the other malcontents, but went immediately to Brittany which he claimed as his *gouvernement* in spite of his recent removal from the position of governor.[12]

There were reports that forces were being raised in various provinces in support of the rebels. Pamphlets were churned out by both sides; Paris was

---

[10] Pontchartrain, *Mémoires*, pp. 328–329. B.N. MS fr. 4067, fols. 6v–8v (Puisieux to François-Annibal d'Estrées, marquis of Coeuvres, January 21, 1614). B.N. Cinq Cents 88, fols. 295v–296r. Cinq Cents 89, fol. 221v. B.N. MS fr. 3713, fols. 1r–6r (instructions for Ventadour and Boissise). Epernon and Guise, after some wavering, remained loyal to the crown for a price in money and power. Guise became Lieutenant General of France. Epernon settled for preferment for his children; one of these rewards, the diocese of Metz for his third son further entangled France in a quarrel with the Empire and Rome. B.N. MS fr. 15581, fols. 184r–184v, 186r–188r, 192r–193v, 217r–217v. B.M. Stowe MS 174, fols. 229v, 252v, 269r. Guise also maintained contacts with James I, *Ibid.*, fols. 229r, 279r. Life went on as usual at court during January, perhaps to keep the pretence that all was well, with ballets being performed on January 23 and 30. Paul Lacroix, ed., *Ballets et mascarades de cour de Henri III à Louis XIV, 1581–1652* (Geneva, 1868–1870), II, 1–23.

[11] [Claude Malingre], *Remarques d'histoire*, p. 219. Pontchartrain, *Mémoires*, p. 328. *Mercure françois*, III, part 1, 312–317. *Discours de ce qui s'est passé à Mézières* (n.p., n.d.). B.N. Cinq Cents 12, fols. 184r–200r (justifications of Nevers and Condé concerning what happened at Mézières; these were sent to De Thou as noted in his hand). B. M. Stowe MS 174, fols. 261r–263r (Bouillon to James I from Sedan and Mézières describing the situation).

[12] François de Malherbe, *Oeuvres de Malherbe, poésies et correspondance* (Paris, 1865), pp. 473–475 (letter to Peiresc of February 20, 1614). Malherbe can usually be counted on for the minutiae of court life. Vendôme was also upset by the order to dismantle his coastal fortress of Quilleboeuf, A.N. E 43A (January 11, 1614).

filled with talk of war. In spite of initial problems Marie, Villeroy and Jeannin were gaining the upper hand. The Regency had been collecting information on the movements and strength of the departed nobles and by the second week in February Marie de Médicis was in full action against them. She ordered one of her commanders to pursue Vendôme, but he was sent in the wrong direction toward Mézières. On February 20 Concini was sent to Picardy and the Duke of Montbazon to Nantes to secure those areas. In the next few days orders were sent to call back M. Boucare who was searching for Vendôme, the governor of Bourbonnais was ordered to Paris, and M. de Jeuffreville, a member of the royal council usually resident in Paris, was ordered to return to his *gouvernement*.[13]

In the meantime the army was built up, especially by the recruitment of Swiss mercenaries. Letters in Marie's hand were filled with orders to various commanders to move the troops here and there to keep the rebels contained. Cities in threatened areas such as Angers were ordered to fortify themselves. The Marquis of Coeuvres was informed on February 12 that no troops could be sent to Italy until Guyenne was safe. Throughout the spring the orders flowed, not only from Marie but from other members of the government. Judging from the failure of the nobles to raise substantial troops in France or to stage any important battles, these maneuvers were successful.[14]

The money spent on troops and on special missions to the areas that were endangered by Condé, or suspected of disloyalty, is recorded in the accounts of the *Trésorier de l'Epargne*. These figures confirm that the government

---

[13] B.N. MS fr. 15581, fols. 183r–183v (report to Villeroy from Orléans of January 26 on movements of Condé's family and their aims). *Ibid.*, fols. 200r–200v, 209r–209v, 218r–219v, 222r–223r (reports to Villeroy in February, March and April on the movements of the rebels' relations). B.N. Cinq Cents 89, fols. 224r–225r, 227v (three letters in Italian from Marie to Boucare). *Ibid.*, fols. 227r, 229v. Pontchartrain, *Mémoires*, p. 329. B.N. MS fr. 3800, fol. 1r (Concini's problems in Picardy). *Apologie pour Monsieur le Prince de Condé sur son départ de la cour* (n.p., 1614); according to B. M. Stowe MS 174, fol. 254r the author was named Pelletier. J.L.P.S., *A Monseigneur le Prince* (n.p., n.d.). For Picardy see B. Mun. Amiens BB 59.

[14] B.N. Cinq Cents 89, fols. 231r–232v, 244v–245v. B. M. Stowe MS 174, fols. 226r–227r (Beaulieu to Edmondes February 4/14 on troop arrangements). Jean Louvet, 'Récit véritable de tout ce qui est advenue de mémoire, tout en la ville d'Angers, pais d'Anjou et autres lieux avec un journal allant de 1583 à 1634', *Revue d'Anjou et de Maine-et-Loire*, I (1885), 53–55. B.N. MS fr. 4067, fol. 15v (Puisieux to Coeuvres). B.N. MS fr. 3788, fol. 6r; MS fr. 3797, fols. 6r–9r (May-June troop movements), B.N. MS fr. 3800, fols. 4r (letter of Louis XIII of April 13), 6r–6v. Rott, *Histoire*, III, 112, 118. B.N. MS fr. n.a. 23369, p. 373 (Lomenie to La Force, Feb. 19, 1614). François de Bassompierre, *Journal de ma vie...*, I, 367–374. To make clear the status of the Prince as a rebel, the King issued ordinances on March 4 and 5 forbidding transportation of war supplies and levying of troops without the express permission of the King. Philippe Du Plessis–Mornay, *Mémoires et Correspondance de Duplessis–Mornay*, ed. Pierre René (Paris, 1825), XII, 540–542.

action began seriously about February 15, and that February and March were the months of greatest stress. For example, the number of missions sent to the troubled areas rose by steps from thirty-one between February 15 and March 1, to a hundred between April 19 and May 10, then dropped sharply. The military expenses began to rise in the first period, reached a peak between March 15 and April 5 (400,000 *livres*) and then steadily declined until by early June almost no money was being spent for these purposes. A comparison of military expenses in 1613 and 1614 shows the magnitude of the expense necessary to end the revolt and the aptness of Jeannin's comments on his preference for paying for gifts rather than for a war.[15] On January 27, 1611, when Sully retired, it was certified that there were five million *livres* stored in the Bastille. Until the open rebellion of February, 1614, the government had not touched this reserve. But the Bastille was emptied by the end of 1615 as the policies of the Regency were brought to a successful conclusion. The money was used to pay troops and to cover extra expenses connected with the royal marriages in the autumn of 1615. In addition 440,000 *livres* were borrowed from Antoine Feydeau, Farmer General of *Aides*, and 220,000 *livres* from the Five Great Farms. It was stipulated that the Estates General would be asked to provide means for repaying these loans, but this was not done.[16]

As far as it can be determined, the decision of the Princes to leave the court had been made about the middle of December 1613 under the influence of Bouillon. Not even the English ambassador had any idea that this was anything other than an almost routine attempt to put pressure on the government. The various malcontents had no common purpose. Each had his own grievances, his own plan to gain preferment, though the recent appointment of Concini as Marshal of France bothered them all. The only unifying force at this point was Bouillon, who after urging action, kept quiet until everyone had left Paris. He then appeared before Marie in the role of honest broker to list the grievances of the Princes, which were basically that they wanted a greater role in the government. Only when he was not permitted to assume the role he had chosen for himself did he openly join the rebels. After this he allowed Condé to serve as leader since he had the strongest claim to power. As time went on, Bouillon again found that Condé would neither provide any effective leadership nor accept anyone's advice. At this

[15] B.N. Dupuy 826, fols. 44r–56r, 68r–83v, 96r–112v, 128r–151r, 159r–189r; A.A.E. France 769, fols. 88r–93r, 306v–313r.

[16] A. de Boislisle, *Chambre des Comptes de Paris. Pièces justicatives*, 1566–1701 (Nogent-le-Rotrou, 1873), pp. 298–306. Battifol, 'Le Trésor', pp. 200–209. B.N. Cinq Cents 43, fols. 117r–139r. A.N. E 46B–47A, fols. 358r–360r. A further 30,000 *livres* was borrowed on April 1, 1615. A.N. E 48B–49, fol. 1r.

point, in late spring, Bouillon began to align himself with the government in an effort to gain what he could.[17]

On February 18, the rebels made their demands public in letters to Marie de Médicis and the *parlements* of France. These letters, signed by Condé, began with the same protestation that would be used throughout the revolts of 1614–1616, that in reality the nobles were loyal and were acting only for the welfare of the King. The letters said that the advice of the important nobles should carry more weight than that of the present councilors, and that an Estates General should be called during the minority of the King to review the state of affairs and propose reforms as was customary. The planned Spanish marriages also displeased the rebels, as did the growing power of *Parlement*. A number of minor grievances were presented with emphasis on the assertion that no important steps should be taken until an Estates General had met and the King had reached his majority.[18]

Marie had anticipated the complaints of the rebels. On February 12 she had written to Cardinal de Sourdis that she planned to call an Estates General when the King attained his majority in October, 1614. On February 12, 13 and 14 she wrote to the governors, important towns, and *parlements* of France as well as to some of the important nobles such as Lesdiguières, a Huguenot and vice-governor of Dauphiné, informing them of the course of events and soliciting their support. The governors were told of her plan to call an Estates General and were commanded to inform everyone of this.[19]

Upon receiving Condé's letter Marie immediately began to prepare an

[17] B. M. Stowe MS 174, fols. 197v–199r, 203v (Edmondes, dispatches of December 3/13 and December 14/24, 1613); B.N. MS fr. n.a. 23369, pp. 361–362 (Lomenie to La Force, February 10, 1614, on Bouillon's appearance at court). *Discours de ce qui s'est passé à Mézières* (n.p., n.d.). Further indication of Bouillon's influence can be found in Charles Pradel, ed., *Mémoires de J. de Bouffard-Madiane sur les guerres civiles du Duc de Rohan, 1610–1629* (Paris, 1897), p. 9.

[18] Henri II de Bourbon, Prince de Condé, *Double de la lettre escrite par Monseigneur le Prince de Condé suivant le vray original. A la royne régente mère du roy, le 19 février mil six cens quatorze* (Paris, n.d.). The usual date given for this letter is February 19, but B.N. MS fr. 3654, fols. 62r–64v contains a copy of this letter signed by Condé, dated February 18. See also Condé, *Lettre de Monseigneur le Prince à MM. de la cour de Parlement* (n.p., 1614). This letter also carries the date of February 18.

[19] B.N. MS fr. 6379, fols. 177r–177v (letter to de Sourdis). Marie de Médicis, *Copie de la lettre escritte à Monsieur Desdiguie par la Royne* (n.p., 1614). Lesdiguières did not condescend to answer this plea until he wrote to Jeannin on May 2, but there should have been no worry about the loyalty of the 'King of Dauphiné'. François de Bonne, duc de Lesdiguières, *Actes et correspondance du connétable de Lesdiguières*, ed. Douglas and Roman (Paris, 1878), II, 58. Marie de Médicis, *Lettre de la Royne au Parlement de Bretagne* (Paris, 1614). *Du 14ᵉ jour de février 1614. Avis aux trois estats de ce royaume sur les bruits qui courlt à présent de la guerre civille* (Blois, 1614). B.N. MS fr. 3654, fols. 57r–58v (letter to Brèves from Marie de Médicis of February 14). Augustin Thierry, *Essai sur l'origine et des progrès du tiers état* (Paris, 1863), III, 6, footnote 1. [Malingre], *Remarques*, p. 219. *La Harangue de Alexandre Forgeron, prononcé*

answer. Jeannin and Villeroy were each asked to draft a reply. Marie decided to use Villeroy's, and it was sent from Paris on February 27. This letter promised that an Estates General would be called, noting that the Regent had decided on this action before Condé's letter arrived. The various other grievances were then discussed. Satisfaction was promised, and the admonition added that if Condé wanted anyone to believe that he was sincere he should return to the court.[20]

The advice given Marie by Villeroy, Jeannin and Sillery during the crisis is extant. From this and the pamphlets and memoirs it would seem that both Villeroy and Jeannin encouraged energetic action against the rebels, while Sillery and his new ally Concini discouraged it. Villeroy and Jeannin used well the experience they had gained during the Wars of Religion. That Marie was more inclined to a policy of action can be seen from the course she followed and from the favor that Villeroy and Jeannin enjoyed during this period.[21]

From the beginning of the rebellion Condé and Bouillon had sought to strengthen their forces by raising money and troops in Switzerland, the Spanish Netherlands, the United Provinces, England and Savoy. In spite of the Spanish ambassador's worry that the Protestant nations of Europe would conspire to help Condé there were few concrete results from the Princes' appeals. The French ambassador in Switzerland arranged for the arrest of Condé's and Bouillon's emissary. Some troops were raised by Nevers in Liège but the Duke of Lorraine warned the French government of their presence and few got through. The Dutch agreed not to give any help after the Regency government speeded up troop payments. Some arms were shipped to Condé by individual Dutchmen but the government of the United Provinces interfered with this by imposing severe fines on those involved. James I had Edmondes write to Bouillon asking him to break with Condé and con-

---

au conclave des réformateurs (n.p., 1614), p. 8. The idea of holding an Estates General had been put forward by various people since the death of Henry IV. The government had decided by early February that either an Assembly of Notables or an Estates General should be called, B. M. Stowe MS 174, fols. 222r–224v (Beaulieu to Edmondes January 29/February 8, 1614); La Force, *Mèmoires*, III, 385 (Marie de Médicis to La Force, February 8, 1614). Fontenay-Mareuil, *Mémoires*, p. 72, says that the letters were sent on February 3, but there is no other proof of this.

[20] Marie de Médicis, *Double de la response de la royne régente, mère du roy, à la lettre escritte à sa majesté, par le Prince de Condé, le 19 de février 1614* (Paris, 1614). See also B.N. MS fr. 3712. Jeannin's version is to be found in B.N. MS fr. 15644, fols. 12r–18v, and MS fr. n.a. 7262, fols. 98r–101r. Jeannin's letter in keeping with his position emphasizes the financial affairs of the kingdom, stating that during the Regency taxes had been lowered.

[21] B.N. MS fr. n.a. 7262, fols. 102r–107v ('advis donné à la royne par trois des principaux du conseil'). B.N. MS fr. n.a. 7260, fols. 123r–129v (Villeroy's advice). See also J. Nouaillac, 'Avis de Villeroy à la Reine Marie de Médicis, 10 mars, 1614', *Revue Henri IV*, II (1908), pp. 79–81.

centrate on bringing peace to the Huguenot community and good relations with Marie de Médicis to further the English – French marriage negotiations. As usual Charles Emmanuel of Savoy went no further than words. Pope Paul V joined in with a gentle rebuke for Condé's actions.[22]

To counter the possible concentration of troops in Bouillon's semi-independent principality of Sedan which was upriver from Liège, the French government entered into negotiations with the Spanish to provide some troops they had stationed in Luxembourg. To aid in convincing the Spanish to help, Villeroy played on Spanish fears by saying that Condé's victory would mean the disappearance of Catholicism in France and that this would render Spain and Italy prey to Protestantism.[23]

Condé had hoped to receive help from discontented Huguenots, but he was not very successful. The Duke of Rohan, Sully's son-in-law, doubtful of Condé's prospects of success, refused to join him when he found that peace negotiations were already underway. In the meantime he informed the Queen that he remained united with the body of the Huguenots and that if she gave them contentment she need have no worries about their loyalty.[24]

By the time Marie received Rohan's assurance the negotiations for peace were just about completed. During the critical months of February and March there had been fear at court that the Huguenots would join the insurgents. The Huguenots of Languedoc were put under surveillance by the government, but at an assembly in Nîmes they agreed to join Condé under certain conditions. Before negotiations could be completed the opposition of a number of Huguenots and the promises of the Regent forestalled the alliance. The Marquis of La Force, a Huguenot and lieutenant general of

[22] B.N. MS ital. 1767, pp. 26–29 (report of Contarini of March 14, 1614). A.N. K. 1469, nos. 27–28 (Condé and Bouillon to possible Swiss allies, February 22, 1614), no. 69 (Cardenas letters of April 2, 3, 6, 1614), Rott, *Histoire*, III, 112, 980. B.N. MS fr. 15581, fols. 208r-v, B.N. MS fr. n.a. 23369, p. 379. B.N. MS fr. 15581, fol. 252r (Jeannin to Villeroy, May 20, 1614 on Condé's Walloon troops). B.N. Dupuy 744, fols. 177r–180r, A.A.E. Hollande 7, fols. 385r–388r. Ouvré, *Du Maurier*, pp. 214–215; B. M. Stowe MS 174, fols. 244r–245v, 248r–249v, 275r–275v, B.N. MS fr. 20154, p. 1255.

[23] A.N. K. 1428, nos. 38, 41; K 1469, nos. 43–44, 70, 73–75 (Cardenas's reports of March and April). In the end Condé had an army of between 3,000 and 6,500. The royal army had a strength of more than 12,000 men. B. M. Stowe MS 174, fol. 304v. François de Malherbe, *Lettres de Malherbe* (Paris, 1822), pp. 354–356 (letter of March 10, 1614). A.N. K. 1469, no. 48. In contrast with 1614, in 1610 Condé was trying to get support from Spain to stage a revolt in France, Lonchay and Cuvelier, eds., *Correspondance*, I, 389 (Spinola to Philip III, September 23, 1610).

[24] Henri duc de Rohan, *Mémoires du duc de Rohan* in Michaud and Poujoulat, *Nouvelle Collection*, XIX, 503. James I wrote to Rohan in February 1614 urging him to concentrate on religious problems and not to get involved in anything contrary to the obedience he owed his King or that would bring fighting. B. M. Stowe MS 174, fol. 232r. Villeroy received information in late April that Rohan was planning to raise troops for Condé, but this must have been false. B.N. MS fr. 15581, fols. 238r–239r.

Navarre and Béarn, maintained the loyalty of the Protestants of the far south. Cardinal de Sourdis was negotiating with the Huguenots in Guyenne, and as early as February 12 he sent word that he was making progress though he continued working most of the spring. Further north things seemed more secure. For example, the town of Vitry à la Reine, a town with a large Huguenot population in eastern Champagne, sent the Queen Mother assurance on March 5 of its loyalty. On March 22 Sully told Marie that he would remain faithful. So, despite the defection of a few nobles such as Bouillon, most of the Huguenots remained loyal to the government; those in the north because they sincerely wanted to, those in the south because they were too disorganized or saw no advantage in joining Condé. Most of the leaders, La Force, Lesdiguières, Du Plessis–Mornay, and Rohan, chose not to join in a dubious battle.[25]

Sully wrote to La Force on February 22 that 'ceux de la religion' were too disorganized to do anything. An example of this was provided by the political–religious quarrels in Bordeaux. Cardinal de Sourdis, the Marquis of La Force, and Condé were all involved in this confused situation. Part of the trouble came from long-standing demands by Condé for both a fortress and the power to nominate the mayor, but the difficulties raised by the split loyalties of the Huguenots seem to have been most important. In the end Condé failed to gain either his claims or sufficient Huguenot support. La Force was rewarded by obtaining support from the Crown in his personal troubles and Sourdis was warmly congratulated by Marie. Bordeaux was also a source of worry for the government because of the supposed reply of the *Parlement* of Bordeaux to Condé, giving him support. This was later proved to be a forgery. Most of the other *parlements* refused even to open the letters sent by Condé.[26]

In the meanwhile the rebel nobles were kept busy trying to justify themselves in letters to various important officials and nobles, continually main-

---

[25] A.S.F. Arch. Med. 4629 (letter of Matteo Bartolini, the Tuscan ambassador of April 9, 1614). B.N. MS fr. 15581 fols. 296r–296v (the conditions of the Huguenots of Nîmes). A.S.V. Fond. Borgh. II, 242, fols. 3v–5r (Ubaldini to the Curia, January 28, 1614). Dom Claude Devic and Dom Jean Vaissete, eds. *Histoire générale de Languedoc* (Paris, 1889), XI, part 2, col. 918, XII, part 2, cols. 1635–36. A.N. K 111, no. 1, parts 170, 195, 196, 209, 218, 231, 232, 234, 238, 246, 292 (documents concerning La Force), B.N. MS fr. n.a. 23369, pp. 358–364 (Lomenie to La Force, February 10, 1614). B.N. MS fr. n.a. 6379, fols. 180r, 182r, 184r–184v. Georges Herelle, ed., *Documents inédits sur le protestantisme à Vitry-le-François, Epense, Heilly-le-Maurupt, Nettancourt et Vassy* (Paris, 1880), pp. 69–70. B.N. MS fr. 3795, fol. 13 (Sully).

[26] La Force, *Mémoires*, II, 386. Pelletier, *Lettre à Monseigneur le Prince de Condé* (n.p., n.d.). B.N. MS fr. n.a. 23369, p. 394. De Vic, *Languedoc*, XII, part 2, col. 1632. B.N. MS fr. 6379, fols. 216r–217r, 225r–225v. B.N. Cinq Cents 12, fol. 276v. A.N. V⁶ 1223 (*Conseil privé*, May 12, 1614). B. M. Stowe MS 173, fols. 3r–3v, B.N. Cinq Cents 12, fol. 276v. Boutriche, *et al.*, *Histoire de Bordeaux de 1453 à 1715* (Bordeaux, 1966), pp. 317–319. A.C., [Pierre Beaunis] *Le Lourdaut Vagabond rencontré par l'esprit de la cour . . .* (Paris, 1614). Another edition of this anti-Condé pamphlet appeared under the title *Le Lourdaut de Champagne . . .* (Paris, 1614). See also Pierre Beaunis de Chanterain, sieur de Viettes, *Le Hola des gens de guerre . . .* (Paris, 1614).

taining that they were working for the good of the kingdom and that therefore they were forced to do what they were doing.[27]

The Queen Mother sent Jacques de Thou to Condé on March 3 with instructions to arrange for negotiations. De Thou spent most of the month wandering around Champagne trying to find Condé. Finally contact was established at Sedan, and Condé agreed to negotiate at Soissons. Condé arrived in that town on April 5 with four thousand infantry and about six hundred cavalry. On April 6 the negotiators for the government – Ventadour, Boissise, De Thou, Jeannin, and Claude de Bullion – left Paris.[28]

The negotiations began on April 14. But Condé, afraid of the large body of royal troops that were being brought into Champagne, retreated to the town of Sainte-Ménehould and captured it, leaving Mayenne to negotiate at Soissons. Agreement was soon reached on the main issues, but details and additional small demands by the rebels slowed things down. Also hindering progress was the problem of getting Condé to return to sign the treaty. The Queen first offered to send her negotiators as far as Rethel, but finally Condé won the minor victory of having the treaty signed at Sainte-Ménehould. Though the discussions dragged on for a month, governmental correspondence reveals that from the time Condé agreed to negotiate the tension and worry began to disappear, though slowly. There were a number of rumors of troops being raised for Condé in the west, and the makings of an international incident when the French intercepted the reports of the English representative at Soissons, which included James I's advice to Bouillon on the Spanish marriage question.[29]

The treaty of Sainte-Ménehould, signed on May 15, which was to bind all insurgents present or absent, provided that an Estates General would meet in Sens on August 25. Since the King would not reach his majority until

---

[27] *Mercure François*, III, part 2, 329. Fiefbrun was the main courier of Condé to the court and high officials. Condé, *Le Manifeste de M. le Prince envoyé à M. le Cardinal de Joyeuse...* (n.p., 1614). François Cardinal de Sourdis, *Response de Monsieur le Cardinal de Sourdis à la lettre de Monseigneur le Prince* (Paris, 1614). Jacques Davy, Cardinal du Perron, *Lettre de Monseigneur le Cardinal du Perron à Monsieur le Prince* (Paris, 1614).

[28] Malingre, *Remarques*, pp. 221–222. Pontchartrain, *Mémoires*, p. 330; B.N. Cinq Cents 12, fols. 192r–198v (De Thou's letter while in search of Condé). In early March printers and booksellers who sold editions of Condé's letters were imprisoned and the others were forbidden to publish or sell pamphlets on the troubles without permission. B. M. Stowe MS. 174, fols. 276v, 285v. In the period just before Condé began to negotiate there was fear of unrest in Paris, *ibid.*, 315v; *Reg. délib. Paris*, XV, 351–354, 357–358; *Le colonel de la milice de Paris* (Paris, 1614).

[29] B.N. Cinq Cents 88, fol. 299v; B.N. Cinq Cents 12, fols. 237r–238v (report of De Thou's and Condé's agreement of May 2 to finish matters). B.N. Cinq Cents 43, fols. 46r–112v (letters of Marie and commissioners on negotiations). B.N. Cinq Cents 43, fols. 113r–117r (the first president of the *Parlement* of Paris reports to the *Parlement* on the meeting of the Council of May 5, concerning the final details of the treaty. The last thing that the Council decided, after much discussion, was to give Condé the fortress of Amboise). B.N. MS fr. 3799, fols. 26r–27r,

October 1, this was a seeming victory for Condé. The text of the treaty stated that the Queen Mother and Condé had reached a secret agreement on the Spanish marriages. The citadel of Mézières was to be demolished, but Nevers would be given money to build another residence. Blavet and the new fortifications in Brittany were to be destroyed. Within twelve days the foreign troops of both sides were to be sent home and the French soldiers were to return to their posts. Condé was to be given the Château of Amboise in trust until the Estates General should meet. When Vendôme, who was absent, rendered his obedience to the King he would be restored to the governorship of Brittany and his other honors. With a few exceptions the fortifications built since January 1 were to be razed. It was to be officially proclaimed that none of the Princes had acted contrary to the service of the King. There were several smaller concessions, and Condé was given 450,000 *livres* to be divided as he saw fit.[30]

The treaty was greeted with the unanimous approval of the pamphleteers. However, the Duke of Rohan summed up the treaty by saying that the particular interests buried the general. Cardinal Ubaldini was dismayed by the treaty, saying that it gave too much power to Condé and the Huguenots, that the *parlements* had been permitted to play too big a role in the negotiations, and that the Spanish marriages were in danger. Marie de Médicis had other ideas about this. As Jeannin wrote to Villeroy on April 16; if each prince gets what he wants they will forget their public demands.[31]

Louis XIII approved the treaty on May 25. The *Parlement* of Paris was thanked on May 31 for its services. The letters patent exonerating Condé

29r–29v, 32r–32v, 38r–49r, 55r–93r, 96r–96v (110 letters on the negotiations, mostly between Jeannin and Villeroy). B.N. MS fr. 15581, fols. 224r–255v (Jeannin to Villeroy, April 10 – May 20). B.N. MS fr. 6379, fols. 200r–210r (Pontchartrain to Sourdis), 212r, 213r–213v (Villeroy to Sourdis), 210r (Pontchartrain to Sourdis on April 21, reporting that the end of the negotiations was just about reached, but that the Queen wanted them to drag on to keep things quiet). B.N. MS fr. 3799, fol. 119r (Bouillon to Jeannin, May 27). A.N. K 110, no. 29³ (Condé's declaration of April 14, 1614). A.N. G8* 635, p. 4. B.N. MS fr. 15581, fols. 240r–245r (the French account of the interception, including some of the English documents). These documents are also in B. M. Stowe MS 174, fols. 306r–309r, 312r–312v. *Ibid.*, fols. 330v, 340v (English account). B.N. MS ital. 1767, pp. 62–65, 67–69 (Contarini's dispatches of April 29, 30, May 9). Jeannin played the most important part in the negotiations. He was trusted by Condé and Bouillon as was De Thou, while Villeroy was not.

[30] B. M. Stowe MS 174, fols. 317r–319v. *Articles de la paix* (Paris, 1614). B.N. Cinq Cents 1, fols. 348r–350v. A.N. AD + 156 (May 15, 1614). A.A.E. France 769, fols. 157r–157v, 158r–158v (signed copy of the Treaty).

[31] *Le Certification de la paix* ... (Paris, 1614); *Projet des principaux articles de la paix* ... (Paris, 1614); *Remerciements à la Royne* ... (Paris, 1614); *Le resjouissance de la France pour la réconciliation de messieurs les princes* (Paris, 1614). Rohan, *Mémoires*, p. 503. Ubaldini's dispatch of May 8 is in François T. Perrens, *Les mariages espagnols sous le règne de Henri IV et la régence de Marie de Médicis* (Paris, 1869), pp. 508–509. B.N. MS fr. 15581, fol. 231r (Jeannin to Villeroy, April 16).

and his followers were registered in that same body in July 4. On June 7 the Queen began a new series of moves. The letters announcing the Estates General were published throughout the kingdom, but the meeting was set for September 10 at Sens. The date would later be postponed until October 10 and the meeting would be transferred to Paris. When the Estates General finally met in Paris at the end of October the deputies would be meeting under the direct supervision of the government and after the declaration of the majority of the King.[32]

The period from January through May 1614 was characterized by the large numbers of pamphlets that were published. There are 858 pamphlets on political affairs in 1,425 editions that have survived from the years 1614–1615. Of these editions 21% were published between January and May, 1614. The Princes found little support for their cause in these pamphlets beyond the published versions of their own letters.[33] The criticism of the rebels ranged from moderate rebukes of their actions such as that contained in *Le Conseiller fidelle à Monsieur le Prince* to statements in favor of Regency policy such as *Discours sur le lettre de Monsieur le prince* or *Avis aux gens de bien* to violent satire of their pretensions. Typical statements were that the princes had no popular support,[34] that above all people wanted the continuation of the peace that Henry IV had brought to France,[35] and that:

the sickness that exists can only be cured by gentle remedies and he who looks for others and wishes to use violent and corrosive ones only increases and irritates the sickness. Above all, Monsieur le Prince should remember that between Divinity and Royalty there is no middle power; no one shares authority with kings.[36]

---

[32] A.N. K 110, no. 129 (approval of Louis XIII). Marie de Médicis, *Lettre de la royne régente à Messieurs du Parlement* (Paris, 1614). Lalourcé and Duval, eds., *Forme générale et particulière de la convocation et de la tenue des assemblées nationales ou Etats généraux de France, justifiée par pièces authentiques* (Paris, 1789), II, 41–44. A.N. AD + 156 (July, 1614). This includes a contemporary pamphlet that gives the date of verification as July 4. See also A.N. XIA 8648, fols. 43r–44r.

[33] Only six pamphlets excepting the published letters can be said to have been favorable to the Princes: *Advis à Monseigneur le Prince* (n.p., 1614). *Apologie pour Monsieur le Prince de Condé sur son départ de la cour* (n.p., 1614). *Le bon françois* (n.p., 1614). S.B.S., *Considérations sur l'estat de la France* (Paris, 1614). *Discours sur les calomnies et médisances publiée contre M. les princes* (n.p., 1614). *Discours sur les mariages de France ...* (n.p., 1614). One pamphlet, *Exhortation aux Parisiens* (Paris, 1614), evidently written after the peace treaty, managed to praise both the Princes and the government. Some unprinted support for Condé can be found in B.N. MS fr. 9225, fols. 46r–47v.

[34] *Le cabinet de Vulcan* (n.p., n.d.), pp. 4–5.

[35] *Ennuis de Paysans champestres ...* (n.p., 1614), pp. 1–5.

[36] *Discours sur la lettre de Monsieur le Prince* (n.p., n.d.), p. 25. See also *Libre Harangue faicte par Mathault* (n.p., 1614), *Résolution à la paix au service du Roy* (Paris, 1614), *Lettre de Jacques Bonhomme paysan de Beauvais à Messeigneurs les Princes retirés de la cour* (Paris, 1614), *Discours de Maistre Jean Joufflu sur les débats et divisions de ce temps (n.p., 1614), and Pierre Beaunis Sapience manifestée ...* (Paris, 1614).

The satirical pamphlets varied from the comparatively gentle joking of Jacques Bonhomme[37] to the more biting *Poule* series – the Princes say they are saving France when it seems that they only want to eat us, as the hens of Champagne and Brie have testified.[38] The strongest attack on the rebels' dignity was levelled against the returning nobles in June 1614 in *Discours véritable des propos tenus entre deux marchâdes du Palais*. This is a dialogue between two women, one a seller of linen, the other of hats. The women were happy that the great nobles had returned to court since they often came to use a room at the rear of the linen shop 'where assuredly you can show the entire display of your merchandise'. The two were particularly happy that the Princes had returned when they did because they were beginning to be approached by various scoundrels offering their 'services' thinking that they were 'going to waste'.[39]

The only match for the women was *Extraict de l'inventaire . . . de môsieur le Chevalier de Guise* which ridiculed the nobles of both parties and the Regency government and concluded:

Discours du procez intenté pardevant les Dames de la Cour d'un certain François demanduer en requeste tendant en fin que deffences soient faites à tous estrãgers de ne labourer les jardins dedites Dames ny semer de leurs graines, veu les parties naturelles des François avec l'arrest desdites Dames par lequel il est dit que les parties produierent leurs pièces pardevant elles pour icelles veuës, visitées & meurent considerées faire droict, ainsi que de raison.[40]

The evidence of the pamphlets strengthens the general impression of January to May 1614 – most Frenchmen did not want war. They were not perfectly happy but they were quite willing to live in their relative prosperity and hope for eventual reform rather than risk another civil war. Beginning in 1615 there was to be a change in this attitude but this came as a result of the

---

[37] *Conjouissance de Jacques Bonne Homme paysan de Beauvoisis avec Messeigneurs les Princes reconcilées* (Paris, 1614); *Le Réponse du crocheteur de la Samaritaine à Jacques Bonhomme* (Paris, 1614). See François Dumont 'Recherches sur les ordres dans l'opinion française sous l'Ancien Régime', *Album Helen Maude Cam*, I, 187–201.

[38] *Remerciement des Poules à Monsieur de Bouillon* (n.p., n.d.), pp. 3–4. *Discours de M. Guillaume et Jacques Bonhomme sur la deffaicte de trente cinq poulles . . .* (Paris, 1614).

[39] *Discours véritable des propos tenus entre deux marchâdes du Palais estant aux estuves près S. Nicolas de Champs . . .* (Paris, 1614), pp. 7, 14.

[40] *Extraict de l'inventaire que s'est trouvé dans le coffre de môsieur le Chevalier de Guise* (n.p., 1615), pp. 6–7. Mock legal style was also adopted by the writer of *Jugement définitif donné par Mathault . . .* (n.p., 1614); a less violent satire of both the princes and the government was *Sentence arbitrale de M. Guillaume* (n.p., 1614). Some satirical pamphlets that seem to have disappeared are noted in L. A. Caraccioli, *Notice intéressante et curieuse des ouvrages satyriques que parurens à l'époque des Etats généraux tenus en 1614 . . .* (Paris, 1789), pp. 3–19.

Huguenot fear of the Spanish marriages and the decay of the central government after the meeting of the Estates General. The conditions that proponents of the general crisis theory and theorists of peasant rebellions have described had not arrived in 1614. Despite their supposed control of large areas of France, the popular memory of the civil wars and prosperity rendered the rebels powerless.

Once the treaty was signed the next step was to induce as many rebel nobles as possible to return to court through the usual promises of preferment and money. Longueville and Mayenne returned at the beginning of June, and by July 8 Bouillon was writing to Condé urging moderation. Nor did Marie forget those who had helped her during the troubles. During the second week in June she wrote seven letters thanking various people for their aid. The same month she began her preparations to control the elections for the Estates General.[41]

The man most surprised by all this was César de Bourbon, Duke of Vendôme. He had not signed the treaty and he felt that he had been betrayed by Condé. Condé was not too dismayed by this, probably because Vendôme had never really been part of his group and because Vendôme was clearly the most touchy and unreasonable of nobles. Rohan was approached by Vendôme in hopes of getting support, but was advised to quit before he ruined himself completely. Nevertheless, Vendôme along with the Duke of Retz spent the summer conducting raids against areas loyal to the King in Brittany and Anjou, claiming, of course, that he was only doing his duty as governor of Brittany.[42]

At first Condé placed his hopes in securing the election of deputies to the Estates General who favored him, but it must soon have become evident that the Queen was outmaneuvering him. Condé tried to build support by traveling in the west but with little success. An excuse to begin agitating again came near the end of June at Poitiers during the preliminaries of the mayoralty election that involved Condé's friends. The whole process was very complicated, but in the end, despite Condé's attempts to interfere, the city was barricaded against him and a battle seemed imminent. At first Marie only sent a representative to Poitiers, but it soon became evident that something drastic had to be done to stop both Condé and Vendôme and to secure the loyalty of Brittany and the Loire region.[43]

---

[41] Pontchartrain, *Mémoires*, p. 331. Duc de Bouillon, *Lettre de M. de Bouillon à M. le Prince sur l'affaire de Poitiers* (n.p., 1614). B.N. Cinq Cents 43, fols. 143v–145r.

[42] Pontchartrain, *Mémoires*, p. 331. Rohan, *Mémoires*, p. 503. Estrées, *Mémoires*, pp. 107–108. Louvet, 'Recit veritable', pp. 129–137. Duc de Vendôme, *Lettre de Monsieur de Vendôme à la Reine* (Paris, 1614).

[43] Richelieu, *Mémoires*, I, 73. Pontchartrain, *Mémoires*, pp. 331–332. Estrées, *Mémoires*, pp. 107–108. B.N. Cinq Cents 12, fols. 256r–360v (original, signed account of Louis Gouffier, Duke of Roanes, the Governor of Poitiers, on the events at Poitiers). B.N. Clairambault 364, fols. 161r–164v, 223r–224v (letters of Condé to Marie on Poitiers).

It was decided that the King and Queen Mother would make a journey through the Loire country. According to the letter of the English ambassador to James I of August 22, 1614, this was Villeroy's idea. Edmondes also stated that Jeannin and Sillery lost some credit with the Queen because of their advice against the trip.[44]

Upon hearing of the plan Condé wrote to Marie saying that Vendôme would capitulate and that therefore it was not necessary to leave Paris. All that was necessary was the disbanding of the royal army as had been promised. Condé stated that if the trip were made it could only be construed as an attack on him. He implored the Queen not to believe the reports that he was trying to ruin the Estates General.[45]

Needless to say, Marie was not willing to believe Condé. Villeroy, who was sick, did not make the journey, but the Council and a large entourage accompanied the King and Queen Mother. The personal physician of Louis XIII, Jean Héroard, kept a complete journal of the trip that not only records the official business but also provides a very interesting portrait of the King behaving like a twelve year old boy – playing with guns, going fishing and hunting, reviewing the troops whenever the whim struck him, and so forth. However, Louis was taken on this journey for very special reasons, not only to win support for the Regency, but to prove that the King, contrary to the predictions of Morgard and the stories that abounded, was healthy.[46]

The royal party left Paris on July 5 and during the next month visited Orléans, Blois, Tours, Châtellerault, and Poitiers. During August it traveled

[44] B.M. Stowe MS 174, fols. 363r–364r (Beaulieu to Edmondes, June 25/July 5). Throughout the summer Jeannin was in contact with Condé, Nevers and Sully, trying to get Condé to end his opposition, and trying to keep Nevers happy. B.N. MS fr. 3799, fols. 6r–18r (seven letters from Condé to Jeannin), 123r–124r, 128r, 135r, (Sully to Jeannin). Lesdiguières also wrote to Jeannin three times during the summer (fols. 121r, 126r, 130r). Pontchartrain, *Mémoires*, p. 334. It seems evident that as late as July 22 Marie was planning to return to Paris after visiting Poitiers; François de Malherbe, *Letters inédites de Malherbe* (Paris, 1841), pp. 20–21. The *Parlement* of Paris was given notification of the plan to continue to Nantes on August 7 and told to remain in session in case something important came up, A.N. X1A 8648, fols. 102v–103v; A.N. AD + 157, no. 1. The *Parlement* was finally given permission to take its vacation on October 8, and it began October 10; A.N. X1A 8648, fols. 116v–117r. Edmondes's report of August 12/22 was his first on returning to France, B. M. Stowe MS 175, fol. 9v. Edmondes was worried that the French might be getting suspicious of English activities, *ibid.*, fol. 12r.

[45] B.N. MS fr. 7794, fols. 520r–522r. Condé, *Dernière lettre escrite à la royne par Monseigneur le Prince* (n.p., 1614). See also B.N. MS fr. 15581, fols. 256r–257r, 266r. A regiment of the Swiss Guard was kept in the west throughout 1614. Rott, *Histoire*, III, 118. Condé kept up his contacts with Holland and England during the summer. The Dutch refused to listen to him. James I was more open as will be seen. Ouvré, *Du Maurier*, pp. 217–218, Ballesteras Beretta, *Documentos*, IV, 200 (Gondomar to Lerma, July 3, 1614).

[46] B.N. Clairambault 364, fols. 260r–265r (negotiations with Condé during the trip); François de Bassompierre, *Journal*, I, 374–376. Jean Héroard, *Journal de Jean Héroard*, ed. E. Soulié and E. de Barthélemy (Paris, 1868), II, 143–159. Pontchartrain, *Mémoires*, p. 333. The King often rode on horseback to prove his health.

to Loudun, Saumur, and Angers. When it became evident that Vendôme was not sincere in his offer of surrender, the entourage proceeded to Nantes on August 12, where the King and Queen Mother presided over the Estates of Brittany. This maneuver forced Vendôme to capitulate and made sure that the deputies elected to the Estates General by the Estates of Brittany would be loyal to the King. Between August 29 and September 16 Angers, La Flèche, Mans, and Chartres were visited.[47]

The journey was a complete success. From the letters to and from Marie during the trip it appears that every noble of importance in Orléans and Brittany came to pledge loyalty to the Crown. The populace of the towns, both Catholic and Huguenot, were won over. Vendôme and Retz submitted, and Condé's attempts to win deputies for the Estates General were seriously hindered. The re-entry to Paris on September 16 was an occasion for great ceremony that lasted for most of the day. Paris belonged to the King, and so did France.[48]

Between June 21 and September 22, 1614 the Regency government spent 93,700 *livres* on 220 trips made to all parts of France by envoys whose purpose was to influence the elections. The treasury accounts note that the king called a number of other people to him for similar purposes during the royal tour of July and August. In June, Marie sent Sully's son the Marquis of Rosny to various lieutenants general and other important local officials to see that loyal men were elected. She sent letters in her own hand to those to be visited by Rosny urging them to elect good subjects of the King and hinting that their efforts would not go unrewarded. Marie's letters went to all areas of Normandy where she held the position of governor and to localities along a line between Nantes and Sens, from southern Brittany to western Champagne. Letters to the same men late in the summer show that Marie's efforts were successful;

---

[47] Boislisle, *Chambre des Comptes*, pp. 301–302. (Audience of the *Chambre des Comptes* with the Queen on day of departure). Héroard, *Journal*, II, 143–159. Bassompierre, *Journal*, I, 375. *Le Triomphe de la Fleur de Lys* ... (Paris, 1614), A. A. E. Hollande 7, fols. 404r–407v. Marie had made a similar trip with Henry IV in 1605 to head off a rumored uprising engineered by Bouillon, *LMHIV*, VI, xii–xiii. By the summer of 1614 Bouillon returned to his pose of middleman; Bouillon to Condé in *Mercure François*, IV, 2–4. For defense preparations in Paris during the royal journey see *Reg. délib. Paris*, XV, 365, 367.

[48] B.N. MS ital. 1767, pp. 167–168 (report of Contarini, Sept. 16, 1614). B.N. MS fr. 4121, fols. 94r–96v. B.N. MS fr. 6379, fols. 234r–234v, 235r. B.N. Cinq Cents 89, fols. 274v–275r, 277r. Pontchartrain, *Mémoires*, p. 333. The *gouvernement* of Orléanais in which most of the trip took place had a significant Huguenot population and was also an area in which was found much of the support of the rebel nobles. Theodore Godefroy, *Le cérémonial françois*, ed. Denis Godefroy (Paris, 1649), pp. 970–971. Dom Michel Félibien, *Histoire de la ville de Paris*, ed. D. Guy-Alexis (Paris, 1725), II, 1299–1300. Armand Baschet, *Le Roi chez la Reine ou histoire secrète du mariage de Louis XIII et d'Anne d'Autriche*, 2nd ed. (Paris, 1866), pp. 85–87.

she expressed her gratitude for the success of their efforts. Other letters to and from Secretary of State Paul Phelypeaux, *seigneur* of Pontchartrain, show that the elections in Guyenne were being controlled by François de Noailles and Cardinal de Sourdis. In Picardy Concini was active. Even Sully and Queen Marguerite helped. On the basis of these letters and other reports of success the elections in at least the governments of Guyenne, Orléanais, Brittany, Normandy and Picardy seem to have been favorable to the government.[49]

But the battle was not yet won. If Condé was lacking in ideas of his own he was soon to get help. King James I had tried to hold Bouillon back from civil war but the success of the Regency government during the summer of 1614 worried him. Having received information previously from Bouillon and Edmondes, he had the Earl of Somerset write to Edmondes, who had returned to Paris. Edmondes was to point out to Condé through Bouillon that the treaty of Sainte-Ménehould was not being honored since the Estates General was now to be held at Paris under the Queen's control. The deputies who had been elected were favorable to the Queen. The Prince was to be encouraged to 'interest himself and assume that right in managing the effayres, which properly belongs to him in ryght of his place, that they fall not back again and into the former absolute government of the . . . ministers'.[50]

Nor was James I to be the government's only worry. The summoning of an Estates General was bound to stir up interest in conditions and institutions that needed reform. Frenchmen who were loyal to the government and who had no use for the Princes, such as the author of *Anatomie des Trois Ordres*, knew from personal experience that many changes were desirable. Laymen held benefices while good priests starved, nobles equated money and honor, justice was exiled from France, offices were sold.[51] The danger was that these basically loyal subjects would want to do something through the Estates General about these evils.

[49] B.N. Cinq Cents 89, fols. 254v–256v, 267v, 273r, 276r–277r, 278r, 282r–282v (15 letters by Marie de Médicis); B.N. Dupuy 826, fols. 277v–287v, 312r–378r (treasury records); B.N. Clairambault 364, fols. 266r–266v, 268r, 277r–280r, 288r, 290r–290v, 299r–299v (letters of Noailles, July-August 1614); B.N. MS fr. 6379, fols. 227r–228r (letters to Sourdis July 12, 1614); A. C. Amiens BB 59, fols. 180r–194r, 199v (Amiens elections); A.N. E 46B–47A, fols. 166r–166v (Ponthieu). Sully wrote to Richelieu on June 23 encouraging the election of loyal deputies, A.A.E. France 769, fols. 169r–169v. The full extent of the government's actions in controlling the elections to the Estates General will be discussed in the following chapter.
[50] B.M. Stowe MS 175, fols. 58r–59r (letter of September 27/October 7). If Bouillon would not relay the message someone else was to be found. Bouillon was still keeping apart from Condé, *ibid.*, fols. 56r, 68v, 89r–91r. Condé returned to Paris on September 29; Vendôme also came at about the same time. [Malingre], *Remarques*, p. 225.
[51] *Anatomie des trois ordres de la France sur le sujet des estats* (n.p., 1615). pp. 4–6, 10–18, 19, 23–24, 35.

73

5

ELECTIONS AND DEPUTIES: JUNE TO OCTOBER 1614

Control of the elections to the Estates General of 1614 was crucial to the continued existence of the Regency government. At the same time it was vastly important that the Estates should be free Estates and that all traditional forms should be strictly adhered to. This chapter is primarily concerned with a description of the methods used to control the elections and with the results of the compilation of data on the 474 deputies who were finally sent to the meeting at Paris in October 1614. The information about the background of each deputy available in printed sources has been catalogued in Appendix 3. Analysis of this data provides considerable information about the nature of social and political life in France in 1614.

Between June 7 and 10 the King and Marie de Médicis each sent letters to the governors, *baillis*, seneschals, lieutenants general, and other important local officials announcing a meeting of the Estates General for September 10 in Sens. The recipients of the letters were ordered to convoke the three estates of their particular jurisdiction in the accustomed manner and as quickly as possible. *Cahiers* were to be drawn up and the traditional number of deputies were to be sent with these to the Estates General. It was emphasized that the deputies should be men of integrity and intelligence who were sincerely interested in the welfare of the King and the people.[1]

These letters initiated a long process that was to take most of the summer, and even part of the autumn in some remote areas, to complete. Although the process is too complicated to describe in detail, because of the many variations in different areas and estates, a simplified outline follows. An official, upon receiving the letters of the King and the Regent, notified his subordinates of the impending election. They in turn notified those below them. Important persons received individual summons from local authorities.[2] Then began the slow march back upward to the Estates General. In those rural parishes which were permitted to vote, the assembly, usually composed of the 'greater and

[1] B.N. MS fr. 20154, pp. 1251–53 (original, with signature, of the King's letter). A. C. Marseille AA 118 (original, with signature, of the Queen's letter). Many other copies of these letters exist in local archives, for example A.D. Somme B 17, fols. 28r–29v; A.D. Seine Maritime A 22, fols. 402r–408r; A.D. Ile-et-Vilaine C 2648, pp. 606–608.

[2] An example of the letters sent can be found in A.D. Yvelines 47 J 4.

saner part' of the male inhabitants, met after the High Mass in front of the church, the *curé* having announced the meeting during Mass. One or two men were elected to carry the grievances of the parish to the meeting of the next higher jurisdiction, whether town or *bailliage*. In the towns the officials, and sometimes but not always (especially in the Midi) some of the townsmen, met and chose deputies and a committee to draw up a *cahier* that was supposed to incorporate the rural parish *cahiers* as well as the complaints of the town. The deputies then went to the *bailliage* assembly with the new *cahier*. The final step was the Estates General except in areas where there were provincial estates where the process of refinement was repeated one more time. The clergy usually met by diocese (most often in the Midi) or by *bailliage*. The nobles met by *bailliage*.

Slowly the process of election and refinement of grievances into successive *cahiers* went on. Sometimes only one or two stages had to be gone through, but the complaints of a rural parish in a secondary *bailliage* had to be processed three times before reaching the Estates General, where they would go through two more stages of refinement.[3] The result of this process is not surprising; the grievances of the peasants and small towns, almost solely concerned with local affairs, soon disappeared as did their deputies, to be replaced by more important men and their grievances.[4]

One of the major problems in describing the elections for the Estates General of 1614 is to determine the electoral districts. The continual growth

---

[3] An excellent example of the elections and *cahier* preparations for a secondary *bailliage*, that of Ferté-Alais, subordinate to the *Prevoté* of Paris in the Ile de France, is to be found in A.D. Yvelines 6 B 304. This *bailliage* tried to act on its own in 1614 by sending deputies to the Estates General, but it was unsuccessful.

[4] J. Russell Major, *The Deputies to the Estates General of Renaissance France* (Madison, 1960), pp. 1–131 contains the best description of the process. Additions to and in some cases corrections of this material can be found in A.N. G8, no. 87 (dossiers on twenty-seven elections, mostly for the First Estate, fourteen of which have new material); A.N. E 47B, fols. 8r (Auxerre), 250r (Poitiers), 272r, 504r–505r (Montpellier); B.N. Moreau 1427, fol. 183v (chapter of Noyon); A.D. Ariège A 12 (Foix), see also Louis Dupin, ed, *Recueil de pièces concernant l'histoire de Louis XIII* (Paris, 1716), I, 205–207; A.D. Calvados, Series F (nobles of Orbec); A.D. Charente-Maritime, minutes de Masset, 1614, fols. 152r–156v (la Rochelle); A.D. Dordogne 6 C 1 (not C 14 as Major says) for Périgueux; A.D. Loire C 32, piece 5 (nobles of Forez); A.D. Maine-et-Loire, I, B G nos. 1–3 (clergy of Anjou); A.D. Seine Maritime D 110 (clergy of Pont-St-Pierre); A.D. Yvelines 6 B 304 (Ferté-Alais); Gabriel Le Roy, note in *Revue des Sociétés Savantes des Départements* series 5, 11 (1870), 354 (Melun); Yves Durand, ed., *Cahiers de doléances des paroisses du bailliage de Troyes pour les Etats généraux de 1614* (Paris, 1966), *passim*; Tyrell, *Poitou*, pp. 74–75, 86–95, 104–117, 125. It should be noted that it was not unusual for the deputies of a *bailliage* to elect someone who was not there. It was definitely not unusual for many who were supposed to come to fail to appear. Despite a ruling to the contrary, voting by proxy was permitted in a number of places. For example Villeroy was represented by a proxy at Magny-en-Vexin (A.N. G8 87, no. 10).

of administrative subdivisions within France is notorious. Although much of this was to take place in Richelieu's time and later, there was considerable confusion in 1614. In calling for the elections in the summer of 1614 the royal secretaries had taken the easy way out. The letters of the King and Marie de Médicis were sent to all important local officials. They were told to carry out the elections in the usual manner. They were to decide such details of the complicated protocol as which *bailliages* and towns could send deputies directly to the Estates General, which other localities, if any, they were to consult, where provincial estates were to be held, and which localities belonged to which electoral district. In the majority of cases this method somehow worked, after a mountain of correspondence had been exchanged between *baillis*, governors, lieutenants general, bishops, town officials, and so on. When there were disputes, recourse was had to tradition.[5]

Serious debates over two elections in one area, the claims of newly important towns or long-feuding districts usually reached the *Conseil d'Etat et des Finances*. The Council in its decisions of August, September, and October almost always fell back on the procedure followed for the Estates of Blois in 1588. But if the feud was too bitter or, as happened in a few cases, was carried on into November or even December, the Council found a compromise, usually giving a seat to some of the deputies of each of the districts or giving precedence to one deputy over another 'for this time only'. In other words, when pressed, the Council instead of trying to grapple with the mass of contradictions merely temporized adding another bit to the traditional confusion.[6]

Part of this attitude was the result of the frustration of a busy Council faced with a maze of claims and counter-claims, but another reason undoubtedly was to be found in the attitude of the government toward the Estates General. The meeting was for show not reform; the sooner the disputes were settled and the Estates General got under way the sooner it would be over and the danger of embarrassment lessened.

Confusion over electoral districts severely handicapped those who tried to draw up lists of the deputies in 1614 and in later years. On November 15, 1614 the King settled a long-standing dispute by defining the twelve *gouvernements* of France and by assigning to them a voting order based on tradition, privilege, and the order in which each area had become part of France. The voting order was Ile de France, Burgundy, Normandy, Guyenne,

---

[5] Lalourcé and Duval, eds., *Forme générale*, II, 20–90 gives many examples of the complicated procedure. Only tradition, rigidly followed, saved the process from utter confusion.

[6] A.N. E 46B–47A, fols. 166r–166v, 173r–174v, 184r–184v, 274r, 282r, 352r, 353r, 355r–355v, 368r, 387r, 388r–388v, 409r, 410r–410v, 433r, 438r, 440r, 478r–478v; E 47B, fols. 18r–18v, 116r–116v, 329r, 332r–332v, 526r–527r. Major, *Deputies*, refers to a number of other examples found in local records. A good illustration of the problems can be found in A.C. Saint Flour, Chap. v, art. 1, nos. 15, 21–23.

Brittany, Champagne, Languedoc, Picardy, Dauphiné, Provence, Lyonnais, Orléanais. This decision was announced in the decree which ordered that voting in the Estates General should be by *gouvernement* instead of by *bailliage*. For the most part the question of precedence was not settled. Within the Estates General itself the necessity of moving from procedural questions to the business at hand led to a variety of compromises, different in each estate. In a few disputes which could not be settled the Council was again consulted and, if the precedent of 1588 did not suffice, a temporary decision was rendered.[7]

In the royal letters convoking the Estates General of 1614 those written in the King's name had stressed that it had always been the intention of the government to call the Estates General when the King reached his majority, that the Estates General should be free, and that action would be taken on the recommendations of the deputies. Those written by Marie de Médicis emphasized that loyal subjects should be chosen as deputies. The Queen Mother used every means at her disposal to ensure that this would be the case.

At the same time care had to be taken to preserve form. For example, there were complaints that the delegation from Bordeaux had not been elected fairly, so the Queen Mother ordered a new election. Even though those elected the first time were known to be loyal, it must be remembered, she said, that 'the Estates, which must be free Estates', could only accept delegations chosen by the ancient form.[8] Throughout the preparations and the actual meeting of the Estates General Marie de Médicis was most careful of this point – that the Estates General should appear to be free. That its purpose was merely to serve the crown in time of need she did not doubt, but if this service were to be effective then all the formalities and forms had to be correct.

At times Marie intervened directly in an election, though still maintaining the appearance of not doing so. During the meeting of the Second Estate of the *bailliage* of Berry in Orléanais the representative of the Prince of Condé tried to put pressure on the nobles to elect Henri de la Chastre, Count of Nancey. The first line of defense of those directing the election was the *arrêt* of July 21 forbidding the admission of procurations (representation by proxy). Though the *arrêt* was obeyed, the Count of Nancey was still elected. However. Marie wrote to inform Nancey on August 7 that Guillaume Pot, *seigneur* of Rhodes and Master of Ceremonies of France, was coming to help draw up the *cahier*. She hinted very strongly that it would be well if Rhodes were also

[7] Lalourcé and Duval, eds., *Recueil de pièces originales et authentiques concernant la tenue des Etats généraux* (Paris, 1789), V, 141–143. A.N. E47B, fols. 8r, 18r–18v, 24r–24v, 29r, 114r–114v, 116r–116v, 250r, 272r, 329r, 332r–332v, 340r, 526r–527r. These disputes lasted into December 1614.
[8] B.N. MS fr. 6379, fols. 234r–234v.

chosen as a deputy for the Estates General. He was, and so Nancey's vote was canceled.[9]

There is no doubt that Condé was upset at the way the elections were going. He found that he had nothing to offer to prospective deputies that interested them. War was his only bribe. Marie had the popular desire for peace on her side plus the possibility of quite tangible rewards.[10]

The court, however, could not be sure of the people's reaction to Condé. A possible coalition of Huguenot deputies with Condé's supporters in the Estates General posed a serious threat to the Regency. When the revolt had broken out in early 1614 Marie feared that the Huguenots would join Condé. Even though they had not joined the revolt and had protested their loyalty, Marie was not satisfied. This fear was later justified by the part the Huguenots took in the revolt of 1615–1616. The Spanish ambassador Inigo de Cardenas reported to Madrid on July 7 and 8 that the Huguenots were demanding more representatives in the coming meeting of the Estates General. Since Condé was supporting their demands, this was a potentially dangerous situation. But by the end of July Cardenas reported that the Huguenots were no longer a source of worry. This was because of the election efforts of the government.[11]

The contemporary impression as recorded in La Mercure François was that there were many Huguenot deputies in the Second and Third Estates. How many there actually were can not now be determined. However, it is possible to identify positively nine Huguenots among the 135 deputies of the Second Estate. In February eight of the nine led by Prejen de la Fin, Vidame of Chartres, refused to sign the cahier of the Second Estate because it called for the inviolable maintenance of the Catholic religion. They issued a signed protest which identifies them as Prejen de la Fin, deputy of Chateauneuf-en-Thimerais; René de Tallansac, the deputy of La Rochelle; Jean du Mas, one of the six deputies of Brittany; Jean de Puy-Montbrun, one of the three deputies of Dauphiné; Henri Poussart, one of the two deputies of Basse Marche; Marc Antoine d'Avessens, one of the two deputies of Lauragais; Jean Degar-

---

[9] B.N. MS fr. 3328, fols, 58r–67v. Another example of Marie's intervention, this time in the election of nobles in the Prevoté and Vicomté of Paris is noted i . A.N. K 1469, nos. 120–126, 143.

[10] Condé probably never had a consistent election strategy beyond the hope that everyone would line up behind him. See A.N. K 1428, no. 44 (Spanish Council of State, June 30, 1614). But many contemporaries tried to provide him with one after the fact. See Richelieu, Mémoires, I, 249, 300. Estrées, Mémoires, p. 109.

[11] A.N. K 1428, nos. 46, 49. The demands of the Huguenots and steps to please them were also reported in the English diplomatic correspondence, B.M. Stowe MS 174, fols. 348r–348v, 357v; Stowe MS 175, fol 52v. By August 24, according to Cardenas, Marie de Médicis was quite confident about the success of the Estates General, A.N. K 1469, no. 150. See also K 1428, no. 53 (Spanish Council of State, September 6, 1614).

dieu, one of the two deputies of Montpellier; René de la Tour de Gouvernet, one of the two deputies of Beaucaire and Nîmes.[12] One Huguenot in the Second Estate, Odet de la Noüe of Poitou, did not sign the protest.[13]

In the Third Estate there may have been Huguenot deputies from those *bailliages* and *sénéchaussées* which elected no deputy for the First Estate: Albret, La Rochelle, Châtellerault, Calais, Haute-Marche, Puy-en-Vellay, and Lauragais. Daniel de Gallière of Montpellier and Jean Guérin of Rouergue were definitely Huguenots.[14] Jean du Broca of Albret was most probably a Huguenot as were one of the deputies of Loudunois and possible one from Châtellerault.[15] There is inconclusive evidence that eight other members of the Third Estate were of *la religion prétendue réformé*. Most interesting in light of the Regency's election strategy are the areas from which the Huguenot deputies of both the Second and Third Estates came. Orléanais and Languedoc supplied the largest number and there is evidence that others were elected in Burgundy, Guyenne, Lyonnais, Picardy, Brittany, and Dauphiné.

Very few of the deputies actually elected to the Three Estates were supporters of the Princes. Rapine reports that all the deputies of Nivernois favored the Duke of Nevers. Since Chateauneuf-en-Thimerais was part of Nevers's territory the deputy of that *bailliage* may have been under his influence. The nobles of St Pierre-le-Moutier were friends of Nevers and may have been his supporters. Théophile de Damas, the deputy of Charolais, was ensign of one hundred men of arms under the Duke of Mayenne and may have favored him. The deputy to the Second Estate from Gien, Henri de Postel, was a gentleman ordinary of the chamber of the Prince of Condé. Further evidence for Gien's disloyalty is that its *bailli* was Henri de la Chastre, the man whose election the Regent had wanted to prevent in Berry. One other unfriendly deputy can definitely be identified – Louis de Montmorency, the *seigneur* of Bouteville, who protested against Marie's forcing of the election of the president to the Second Estate in October 1614.

This is not an impressive showing of strength, especially when the intrigues of Condé and his allies are remembered. But an analysis of all of Marie's actions shows why the result was so niggardly. The areas with the greatest potential for causing trouble, either because of suspected support for Condé or because of a significant Huguenot population, were those to which Marie devoted most of her attention. Particularly important was the *gouvernement* of Orléanais where Condé had extensive territory. At least part of the happiness that Marie

---

[12] B.N. Dupuy 323, fol. 192r (original of the signed protest).

[13] Eugène Haag and Emile Haag, *La France Protestante* (Paris, 1846–1859), VI, 273–304. See Chapter 9 below.

[14] A.N. E 47B, fols. 504r—505r, E 48A, fol. 338r. B.N. Clairambault 364, fol. 299r. Châteauneuf-en-Thimerais had no deputy for either the First or Third Estate.

[15] A.N. E 46B–47A, fols. 410r–410v, 352r.

continually expressed on the success of her summer trip through that area must have come from the fact that she had either controlled the elections or influenced the deputies in the areas she visited. The royal party had visited the towns of Orléans, Blois, Tours, Châtellerault, Poitiers, Loudun, Saumur, Angers, Mans and Chartres in the *gouvernement* of Orléanais. It is significant that the delegations for all three estates from these ten *bailliages* were controlled by royal officials. There still remained pockets of resistance in Orléanais, but when the elections were over they were so submerged that they were rendered powerless in the meetings in Paris. Further proof of the confidence Marie had in her control of the *gouvernement* of Orléanais is evident in the decision of the *Conseil d'Etat et des finances* on October 25 that the deputies of the *bailliage* of Nivernois, all of whom were clients of the Duke of Nevers, should sit in the Estates General with the deputations of Orléanais, even though Nivernois was part of Lyonnais. As a result the votes of Nevers's supporters were swallowed up by those of the loyal delegations of Orléanais.[16]

All the 474 deputies to all three estates and all their offices are listed in Appendix 3. Analysis of this list reveals that a large number of the deputies, far more than was the case in any other meeting of the Estates General, were royal officials. Marie's activities had been directed toward obtaining the election of loyal deputies to the Estates General. Considerable evidence indicates that, as in the case of Orléanais, a significant number of those she depended on held royal office. The fact that royal officials controlled a deputation to the Estates General did not guarantee that the deputation was loyal to the Crown nor was the reverse necessarily true.[17] But the information gained from this analysis, when combined with the evidence discussed above, reveals a definite pattern as will be seen and provides a fuller answer to the question of what areas Marie controlled. Tables 1 to 3 will aid the discussion.[18]

The great problem in any study of office-holding in the *Ancien Régime* is that very many officials held more than one office. In the present circum-

---

[16] *Ibid.*, fol. 433r. For Nivernois and Saint Pierre-le-Moutier see Rapine, *Rècueil*, pp. 2–5, 347.

[17] A number of examples where men who were not royal officials and yet are known to have been loyal could be cited, for example the delegation of Rouergue (B.N. Clairambault 364, fols. 299r–299v). Perhaps another reason why royal officials were not to be found in the delegations from Dauphiné, besides the independence of the provincial estates, was that allies of Condé, the Soissons family, formerly had the right to name most royal officers in that government. Mousnier, *Venalité*, p. 290.

[18] The tables are based on material found in Appendix 3. The reasons given for the presence of the large number of royal officials at the Estates General of 1614 are not meant to deny the long-term struggle between royal and local officials, demonstrated by J. Russell Major. It simply means that in this one instance the significant jump in the numbers of royal officials is best explained by Marie's action.

stance, when the holding of royal office is a crucial factor, the problem is particularly acute because the same man could hold both royal and non-royal offices in a variety of combinations. On the basis of the evidence preserved it is futile to attempt to decide either which office a particular individual considered most important or which position, if any, influenced his decision on matters of royal policy, local privilege, or office-holder's rights.[19] To overcome this problem in the analysis that follows the office rather than the office-holder is the focus of attention. Royal offices have been designated as effective or non-effective depending on whether the incumbent was likely to feel any particular loyalty to the monarch because of his office. The *Parlement* offices, the position of *bailli* or seneschal and the honorary post of *Conseiller du roi* have been considered non-effective. Then for each *gouvernement* in each estate the relationship of the total number of royal offices held to the number of deputies present in the *gouvernement* has been calculated. In this tabulation each of a man's offices has been counted separately. Given the evidence of the Regency's predilection for royal officials, those *gouvernements* with the highest ratio of royal offices per deputy have been designated as those *gouvernements* where the elections were best controlled by the Crown.

The results of this study show that the ratio is the highest for the First, Second and Third Estates in the Ile de France and Orléanais, for the First and Third Estates in Normandy, for the First and Second Estates in Dauphiné, Languedoc and Guyenne (in the Third Estate of Languedoc and Guyenne royal officials were neither dominant nor submerged), for the Second and Third Estates in Picardy, for the Second Estate in Brittany and for the Third Estate in Lyonnais and Champagne.

To complement this method the number of *bailliages* in each *gouvernement* whose vote was controlled by men holding effective royal offices was computed. This study shows that the strongest control by royal officials in the First, Second and Third Estates was in Languedoc, the Ile de France, Guyenne and Orléanais; for the First and Third Estates in Normandy, for the Second and

---

[19] For a discussion of various attempts to make these distinctions see J. Michael Hayden, 'Deputies and *Qualités*: the Estates General of 1614', *French Historical Studies*, III (1964), pp. 507–510. The analyses mentioned in the article cited and others differ so much because of either miscalculation of the number of deputies or arbitrary choosing of one of the elements of a deputy's *qualité*. In addition to the studies mentioned in 'Deputies and *Qualités*' see Roland Mousnier, 'L'évolution des institutions monarchiques', and 'Le participation des gouvernés à l'activité des gouvernements dans la France des XVIIe et XVIIIe siècles', both reprinted in Mousnier, *La plume*, pp. 216, 232–235; C. Soule, *Les Etats généraux de France, 1302–1789*, (Heule, 1968), pp. 233–237; François Dumont, 'La représentation de l'ordre du clergé aux états français', *Journées internationales, Paris, 1957* (Louvain, 1957), p. 46; Lalourcé, *Pièces justicatives*, II, 54. The comparisons below with previous Estates General are made with the aid of Major, *Deputies*, pp. 132–142, 163–166.

TABLE I *Office-holding among the Clergy at the Estates General of 1614*[a]

	I. de F.	Bu.	N.	G.	Bri.	C.	La.	Pi.	Da.	Pr.	Ly.	O.	GA.	Total
Councilors of State	4%												.	1
Councilors of the King, state and private	30%	15%	40%	30%	17%	9%	56%		50%	100%	25%	32%		41
Councilors of the King	13%	15%	10%	35%	33%	18%	22%					14%		30
Councilors in Parlement	9%	8%			17%							4%		5
Councilors in Bailliages	4%													1
Number of votes	23	13	10	23	6	11	9	7	2	6	16	28	2	156
Actual number of deputies	22	13	10	22	6	11	9	5	2	2	12	26	2	142[d]
Ratio of royal offices per deputy	0·61	0·38	0·50	0·65	0·67	0·27	0·78		0·50	1·00	0·25	0·50		0·52
Ratio of effective royal offices per deputy[b]	0·39	0·15	0·40	0·30	0·17	0·09	0·56		0·50		0·25	0·32		0·29
Total Bailliages	15	12	7	15	1	8	5	6	1	3	8	16		97
Number controlled by royal officers[b]	5	1	3	5	1	1	3					3		21
Number with split control or doubtful[c]	4	3	1	4	1	1	2		1	3	3	4		26

[a] The only duplication of office in this table is in Orléanais where Bishop Frémiot was both a Councilor of State (S and P) and a member of *Parlement*. The percentages are figured by vote: a deputy's position was counted for each vote he had. The position of Almoner of the King was not included since most of these were honorary and since there are too many contradictions between the Estates General records and those in Griselle. The abbreviations along the top of this and following tables stand for the twelve *gouvernements* in the order listed on pp. 76–77 above. GA represents the General Agents of the clergy.

[b] Councilor of the King and the *Parlement* offices are excluded here.

[c] When the only deputy for a *bailliage* was a councilor of the king that *bailliage* was listed as doubtful.

[d] Bishop Hurault of Chartres sat in the delegations of the Ile de France and Orléanais, so there were only 141 deputies present.

TABLE 2 *Office-holding among the Nobles at the Estates General of 1614*

	I.de F.	Bu.	N.	G.	Bri.	C.	La.	Pi.	Da.	Pr.	Ly.	O.	Total[a]
Lieutenant of the King		8%			17%								2
Baillis and Seneschals (only)	36%	15%	25%			13%	10%				20%	14%	17
Baillis and Seneschals and/or Governors of towns and places	14%	8%	13%	20%	33%		30%	50%			7%	14%	20
Councilors of State	21%			20%				17%				23%	13
Councilor of the King (S & P)	21%	8%	8%	15%	17%	13%	40%	17%	50%		7%	27%	23
Councilor of the King												5%	1
King's Household	14%	23%	25%	10%		25%	10%		25%		7%	14%	17
Other royal officials	7%	7%		5%								5%	3
Royal Military Office	43%	15%	13%	15%	67%	13%	40%	50%	25%		7%	23%	31
Number of votes	14	13	8	20	6	8	10	6[c]	4	9	15	22	135
Actual number of deputies	14	13	8	20	6	8	10	6	4	9	15	22	135
Ratio of royal offices per deputy	1·57	0·77	0·75	0·85	1·33	0·63	1·30	1·33	1·00		0·47	1·23	0·94
Ratio of effective royal offices per deputy[b]	1·07	0·38	0·25	0·75	1·33	0·25	1·10	1·33	0·75		0·20	0·91	0·68
Total Bailliages	14	12	7	15	1	8	7	5	1	3	9	18	100
Bailliages controlled by royal officers	8	2	1	7	1	1	3	3	1		1	8	35
Control split		1	1		1	1	3	3			2	3	10

[a] Since all elements of *qualité* are tabulated the totals reflect the number of votes not the number of deputies.
[b] *Baillis* and seneschals only, Councilor of the King and King's household are not included.
[c] Estourmel had only one vote and has been counted only once.

TABLE 3   *Office-holding among members of the Third Estate at the Estates General of 1614*

	I.de F.	Bu.	N.	G.	Bri.	C.	La.	Pi.	Da.	Pr.	Ly.	O.	Total[a]
Secretary of King, Household and Crown													1
Secretary of the King		5%	10%										2
Treasurer of France							8%				4%	3%	3
Baillis and seneschals					14%						4%	5%	4
Lieutenants of baillis and seneschals	4%											3%	2
Lieutenants general, presidents of presidial seats, juges mages	38%	19%	20%	32%		25%	25%	71%			35%	34%	58
Avocats and procureurs of King and Sovereign Courts				3%									1
Lieutenants particular, civil and criminal	12%	10%		6%	14%	17%	8%	29%			4%	3%	13
Avocats and procureurs of the King in Bailliages and Sénéchaussées	4%		10%	3%	14%	8%	8%				4%	21%	17
Other royal officials	19%	29%	20%	10%	14%	17%	8%				22%	16%	31
Councilors of State												3%	1
Councilors of King (S & P)	8%										4%		3

													Total
Councilors of the King	46%	38%	60%	39%	57%	50%	42%	57%	40%	50%	35%	45%	80
Parlement officials	4%	10%	10%	10%		8%	17%		20%	17%	9%	3%	17
Officers of Estates	4%	10%	20%		14%								5
Officers of Nobles	4%	10%										3%	2
Mayors					14%	17%		14%			9%	11%	12
Echevins and Town Councilmen	15%	10%	20%	32%		8%	50%		40%	17%	13%	3%	32
Syndics		5%	10%	13%	14%				20%	17%	9%	3%	12
Other local officials		5%	10%							50%	4%		6
Doctors of medicine	12%						8%						1
Avocats		19%	10%	6%		8%	8%			16%	13%	3%	17
Merchants	4%	5%	10%									5%	2
Bourgeoisie only			10%	3%								3%	5
Rural inhabitants			10%										1
Law degrees	4%	5%	10%	19%			25%		20%	16%			13
No. of votes	26	21	10	31	7	12	12	5	5	6	23	38	196
Actual no. of deputies	26	21	10	31	7	12	12	7	5	6	23	38	198
Ratio of royal offices per deputy	1·35	1·10	1·30	1·03	1·14	1·25	1·17	1·57	0·40	0·50	1·22	1·34	1·19
Ratio of effective royal offices per deputy	0·85	0·62	0·70	0·55	0·43	0·67	0·58	1·00			0·74	0·82	0·67
Total Bailliages	15	12	8	15	1	8	7	5	1	3	9	19	103
No. controlled by royal officials	10	4	3	6		4	3	5	1	3	6	10	51
Split	3	3	1	4		3	3	5			1	7	22

[a] Because of multiple office-holding the totals reflect the number of votes but not the number of deputies.

Third Estates in Picardy, for the Second Estate in Brittany and for the Third Estate in Champagne and Lyonnais.

A comparison of the two results indicates that the delegations in all three estates from the Ile de France and Orléanais were distinctly loyal, as was most probably the case in Guyenne and Languedoc. In the First and Third Estates Normandy seems to have been assured for the Crown; in the Second and Third Estates Picardy; in the Second Estate Brittany and in the Third Estate Lyonnais and Champagne. These findings correspond to the evidence of direct intervention by the Regency in the elections and also correspond with the known areas of discontent. In other words the royal government directly intervened and worked successfully to control elections in those areas which were most likely to cause trouble because of suspected influence of either the princes or the Huguenots.

When the Estates General met, the government could count on at least five of the twelve *gouvernements* in the First Estate, six in the Second Estate and eight in the Third Estate. What of the other *gouvernements*? It is certain that Brittany was safe for the Regency.[20] There were few royal officials in the deputations of Dauphiné and Provence because the provincial estates controlled the final selection of deputies. In neither case is there any evidence of any intrigue by Condé or any support for his cause. Further, their *cahiers*, particularly those of Provence, show distinct loyalty to the Crown. Burgundy may have been ignored by Marie in her effort to control the more troublesome areas. It may also be that the Burgundians had the most open elections and simply ignored attempts at royal control. This attitude of disinterest toward the central government is also reflected in the Burgundian *cahiers*. Again there is no evidence of loyalty to Condé. The royal government seems to have distinctly failed only in the First and Second Estates in Champagne, perhaps in the First Estate of Picardy and in the Second Estate of Normandy.

How real was the seeming control of the deputies elected to the Estates General? This is difficult to assess. The election of deputies who were essentially loyal to Louis XIII and Marie de Médicis did not ensure that these deputies would support the government beyond matters of broad policy. It did not ensure that they would not bring up questions that would prove embarrassing. A further analysis of the data collected in Appendix 3 will give some indication of what Marie de Médicis and her advisers would face when the Estates General met.

As has been said, France was a society of orders rather than of castes or classes in the first part of the seventeenth century.[21] That is it was a society

---

[20] P. Thomas-Lacroix, 'Les Bretons aux Etats généraux de 1614', *Mémoires de la société d'histoire et de archéologie de Bretagne*, XV, (1943), 2–3.

[21] R. Mousnier, J.-P. Labatut, Y. Durand, *Problèmes de stratification sociale: Deux cahiers de la noblesse, 1649–1651* (Paris, 1965), pp. 9–25. See also François Bluche, Pierre Durye, *L'Anoblissement par charges avant 1789*, 2 vols. (n.p., 1962).

in which a person's importance was derived from the honor and dignity attached by society to his social functions.

Social function included first of all the estate to which one belonged and secondly the office one held, or, for the lower ranks of the Third Estate, one's profession, craft or occupation. Since many men held more than one office, since the precise ranking of offices in the social hierarchy was a matter of contention, and since the lines between the three estates were not clear, exact ranking of social importance is impossible. A president of the *Parlement* of Paris was a *chevalier*, a nobleman; yet if he were to be elected to the Estates General he would sit with the Third Estate. A bishop could be a noble by birth. By entering the First Estate he could claim both spiritual ascendancy and temporal importance, a harder task for one of his fellow bishops who was not born a noble. The members of the Second Estate considered themselves the social betters of such clerics. A member of the Third Estate could hold several offices simultaneously, each with a different rank, and even add to this a claim to nobility either from one or more of his offices as such or because it had been held continuously by himself, his father and grandfather. If his office did not permit such a claim for either reason he might still attempt to claim nobility through possession of a noble fief. A higher ranking official might lay claim through both office and land. The member of the Third Estate might or might not gain the final proofs of his claim by being freed from payment of both the *franc fief* and the *taille* but he could still make his claim and hope that eventually he or one of his descendants would get the exemption. For those who could not find a means of calling themselves *écuyer*, the lowest rank of the nobility, there were still the possibilities of claiming to be a *seigneur*, a *sieur*, or in the last resort a *noble homme*.

Faced with this type of society the only solution for the historian is to accept the fluidity of the system and rank the deputies to the Estates General by all of their claims to social importance at once. For purposes of simplicity these claims will be referred to collectively as the person's *qualité*; that is the group of titles, dignities, honors, privileges, degrees and offices that an individual managed to amass. In ranking *qualité* two separate scales will be used: that of nobility, claim to nobility, or incipient nobility; and that of office.

This method of ranking the members of the Estates General of 1614 does not lend complete support to the Mousnier school, though it tends to confirm its theories more than those of the Porchnev-Lubinskaia school. The important thing is that the system gives adequate expression to the social realities of the era. The years around 1614 were a time of special confusion. The government was trying to make rules to limit the claims of the Third Estate to noble rank at a time when there was an extraordinary push by members of that estate to raise themselves to noble rank – a push as yet not fully explained. At the same time there was a strong reaction by members of all three estates

87

against this tendency. There existed in France in the late sixteenth and early seventeenth centuries a mobile society with conflicting standards, which like everything else in the *Ancien Régime* was not planned but just happened; in 1614 the process had not sorted itself out. This is amply illustrated by Tables 1–3 above and Tables 4–6 which follow.

In turning from the theoretical to the actual, the best place to begin is with the First Estate. Because of the clerical predilection for the making and preserving of records it is possible to get a much clearer picture of the clergy at the Estates General of 1614 than of the other two estates. The most striking fact about the clergy at the Estates General was their organization. From the beginning the First Estate moved with more direction and ease than the nobles or Third Estate. Part of the reason was the prior experience of the members of the First Estate. The clergy had a tradition of frequent national assembly dating back to 1561 when the first Assembly of the Clergy met. A number of the deputies of the clergy in 1614 had participated in such meetings. Few members of any estate had participated in prior meetings of the Estates General.[22] Perhaps even more important for the organization of the clergy was the predominance of bishops. Of the 141 deputies to the First Estate there were fifty-nine bishops or archbishops including five cardinals present either by election or, in the case of Cardinals Joyeuse and Bonzy, Archbishops La Valette and Louis of Lorraine and Bishop Gondi, by invitation. Because of a number of instances of multiple representation the bishops had seventy votes. This, when added to the influence of clerical discipline and an unusual combination of administrative ability and zeal on the part of at least sixteen

[22] Those that have been identified are:

For the First Estate: Nicholas Boucherat, Dijon – 1576; Cyrus de Tyard, Chalons-sur-Saône – 1593; François de Pericard, Contantin – 1593; François de la Rochefoucauld, Auvergne – 1588 (Senlis – 1614); Henri de Lamartonie, Haut Limousin – 1588.
For the Second Estate: Antoine de Brichanteau, Melun – 1588; Jean de Buzet, Condomois – 1588 (?); Eustache de Conflans, Vermandois – 1588; Jean de la Valette, Toulouse – 1588 (?); Florimont de Dormes, St Pierre-le-Moutier – 1588 (?).
For the Third Estate: Philibert Venot, Autun – 1588; Robert Choquel, Peronne – 1576, 1588; Jean Courtin, Blois – 1588; Louis Trincaut, Loudunois – 1576; Claude Maleteste, Charolais – 1588; Noel Rafron, Montfort-Lamaury – 1576; Jean Picot, Brittany – 1588(?).

On the other hand there was a tradition of sorts for some of the deputies of all three estates to fall back on since a number of them came from families that were traditional representatives of their area. See Major, *Deputies*, pp. 137–141, 188, and the deputy lists in the books cited in Appendix 3. The role of the deputies of 1614 in future assemblies is also interesting to note. Thirteen members of the First Estate were to serve in the Assembly of Notables of 1617 or 1626, six of the nobles did so and only one of the members of the Third Estate. Membership in these bodies was established in such a way that the deputies of the Third Estate in 1614 had little chance of being called, especially since the members of the Parisian *Parlement* and *Chambre des Comptes* had refused to take part in the Estates General of 1614.

TABLE 4 Qualité *among the Clergy at the Estates General of 1614.*

	I.de F.	Bu.	N.	G.	Bri.	C.	La.	Pi.	Da.	Pr.	Ly.	O.	GA.	Total[a]
Cardinal-Archbishop						9%								3
Cardinal-Bishop	4%													2
Archbishop			10%	4%			11%	14%	50%	50%		7%		11
Bishop	22%	31%	50%	65%	33%	27%	11%		50%	50%	19%	29%		54
Chapter Members	30%	15%	20%	26%	17%	18%	78%	57%			56%	25%	100%	43
Diocesan Officials	9%	15%	10%	4%		18%					6%	14%		12
Curés	13%	15%	10%	4%		18%		14%			6%	11%		13
Regular Abbots, Priors, Superiors	13%	23%				9%					6%	11%		11
Other members of religious orders	4%	15%	10%	4%										5
Abbots and Priors in commendam[b]	43%	23%	40%	4%	50%	36%	33%	43%	50%		19%	29%	100%	49
Theology degrees	17%	23%	10%	9%		45%	33%	29%			6%	25%	100%	28
Law degrees	26%	8%		30%	50%	9%	22%	29%	50%		25%	21%	50%	34
Number of votes	23	13	10	23	6	11	9	7	2	2	16	28	2	156
Actual number of deputies	22	13	10	22	6	11	9	5	2	2	12	26	2	142[c]

[a] The totals in the right-hand column represent the number of votes for each category and each element of a deputy's *qualié* has been counted separately. Thus for example there were 59 bishops and archbishops actually present though they had seventy votes. The percentages in the case of the first estate represent percent of votes because of multiple representation. For the third estate they represent percent of deputies. In the second estate represent percent of deputies and number of voters is always the same.

[b] Includes bishops known to have retained monasteries *in commendam* after their consecration.

[c] Bishop Hurault of Chartres sat in the delegations of both Ile de France and Orléanais, so there were only 141 deputies present.

TABLE 5   Qualité among the Nobles at the Estates General of 1614

	I.de F.	Bu.	N.	G.	Bri.	C.	La.	Pi.	Da.	Pr.	Ly.	O.	Total[a]
	(%)	(%)	(%)	(%)	(%)	(%)	(%)	(%)	(%)	(%)	(%)	(%)	
Peer													0
Prince												5	1
Duke													0
Marquis	7			10		25	10			11	7		8
Count	14	8		25	17		10		25	11		9	14
Viscount	14			5	17		20						6
Vidame												5	1
Baron	22	31		30	17	37	10		25	11	33	14	28
Chevalier-Seigneur	43	62	100	25	50	37	30	67	50	56	53	63	69
Chevalier-Sieur							10						1
Chevalier only											7	5	2
Ecuyer Seigneur													0
Ecuyer-Sieur													0
Ecuyer only										11			1
Seigneur only				5			10	33					4
Sieur only													0
9th–12th[b]	31	45	13	29			50	33	50	25	20	20	26%
13th	8	33	13	7			33	17	50	25	20	20	19%
14th	38	22	50	21	67	83		33		13	20	27	28%
15th			13	14				17		25	30	20	12%
16th	23		13	29	33	17	17			13	10	13	15%

[a] These figures represent not only the total of votes for each category but also the actual total of deputies for each category.
[b] These percentages apply to the 74% of the deputies whose ancestry can be precisely determined. The dates refer to the century to which a family's nobility can be traced.

	I.de F. (%)	Bu. (%)	N. (%)	G. (%)	Bri. (%)	C. (%)	La. (%)	Pi. (%)	Da. (%)	Pr. (%)	Ly. (%)	O. (%)	Total[a]
Viscount													0
Baron			10	6									1
Messire-Seigneur	8							14					2
Messire-Sieur								14					2
Messire only	3	9						14			4	3	1
Noble homme, Messire			10										6
Ecuyer-Seigneur													1
Ecuyer-Sieur	19			6	14	17					4	10	14
Maître, Ecuyer-Sieur or seigneur			10			8		14				3	5
Ecuyer only	8						8	43			4		7
Seigneur only				6							4		3
Sieur only		5		3						17			3
Noble-Seigneur			10										1
Noble only		5					8						2
Noble homme, Maître-Seigneur												3	1
Noble homme, Maître-Sieur												5	2
Noble homme, Maître only	3	5					8				4	5	6
Noble homme-Seigneur	8		10	3	86				20		9		5
Noble homme-Sieur	8		10	10						17	4	3	13
Noble homme only	15	14	10				8		60			10	18
Maître-Seigneur		5										8	3
Maître-Sieur	8	9		13		8					18	8	17
Maître only	12	48		49		67	59		20	66	39	42	73
Sire												3	1
Honorable homme			10										1
No prefix or title	8		10	3			8				9	5	9

[a] The totals represent the actual number of deputies with the title in question since each deputy has been counted only once.

bishops, made them the dominant group.[23] The bishops who sat in the First Estate are the one group who can be compared to all the other members of their rank in French society. When they are compared with the other fifty bishops in office in France in 1614 it is found that 32% of the bishops who were deputies and 22% of those not elected held law degrees (usually canon law or a degree in both canon and civil law); about the same percentage had theology degrees (17% of the deputies, 18% of the others). Both groups held monasteries *in commendam* despite provisions against this (34% for each). What is most striking is that almost all foreigners and members of religious orders who were bishops were not elected as deputies (5% of the bishops at the meetings belonged to religious orders; 26% of those not elected were members of religious orders).[24]

An indication that a spirit of religious reform was growing in France was the increasing frequency of the holding of diocesan synods. The period 1601 to 1625 was a time of definite increase in the holding of synods in France.[25] Of the eighty-seven diocesan synods held between 1610 and 1624 the bishops

[23] For the reformers see Blet, *Clergé* I, 15—21 and Paul Broutin, *La réforme pastorale en France au XVIIe siècle* (Brussels, 1956), I, *passim*. The strangest thing about these men was that many of them had gained office through royal service in the usual way. As a group they were jealous of their authority, were often harsh in dealing with opponents and yet were true reformers. Also see Louis Pérouas, 'La réforme Catholique au diocèse du Maillezais dans le premier quart de XVII siècle', *La Revue de Bas-Poitou*, LXIX (1958), 340—346 and Marcelle Forman, 'Henri-Louis Chasteigner de le Rocheposay, évêque de Poitiers (1612—1651)', *Bulletin de la Société des Antiquaires de l'Ouest et des Musées de Poitiers* (1955), pp. 165—231.

[24] G. van Gulik and P. Gauchat, *Hierarchia Catholica Medii et Recentoris Aevi* (Munster and Regensberg, 1923 and 1935), III, IV, *passim*. See Jacques Dubois, O.S.B., 'La carte des diocèses de France avant la Révolution', *Annales: Economies, Sociétés, Civilisations*, XX (1965), 680—691 and map. Four sees were vacant.

[25] The average number of synods per year in France from 1401 to 1789 is as follows:

1401—1425	2·12 per year	1601—1625	5·40
1426—1450	1·92 per year	1626—1650	6·40
1451—1475	1·60 per year	1651—1675	8·92
1476—1500	2·56 per year	1676—1700	9·69
1501—1525	3·72 per year	1701—1725	4·92
1526—1550	3·72 per year	1726—1750	4·24
1551—1575	2·92 per year	1751—1775	1·84
1576—1600	3·08 per year	1776—1789	1·36

These averages were compiled from the diocese-by-diocese listing in A. Artonne *et al.*, *Répertoire des statuts synodaux des diocèses de l'ancienne France du XIIIe à la fin du XVIIIe siècle* (Paris, 1963). See also the correction of Artonne in L. E. Halkin, 'Les statuts synodaux de l'ancienne France', *Revue d'Histoire Ecclésiastique*, LXII, 2 (1967), 429—436. During the period 1601 to 1625 there was a continual increase; from 1611 to 1617 the average was 6·43; during the years 1613 to 1620 the average was 7·12 per year. See also Jacques Gadille, Dominique Julia, Marc Venard, 'Pour un répertoire des visites pastorales', *Annales: Economies, Sociétés, Civilisations*, XXV (1970), 561—566.

who were deputies in 1614 presided at or authorized fifty-three. In other words 52% of the bishops held 61% of the synods.[26]

In the final analysis, then, the bishops who attended the Estates General were better educated in law than the bishops not there, were predominantly members of the secular clergy and tended to hold more synods which indicates their interest in reform. On the other hand they shared the fault of plural and *in commendam* benefice-holding equally with their absent confreres. A comparison of the possession of benefices by French bishops in the period 1540–1560, 1614 and 1640–1660 shows that the number of bishops holding benefices was fairly constant and tended to follow a diocesan pattern. But what set the 1614 bishops off from the other bishops were the sixteen or so men who provided leadership for the Catholic Church in France at the beginning of an age of reform. They were pastoral reformers, supporters of new and reformed religious orders and congregations and, what was more unusual, they were ultramontanes. These men would propel the First Estate toward the goal of using the Estates General as a means of introducing the reforms of the Council of Trent into France, a goal that would not please the royal government. The list of their names includes from the Ile de France, Cardinal de la Rochefoucault; from Burgundy, Bishops Gaspard Dinet of Mâcon, François de Donadieu of Auxerre and Jean-Pierre Camus of Bellay; from Normandy, Cardinal Joyeuse and Bishops Jacques Camus de Pontcarré of Séez and Jacques d'Angennes of Bayeux; from Guyenne, Cardinal de Sourdis and Bishops Octave de Bellegarde of Couserans, Gilles Souvré of Comminges and Jean-Jacques du Sault of Dax; from Champagne, Cardinal Du Perron and Bishop René de Breslay of Troyes; from Orléanais, Bishops Armand Jean du Plessis of Luçon, Charles Miron of Angers and Gabriel de l'Aubespine of Orléans.

The second largest group of clergy present were members of cathedral chapters. As a group they were relatively weaker than they had been in previous Estates General. This probably corresponds to the increasing strength of the bishops as a group and it corresponds to the predilection of the royal government for deputies who held royal office. Bishops were more often *Counseillers du roi* than canons. Nevertheless the canons were still influential, representing 27% of the total vote. Their demands for Gallicanism and local privilege and their opposition to reform were to make themselves felt during the course of the Estates General. Sixteen members of ten religious orders were present, but altogether they controlled only 10% of the votes and these were too widely scattered among the *bailliages* to have any real effect. There

---

[26] The present location of the printed synod statutes of the 1614 bishops are cited in Artonne, *Répertoire*, pp. 23–24, 34, 56, 60, 79–80, 91, 122–123, 142–146, 150, 193–194, 204, 206–207, 211–212, 219, 231, 264, 266, 276–277, 280, 290–291, 293, 298, 305, 345–346, 355–356, 370, 373, 381, 384, 399–400, 410–411, 413, 415, 417, 442–444, 465, 469, 474.

were thirteen *curés* present, more than in any other meeting of an Estates General. However, only seven of these were simple *curés* without any other office and only two of the *curés* held no academic degree. The mass of the poorly educated rural clergy had no real voice in the First Estate. Forty percent of the deputies of the clergy had either a theology or law degree. The best educated clerical deputies came from Languedoc, Picardy, Champagne, Dauphiné, Ile de France and Orléanais. The most poorly educated came from Provence and Normandy. Finally it would seem that two of the clerical deputies, Estaing of Auvergne and Espinay of Brittany, were only subdeacons while Sublet of Vendôme and perhaps Zamet of Sens held neither major nor minor orders.

The noble deputies were the most poorly organized and least prepared. They had no tradition of noble assembly. Their natural leaders, *les grands*, had been involved in the rebellion of 1614 and were not present at the meetings. Of the 135 deputies of the Second Estate in 1614 twenty-seven were *baillis* or seneschals, but this office had lost its importance. The governors and lieutenants general were now the most important local royal officials. Twenty of the noble deputies (including ten of the *baillis* or seneschals) were governors; none were lieutenants general. There were fewer councilors of the King among them than among the deputies of the First and Third Estates. On the other hand they did have more *Conseillers d'état* than the other two estates. Seventeen of the nobles were members of the King's household; thirty-one held royal military office and three held other minor royal offices.

The position of the ordinary nobles in the fluid society of 1614 was unstable and ambiguous. Theoretically, they were the leaders of the secular life of France. But the members of the Third Estate were moving into their ranks at what must have seemed an alarming rate. At the same time the members of the Second Estate found themselves cut off from all important administrative, judicial, and financial offices. The *paulette* encouraged the selling and reselling of offices for a profit and raised their price beyond the means of the nobles whose incomes were already limited by the effect of inflation on fixed rents and feudal dues. Many of the appointive offices of the court were held by the clergy. The nobles had such positions as were left – gentlemen of the King's chamber and the like. They held military offices, but commoners were even making inroads into the higher echelons of the army. The nobles retained their social and tax privileges, which at times were threatened, and their pride. They could complain, which they did, or attempt revolt, as some had under Condé, or depend on feudal income and subsidies from the Crown and live the life of courtiers or local grandees.[27]

The position of the majority of the noble deputies in the hierarchy of their

---

[27] Birch, *An Historical View*, pp. 425–429, 447–457. Mousnier, *Venalité*, pp. 506–517, 566–568, 622–624.

class was quite low. For example, 54% of them could claim only the titles of *chevalier* or *écuyer*; 3% could only call themselves *seigneur*. An additional 21% held only the lowest of the named titles, that of baron. On the other hand there were proportionately more higher nobles than there had been in previous meetings of the Estates. Far more important, of the 74% of the noble deputies whose ancestry can be precisely determined 73% could trace their nobility to the fourteenth century or earlier, and 45% to the thirteenth century or earlier. The *chevaliers-seigneurs* of the Second Estate were the backbone of the nobility, members of the old lower nobility; men of exactly the same class as Sully whose father was a *chevalier-baron*. Furthermore many of them came from families whose fathers and grandfathers had represented their districts in the Estates General since 1560. They were the leaders of the local nobility, some of whose descendants would still be representing their area in 1789. They were not men who became famous but they were related to many who did, from Henri de Balsac of Dreux, who was a cousin and nephew of two famous royal mistresses, to relatives of the main branch of the Coligny family, the brother of the killer of Concini, the Marquis of Vitry, and the brother of the novelist Honoré d'Urfé.[28]

The twelve delegations of nobles can be described in the following way: Those from Normandy and Picardy represented the lower and older nobility, that from Burgundy the lower and oldest. The delegations from Orléanais and Provence were from the lower nobility but were divided between representatives of old and new families. The Lyonnais delegation had the same and Provence were from the lower nobility but were divided between rephiné and Languedoc were represented by nobles from the older families, half of whom came from the higher ranks. Brittany's delegation was similar in rank but more diverse in age. The delegations from Champagne and Guyenne had the largest proportion of higher ranking members. The bulk of Champagne's deputies traced their ancestry to the fourteenth century; those from Guyenne came from younger families. The delegation from the Ile de France was divided in both age and rank. When this division is compared with the makeup of the delegations of the First and Third Estates it can be seen that the deputies from the Second Estate were by far the most representative of their order in the country as a whole.

[28] Some of the men of the First Estate had these types of relationship too; Bishop Frémiot was a brother of Ste Jeanne de Chantal. The most complicated inter-relationship involved all three Estates: the son of Louis de Montmorency, deputy for Senlis in the Second Estate, was involved in the death of the son of Charles d'Amboise, deputy of the same estate for Vitry-le-François in the famous duel of 1627. As a result Montmorency's son was executed by order of the deputy of Luçon, Richelieu. Eventually Henri de Mesmes, deputy for the Third Estate of the *prévôté* of Paris married the widow of Charles d'Amboise. For other examples of relationships see Charles Dangibaud, 'Louis de Bassompierre, évêque de Saintes', *Revue de Saintogne et d'Aunis* XLV (1933–1935), 76–78.

The nobles of the First Estate were to be found among the bishops and canons. The evidence shows that 66% of the bishops who were deputies and 34% of the canons were from noble families. Of all the bishops in France in 1614, 56% were noble. The First Estate had the largest number of family relationships with members of the other estates. Bishop Brichanteau was the son of the Brichanteau of the nobility. Bishops Angennes, la Vallette Cornusson, Barrault, Glandesves and Hurault de l'Hôpital had brothers in the Second Estate. Archdeacon Foucault had brothers in the Second and Third Estates while Bishop Goualt had a brother in the Third Estate.[29]

The lowly Third Estate in 1614 included one viscount and two barons as well as many men who had at least pretensions to nobility.[30] Of the deputies of the Third Estate, 37% styled themselves as *maître* and an additional 6% were of lower rank or had no honorary prefix for themselves. This means that the remaining 57% of the deputies of the Third Estate were trying to push themselves into the ranks of the nobility, though only 25% had any definite claim to that rank and only 20% a completely valid claim. The attempt to move upward into the nobility is fully evident in the long string of permutations and combinations of honorary prefixes and titles in the list of *qualités*. Whatever the reason, the majority of the Third Estate wanted to be considered as nobles.

But if the important members of the Third Estate were moving into the ranks of the nobility of the robe, they had not left behind them their practical abilities. The Third Estate was by no means as well organized as the clergy, nor was it equipped with a tradition of experience in national assemblies. But in 1614 a great number of deputies of the Third Estate came to Paris prepared with valuable experience. Seventy-one deputies were lieutenants of the king (general, particular, civil, or criminal), presidents of presidial seats, or *juges majes*. Seventeen were members of the *parlements* of France. Three were Treasurers of France, twelve were mayors, and thirty-two were town councilmen. Only nineteen deputies held no administrative, judicial, or financial offices, and nine of these were lawyers. Five of the remaining ten called themselves bourgeoisie, one was a merchant, one a rural inhabitant, and three were listed only as *sieurs*.

This comparison of the deputies helps to explain why the great clashes during the meetings were to come between the members of the First and Third

---

[29] Bishop Péricard of Cotantin was the uncle of the Bishop of Evreux. The two Apchons and Jacques and Anne de l'Hôpital of the Second Estate were cousins. François de Nompar de Caumont and Giles de Léaumont were brothers-in-law of Antoine de Gramant and the Barrault brothers respectively. Geoffrey de la Roche Aymont was the son-in-law of Philibert de Serpent and Adrien de Breauté was the son-in-law of Pierre de Roncherolle.

[30] During the meeting of the Estates General the Lieutenant Civil of the provostship of Paris would say 'qu'il ne falloit pas que la Noblesse se relevoit si haut par dessus le Tiers Estat, veu qu'il promettoit de tirer un quart de la noblesse du Tiers Estat et qu'un quart du Tiers Estat estoit tiré et sorty de la Noblesse'. Rapine, *Recueil*, p. 162.

Estates. These two estates consisted of men used to office and authority, men with far greater governmental experience than the representatives of the nobility.[31] The nobles came from a rich tradition and they had a sense of their own importance. But their latent desire to restore a feudal state was to be overwhelmed by the conflicting desires of the other two estates. The clergy sought to re-establish elements of an ideal medieval ecclesiastical state concerned with Christendom as a whole while the Third Estate desired to strengthen a modern bureaucratic state concerned primarily with its own glory. Yet at times the nobles could make themselves heard and were to contribute their share to the problems that would face the Regency government when the Estates General met.

Every level of French society had some representation in the Estates General of 1614 from bishops and religious orders to simple *curés*, from peers to *sieurs*, from members of the *parlements* and lieutenants general to town councilmen, from the bourgeoisie to the peasants. However, the representation was very unequal. For example only eleven deputies (one rural inhabitant and ten syndics) could be said to represent in any way 85% of the population, the peasants.[32] But the representatives of the people who counted were there. The two exceptions were the supporters of Condé and the most important supporters and officials of the monarchy. The first group was absent because of the policy of the government. The members of the other group were on hand in Paris to help the government if necessary. This help would be needed. The Estates General refused to follow its assigned role of showpiece.[33] It refused to go home meekly after a few months, and above all it demanded a comprehensive program of reform.

[31] Of the deputies in 1614 two bishops gained a permanent reputation in intellectual history: Camus as a novelist and to a lesser extent as a philosopher, Du Perron as a poet and a theologian. The other writers among the deputies such as Savaron and Ribier of the Third Estate were of lesser rank.

[32] Comparing the delegations in all three estates it can be said that the largest cross-section of the population was represented by the deputies from the Ile de France; to a somewhat lesser extent this was true of Orléanais, Normandy, Lyonnais and Guyenne. The deputies from Provence and Dauphiné were the least representative. On the other hand the lower strata of the estates were best represented in Burgundy, fairly well in Champagne, Orléanais, Lyonnais and Provence. These groups were least represented in Brittany and Dauphiné and were not very well represented in the Ile de France and Guyenne. Any attempt to go beyond this to decide which areas had the most open elections in 1614 is thwarted by the fact of royal influence. The government wanted loyal deputies and chose royal officials as the most likely to be loyal. This was bound to interfere with the proportions of groups represented. This was evidently true, though to a lesser degree, in preceding estates general. Nevertheless, Professor Major's conclusions, based on local records, that elections in Northern France tended to be more open and that there was a progressive development of this openness seem to be true.

[33] The best proof of this in the Third Estate would be the fight over the proposed *cahier* article supporting the absolute power of the King. The deputies of the Ile de France, Orléanais and Picardy were such strong supporters of royal power that they would resist the government's attempt to avoid the issue.

6

THE OPENING OF THE ESTATES GENERAL: OCTOBER 1 TO NOVEMBER 13

In a letter to Cardinal Borghese nine days after Louis XIII triumphally re-entered Paris on September 16, Cardinal Ubaldini reflected the complacency of the French government. The elections and royal tour during the summer of 1614 had brought to a successful conclusion eight months of effort by Marie de Médicis and her advisers.[1] The letters of Louis, Marie and government officials during most of September give the same impression – all is well; Condé is under control; foreign affairs are proceeding smoothly; the deputies to the Estates General will be submissive.

At times everything did seem to be going the government's way. Condé, despite rumors to the contrary, returned to Paris at the end of September and did not seem to be involved in any intrigues. Nevers and Bouillon were slower to return, but to everyone's relief they appeared as the Estates General got under way.[2]

The problem was that not only was James I ready to encourage *les grands'* troublemaking but the Venetian ambassador, upset by Lesdiguières's unofficial aid to the Duke of Savoy and France's interference in Switzerland, had quietly begun to open lines of communication with Nevers and Condé.[3] However, these intrigues would not become serious until early 1615. Then the government would find itself involved in a whole series of external and internal difficulties.

In the meantime the pressure of foreign affairs had definitely been reduced. On September 20 the Marquis of Rambouillet was sent to negotiate a settlement between Savoy and Mantua and a treaty was signed on November 17. With the assistance of the French and English ambassadors the treaty of Xanten was signed on November 12. Though problems still remained this

---

[1] A.S.V., Fond. Borgh. II, 242, fol. 67r (Ubaldini to Cardinal Borghese, September 25, 1614).

[2] B.N. MS ital. 1767, p. 167 (report of Venetian Ambassador of September 16, 1614). A.S.F., Arch. Med. 4853, fol. 138r (report of Florentine Ambassador of October 4, 1614). B.N. MS ital. 38, fol. 192r (Ubaldini's report of November 4, 1614). B.N. MS fr. 15581, fols. 276r–279r (Villeroy's copies of letters between Condé, Bouillon and Nevers, October 3–8).

[3] B.N. MS ital. 1767, pp. 202–208, 209–211 (letter of October 28).

treaty did bring a truce in the Jülich area. The Spanish border treaty was signed by France on December 5.[4]

In spite of the government's success foreign negotiations caused much debate during 1614–1615. Pamphlet warfare raged in which strong sentiments were expressed for and against the royal policy. The complaints of the Gallicans, the Huguenots, and the Princes were published along with denunciations of the supposed betrayal of the German Protestant princes, old Italian allies and the anti-Spanish tradition. *Cassandre française* summed it up by saying France would end up as Concini's fief and a Spanish slave. Supporters of the government praised the alliance with a Catholic power and the promise of continued peace.[5]

Marie and her advisers were beginning to realize that even an Estates General for which the election had been controlled provided an opportunity for those who wished to air their grievances and to seek public support for for their causes. By the end of September the government must have realized that it was impossible to relax. Two important alterations in plans were made: the Estates General was postponed until after the majority of the King could be officially proclaimed on October 2 and the meetings were moved from Sens to Paris. Once the Estates began the government kept close watch on developments. As the French representative in Germany was informed it was known that there were those who were trying to make the Estates General work against the King and to exaggerate the problems that faced France.[6]

The first step in securing the situation was the proclamation of the King's majority. This was confirmed at a *lit de justice* in the *Parlement* on October 2, with Condé and most of the disaffected nobles in attendance. (Longueville had quareled with Concini and had left the court.)[7] At the ceremony of the proclamation the *Parlement* of Paris, in spite of its Gallican opposition to the Spanish marriages, voiced its support for the Regency government. President Servin's speech praised the King and urged Louis to continue to follow the Queen's counsel. There was no need for the urging. Louis told the assembly

---

[4] See Chapter Three above and B.N. MS fr. 15581, fols. 290r–290v, B.N. MS ital. 1767, pp. 165–187 (Venetian Ambassador's reports of September 16–30). A.N. K 1469, no. 162; K 1634, nos. 11–12, 15–16 (Navarre Border treaty).

[5] *Cassandre françoise* (n.p., 1615). *De France et d'Espagne* (n.p., 1614). *Discours sur les mariages de France et d'Espagne contenant les raisons qui ont meu Monseigneur le Prince à demander la surséance* (n.p., 1614). *Discours sur l'alliance faicte par le roy très-chrétien, avec le roy catholique* (n.p., 1615). *Lettre de Guillaume sans Peur envoyée aux desbandéz de la cour* (n.p., 1615). *Réfutation du discours contre les mariages de France et d'Espagne* (n.p., 1614). *Les terreurs panniques de ceux qui pensent que l'alliance d'Espagne doive mettre la guerre en France* (Paris, 1615). *La harangue de Achior l'Ammonite . . .* (n.p., 1614) which was a reply to *La harangue de Alexandre le Forgeron . . .* (n.p., 1614).

[6] B.N. MS fr. 4121, fol. 106r (Puisieux to Sainte Catherine, October 21).

[7] Isambert, *Recueil*, XVI, 52. Estrées, *Mémoires*, p. 282. Pontchartrain, *Mémoires*, p. 336. B.N. MS Depuy 76, fols. 51r–52r (list of those present).

that he intended to demand the respect and obedience due him; then turning to his mother he said, 'Madame, I thank you for the great pains which you have taken for me; I ask you to continue to govern and to command as you have before. I wish and expect that you be obeyed in everything and everywhere, and that after me you should be the head of my Council'.[8]

The first acts of the thirteen-year-old King were the renewal of edicts condemning blasphemy, protecting the Huguenots, forbidding dueling, outlawing the formation of leagues, and decreeing the pacification of the kingdom. He ordered every Frenchman to refrain from serving any prince or lord except himself. Louis further emphasized his support for his mother and her policies, stating that these policies were in accord with those of his predecessors, and that any attempt to subvert them was contrary to the tradition of France.[9]

In the meantime the opening of the Estates General was postponed until after the proclamation of the King's majority, and on the pretext that many of the deputies were already in the capital for that ceremony, the Estates General was transferred to Paris. That this was dictated by more than impulse is indicated by the fact that James I knew of the changes at least by the end of September. As a further precaution royal troops were stationed around Paris as the deputies began to assemble. On October 13 it was publicly proclaimed that a preliminary meeting of the Estates General would be held the next day at the monastery of the Grands Augustins. The formal opening of the Estates General had at first been scheduled for October 10, but it had to be postponed because renovation of the hall of the Hôtel de Bourbon took longer than expected. During the interim the deputies were ordered to take care of details of organization at the Augustins. After these preliminary meetings the three estates were to meet in separate buildings: the clergy were to continue to meet at the Augustins (across the Seine from the King's residence in the Louvre), the nobles at the monastery of the Cordeliers (a short distance west of the present Boulevard Saint Michel), and the Third Estate at the Hôtel de Ville.[10]

[8] Isambert, *Recueil*, XVI, 52. Louis Servin, *Action des gens du roy sur la déclaration de Louys XIII roy de France et de Navarre séant en son lict de justice en sa cour de Parlement au jour de sa majorité* (Paris, 1615), pp. 1–27. It should be noted that though Louis XIII's name will now appear more frequently, Marie, as Louis said, was still in charge. Louis did as Marie and her advisers decided.

[9] Pontchartrain, *Mémoires*, p. 336. Servin, *Action des gens*, pp. 27–64.

[10] B.M. Stowe MS 175, fols. 58r–59r (James I to Edmondes, September 27/October 7). A.N. K 674, no. 25 (the proclamation of October 13, signed by Louis). B.N. MS fr. 3788, fol. 10r; B.N. MS fr. 3797, fol. 16r; B.N. MS fr. 3800, fol. 25r (all concerning troop movements). Birch, *Historical View*, pp. 381–382 (Edmondes to James I on October 28, 1614, concerning preparations for the Estates General). A diagram of the monastery of the Grands Augustins is to be found in Emile Raunie, *Epitaphier du vieux Paris, Histoire générale de Paris* (Paris, 1890), I, 50–51. See also Malherbe, *Letters*, p. 415. Malherbe reported to his friend Peiresc on October 17 that he was hard at work on the hall of the Hôtel Bourbon, but that he did not think that it would be ready for two weeks.

The preliminary sessions lasted from October 14 to October 25 and were devoted mainly to the exchange of formal, complimentary greetings among the three orders, the accepting and accrediting of deputies, the arranging of matters of precedence and procedure. None of the estates had its full complement of deputies on October 14, and there were many disputes among rival claimants from the same *bailliage*.[11] The nobles did not get most of their members accredited and sworn in until November 17, and even after this latecomers would appear. The other orders had somewhat more success, but the Estates General moved slowly at first.[12]

[11] For the development of the process of verification of powers and problems of ranking see Jean-Paul Charnay, 'Naissance et development', pp. 556–578. The action of the King's Council in helping to solve the problems that arose can be seen in A.N. E 47B, fols. 8r, 18r, 24r–24v, 29r, 114r–114v, 116r–116v, 250r, 272r, 329r, 332r–332v, 333r, 504r–505v, 526r–527r; E 48A, fol. 338r. It took until the end of December to sort things out. Also see Rapine, *Recueil, passim*, especially pp. 30–102, and the letters of Guy Goualt of October 29 and November 8 in A.D. Morbihan 87 G 4. The slowness of the deputies to arrive can be illustrated by the following: The deputy for Dijon was not elected until October 16 (A.D. Cote d'Or C 3473); the deputy for La Rochelle was not chosen until November 19 (A.D. Charente-Maritime, Minutes de Masset – 1614, fol. 152r–155v); the *cahier* for Toulouse was not ready until October 27 (A.D. Hérault C 7673); the deputies of Haute Auvergne did not leave for Paris until November 10 (A.C. Saint Flour, Chap. V, Art. 1, no. 24). On the other hand at least one deputy tried to leave in early December since his *cahier* had been studied by the *gouvernement* of Orléanais (Rapine, *Recueil*, p. 186).

[12] In following the course of the Estates General of 1614 the three accounts printed in Lalourcé and Duval, *Recueil de pièces*, VI, VII, VIII (Behety and Breteville, secretaries of the clergy, Montcasin, secretary of the nobles, Clappisson, assistant secretary of the Third Estate) have been used as the basic sources since they are the most readily available. In each case these *procès-verbaux* have been checked with the extant manuscript copies, and found accurate except for some mistakes in dating which also appear in many of the MSS. For the First Estate one other *procès-verbal*, that by Charles de la Saussaye of Orléanais, has been found and is used (B.N. MS fr. 4082). For the Third Estate six other *procès-verbaux* are used. Two have never been used before: B.N. MS fr. n.a. 7254, the account of the secretary of the Third Estate, Jacques Hallé, which is particularly useful for finding the membership of the deputations which were sent to the other two estates and for fuller details on the process of compiling the general *cahier*; B.N. MS fr. 18256, an eighteenth century copy of the account of a member of the delegation from the Ile de France which is the best source for determining the governmental votes and the content of speeches. Another account has been identified for the first time: B.N. MS fr. 10876 which, though it ends on January 23, is particularly good for provincial affairs. It was written by a member of the delegation from Burgundy, most probably Guillaume Prisque. In addition, the following have been used: Bibl. Ars. MS 4255, the account of Etienne de Lalain of Vermandois and B.N. MS fr. n.a. 1395, the account of Claude le Doux of Normandy. This latter account was published by Charles Molle in 'Journal,' *Recueil des travaux de la société libre d'agriculture, sciences, arts et belles lettres de l'Eure*, series 4, VIII (1889–1890), but because of the MS he used there are a number of dating errors in this printed edition. Le Doux's account could be described as very favorable to the Regency government. The most hostile was the account of Florimond Rapine of Lyonnais. *Recueil très-exact et curieux de tout qui s'est fait et passé de singulier et memorable en l'assemblée des Estats tenus à Paris en l'année 1614 et particulièrement en chaque séance du tiers ordre* (Paris, 1651). The account printed in L. Cimber and F.

The clergy had held ten preliminary meetings by October 25 mostly concerned with the ceremonies for the procession and formal opening of the Estates General. The early meetings also dealt with conflicts over representation. The latter problem was usually settled by letting both claimants represent the *bailliage* in question. After much argument a definite seating order was agreed on. No solution was found for the questions of protocol raised by the opening ceremonies. In desperation it was decided that in the procession the clergy below the rank of bishop would line themselves up without distinction, except for the abbots of Citeaux and Clairvaux, who were heads of religious orders. It was further agreed that each Sunday one bishop would say Mass and another would preach a sermon for all the estates in the chapel of the Augustins. The clergy accepted the procedure of voting by *gouvernement* rather than by ecclesiastical province, *baillage*, or individually. Finally on October 24 the promoters and secretaries were elected. In this hierarchical assembly no formal election for president was held. Cardinal Joyeuse, the senior French cardinal, presided by right. But because of age and illness his place was filled, after the first meeting, by the next two ranking cardinals, Rochefoucault and Sourdis, the favourite of the Queen. The debates over these matters were carried on in the midst of such tumult in the cloisters that on October 22 it had to be ordered that no deputy could bring more than one servant or page with him, and that he should be left in a coach or on horseback during the meetings.[13]

Questions of rank and the election of officers dominated the meetings of the Second Estate. The first piece of business was to obtain the aid of the clergy in presenting to the King a petition for permission to continue meeting in the Augustins. The First and Second Estates presented this petition on the afternoon of October 14. Meetings were then suspended until October 17, to wait for more deputies to arrive. Between October 17 and 25 disputes over representation and seating, which depended on recognition of rank and privilege, were constant and heated. At one point swords were drawn. In the midst of one of these violent arguments word was received that a deputation from the Third Estate was on its way to the chamber of the Second Estate. Having

Danjou, eds., *Archives curieuses de l'histoire de France* (Paris, 1837), series 2, I, 7–225 and Collin, *Relation imprimée par un contemporain de tout ce qui s'est passé aux Etats généraux convoqués en 1614* (Paris, 1789) are essentially the same and are copies of the material that originally appeared in *Mercure françois*, III, Part 2, which seems to be based mainly on the *procès-verbaux* of the First and Third Estates. The *Journal de ce qui s'est passé aux Etats généraux de 1614* ... (Paris, 1789) is a reworked version of the same material. To facilitate footnoting, the account of the first Estate by Behety and de Breteville will be cited as PV–1, that by Montcasin as PV–2, and that by Clapisson as PV–3. Rapine's account will be cited as Rapine and the MSS copies by their numbers.

[13] PV-1, pp. 2–58. B.N. MS fr. 4082, fol 3r.

heard that the Third Estate had complained that the nobles had not received their earlier delegations with as much ceremony as the clergy had accorded them, the nobles decided that they could not be outdone. They sent one more emissary than the clergy had to escort the deputies of the Third Estate into their chamber. The delegation so favored asked the nobles to help the Third Estate in a petition to the King to permit them to continue to meet in the monastery of the Augustins. After it was ascertained from the clergy that they had agreed to help the Third Estate, the nobles assented. After many intrigues Henri de Bauffremont, the Baron of Senecey, the deputy of Chalons-sur-Saône was finally elected president of the Second Estate on October 23 by a vote of eleven *gouvernements* to one. The next day Louis de Montmorency, the *seigneur* of Bouteville, protesting against the election, complained that remarks he had made in a meeting of the delegation of the Ile de France when told that Senecey had been the Queen Mother's choice for president, had been reported to Marie. He demanded that everything that was said in the meetings of the Second Estate be kept secret. In the midst of loud protests that the election had not been influenced by the Queen Mother, Senecey suggested the election of a second president, saying that there were other deputies who were more capable than he. Henri de Clermont of Dauphiné was elected, but the leadership remained in Senecey's hands. During all of this deputies had not been able to reach a decision about the voting and speaking order, and had finally decreed that, in the interim, no order used implied prejudice to rank. The continuing argument was taken to the Council, where on October 25 it was decided that the procedure of the last Estates General in 1588 should be followed except in very special cases.[14]

In the Third Estate the role to be played by the deputies from Paris overshadowed concern with either rank or ceremony. The roll for the first meeting of the Third Estate was called according to the method used in the Estates General of 1576. Henri de Mesmes, the lieutenant civil and deputy of the provostship and viscounty of Paris, was accepted as chairman since he was the ranking member of the Ile de France delegation until the deputies from the City of Paris should arrive. When a group of Parisians appeared their spokesman Robert Miron, provost of merchants (mayor) of Paris, said that the *cahier* of Paris was not yet ready but that the King had sent them as interim delegates. After a short argument Miron was elected as temporary

---

[14] PV-2, pp. 6–47. There is ample evidence of the exaggerated compliments that each order paid the other during the preliminary sessions, but Montcasin, secretary of the nobles noted that he did not record the praise verbatim so that no scandal would be given to any historian who wanted to write an account of these meetings. PV-2, p. 36. Precedent played a large role in deciding the organization and actions of the Estates General. Examples of this can be found in Griffith, *Representative Assemblies*, pp. 178–196, 206–211. See also J. Russell Major, 'The Loss of Royal Initiative and the Decay of the Estates General in France, 1421–1615', *Album Helen Maud Cam II*, 254–258.

president. When it was time to elect a secretary, a great uproar arose over the alleged attempt of Paris to dominate the assembly. The field was eventually narrowed to three candidates, but the arguments continued until two o'clock in the afternoon when the meeting was finally adjourned. Miron persuaded the assembly to postpone the next meeting until Paris was ready to send its regular delegation. The next meeting was held on Saturday, when the argument over elections continued. Finally, at the third meeting, on Monday, October 20, Miron was elected permanent president and Jacques Hallé, the candidate of the Norman delegation, was elected secretary. Mesmes was chosen to serve as president if Miron were absent. The same day two assistants to the secretary were elected, Léonard Chastenet of Limoges and Pierre Clapisson of Paris. On October 21 the Third Estate took the oath of fidelity and secrecy devised by the clergy for all three orders. Permission to continue meeting in the monastery of the Augustins was received from the King on October 23, six days after the nobles' request had been granted. The Third Estate also dealt with problems of representation and arrangements for the procession for the formal opening. The Third Estate handled these problems much more efficiently than the other two estates. Rather than having the whole assembly decide every case each *gouvernement* was to handle all but its most difficult controversies. The deputies, fully conscious of their own dignity and importance, were concerned with discussing what should be worn in the procession. Miron said that he had the King's permission to wear the robes of the provost of merchants of Paris, but Mesmes contended that if Miron did this his own office of lieutenant civil entitled him to first place in the procession. Finally, it was decided that everyone should wear plain serge. The clergy, fearing that the Third Estate might upset the order of the procession, sent Gilles Souvré Bishop of Comminges on October 24 to tell them rather curtly to wear something decent and to follow the orders of the King's master of ceremonies.[15]

On Sunday morning, October 26, the opening procession wound its way from the Augustins to Notre Dame, proceeding along the left bank of the Seine to rue Saint Jacques and then on to the *Ile de la Cité*. First came the royal archers carrying torches, then the representatives of the parishes of Paris, the chapters, the rector of the University of Paris, the King's household and troops, and the deputies carrying candles. The Blessed Sacrament was carried before the King and Marie de Médicis, who were followed by various

---

[15] PV-3, pp. 1–17. Bibl. Ars. MS 4255, fol. 1v. Rapine, pp. 1–38. There can be no doubt that Miron was the candidate of the Queen Mother. A.N. K 674, no. 32 (permission of the King for the Third Estate to meet at the Augustins). On December 13 a third president, Mochet of Burgundy, was elected in the Third Estate, Rapine, pp. 194–195. Le Doux was the deputy who came supplied with the 1576 *procès-verbaux* which was used as a guide for the roll call. B.N. MS fr. n.a. 1395, fols. 1v–2r.

nobles, the *Parlement* and the important officials of Paris. At Notre Dame, which was richly decorated, Mass was sung and Cardinal de Sourdis preached a sermon on the text from Saint Peter – 'Fear God. Honor the King'. The deputies had arrived at the Augustins at eight in the morning, the procession had finally started about eleven, and all of the ceremonies were not completed until four in the afternoon. All of this must have been very impressive, if tiring, for the deputies from the provinces, but according to Malherbe, the blasé courtier, 'It was not much at all'.[16]

The next day the Estates General was officially opened in the great hall of the Hôtel de Bourbon. This, the largest hall in the kingdom, about 230 feet long by 60 feet wide, was used for important balls, ballets, and spectacles of the royal court. For the opening of the Estates General the vast ceiling and the walls had been entirely covered with painted fleurs-de-lis. At the head of the hall, on the Saint Germain l'Auxerrois side, was a large platform raised three steps above the floor on which seats were provided for important nobles and the cardinals. In the rear of this, elevated two steps, was a second platform where the royal family sat. In the center the King's throne was raised a further three steps. The whole reserved area was covered with violet velvet embossed with golden fleurs-de-lis. In the hall itself, behind various state officials sat the deputies of the Estates General. The banks along the walls and the balconies were crowded with courtiers.[17]

The King spoke first:

Messieurs, I wished to hold this great and notable assembly at the beginning of my majority to let you hear the present state of affairs, to establish good order by means of which God will be served and honored, my poor people comforted, and so that each person will be able to be maintained and conserved in that which is his, under my protection and authority. I pray and beseech you to employ yourselves as you

---

[16] Lalourcé and Duval, *Recueil de pièces*, v, 84–86, 91–94. B.N. Cinq Cents 139, fols. 186r–189r. Two arguments broke out during the procession – the first when the cardinals wanted a place nearer the King, the second among the nobles who wanted the procession to start earlier than arranged because they were afraid that rain might fall and ruin their plumes. Lalourcé and Duval, *Recueil de pièces*, v, 98–99. Malherbe, *Lettres*, p. 415. Perhaps Malherbe's ennui came from the fact that this was the third royal procession in the last month and a half.

[17] B.N. MS fr. 10876, fols. 6v–7v. B.N. MS Clairambault 1129, fol. 37, etching of opening which shows Condé, hand on hip, insolently watching the proceedings. Robert Arnauld d'Andilly, *Journal inédit de Arnauld d'Andilly, 1614–1620*, ed. Achille Halphen (Paris, 1857), pp. 10–11. Lalourcé and Duval, *Recueil de pièces*, v, 118–126. *Mercure françois*, III, part 2, pp. 29–52. Malherbe, *Lettres inédites*, pp. 21–23. From the care taken with his diagram and description of the opening, Malherbe was evidently proud of his work and at least a little impressed with this ceremony. On the other hand Guy Goualt, deputy of the Third Estate from Brittany, described all the ceremonies and processions in a sober, matter of fact way to his brother, A.D. Morbihan 87 G 4 (letter of October 29, 1614).

should for such good work. I solemnly promise you that I will ensure that everything resolved and advised by this assembly will be observed and executed. You will hear my will more fully through what the Chancellor will say to you.[18]

Chancellor Sillery then spoke for an hour, masterfully outlining the Regency's successful handling of foreign and domestic affairs.[19] Denis de Marquemont Archbishop of Lyon followed, speaking for the clergy. He praised the King and the Queen Mother and lauded the loyalty of his own order as did the other speakers. The Archbishop made clear the clergy's conception of itself, '... dispensers of His sacraments and of His mysteries, shepherds of the sheepfold of God, interpreters of His oracles; we have the tables of the law to teach the people fear of God and obedience to the King, the rod to lead them, the manna to feed them'. Pierre de Roncherolle Baron of Pont Saint Pierre, deputy for Chaumont-en-Vexin, spoke for the nobles. Rapine's accurate comment was that the Baron was long-winded and took the opportunity to point out how inferior the members of the Third Estate were to the nobility. Robert Miron's speech ended the ceremony. As usual he managed to include praise for Paris, but the main thrust of his short oration was a far stronger plea for reform than those of Marquemont or Roncherolle.[20]

The Estates General was now officially in session and its task had been set. The deputies were to decide what should be done to put the kingdom in good order. The King had promised to heed their advice. The traditional (though not established) rights and duties of an Estates General were that it should be asked for counsel on general policy, that unusual subsidies should have its approval. The deputies had some power over the King's attempts to alienate parts of his domain. They could present their grievances to the King, but the King could answer them or not as he pleased. The Estates General had not suffered any limitation of its traditional powers. In fact these seem to have been widened by the statement of the King, but whether this extension would

---

[18] Isambert, *Recueil*, XVI, 53. The royal speeches at the beginning of the Estates General of 1576 and 1588 reveal a France in far greater difficulty than the France of 1614. *Proposition faicte par le roy ... le vie décembre 1576* (Paris, 1576); *La harangue faicte par le roy ... le seizième jour d'octobre, 1588* (Paris, 1588).

[19] See A.A.E. France 769, fols. 207r–213v and Chapter 3 above.

[20] Rapine, pp. 49–53. PV-1, pp. 62–67. PV-2, pp. 53–55. PV-3, pp. 19–21. B.N. MS fr. 10879, fols. 1r–6v, 7r–12r, 12v–15v (the speeches). Lalourcé and Duval, *Recueil de pièces*, V, 127–141. All was not serene during the opening as everyone tried to push into the hall. At the beginning the nobles and clergy, after complaining of the placing of their seats with relation to government officials were allowed to move some of their benches forward. The speeches of Marquemont, Roncherolle and Miron were each published as pamphlets.

be honored or whether even basic rights would be respected was yet to be seen.[21]

The beginning of the Estates General produced the usual flood of pamphlets. There are 191 pamphlets in 270 editions that have survived from the period during which the Estates General was in session. Of the pamphlets that were written to give advice, 71% directed their attention to the deputies rather than to the King, though the King was usually regarded as the ultimate source of reform. Typical examples of advice and argument were contained in *Le chevalier errant, Le surveillant Français, Advis au roy sur la réformation générale*, and *Discours à messieurs les députéz aux Etats généraux de France*. The last of them reminded the deputies that they were advisers, not judges, that they were to present remedies for such problems as venality, finances, offices, pensions, and the over-abundance of fortresses and garrisons. The King would judge whether or not the remedies were good ones. The author of *Advis au Roy* spoke in a similar vein, summing up the thoughts of many Frenchmen in 1614:

> Be advised then Sire and begin to see that God is served in this kingdom; chastize the evil clergy, judges, and financiers. Then you will see how the torrent of divine grace will overflow on all sides on the people of your kingdom. On this subject, with all the extent of my soul, I pray that the King of Kings will pour forth the sacred dew of His love on your head, so that loving Him you will love His Church, render justice to everyone without charge, and in fine comfort, throw out, and raise up His people from the evil state to which the great subsidies have reduced them.[22]

Along with these pleas for reform there were pamphlets which presented the special cases of various groups such as *Copie de la harangue* which spoke for the Huguenots.[23]

The problem for the deputies was to transcend the conflicting viewpoints of special interests, and to go beyond the platitudes of the purveyors of general advice toward a concrete program of reform. The deputies of course were not united in what they wanted. This would be made clear

---

[21] Olivier-Martin, *Histoire du droit*, pp. 373–377. André Lemaire, *Les lois fondamentales de la monarchie française d'après les theoriciens de l'Ancien Régime* (Paris, 1907), pp. 279–283, 304–309.

[22] *Discours à messieurs les députéz aux Estats généraux de France* (n.p., n.d.), pp. 3–8, 42, 59. *Advis au Roy, sur la réformation générale des abus ... en son royaume* (n.p., 1614), p. 16.

[23] *Copie de la harangue fait en la presence du roy à l'entrée des Estats, par les députéz de la Rochelle, pour les églises réformées au raport de Mathoult* (n.p., 1615). In 1588 the deputies had been received with pamphlets that painted a far darker picture. See for example *Advis au Roy* (n.p., 1588); *Advis à messieurs des Estats sur la réformation et le rétranchement des abus et criminels de l'estat* (n.p., 1588); *Le dispositif ... advis à messieurs les députéz ...* (n.p., 1588).

not only in their debates but in the pamphlets that deputies themselves wrote and published during the course of the meetings.[24]

The pamphlets written by members of the First Estate were aimed primarily at refuting the arguments set forth by proponents of the proposed first article of the *cahier* of the Third Estate concerning the power of the king and at obtaining official acceptance of the decrees of the Council of Trent in France. The clergy were also eager to effect the incorporation of Béarn and Navarre into France so that Catholicism could be fully restored in those areas.[25] Of special interest are three pamphlets written by Jean Camus, bishop of Bellay. Delivered originally as sermons to the assembled members of the three estates and quickly printed by Claude Chapplet, these pamphlets contain the most balanced assessment of the problems facing the Estates General of 1614 to be found among contemporary writings. In some of the plainest language to be heard during the meetings Camus criticized the deputies and emphasized the inherent weakness of the Estates General. The 'Homily of the Three Simonies' excoriated the First Estate for not resisting the temptation to buy and sell church offices and the Third Estate for selling justice by permitting the venality of office. He commiserated with the nobility over the selling of military offices saying 'O venal France! Will it soon perish if it finds a buyer?'. The remedies for these abuses fell only partially within the competence of the Estates General, said Camus, but the deputies should beg the King to end venality of ecclesiastical, military, judicial, and financial offices and the King should act. In the 'Homily of the Three Scourges' Camus attacked the three estates with even more vigor, threatening to pour three phials full of the ire of God on the deputies' heads. The scourges which afflicted the clergy were heresy, caused by the ignorance and vice of the pastors, and the threat of schism. He recommended the enforcement of the decrees of the Council of Trent concerning doctrine and morality as the remedy. As for the nobles, Camus charged that with their dueling they profaned the peace with greater carnage in one year than there was in two years of war. The final scourge was famine which affected the ordinary people of France. The causes were high taxes and especially the existence of a multitude of officials. Again Camus said that it was the King who must cure these evils. Using the parable of the wheat and the tares as his text Camus began his final sermon 'Homily of the Disorders of the Three Orders of this Monar-

---

[24] At least forty-one pamphlets were written by deputies during or immediately after the Estates General.

[25] Cardinal Du Perron, Bishop Marquemont and Richelieu all immediately published speeches they gave during the Estates General. Other examples of pamphlets by clerical deputies include *Article de l'église apporté au Tiers Estat* ... (n.p., n.d.); *Copie d'une lettre d'un prélat* ... (n.p., 1615) and *Le décret du concile de Constance* (n.p., n.d.).

chy' by excusing himself for concentrating on the imperfections of the three estates while the other preachers had been praising the deputies. However, it had to be done, he said, and after his usual excursions into classical literature Camus set out to criticize each estate for its way of life. The bishops held *in commendam* benefices, clerics hunted, neglected to wear their clerical tonsure and quarreled about their prerogatives. In short the clergy were not faithful to their vocation. The nobles, as confused in ranks as 'rats in a frying pan', had lost their offices and spent all their time in playing, hunting, dancing, and singing. They had no military discipline. And the Third Estate: What was to be done with them, Camus asked; these nobles gathered around him, these poor people in robes of silk? Let them go into the Second Estate where they belonged and stop pretending to be men of the people. Further, let them not concern themselves with sacred matters. As for the abuses in the administration of justice and finances, Camus found that these were too great to be discussed in one sermon. He closed his final sermon with another plea for the poor and a last reminder that only the King had the power to bring reform to France.[26]

The nobles who turned to the writing of pamphlets usually did so to protect the privileges of their class or to protest against the bureaucrats of the Third Estate. Typical was Gentilhomme Français, who addressed his pamphlet to the First and Second Estates to urge them to maintain the privileges of the nobility. He pointed to the officials of justice and finance as the cause of all the woes of France. Another anonymous author joined him to complain to all three estates that royal officials took all the best land for themselves and raised the price of offices beyond the reach of those who deserved them. The various branches of the government must be investigated. Tax collectors must be kept under tighter control, and *tailles* and pensions must be lowered. The lengthy pamphlet *Advis, remonstrances et requestes aux Estats généraux tenus à Paris, 1614 par six paysans* is especially interesting for its expression of the nobles' fierce pride in class and hereditary privilege and their determination to bar all newcomers from their ranks. For themselves the nobles demanded more offices, the re-establishment of the importance of the offices of *bailli* and seneschal, and the downgrading of officials who were members of the Third

[26] Jean Pierre Camus, *Homélie des trois simonies, ecclésiastique, militaire et judicielle* (Paris, 1615). Camus, *Homélie des trois fleaux des trois estats de France* (Paris, 1615). Camus, *Homélie des disordres des trois ordres de cette monarchie* (Paris, 1615). These three sermons given on November 30 and December 28, 1614 and February 8, 1615 are also collected in Abbé Minge, ed., *Collection intégral et universelle des orateurs sacrées* (Paris, 1844), I, cols. 11–88, and have been thoroughly analyzed in Jean Pierre Camus, *Homélies des Estats Généraux (1614–1615)*, ed. Jean Descrains, (Geneva, 1970). Descrains conveniently lists the other preachers for the official masses of the Estates General, *ibid.*, pp. 81–85. Details of some of the other sermons can be found in B.N. MS fr. 10876, *passim*.

Estate. While the only reforms proposed for the nobility were the outlawing of dueling and the abolition of some military offices, the pamphlet was generous with proposals for reforming the Third Estate and also had some ideas for the improvement of the First Estate.[27]

In general the pamphleteers of the Third Estate, whether deputies or not, begged that the people be freed from excessive taxation, violence, and restrictions on business. Royal officials added their part to the controversy in replying to the numerous attacks on the faults of their class. Often their defence was the rather weak one that there were other abuses in France. The most telling points were made against the pensions received by the nobles. The Third Estate had its Camus in the person of the prolific writer Jean Savaron, lieutenant general of Clermont and deputy from Basse Auvergne, who published six pamphlets in 1614–1615. In his view, there were three steps that must be taken. The King must fulfil his duty in disciplining the Church, justice must be re-established, and in the future reforms must be strictly enforced. Benefices and simony were great causes of evil, as was venality. Taxation was too great; consequently pensions and gifts must be reduced.[28]

During the Estates General even the King was not exempt from criticism. The pamphlets with the name Caton in the title criticized the Regency, its councilors, and its policies, especially the Spanish marriages. The government found supporters in Diogenes, Guillaume sans Peur, and others, who

---

[27] Discours d'un genti-homme françois à la noblesse de France, sur l'ouverture de l'assemblée des Estats généraux dans la ville de Paris en ceste anné . . . (n.p., n.d.). Mémoires adressés à messieurs des Estats pour présenter à sa majesté, contenants les fautes, abus, et malversations comises par les officiers de finance, partisans et payeurs des rentes en l'estendue de ce royaume (n.p., n.d.), pp. 1–7. Advis, remonstrances et requestes aux Estats généraux tenus à Paris, 1614 par six paysans (n.p., n.d.), pp, 21–35. The last was reprinted in another edition with only these pages, the introductory material being deleted. Despite the title, there can be no doubt that this was written by a noble; most of the pamphlet is in the spirit of the nobles' general cahier. Davis Bitton is wrong in ascribing this pamphlet to someone who wanted to restrict the nobles, The French Nobility in Crisis, 1540–1640 (Stanford, Calif., 1969), p. 54.

[28] Harangue de l'amateur de justice aux trois estats (n.p., 1615). Humble suplication au roy pour le soulagement du tiers Estat (n.p., 1614). Discours pour la conservation de l'annuel des offices (n.p., n.d.). Le financier à messieurs des Estats (n.p., 1615). Très humbles remonstrances faictes au roy par les thrésoriers de France . . . sur la continuation du droict annuel (Paris, 1615). The claims of the officers were countered by many other writers, for example, Libre discours et véritable jugement sur l'hérédité des offices insinuée en France, dans le doux venim du droict annuel (Paris, 1615). Jean Savaron, Advis donné au roy par le président Savaron député du Tiers Estat d'Auvergne aux Estats généraux tenus à Paris l'an 1615 pour la réformation du royaume (n.p., n.d.). Other examples of pamphlets by members of the Third Estate include Au clergé (n.p., n.d.), which summarized important speeches given by members of the Third Estate to the clergy, nobles and Louis XIII; Articles présentés au Roy . . . (n.p., n.d.), and B.L.D. Franc et libre discours (Paris, 1614). Robert Miron, Pierre Marmiesse, Guillaume Ribier and Balthazar Vias all published speeches they gave during the Estates.

attempted to direct public wrath toward the Huguenots, Condé, and the radical Gallicans.[29]

There was more to be done, though, than write and read pamphlets. During the first two weeks in November time was still devoted to battling over representation, but general meetings were few in number as the deputies of each *gouvernement* in each estate met separately to draw up governmental *cahiers*. These were compilations of the *bailliage cahiers* which the deputies had brought with them. When completed the governmental *cahiers* would be used as the basis of the general *cahiers* which each estate would present to the King at the end of the meeting of the Estates General.[30]

Though each estate was a separate entity, the deputies realized that their best hope for success lay in presenting a unified program of reform. Throughout the meetings there would be a continual process of sending delegations from one estate to another. The First Estate relied on twenty-two bishops as its spokesmen. Six of these, Péricard of Avranches, Potier of Beauvais, Richelieu of Luçon, Valette Cornusson of Vabres, Sainte-Croix of Grenoble and Glandèsves of Cisteron were used for missions to both the nobles and the Third Estate. Potier of Beauvais was used most often in delegations to the Third Estate. Paul Hurault de l'Hôpital of Aix, Claude Gelas of Agen and Saluat d'Iharce of Tarbes were also frequently sent to the Third. When really important issues were involved Cardinals de Sourdis and Du Perron were sent. For missions to the court, Joyeuse, Sourdis, Hôpital, de la Croix and Miron of Angers were called on. In other words the clergy fit the speaker to the occasion by using its best orators and by choosing men who had relatives in the estate concerned or who had particular influence at court.[31]

---

[29] *Le Caton françois au roy* (n.p., 1614). *L'image de la France représentée à messieurs des Estats avec la réfutation d'un libelle intitulé le Caton françois, faict contre ceux qui maintennent la religion et l'estat le tout devisé en trois parties* (n.p., n.d.). *Lettre de Guillaume sans Peur envoyée aux desbandéz de la cour* (n.p., 1615). *Le recontre du Caton et Diogne . . . sur le sujet des Estats tenus à Paris en l'année 1615* (n.p., n.d.). One pamphlet, *L'hermaphrodite de ce temps* (n.p., n.d.), outdid all the others, defending the King by railing at almost everyone but the King.

[30] The presidents of the twelve *gouvernements* of the Third Estate who conducted the meetings that compiled the governmental *cahiers* were Ile de France: Miron; Burgundy: Mochet; Normandy: Le Doux and Vauquelin; Guyenne: Raymond de Montagne; Brittany: Guy Goualt; Champagne: Jean Bazin; Languedoc: Jean de Louppes; Picardy: Pierre Pingré; Dauphiné: Louis Masson; Provence: Jean-Louis de Mathaon; Lyonnais: Pierre Austrein; Orléanais: François de Beauharnois. See B.N. MS fr. 3715, fols. 108v–109r. The names of only two of the provincial secretaries are known, Ile de France: Philippe Loisel, and Lyonnais: Jean de Champfeu. No *procès-verbaux* of governmental meetings seem to have survived though there are references to them in the accounts of the general meetings and in the letters of Guy Goualt. It is interesting to note that the eastern *gouvernements* chose members of the *Parlements* as presidents, those of the North mayors, and those of the West lieutenants general.

[31] For Le Doux's favorable comments about Jean Camus and de la Croix who had served for a long time in the *Parlement* of Grenoble, see B.N. MS fr. n.a. 1395, fols. 7r, 47r.

The Second and Third Estates were not as selective in general as were the clergy. However Charles d'Angennes of Chartres and Prejen de la Fin of Chateauneuf-en-Thimerais were used by the nobles as representatives to both the other estates. Louis de Montmorency, deputy from Senlis, and Jean de Murines of Dauphiné were sent most often to the Third Estate.[32] Rotation played a big role in the Third's choice but five men, four of them lieutenants general, were used to speak to both the clergy and nobles: Raymond de Montagne of Saintogne, Guillaume Ribier of Blois, Jean le Couturier of Mantes and especially the two most talented orators Pierre Marmiesse, capitoul of Toulouse, and Jean Savaron of Clermont. François Lanier, Lieutenant General of Anjou, was sent a number of times to the Second Estate while Julian le Bret, Viscount of Gisors, spoke to the clergy on three occasions.

The ceremonies of reception of the various delegations quickly became ritualized and care was taken not to cause offense. For example, the clergy greeted noble delegations several steps in front of the door of their chamber while they waited at the door itself to greet representatives of the Third Estate. However, all was not serene. On October 29 the clergy invited the other two estates to join them in receiving Holy Communion at Notre Dame on November 1, All Saints' Day. The nobles took the opportunity to abuse the Third Estate, trying to prevent the clergy from arranging a special seating place at the Mass for the leaders of the Third Estate.[33]

On Thursday November 6 the clergy requested that the King permit matters of special importance to all three orders to be discussed jointly and then presented to the King before the *cahiers* were ready. On November 7 the clergy voted that the acceptance of the decrees of the Council of Trent should be the first item on the list of items of special importance. At the insistence of the delegates of cathedral chapters this was modified the next day to include the statement that the acceptance of the decrees of the Council of Trent was in no way to interfere with the rights of the Gallican Church. The Third Estate was very worried by the clergy's plan because of the context in which the First Estate was making its request. The deputies of the Third Estate knew that the First Estate was beginning a general campaign for the acceptance of the decrees of the Council of Trent which they opposed on the grounds of Gallicanism. They were visibly relieved when the King rejected the clergy's plan on November 8. The three estates were told to proceed separately and quickly with their traditional work, the preparation of their *cahiers*. However, through the influence of Cardinal Joyeuse, who visited Villeroy, who in turn spoke to the King and Queen Mother, the clergy won permission to present

---

[32] On one occasion the Third Estate complained that Murines was obscuring the issues with his flowery language. *Recueil d'un réponse du Tiers Estat rendue à la chambre de la Noblesse . . .* (Paris, 1615).

[33] PV-1, pp. 67–82. PV-2, pp. 55–61. PV-3, pp. 21–22. Rapine, pp. 58–60.

some special pleas, and if Their Majesties and the Council thought it proper, they would look into them.[34]

On Saturday, November 8, the Second Estate discussed two proposals that were to have repercussions. The nobles decided to ask the King for a delay in the payment of the *paulette* until February so that the Estates General would have time to discuss it, and a commission was appointed to discuss financial abuses.[35]

Much of the debate in the Third Estate continued to center around Miron and the alleged undue influence of Paris in the assembly. There was great objection to Miron's taking orders from the Queen as to what should be discussed by the Third Estate. Then on November 7, on the initiative of Picardy, the deputies decided to ask the First and Second Estates to join them in a proposal put forward by Champagne that extraordinary commissions be suspended and appointments to various new offices be postponed while the Estates General studied their effect on the people. The next day the nobles agreed to back these requests, but the clergy said they needed more time to study the problem.[36]

The following week the nobles asked the clergy to support them in asking for the suspension of the *paulette*. The clergy, trying to organize the three estates (at least partly for their own purposes), decided that the Third Estate should be informed. The request of the nobles was presented to the Third Estate on November 15 and all of a sudden the Estates General was jolted into full action. The details of representation and precedence fell far into the background as the deputies grappled with their first real issue – venality and the role of royal officials in the life of France.[37]

[34] PV-1, pp. 82–107. Pierre Blet thinks that the Third Estate by failing to accept the clergy's plan missed a chance for the Estates effectively to pressure the government. The Third Estate saw both Trent and the danger of early dismissal as reasons for refusal. Further, when the three estates did present pleas together they got little for their efforts. See Blet, *Clergé*, I, 23–24 and Rapine, pp. 76–86. Etienne Lalain put the Third's case simply: 'few liked this proposition which would be judged *prima facie* suspect . . .', since it was not traditional. Bibl. Ars. MS 4255, fol. 11v.

[35] PV-2, pp. 61–69.

[36] PV-3, pp. 22–39. Rapine, p. 87. B.N. MS fr. n.a. 1395, fol. 20r.

[37] PV-1, pp. 104–107. PV-2, pp. 69–71, PV-3, pp. 39–44. The deputies were being encouraged to act from outside also. On November 10 all three estates found in their meeting rooms a letter addressed to them which made fun of the lack of progress and their vain ceremonies; Rapine, pp. 95–96. Similar sentiments were expressed in a pamphlet published in 1615: *Le catholique christianizé* (n.p., 1615); it included the quatrain

Dieu vous bénisse Messieurs si vous rompez l'annuel
Autrement toutes vos femmes seront menées au bordel
Pour y passer nostre temps n'ayons poinct d'autre exercice
Puis que vous autres veaux d'or possédez tous les offices.

113

7

OFFICES AND FINANCES: NOVEMBER 14 TO DECEMBER 14

French government in the last centuries of the Old Regime was government by officials. The Kings, in effect, gave up a significant part of their sovereign power to a new caste of administrators and judges. Originally an official served simply as an administrator of part of the King's domain but, as the notion of the 'state' became more precise, the official was considered to have been delegated part of the public power by the King. Thus at the same time that the Kings were slowly gaining control over functions formerly in the hands of the nobility they were losing it again.

The turning point in this development that is commonly cited is the ordinance of Louis XI of October 20, 1467 which provided that an office returned to the disposition of the King only upon the death of the office-holder, his resignation, or judicially proved forfeiture of the office. In spite of all attempts to modify the provisions of this ordinance they remained in force. To counteract partially this loss of power the Kings created a new form of office, one over which they had more control, the commission. The commissioner was given a special task for a limited time by the King; his function and office could be revoked at any time at the will of the King. These officials became more and more common in the sixteenth century as judicial commissioners, as representatives of the King at provincial estates, as collectors of various taxes. When the practice was extended to administrative affairs, the precedent that resulted in the appointing of intendants by Richelieu was established.[1]

In spite of a clear realization on the part of the Crown of the disadvantages

---

[1] The history of the development of the commissioner system remains to be written. At present it is impossible to provide even a commonly accepted vocabulary. It should be noted though that extraordinary commissions, the source of so many complaints by the deputies and others, were not the same as commissions. The former were usually investigative in nature, but served most often simply as a means of profit for the holder of the commission. He used his powers to force payments from anyone he could find who was guilty of the abuse he was investigating such as failure to pay a certain tax or violation of weights and measures regulations. The procedures used in the investigations were often very arbitrary. See R. Doucet, *Les Institutions de la France au xvie siècle* (Paris, 1948), I, 430 and Buisseret, *Sully*, pp. 99–100.

of the older system it was not abandoned in favor of the commissioner system because the Kings needed money, and the selling of offices that could not be readily abolished was an easy means of raising money. The practice of selling offices had originated in the Middle Ages and was not limited to France, but with the growth of the power of French royal officials venality became more than a questionable means of raising money for the central government. The buying and selling of offices became a profitable private business and an important means of social advancement. The welfare of France suffered, many of the powers of the King were exercised by unworthy men; but the system had too many supporters and the Kings had too many debts.[2]

The modern development of venality began in the early sixteenth century. Francis I's pressing need for money led him to create and sell large numbers of offices. He regularized the system in 1523 when he established the *Recette générale des Parties Casuelles* which handled the revenues gained from selling offices. Under Henry III many unnecessary and minor positions were raised to the dignity of royal office. The practice of inventing royal offices continued openly throughout the Old Regime, in spite of continual attempts to hide the reality by edicts which were laxly enforced or to which exceptions were granted for a price.

Developing along with delegation of authority and venality was a usage adapted from ecclesiastical practice, that of resignation of benefices. It became the custom that a man could resign an office to a person of his own choosing without interference from the King. As a logical extension of this, *survivance* (reversion) became common, whereby the official could pass his office on to someone in his last will. An office became a personal possession. In the fourteenth, fifteenth and sixteenth centuries there were growing protests and a number of laws were enacted against this system, especially near the end of the fifteenth century when judicial officials more and more were permitted to avail themselves of these practices. In an attempt to regulate resignations and reversions, which accounted for much of the traffic in offices, Francis I forbade the latter and had inserted in the letters of provision to an office what became known as the 'clause of forty days'. Thereafter if a man who resigned an office died within forty days of this resignation the office reverted to the disposition of the King.

The clause of forty days favored the King since the money to be gained from re-selling an office was much more than that received from the resignation tax. However, the protests of office-holders and the need for immediate money created by the Wars of Religion led to a gradual finding of ways around the

---

[2] On the question of the development of recruitment for royal offices and its effect in the fifteenth and early sixteenth centuries see Christopher Stocker, 'Office as Maintenance in Renaissance France', *Canadian Journal of History/Annales Canadiennes d'Histoire*, VI (1971), 21–43.

clause of forty days. In June 1568 Charles IX proclaimed that all officials of justice and finance who paid a tax of one-third the value of their office by December 31 of that year would have the right to resign their office at any time they wished without fear of the clause of forty days. If they died without making provision for passing on their office, their heirs were to be permitted to dispose freely of the office. Similar edicts were promulgated in 1574, 1576, and 1586.

The government's need for money during the Wars of Religion led to further alterations including the temporary introduction in 1586 of hereditary offices in return for a payment to the government of one-half the value of the office. By the end of the sixteenth century there was a vast complex of contradictory laws applicable to the purchase and disposition of royal offices. It was not until 1598 that legal tolerance was officially granted to the practice of venality itself when the oath formerly required of all judicial office holders to the effect that they had not bought their office was abolished, thus easing a few consciences if not changing reality.

Sully, despairing of significantly reforming the system and himself in need of money, devised with the King and Council in 1604 a new system known as the *droit annuel* or *paulette*. This word was derived from the name of Charles Paulet, Secretary of the Chamber of the King, who obtained the right to collect the new tax for six years in return for a payment of 1,066,000 *livres* the first year and 1,006,000 *livres* in succeeding years. Instead of paying a tax equal to one-third of the value of the office all at one time, the officers were now to pay Paulet a yearly sum equal to one-sixtieth the value set for the office by the Council in 1604. This value was purposely set much lower than the market price. On resignation of an office to someone who was not an heir, an additional tax of one-eighth instead of the former one-fourth of the value of the office was to be paid to Paulet. The clause of forty days was revoked. If the office-holder did not resign before his death, his heirs were allowed to dispose of the office as they wished if the office had been created prior to the time of Henry II. If the official had not resigned his office before his death and it had been created since the time of Henry II it reverted to the tax farmer for resale.[3] In spite of the last provision the security provided by the new system appealed to all office holders.

---

[3] Mousnier, *Venalité*, pp. 1–69, 208–255. For the best short discussion of offices and venality see Doucet, *Institutions*, I, 403–421. See also K. W. Swart, *The Sale of Offices in the Seventeenth Century* ('s-Gravenhage, 1949), *passim*, especially pp. 5–10, 112–127. For the question of Sully's motivation in instituting the *paulette* see Chapter 1 above. The English ambassador, George Carew, wrote in 1607 that France was prosperous because of the wise rule of Henry IV, but that it would be more so '... were it not that all offices being vendible in this kingdom, the merchants employ their money rather in buying offices than in exercising traffick because officers wives go before merchants wives'. Birch, *Historical View*, pp. 434–435.

From 1608 Henry IV reversed his previous policy and began to suppress unnecessary offices, though with inconsistency. The Regency government of Marie de Médicis continued the process of suppression in the same manner. On July 22, 1610 the execution of numerous edicts creating offices was delayed and a number of offices were abolished. This activity further limited the already restricted profits of the farmer of the *droit annuel*. In an effort to make the position more attractive the *paulette* was extended to cover higher offices in September 1611 (first presidents of the *Chambre des Comptes* and *Cour des Aides*, lieutenants general of presidial seats and treasurers of the *Epargne*). The dispensation from the clause of forty days was now to be restricted to officials who passed on their offices to a son or another relative. This meant that there would be more 'vacancies through death' and more resignations, both of which were a source of profit to the farmer of the *paulette*. A further result of the new regulations would be the selling of offices by the tax farmer at a lower price than prevailed on the open market. These measures lessened the advantages of the *droit annuel* for the royal officials who made a great profit in selling their offices but gave hope to the nobility that more offices which they could afford would be open to them. The *parlements* were quick to object, and since the loyalty of the provincial *parlements* was especially necessary for the government, the old conditions were virtually restored on March 29, 1612. This satisfied the officials but not the new farmer of the *paulette*, Claude Marcel, nor the nobles who were practically excluded from any office worth having because of the continually rising prices of these offices.[4]

The monarchy of the Old Regime had never been able to reorganize the financial system because it was faced every day with the shortage of money and therefore the need for credit. There never was a breathing space to allow for reorganization. This fact of life forced Sully to institute the *paulette*. Always there was need for men to advance credit and it would not have been wise to scrutinize too closely the ways in which these men got the necessary money. The grant of indirect tax collection to the Farmers General, the abuses of the underlings of the farmers, and the speculations of royal officials who collected

---

[4] Charles Paulet gave up his right to collect the *paulette* within a year. Between 1606 and the end of 1611 Bénigne Saulnier was the farmer. Claude Marcel gave up in 1613. From then on the *Trésorier des Parties Casuelles* collected the *paulette*. Mousnier, *Venalité*, p. 568, thinks that the complaints of the noble 'clients' of *les grands* concerning the re-establishment of the former conditions in 1612 was one of the reasons for the uprising of 1614. The timing is right, but I have found no evidence to link the two events. These clients and their patrons may also have been upset by the edicts of September 1610 and June 1614 which limited the number of royal and princely officials who could claim exemption from the *taille*. See Pierre Deyon, 'A propos des rapports entre la noblesse française et la monarchie absolue pendant la première moitié du XVIIe siècle'. *Revue Historique*, CCXXI (1964), 343–344.

direct taxes all had the same underlying cause: the treasury had no means of obtaining money without the aid of the financiers and businessmen. Any reform of the financial system had to begin with the provision of an independent source of credit for the government.

The complaints of the French people were centered on the middlemen, the so-called *partisans*, especially their methods of collecting indirect taxes and their fiscal monopolies. But the basic problem was that France was becoming a centralized national state without two necessary prerequisites – public credit and a national bank. There had been an attempt to set up a national bank in 1608, a year before the Bank of Amsterdam was founded, which was approved by the royal council. But the man who had proposed the idea, Pierre de Fontenu, was not able to raise the prescribed capital of 1,500,000 *livres*. Other attempts followed in 1644 and 1674. These failed also. Small wonder; those who benefited from the old system and who had the necessary money to back the new venture – the officials – were very much opposed to any change.[5]

If this was not enough there was the problem of inflation. All of Europe had been faced with this throughout most of the sixteenth century. Though the cost of living had leveled off in France during the last ten to fifteen years, concern remained; a concern that was increased because no one was really sure of the causes or the cures for inflation or the related and still bothersome problem of the relative devaluation of French money.[6]

It was in this context that the three estates became involved in their first set of problems: how to ensure that the king got the money he needed at the least cost to the people, while at the same time the nobles and the clergy remained free from what they considered unjust taxation, and the nobles gained profitable and honorable employment.

The nobles proposed that the King be asked to suspend the *paulette* during the meeting of the Estates General. On November 13 they asked the First

---

[5] Jean Meuvret, 'Comment les français voyaient l'impôt au XVIIᵉ siècle', *XVIIᵉ Siècle*, IV (1955), pp. 74–76. G. Fagniez, *Une banque de France en 1608*, extracted from *Bulletin de la Société de l'histoire de Paris et de l'Ile de France (March–April, 1896)*, pp. 1–8. Paul Harsin, *Crédit publique et banque d'état en France du XVIᵉ au XVIIIᵉ siècle* (Paris, 1933). See also A.A.E. France, 769, fols, 327r–330r. An interesting account of the life and methods of the Farmers General is to be found in P. Heumann, 'Un traitant sous Louis XIII, Antoine Feydeau', *Etudes sur l'histoire administrative et sociale de l'Ancien Régime* (Paris, 1938), pp. 183–223.

[6] For the French and European background see Spooner, *Economie mondiale*, pp. 92–97, 173–190, 303–328. For England see *Cal.St.P.* LXVII, 50–54, 104, LXIX, 7–9, LXX, 39–43, LXXI, 185, LXXVIII, 123–124; for Flanders and Spain see Lonchay and Cuvelier, *Correspondance*, I, nos. 837–838, 848, 1001 (various to Philip III, 1610–1614); Ballesteros Beretta, *Documentos*, IV, 94–99 (Gondomar to Philip III May, 1614). For Spanish interest in European money regulation see A.N. K 1469, no. 165 (Cardenas to Philip III, December 8, 1614).

Estate to join with them in presenting this request to the King. On Friday November 14 the clergy replied to the request and informed the nobles that, although they would prefer to take up the problem of the *paulette* in their *cahier*, they would join in a petition that the *paulette* be suspended until the Estates General could fully investigate the situation. However, the clergy insisted on informing the Third Estate of this decision. Later in the day the clergy agreed to add to the original request a protest against the irregularities in collection of the *gabelle*. The nobles claimed that the methods being used were ruining many of them.[7]

The Third Estate had also been discussing the problem of the *paulette*. On November 13 Pierre Rival, *échevin* of Montbrisson, a deputy from Lyonnais, speaking as a private individual, introduced a plan to abolish the *paulette* and was shouted down by the other deputies including those of his own *gouvernement*.[8] On Saturday November 15 a delegation from the Second Estate entered the chamber of the Third Estate to inform the deputies of the nobles' plan to ask for the suppression of the *paulette* during the meeting of the Estates General. After the delegation from the Second Estate had left, Raymond de Montagne, lieutenant of the *sénéchaussée* of Saintogne, speaking in the name of the *gouvernement* of Guyenne, rose to offer a modification of Rival's plan. He proposed that together with the abolition of the *paulette* there should be revocation of all pensions and a reduction of the *taille*, the principal direct tax, to the level of 1576. The Third Estate spent the rest of the morning in furious debate over the proposal and finally, after a vote of seven *gouvernements* to five, accepted Montagne's plan with two important modifications. The Third Estate then informed the clergy and the nobles that in return for its support the First and Second Estates must agree to Montagne's plan as modified by Orléanais and the Ile de France. Orléanais proposed that all venality and pensions be suspended during the meeting of the Estates General and that the *taille* not be collected until the King had considered the *cahiers* of the Estates General or that it be reduced immediately by one-fourth. The Ile de France added the caution that the clause of forty days was not to be reinstituted while the *paulette* was suspended. The nobles refused point blank to listen to such proposals. The clergy tried futilely to convince the enraged deputies of the Third Estate that for the moment it was unwise to enlarge the issue by

---

[7] PV-1, pp. 108–112, PV-2, pp. 73–74. Jules Gassot, *Sommaire mémorial de Jules Gassot, secrétaire du roi*, ed. Pierre Champion, (Paris, 1934), p. 262. The debate on the suppression of the *paulette* would soon have repercussions outside the Estates General. The sovereign courts joined battle to save the *paulette* on November 21.

[8] As a result of Rival's speech the Third Estate decided that no proposition was to be discussed in the general assembly which had not been first approved by a *gouvernement*. Rapine, pp. 100–101; B.N. MS fr. 10876, fols. 20r-20v.

the inclusion of so many requests. At noon on November 15 the Estates General was at an impasse.[9]

All three orders met again at three o'clock to continue discussing. Communications between the three chambers became so stormy and confused that the secretaries' accounts vary in reporting the order of deputations sent from chamber to chamber. The nobles stood their ground. The clergy, in the privacy of their own chamber, admitted the justice of the Third Estate's position, but tried desperately to convince it that only the nobles' requests should be presented to the King at this time. The clergy were fearful that nothing could be gained unless the Estates General proceeded carefully.

The clergy were able to persuade the Second and Third Estates to remain in session far beyond the usual time in an attempt to reach agreement. But any hope of agreement had already been killed earlier that afternoon by a speech delivered by the lieutenant general of Clermont, Jean Savaron, the voluble deputy from Basse Auvergne. In presenting the case for the Third Estate to the nobles he freely expressed the strong emotions felt by his fellow deputies. He further infuriated the nobles by presenting his own version of France's history. The French people had overthrown Roman rule when taxation became too heavy, he said. Once again the people, largely as a result of the granting of excessive pensions, were too heavily taxed and there was danger that once again the people would arise.

The Third Estate continued to maintain that if it must sacrifice its prerogative in the matter of the *paulette* (as many of the deputies had been commissioned to do by their *cahiers*), then the deputies of the Second Estate must sacrifice their pensions, and the people must be freed of part of their tax burden. The nobles countered that the arguments regarding their pensions were fallacious. They could not be considered in the same context as the *paulette*. Finally at eight o'clock in the evening the clergy abandoned their efforts to reconcile these opposing interests and recessed until Monday. They were followed shortly by the other two estates.[10]

[9] PV-1, pp. 112–117. PV-2, pp. 74–77. PV-3, pp. 44–49. Rapine, pp. 99–100, 103–110. B.N. MS fr. n.a. 7254, fols. 22v–26v. B.N. MS fr. 18256, pp. 35–37. A.D. Morbihan 87 G 4 (Guy Goualt to Pierre Goualt November 15, 19). Contrary to the impression given in some of the accounts Montagne did not present his plan until after the noble delegation had left. Two Burgundian deputies who had been at the Estates General of 1588 said of the morning 'that in all of the Estates there had never been so much confusion'. B.N. MS fr. 10876, fol. 22v.

[10] PV-1, pp. 117–122. PV-2, pp. 77–78. PV-3, pp. 49–51. B.N. MS fr. n.a. 7254, fols. 28r–28v. Rapine, pp. 112–118. A large number of pamphlets, written by nobles, lawyers and officials, on the subject of the *paulette* appeared in 1614–1615. The debate presented no striking ideas: history was appealed to by both sides, the good of France was found to lie with both sides, as was the destruction of France. Suppression was condemned as a noble plot to increase their power, maintenance was seen as a plot of the officials to ruin Frenchmen. Among the pamphlets were *Advis, remonstrances et requestes aux Estats généraux tenus à Paris 1614 par six paysans* (n.p., n.d.); *Advis d'un bon senateur sur la rupture du droit annuel* (n.p., n.d.); *Advis au Roy sur la réformation générale des abus ... en son royaume* (n.p., 1614); *Anatomie des trois ordres de la*

The morning of November 17 was filled with further negotiations among the orders. Cardinal Du Perron explained to the Third Estate that the nobles were so insistent about the *paulette* that the clergy had been forced to support their request, but that this would not prevent the First Estate from joining the Third Estate in its requests later. The nobles refused to discuss the matter further. The Third Estate, through Savaron, maintained that if some venality were to be done away with all must be, including pensions.[11]

At eleven o'clock in the morning representatives from the three estates went across the Seine to the Louvre in two groups. Cardinal de Sourdis spoke to Louis and Marie for the clergy and nobles. He asked that the *paulette* be suspended until the Estates General had fully discussed the matter. He also complained of the salt-tax provisions. Jean Savaron spoke for the program of the Third Estate which included not only suspension of the *paulette* and pensions and reductions of the *taille,* but a proposal that a number of extra-ordinary commissions be revoked. In the process he widened the breach between the orders. He repeated his comments of November 15, emphasized the misery of the ordinary people and added, 'But some ask you, Sire, to abolish the *paulette,* which fills your coffers with the 1,600,000 *livres* your officials pay you each year; however, they do not ask that you suppress the excess pensions which are so outrageous that there are great and powerful kingdoms which do not receive as revenue what you give to your subjects to buy their loyalty. Is it not to ignore and to misunderstand the law of nature, of God, and of the kingdom to serve one's king for money . . . ?'. The King and Queen Mother answered in general terms that the Estates General should hasten the preparation of its *cahiers* and that within a few days contentment would be

---

France sur le sujet des estats (n.p., 1615), most probably by a jurist; *Le conseiler fidèle à son roy* (n.p., n.d.); *Discours pour la conservation de l'annuel des offices* (n.p., n.d.); *Discours sur l'droict annuel* (n.p., n.d.); *Libre discours et véritable jugement sur l'hérédité des offices insinuée en France, dans le doux venim du droict annuel* (Paris, 1615), the anonymous author of which claimed to be a deputy to the Estates General. The satires produced on this subject were for some reason particularly poor. See D.M.B., *Le Tombeau de la polette dédié aux jeunes advocats* (n.p., 1615), *Résurrection et triomphe de la polette dédié à messieurs les officiers de France* (Paris, n.d.). Davis Bitton, 'History and Politics: The Controversy over the Sale of Offices in Early Seventeenth-Century France', in *Action and Conviction in Early Modern Europe,* ed. T. K. Rabb and J. E. Siegel (Princeton, 1969), pp. 390–403 gives some idea of the nature of the debate. But it must be pointed out that the deputies of the Third Estate were sincere in their desire to abolish the *paulette* if their conditions were met. As Etienne de Lalain put it, the Third Estate was very troubled when Guyenne first put forward its proposal, but despite strong protests from officials the majority of *gouvernements* agreed that public interest had to supersede their particular interests. Bibl. Ars. MS 4255, fol. 15v.

[11] PV-1, pp. 123–125. PV-2, pp. 78–79. PV-3, pp. 51–53. Among the six pamphlets that Savaron wrote in 1614–1615 was one on the *paulette* and venality. Starting with a long historical analysis he finished by saying that if the *paulette* were abolished all venality must be done away with or nothing would be accomplished. Jean Savaron, *Traicté de l'annuel et venalité des offices. . . .* (Paris, 1615).

given in what had been asked. They also promised that the Estates General would be presented with an account of finances for the period of the Regency.[12]

On Thursday, November 20, the Estates General was notified by the clergy, who throughout the meetings were in close contact with Marie de Médicis and the Council through Cardinal de Sourdis and Cardinal Rochefoucault, that the King had granted the suspension of the *paulette* during the meeting of the Estates General.[13]

The twelve *gouvernements* of the Third Estate had spent Tuesday and Wednesday in separate assemblies working on the preparation of governmental *cahiers*. By the time the Third Estate met again in full session on Thursday the nobles had lodged a complaint with the clergy demanding that the Third Estate make amends for Savaron's remarks. The clergy sent Richelieu, bishop of Luçon, to the Chamber of the Third Estate to ask the deputies to repair the situation. It was not until four o'clock in the afternoon of Monday November 24 that an acceptable formula could be found, but the delegation from the Third Estate accompanied by a delegation from the clergy did not appear before the nobles until eight o'clock that evening. Henri de Mesmes, Lieutenant Civil of the *prévôté* of Paris, speaking for the Third Estate, repeated the bland statement that his order had meant no offense. However, in his speech he did not neglect the opportunity to reply to a remark made by one of the nobles to the effect that Savaron should be turned over to their pages and lackeys for punishment. He also replied to the aspersion that the members of the Third Estate were only the cadets of France. He said that all three orders were brothers and it sometimes fell to the youngest to fulfil duties left undone by the elders. After Mesmes had left, the nobles complained that they had again been insulted – they were not brothers of the Third Estate! The clergy present agreed that they, too, had been insulted by this statement. The First and Second Estates recessed their meetings in righteous indignation at ten o'clock that evening.[14]

On November 26 the Third Estate learned that the King and Queen Mother had been informed of the trouble in the Estates General and had assigned the clergy the task of making peace. By this time the deputies of the Third Estate

---

[12] PV-1, p. 125. PV-2, pp. 79–84. PV-3, pp. 353–354. Rapine, pp. 132–133. For a complete list of the suspensions requested by the Third Estate see B.N. MS fr. n.a. 7254, fols. 32v–36r. Savaron did not ask that venality of office be suspended.

[13] PV-2, p. 88. The *Cour des Aides* protested against the decision to suspend the *paulette* on November 21, the *Parlement* on January 2, and the *Chambre des Comptes* on January 4, 19, and May 11; Mousnier, *Venalité*, p. 576. A.N. X1A 1867, fols. 112r–112v. Boislisle, *Pièces justicatives*, p. 305.

[14] PV-1, pp. 148–153. PV-2, pp. 85–88, 94–96. PV-3, pp. 54–58, 61–63. B.N. MS fr. 18256, pp. 38–48, 62–73 (many details on the controversy between the Second and Third Estates). The remark concerning Savaron and the lackeys was evidently made by Henri de Balsac of Dreux, B.N. MS fr. n.a. 1395, fol. 30v.

were heartily sick of the whole business and agreed to make satisfaction. The quarrel had become so vexing that at one point some of the deputies of the Third Estate had wanted to stop sending deputations to the nobles, who took offense so easily that soon all members of the assembly of the Third Estate would have been used in the business and would be personally involved in quarrels with the nobles. The clergy, too, had almost given up in their attempts to pacify the nobles, but reminded of the Queen Mother's order by Cardinal de Sourdis they continued to strive for a settlement. By December 3 they had worked out a formula. The Third Estate, upon hearing it, again broke into argument as to whether it was too servile since they had never intended any offense in the first place. But Mesmes admitted that his words had not been well chosen, and finally on December 5 peace was restored. On the suggestion of Chancellor Sillery a delegation from the Third Estate was sent to the nobles to thank them for the support they had given to a project the Third Estate had been working on for a month, revocation of extraordinary commissions. To this expression of gratitude the delegates added some general remarks on the greatness of the nobility without, however, mentioning their own alleged offenses. This was enough for the nobles, not because their pride had weakened, but because they wanted the support of the Third Estate for their new project, investigation of royal financial officials.[15]

The attention of the city of Paris was not focused on the activities of the deputies of the Estates General during the second half of November. As Secretary of State Pontchartrain describes the situation, the great subject of interest in Paris at this time was the affair of the Duke of Epernon. The activities of Epernon in Metz had recently threatened to precipitate a war between the Empire and France, and now in Paris he seemed to be about to provoke further trouble for the government. A member of the Guards, Jean Scaron, had been charged with dueling and had been placed in the prison of the Faubourg Saint Germain des Près. Epernon had freed him by force on November 14 on the grounds that he alone, as provost of the troops, could try Scaron. The case was taken to the *Parlement* of Paris for consideration. On November 19 Epernon, with fifty or sixty of his followers in boots and spurs, marched up and down in the courtyard of the *Parlement* as the members were leaving for the day. The members of the *Parlement* interpreted this action as hostile to their authority. Their resentment was encouraged by Condé, who attended their sessions almost daily during this time. The government feared more serious consequences if the quarrel between Epernon and the *Parlement*

---

[15] PV-1, pp. 163–167, 179. B.N. MS fr. 4082, fol. 26r. PV-2, pp. 102–103, 112–114. PV-3, pp. 63–65, 70, 73–74. Rapine, pp. 153–154, 169–175. On December 10 Pierre Marmiesse would provide more flattery for the nobles and on December 13 Jean de Murines worked hard to flatter the Third Estate. Rapine, pp. 196–201.

continued and prevailed upon the members of the *Parlement* to drop the matter. It was agreed that if Scaron were returned to prison and if Epernon presented his excuses to the *Parlement* then the question of jurisdiction could be settled through regular procedures. Such arrangements were completed on November 28.[16]

In late November and early December Condé, Bouillon, and Nevers were all looking for a pretext to cause trouble for the government. First there had been the attempt to play up to the *Parlement* of Paris. Then on November 27 Condé gave his support to the Third Estate in its quarrel with the nobles. Condé also appeared at court in the guise of a friend of the government. Nevers even offered to give up his pension if that would help the financial situation. At the same time Condé, Nevers, and Bouillon were maintaining contacts with the Venetian Ambassador. Nothing much came of all of this because the government took precautions not only to warn the Estates General about Condé's double dealing but also to conciliate him. The Regency Council of Direction was abolished and Condé and Bouillon were made members of a newly organized Particular Council of Finances which was to meet once a week. The government also began negotiations to gain re-entry to the town of Poitiers for several of Condé's followers, a right finally granted at the end of January.[17]

Paris and the author of *Gazette des Estats et de ce temps* may have dismissed the Estates General and concentrated attention on Epernon and Condé, but the government had to worry about both *les grands* and the deputies. In a letter dated December 1, 1614 Pierre Brûlart, Villeroy's adjunct as Secretary of State, reported to the *Sieur* of Sainte Catherine in Germany that the deputies of the Estates General were becoming insolent and were questioning the affairs of the King and Queen Mother and their advisers.[18]

[16] Pontchartrain, *Mémoires*, p. 337. B. M. Stowe MS 175, fols. 105r–110r (Edmondes to Winwood November 23/December 3, 1614). *Extraict des registres de la cour touchant ce qu s'est passé en l'affaire de Monsieur d'Espernon: vingt-quatriesme novembre 1614* (n.p., 1615). Mathieu Molé, *Mémoires* . . . ed. Aimé Champallion-Figeac (Paris, 1855), I, 5–17.

[17] Rapine, pp. 162, 217–218; Bibl. Ars. MS 4255, fol. 26r. A.S.F. Arch. Med. 4867 (letter of Bartolini of December 16), B.M. Stowe MS 175, fols. 116r–119r (Edmondes to Winwood December 1/11, 1614); B.N. MS ital. 1767, pp. 227–230, 230–234, 248–251 (Contarini's reports of November 25–December 9, 1614); B.N. MS ital. 38, fols. 193v–196r (Ubaldini's newsletter of November 20 and December 2, 1614). Edmondes reported on December 30/January 9 that a lewd libel attacking Condé had been published in Poitiers. B.M. Stowe MS 175, fol. 149v.

[18] *Gazette des Estats et de ce temps du Siegᵗ Gio servitour de Piera Grosa. Traduite d'Italien en François le premier janvier 1615* (n.p., n.d.). B.N. MS fr. 4121, fol. 111r (Brûlart to Sainte Catherine). On December 14 Marie de Médicis had used Le Doux and other deputies that she was sure of to warn the Third Estate that Condé was planning to set himself up as the protector of the Estates General and its ally against the government. On December 15 Le Doux was used as a means of trying to add to the *cahier* of the Third Estate a number of articles attacking Condé and supporting the Regency's foreign policy. B.N. MS fr. n.a. 1395, fols. 45v–46r.

124

The Second and Third Estates continued to press for reforms of offices and finances. Between November 20 and December 1 the nobles worked out a plan to ask the King for establishment of a chamber of justice on finances to investigate the activities of the financiers. They then sought to exert influence to persuade the other orders to join them in this plea. On December 1, when a deputation from the nobles visited the clergy, Cardinal de Sourdis pointed out that the financiers had powerful friends, and that even Henry IV had not been able to bring about their reform. The nobles persisted, and on December 5 the clergy and the Third Estate agreed to meet with them to discuss the proposed financial investigation.[19]

At this meeting held in the chamber of the First Estate on Saturday, December 6, the nobles presented their plan to representatives of the other estates and promised that it could save the King 12,000,000 *livres*. On December 10 the First and Third Estates agreed to join in asking for the establishment of the chamber. The request was presented to Louis and Marie by Archbishop Hôpital of Aix, but it was rejected on December 12. The deputies declined to abandon their project. On December 16 they again presented their plea, this time adding the request that deputies to the Estates General be members of the chamber. Marie de Médicis replied that when the *cahiers* were finished the Estates General would receive satisfaction. If such a chamber were organized at present, she said, it would impede the progress of the Estates General. The nobles, however, continued to plead for the chamber.[20]

The Third Estate had been absorbed in developing its own plan for reform, a memoir asking for the suppression of eighty extraordinary commissions and

---

[19] PV-1, pp. 175–176, 194–196. PV-2, pp. 88–106, 111–114. PV-3, pp. 74–76. A chamber of justice was set up to investigate the methods of the financiers on January 17, 1605, but it was abolished by September of that year. The requests of the nobles in 1614 produced no action. A chamber was again set up in October 1624. The same year exceptions began to be made and on May 16, 1625 the chamber was abolished because too many were found to be guilty. B.N. MS fr. 4310, fols. 97r–303v, 304r–414v. See also *Lettres patentes de commission du roy ... pour la recherche des financiers* (Paris, 1605); *Edict du roy pour la révocation de la chambre royale. ...* (Paris, 1605); *Edict du roy portant révocation de la chambre de justice ...* (Paris, 1625).

[20] PV–1, pp. 211, 233–237. B.N. MS fr. 4082, fol. 27v. PV-2, pp. 121, 131–132, 134–135, 138. PV–3, p. 78. Rapine, pp. 202–203. Pierre Marmiesse, *Remonstrances sur l'exécution des délibérations prises en la chambre du tiers Estat pour le retranchement des tailles, communication des cahiers entre les trois chambres et pour la poursuite d'une Chambre de Justice contre les financiers ...* (Paris, 1615), pp. 38–56. Among the pamphlets written on the subject were *Très-humble requeste au Roy sur la disposition de la Chambre de Justice par un officier des finances* (n.p., 1615), which alternately begs for mercy and warns that no one will accept a financial office any longer, and *Mémoires adresséz à messiers des Estats ... contenants les fautes ...* (n.p., n.d.), which attacks the origins and faults of the financiers and partisans. At this time Cardinal de Sourdis received a letter from Queen Marguerite, the first wife of Henry IV, asking the First Estate to support the chamber on finances; B.N. MS fr. 6379, fols. 236r–238v. Several of the deputies of the Third Estate were her officials. She gave assurances of support to the Third Estate on several occasions. See Rapine, pp. 157–158, 163–164, 176–177, 186, 272–275.

new offices. The deputies had been discussing this project among themselves, with the other estates, and with the government, since November 7. The clergy agreed to join with them in presenting the memoir to the King, if they in turn would support the clergy in their particular requests. But Henri de Mesmes reported to the Third Estate on November 29 that Chancellor Sillery had informed him that, instead of presenting the memoir to the King, six representatives should be sent to confer with the Chancellor on the subject. The other two estates were also instructed to send six representatives each to the meeting. The Third Estate insisted that it should be represented by double that number since it had the greatest interest in the affair. In what might be regarded as a foreshadowing of the events of 1789, the Third Estate won its point and sent twelve deputies to the meeting. The action of the Third Estate may have been prompted by a threat the nobles had made during the debate over the *paulette*, that the clergy and nobles together could outvote the Third Estate. Miron replied at the time that they would see about that when a disagreement arose.[21]

The representatives of the estates met with Sillery on December 4, but little was accomplished at this first meeting.[22] On December 5 the Third Estate was informed that the King, in response to the request of November 17, would enforce the edict of 1610 suppressing certain extraordinary commissions and edicts, but that it was impossible to reduce the *taille* by one-quarter. The Third Estate immediately began again to ask for the reduction of the *taille* and continued to do so throughout the meeting of the Estates General, sometimes alone, sometimes with the support of the other orders. They did so in spite of Miron's warning that this might so exasperate the King that he would not grant anything. On December 10 and 11 Sillery again met with representatives of the three estates who gave him a complete list of the offices to be suppressed. This list was presented to the King and accepted. At the meeting of December 11 Jeannin gave a short account of the state of finances and told the deputies that he would be glad to provide further information. The deputies replied that they were empowered to discuss only the suppression of extraordinary commissions but told Jeannin that the Estates General would like more information on France's financial situation. The Chancellor pointed out that the King was not required to give the information but that he would do so to show his good will. The next meeting was set for December 13.[23]

The major concern of the government was to head off any attempt by the

---

[21] PV–3, pp. 46, 51–69. Rapine, pp. 155, 164. B.N. MS fr. n.a. 7254, fols. 56r–59v.

[22] B.N. MS fr. n.a. 1395, fols. 38v–39v.

[23] PV–1, pp. 186, 197, 215–216. PV–2, pp. 109, 118. PV–3, pp. 72–73. Rapine, pp. 170, 179, 188. B.N. MS fr. n.a. 1395, fols. 42v–49v. On December 20, 1614, the *Cour des Aides* registered an edict of the King of the preceding June that contained thirty-one regulations reducing and stopping exemptions from the *taille*. Various lesser royal officials were affected:

Estates General to launch a full scale financial investigation by getting the deputies to accept a freely offered general statement of the Regency financial policy and the results of that policy. This was the reason for the offers made on November 17 and December 11. Jeannin openly admitted the reason for his concern. In 1588 a full written report had been given to the deputies to the Estates General and as a result the deputies had tried to reorganize the whole taxation system. Under the present circumstances this could only lead to trouble; specifically it would open the way for Condé to foment new intrigues. Jeannin insisted that since a written report had been given only once, no precedent had been established. The duty of the deputies was to inform the King of the abuses that troubled the people, listen to an account of the problems that faced the government and then obediently give their support to the government's plans to solve the problems while the King took care of the abuses listed in the *cahiers*. When Miron replied that general statements of financial problems were of little use to deputies involved in drawing up detailed *cahiers* Jeannin shot back that royal officials should give a good example to the people and avoid any occasion that might open the way for new uprisings.[24] In other words the deputies should present their *cahiers* and go home. There was no need for lists of extraordinary commissions, investigations of financiers or close scrutiny of budgets. The government would take care of the country.

On December 20 the government attempted to placate the deputies. The chief financial officials of the kingdom led by Jeannin came to each of the estates to assure the deputies that the chamber of finances would be granted, but that it would be made up of members of the sovereign courts. The nobles immediately proposed that the Estates General should choose these members of the courts and that one-half of the members of the chamber be deputies. They also asked Jeannin to request the King to publish an edict permitting the Estates General to remain in session until the *cahiers* were answered. Both of these requests were contrary to the plans of the government and both would be side-stepped.[25]

Jeannin presented his promised report on finances to the First and Second Estates on December 20, but the Third Estate refused to listen because the report was not detailed enough. This greatly irritated the court and Jeannin

---

greffiers, taille collectors, and masters of the mines. *Edict du Roy sur le règlement et retranchement des exemptes des tailles* (Paris, 1615). The *Cour des Aides* had tried to resist registering this edict. The King published the edict promised on December 5 on December 16. *Articles presentées au roy par les députés de la chambre du tiers Estat de France avec les responses de sa majesté* (Paris, 1615), pp. 16–31. The Third Estate kept up pressure and there were some further concessions in a series of articles dated between December 16, 1614, and January 12, 1615, *ibid.*, pp. 1–15. Further steps were taken through the decision of council of February 17, *Articles présentés au Roy* ... (n.p., n.d.). See also B.N. MS fr. 10876, fols. 256r–258v.

[24] Rapine, pp. 230–237. B.N. MS fr. 18256, p. 148.

[25] PV–2, pp. 132–156. PV–1, pp. 255–265 (misdated).

tried to overcome the resistance of the Third Estate by informing the deputies that a more detailed though still secret financial report would be given to a select committee from each estate at a later date. The Third Estate finally agreed to allow Jeannin's general report to be read to them after further pressure was exerted by Sillery.[26]

While plans for reforming the office-holding and financial systems had dominated the meetings of the Estates General during late November and early December, each of the estates had also continued to devote attention to matters of particular interest to itself. The clergy had gained the King's promise that investigation of *franc fiefs* would be halted for three months. On November 29 final agreement was reached on the wording of the article of their *cahier* on the Council of Trent. As had been the case earlier in the month the reformers yielded to those, especially the members of cathedral chapters, who insisted that a clause be inserted specifically protecting the rights of the King and the Gallican Church. On December 3 the First Estate decided that the meeting of the Assembly of Clergy should begin on March 1, 1615.[27]

The nobles had continued to appoint a series of committees to evaluate the stream of petitions and pleas for reform that were presented to them. They also interested themselves in trying to find a means of seeking satisfaction in affairs of honor without resorting to dueling. The marshals of France were asked for assistance, but replied that they could not act without the King's permission. The nobles made some progress in making heard their complaints on the *gabelles*. The nobles had also been working on plans for monetary reform, but they formulated their ideas too slowly.[28]

On October 31 President Miron had announced to the Third Estate that the King wished them to discuss France's monetary problems. After discussion the deputies decided on November 5 that they would handle these issues when the *cahiers* were drawn up. Part of the reason for the postponement was that the Third Estate did not like the idea of the King communicating with them verbally through Miron.[29] Whether the Third Estate could have played a role in monetary reform even if it had listened to the King is doubtful. On October 7 Louis had called for a meeting of the officials of the city of Paris and

---

[26] B.N. MS fr. 18256, pp. 136–143. B.N. MS fr. 10876, fols. 54v–57v. Bibl. Ars. MS 4255, fols. 34v–35r. The Third Estate seems to have given in partly out of fear, partly because the deputies hoped that the proposed committee could accomplish something. However, the committee received no information until the end of January. B.N. MS fr. n.a. 1395, fols, 49r–50v. B.N. MS fr. n.a. 7254, fols 93v–96v. See Chapter 9 below.

[27] PV–1, pp. 123–174, 183–184.

[28] PV–2, pp. 78–132. At the end of December the King would augment the wages of the councilors, *greffiers*, secretaries of the king's household and crown, and other officers, taking the money from the revenues of the salt tax. *Edict du Roy sur la règlement et retranchement des exempts des tailles*, p. 18.

[29] Rapine, pp. 55–57, 65.

important merchants to study monetary reforms. This group made proposals which were accepted by the government and published as an ordinance on December 5, 1614. The ordinance set the relative values of French and foreign coins, and prohibited the export of gold or silver from France.[30]

The deputies of the Third Estate had spent their time in debating the quarrel with the nobles and in preparing their memoir on extraordinary commissions. Evidently feeling that the Estates General was drawing to a close, on December 12 they elected President Miron to speak and present the *cahiers* at the closing of the Estates General. The debate over this election was bitter. At first Henri de Mesmes was to have a place in the ceremonies, but Miron, through intrigues, the force of his office, and the intervention of Marie de Médicis, who warned Mesmes to withdraw from the race, was elected as the sole representative of the Third Estate.[31]

During November the deputies had been kept busy beyond the hours set aside for daily general meetings by the continuing compilation of governmental *cahiers*. Within each estate each *gouvernement* held frequent separate meetings usually in the lodgings of its president. The purpose of these meetings was to decide which articles from the *bailliage cahiers* that the deputies had brought with them should be used to form the *cahier* that each *gouvernement* of each estate was required to present to the full meeting of that estate. By early December the *gouvernement* assemblies had completed their work.

The clergy had begun the reading of their governmental *cahiers* on December 5. Instead of reading each *cahier* separately in the general meetings, they chose six general headings and then read all of the relevant articles from each of the governmental *cahiers* concerning each topic. On December 12 Cardinal de Sourdis interrupted the regular work to push through articles for the general *cahier* in support of the Regency policies of Marie de Médicis. This included support for her foreign policy and the Spanish marriages. The First

---

[30] *Reg. délib. Paris*, XVI, 1, pp. 22, 137–138, 140–144, 145. The Bureau of the Hôtel de Ville had already discussed these matters in 1613, *ibid.*, XV, 309–311. For 1614 see also A.N. H 1797 (December 6), A.A.E. France, 769, fols. 219r–234r, 302r–305r. An emissary was sent to Spain to try to reach agreement on the declared values, B.N. Cinq Cents 102, fols. 277r–282r. The ordinance was printed as a pamphlet: *Ordonnance du Roy sur le faict et règlement général de ses monnayes* (Paris, 1615). The pamphlet included pictures of the coins, their worth, and the exchange rates for the newly forbidden coins, *ibid.*, pp. 31–96. For background see A. Magen, 'De l'intervention de la municipalité Parisienne en matière monétaire pendant le premier tiers du XVIIᵉ siècle', *Revue Historique du droit français et étranger*, series 4, Vol. XXXVIII (1960), 430–448, 549–557. In 1617 the *Cour des Monnaies* was still trying to get the 1614 *ordonnance* enforced. *Arrest de la Cour des Monnoyes portât deffèces . . . les pièces estrangères. . . .* (Paris, 1617). There had been attempts to reform money values in 1577, 1602 and 1609. For the last see Bernard Barbiche, 'Une tentative de réforme monétaire à la fin de regne de Henri IV: l'édict d'aôut 1609', *XVIIᵉ siècle*, no. 61 (1963), pp. 3–17 and *Mercure François* 1, 361a–362a. For 1602 see *Edict du Roy sur le faict et règlement général de ses monnoyes* (Paris, 1602), pp. 1–72.

[31] PV–3, pp. 79–81. Rapine, pp. 182–185.

Estate also worked on a proposal to be presented to the King asking for a reform of the Council; they wanted the membership of the Council permanently reduced to a stipulated number of men drawn from all three estates.[32]

Early in December the nobles had begun to read the *cahiers* of each *gouvernement* in full assembly prior to drawing up the general *cahier*. On December 13 the Third Estate was ready to begin reading its governmental *cahiers*. However, Miron and Mesmes were absent at the time conferring with the nobles concerning the chamber on finances. Israel Desneux, a deputy of Paris, tried to preside, but the other members refused saying that Paris had taken too many honors already. Claude Mochet, President of the Burgundian delegation, was elected as President in the absence of Miron and Mesmes. At this the deputies of Paris, whose *cahier* was to be read first and form the model for the general *cahier*, stalked out of the chamber *cahier* in hand. It was impossible to continue with the agenda, but the Third Estate prolonged the session so that the election of Mochet would be confirmed. The deputies listened to a report by Pierre Marmiesse of Toulouse, who was gaining a reputation as an eloquent speaker. He described the speech he had delivered to the Second Estate on December 10, a speech that had repaired most of the damage done by Savaron.[33]

But if the breach between the Second and Third Estates had been healed, the Third Estate was about to take a step that would alienate the First Estate. This time the argument would be much more serious. When the Third Estate began to read the *cahier* of Paris and the Ile de France on Monday December 15 and unanimously approved the first article of that *cahier* calling for the proclamation, as a fundamental law of France, that the King had no temporal or spiritual superior within his kingdom, the whole controversy over Gallicanism, the Jesuits, the sovereignty of the King, and the power of the clergy would be opened. The Estates General of 1614 was on the brink of its most serious debate.[34]

---

[32] PV-1, pp. 174–226.

[33] PV-2, pp. 106–132. PV-3, pp. 69–88. Rapine, pp. 191–202. B.N. MS fr. n.a. 7254, fols. 62v–67r. Pierre Marmiesse, *Remonstrances*.

[34] PV-3, pp. 84–87. Rapine, pp. 205–211. B.N. MS fr. 18256, pp. 103–109. Mousnier, *Venalité*, pp. 570–574 states that the issues of venality and the *paulette* split the Estates and made any effort to limit the power of the government impossible. Pierre Blet, *Clergé*, 1, 39, says that the clergy had been effectively working to reunite the three estates in early December but that the threat of the first article of the Third Estate made them give up the effort. In actuality the breach between the nobles and the Third Estate was healed. While the split between the First and Third Estates would never be completely healed the nobles and clergy worked together quite well and all three estates would in the end agree on a common plan of reform. The fabled breakdown of the Estates General of 1614 was actually a disagreement over methods not purposes. As for the Estates General developing into a means of limiting the power of the monarchy – this was impossible since an Estates General could not meet without the permission of the King. If the deputies had tried to eliminate this barrier to their power they would have failed. They had no means to force the King to remove it. But, in fact, it never was their aim.

8

THE FIRST ARTICLE OF THE
THIRD ESTATE: DECEMBER 15, 1614
TO JANUARY 16, 1615

The text of the first article of the *cahier* of the *gouvernement* of Paris and the Ile de France which was read in the chamber of the Third Estate on December 15 read,

That, to arrest the course of the pernicious doctrine which was introduced several years ago by seditious spirits against kings and sovereign powers established by God and which troubles and subverts them: the King shall be asked to declare in the assembly of his Estates *as a Fundamental Law of the Kingdom, which shall be inviolable and known to all*: that since he is known to be sovereign in his state, holding his crown from God alone, that there is no power on earth whatever, spiritual or temporal, which has any authority over his kingdom, to take away the sacred nature of our kings, to dispense [or absolve] their subjects of the fidelity and obedience which they owe them for any cause or pretext whatsoever. That all subjects, of whatever quality or condition they might be, shall hold this Law to be holy and true as conforming to the word of God, without distinction, equivocation or any limitation. This shall be sworn to and signed by all the deputies of the Estates and in the future by all who hold benefices and all officers of the kingdom before they take possession of their benefices or receive their offices. All tutors, regents, doctors, and preachers shall be required to teach and publish this. That the contrary opinion, that it is lawful to kill and depose our kings, to rise up and rebel against them, to shake off the yoke of their obedience, for whatever reason, is impious, detestable, against truth, and against the establishment of the State of France, which is responsible only to God. All books which teach such a false and perverse opinion shall be held to be seditious and damnable. All foreigners who shall write and publish such are sworn enemies of the crown. All subjects of His Majesty who hold to this, of whatever quality and condition they might be, shall be rebels and violators of the fundamental laws of the kingdom and guilty of treason in the first degree. And if any book or discourse is found which contains a proposition directly or indirectly contrary to this law written

131

by [a] foreigner, cleric or not, the clerics of the same order[s] established in France will be obliged to respond to it, impugning and contradicting it incessantly without deference, ambiguity or equivocation, under pain of receiving the same punishment as above, as abettors of the enemies of this state. And this first (present) article shall be read [in] each year in the Sovereign Courts and in the courts of the *bailliages* and *sénéchaussées* of the said (this) kingdom at the opening of the sessions so that it will be guarded and observed with all severity and rigor.[1]

The intent of the article was clear to all who heard it. The deputies of the Third Estate, the King's *pauvre sujets* as the nobles and clergy persisted in describing them, were saying that the King of France was sovereign over all powers, temporal and spiritual, noble or clerical, within his kingdom. This is what would later be described as political Gallicanism as distinguished from ecclesiastical Gallicanism. The latter was concerned with the relative power of Ecumenical Councils and the Pope and with claims of the French clergy to special privileges (or abuses) in matters of ecclesiastical jurisdiction. Political Gallicanism was the creation of French jurists in the late Middle Age, called into being to aid the French kings in their struggle to gain complete control of their kingdom. Support for the theory had grown during the sixteenth century at least partly in reaction to the chaos of the Wars of Religion. The murders of Henry III and Henry IV had provided the final impetus for the widespread acceptance of Gallicanism among the members of the Third Estate; especially by royal officials whose welfare and fortune were closely connected with that of the King.[2] The election strategy of the Regency government that brought so many royal officials together in one spot was producing an unforseen result – one that the government would have preferred to have avoided. Its officials were determined to be more royalist than was convenient.

The basis of the theory of political Gallicanism was that, to survive, France needed an absolute ruler. Consequently, the King's life had to be protected at all costs. In the popular mind the greatest threat to the King's life came from the Jesuits who were blamed for inspiring the murders of the two Henrys. But there were other reasons for the not very veiled references to the Jesuits in the First Article of the *cahier* of the Third Estate. Three eminent Jesuits had written books between 1599 and 1613, which gave a more definite, if theoretical,

---

[1] Rapine, pp. 205–206, A.D. Morbihan 87 G 4. Words in brackets are not in the copy of the first article of the *cahier* of Paris and Ile de France that Guy Goualt sent to his brother. Words in parenthesis are words used in Goualt's copy instead of the word found in Rapine.

[2] W. F. Church, *Constitutional Thought in Sixteenth Century France* (Oxford, 1941), *passim*. Mousnier, *L'Assassinat*, pp. 47–90. François Perrens, *L'église et l'état sous Henri IV et Marie de Médici* (Paris, 1872), I, 514, II, 301–312. Victor Martin, *Le gallicanisme et la réforme catholique* (Paris, 1919), pp. 320–367; Victor Martin, *Le gallicanisme politique et le clergé de France* (Paris, 1928), pp. 323–328.

formulation of the medieval theory of the right of revolt and tyrannicide. It was these books rather than supposed connections with actual murders that enraged the *Parlement* of Paris which had become the center of vocal, radical political Gallicanism. The *Parlement*'s reaction was condemnation. Juan de Mariana's book *De Rege et Regis Institutione* published in 1599 was condemned on June 8, 1610 and Cardinal Bellarmine's *Potestate Summi Pontificis in rebus Temporalibus* on November 26 of the same year.[3] Faced with this and the general reaction in France against the Jesuits, the General of the Jesuits, Claudio Aquaviva, sent a decree to the Jesuits of France on July 6 and August 14, 1610, forbidding any preaching, teaching or printing of the theory that 'it is allowed for anyone whatsoever, under any pretext of tyranny whatsoever, to kill kings or princes or to plan their murder'.[4] Despite this the Jesuit Francisco Suarez published in Spain in 1613 *Defensio Fidei Catholicae et apostolicae adversos Anglicanae sectae errores* which contained a fully argued defense of the legitimacy of tyrannicide. The book had been encouraged by Pope Paul V as an answer to James I's book on the power of kings, *Basilicon Doron*. Suarez's book was burned in London and on June 26, 1614 the *Parlement* condemned it to the same treatment.[5] Cardinal Ubaldini managed to get the *Parlement*'s *arrêt* suspended on December 16 in return for a promise that the Pope would issue a condemnation of the theory of legitimate tyrannicide. Ubaldini had earlier gotten a suspension of the condemnation of Bellarmine's book.[6] General Aquaviva issued decrees on August 1 and 2, 1614, this time to all Jesuit provincials, repeating the 1610 decrees in stronger terms. But it was not enough nor were Villeroy's words of support for the Jesuits in answer to a letter from Aquaviva. This time the *Parlement* had an ally, the deputies of the Third Estate.[7]

The Third Estate had an issue it believed in. During the voting for the acceptance of the first article on December 15, other *gouvernements* pointed

---

[3] A.N. AD III 20, nos. 48, 53. Under pressure from Spain, Mariana's book on currency reform was placed on the Roman and Spanish Indexes, *De rege* never was. Guenter Lewy, *Constitutionalism and Statecraft during the Golden Age of Spain* (Geneva, 1960), pp. 30–32, 142. During 1610, while the *Parlement* was burning Mariana's book on political theory in Paris, the Spanish ambassador to the Imperial Court was burning his book on monetary theory in Prague. Chudoba, *Spain and the Empire*, p. 188.

[4] Printed in Lewy, *Constitutionalism*, p. 167; see also pp. 133–151.

[5] *Cal. St. P.* LXXV, 28. A.N. AD III 20, no. 67.

[6] A.N. AD III 20, no. 54 (Bellarmine's book). For the 1614 action see the text of the Council's action in M. Bouchitté, ed., *Negociations, lettres et pièces relatives à la conférence de Loudun* (Paris, 1862), pp. xxiii–xxiv. See also B.N. MS fr. 18010, fols. 6r, 8r–9r (Tresnel to Louis XIII and Marie de Médicis, January 7, 1615).

[7] Lewy, *Constitutionalism*, pp. 167–168. Henri Fouqueray S. J., *Histoire de la Compagnie de Jésus en France, 1582–1763* (Paris, 1922), III, 340–341. B.M. Stowe MS 175, fol. 130v (Edmondes to Winwood, December 12/22). Both Aquaviva's decrees and the renewal of the decrees of the Council of Constance by Pope Paul V left loopholes that were immediately apparent.

out that their *cahiers* contained similar provisions. In the *cahier* of Normandy the third article in the chapter on the church stated that the King was sovereign in his state and that no power on this earth had any control over the temporal authority of the King. The fifteenth article of the *cahier* of Champagne and articles in the *cahiers* of the *bailliages* of Troyes and Vitry declared that the King's power was absolute and that the rights of the Gallican church should be upheld. An article in the *cahier* of Lyonnais defended the King against any attack on his life as did one of Orléanais's articles. Of the twelve *gouvernements* only Guyenne and Orléanais expressed any objection to the article. Guyenne, however, withdrew its reservation about the wording. Orléanais's only objection was to the designation 'fundamental law'.[8]

The deputies of the Third Estate were tired of the attempts of the clergy to control the direction of the Estates General. Many of the deputies must have known that their article would evoke interest outside the Estates General. But most of them were not aware of the strength of the forces that their action was unleashing. The *Parlement* of Paris was vitally interested in Gallicanism. The members of the *Parlement* felt that it was their private concern since ultramontanism posed a threat to their growing control over ecclesiastical courts. They could be counted on to become involved. Further strong support existed within the University of Paris.[9]

The sixteen reforming bishops who dominated the First Estate were loyal to the King; such loyalty was part of their heritage and essential to their

[8] Rapine, pp. 207–211. B.N. MS fr. 18256, pp. 103–108. Guy Goualt, who sent a copy of the *cahier* of Paris and the Ile de France to his brother, indicated that from the start a number of the deputies of the Third Estate were worried about what they were getting involved in. A.D. Morbihan 87 G 4 (letter of December 17). The *cahier* of the city of Lyon unlike the governmental *cahier* does not have an article similar to the First Article of the Third, A. Mun. Lyon AA 146, fols. 1r–22v. The *cahier* of the nobles of the city, provostship, and viscounty of Paris includes an article saying that the King has no superior in his kingdom and is subject to no temporal power, A.N. H, no. 747². The provincial estates of Provence of June, 1615, supported the First Article of the Third, B.N. MS fr. 4131, fols. 106r–109r; the governmental *cahiers* for the Estates General of the nobles and the Third Estate of Provence give limited support to the First Article. Only the preliminary notes remain for the governmental *cahier* of Champagne and they do not include anything like the First Article; Durand, ed., *Cahiers Troyes*, pp. 247–300. The other *cahiers* mentioned no longer exist. Malingre prints articles similar to the First Article from the *cahiers* of the clergy and nobles of the *bailliage* of Dourdan, *Histoire du règne de Louis XIII* (Paris, 1646), pp. 457–459, but no trace of them has been found. Malingre also claimed that at first the general *cahier* of the nobles had an article similar to the first of the Third, *ibid.*, p. 460.

[9] The original *cahier* of the University of Paris prepared for the Estates General of 1614 had an article similar to the First of the Third, but this article was repudiated by a full meeting of the faculties and withdrawn. The *cahier* of the university that Rapine published was the original one not the final one. See Charles Jourdain, *Histoire de la Université de Paris au XVIIᵉ siècle* (Paris, 1862), pp. 79–81, *pièces justicatives*, nos. 40–43.

careers. But the bishops could not allow laymen to involve themselves in what they considered a theological matter. Further, these men were ultramontanes. Their devotion to reform carried with it a devotion to the Pope. In the world of the Counter Reformation the triumph of Catholicism meant the exaltation of the power of the Pope. Only an all powerful Pope could crush the abuses of regional Catholicism which had opened the way for the Protestant Reformation; only an all powerful Pope could lead the force of missionaries to a re-conversion of Europe. The bishops' reaction to the First Article of the Third Estate was strengthened by the fact that the Jesuits, the leaders of the mis-sionary effort, were singled out for condemnation by the Third Estate. Further, these bishops were worried because some of the members of their own estate were partial to political Gallicanism because of their devotion to ecclesiastical Gallicanism which was the sole support of what they described as their privileges – practices such as multiple benefice-holding, which had been condemned by the Council of Trent. Such feeling was particularly strong among members of cathedral chapters. The bishops found themselves faced with the problem of finding a way to oppose the Third Estate's article without antagonizing members of their own estate or the nobles or appearing disloyal to the King.

The ambassadors in Paris knew that something quite important was begin-ning within the halls of the Augustins. Thomas Edmondes and Cardinal Ubaldini were the two most interested in the events. The papal nuncio saw a threat to the power of the Pope and Edmondes knew that James I would find the ideas of the Third Estate congenial and that the English were being blamed for inspiring the article.[10]

At various times Cardinal Ubaldini placed the blame for the First Article on the *Parlement* of Paris, the Rector of the University of Paris who formulated the original *cahier* of the University in 1614, Edmond Richer former syndic of the University of Paris and author in 1611 of an anti-Jesuit, pro-Gallican

---

[10] Edmondes, with his excellent contacts, was the first to report home on the subject shortly after the *gouvernement* of Ile de France began to draw up its *cahiers*, B.M. Stowe MS 175 fols. 101r–104r (Edmondes to Winwood November 8/18 1614) while Ubaldini first men-tioned it on December 18, A.S.V., Nunz. fr. 56, fols. 140v–141v. (Also in B.N. MS ital. 1200, fols. 33r–33v.) A sign of Ubaldini's involvement once the controversy got going is the fact that from December 30 to January 16 he sent no report to Rome, a most unusual lapse of time for him. His desk must have been piled high with unfinished business by the time the crisis was over because Rome continued to send him all sorts of routine correspondence. A.S.V., Nunz. fr. 296, fols. 6r–16v. Edmondes's wife had just died; he had to continue negotiations to free an English ship seized at Dieppe and keep open the marriage negotiations. But he knew what James I's major interests were and through his reports presented the best summary of events from outside the Estates that exists. The English were continually blamed for the trouble. Paul V spoke of 'flamma ex miserabili anglicano incendio', A.S.V., Arm. LXV, 10, fols. 94v–96r (Paul V to the First Estate, February 28, 1615).

book *Libellus de theologica et politica potestate*, Condé, the Huguenots and James I.[11] There seems to be no doubt, however, that the article used by the Third Estate first saw light in the *cahier* drawn up by an assembly at the Hôtel de Ville of Paris during the summer of 1614 and that there was no significant outside influence.[12] The first discussion noted in the records of the Hôtel de Ville was on August 18, 1614.[13] Supposedly the matter came up because of a request found in the box placed in front of the Hôtel de Ville for Parisians to deposit their ideas for the *cahier* of the city. Two requests from that box support what became the First Article. But one of them, the fullest expression, was not written until after September 22. The other gives only vague support.[14] This would seem to indicate that the inspiration for the article came from the commission that was given power to draw up the articles for the *cahier*. In its final form the article was approved by the full assembly which included representatives of the bishop of Paris and seven religious orders.

The records do not allow any definite statement concerning the source of the article within the commission. It is possible that it came from the members of the *Parlement* of Paris who were on the commission and that this was part of their long-term fight in favor of Gallicanism and in particular against the Jesuits.[15] It is significant that the man originally placed in charge of precisely formulating the article was Antoine Arnauld and that he was followed by a councilor in the *Parlement* and finally by an *avocat* in the *Cour des Aides*. But to deduce from this that the *Parlement* was responsible for the whole affair is

[11] B.N. MS ital. 1200, fols. 33v–34r. A.S.V., Nunz. fr. 56, fols. 142v–143r. A.S.V., Fond. Borgh., II, 244, fol. 2r. The First Estate was keeping an eye on developments at the University of Paris through Charles de la Saussaye, a member of the theology faculty. B.N. MS fr. 4082, fol. 32r. Pierre Blet mistakenly refers to Saussaye as the Dean of Auch, *Clergé* I, 49.

[12] Concerning this see the testimony of J. A. de Thou in Mastellone, *Reggenza*, pp. 203–204 and B.N. MS Dupuy 950, fols. 311r–315r. The Third Estate accepted the article *in toto* from the *cahier* of the *gouvernement* of Paris and the Ile de France. That *gouvernement* in turn accepted the article *in toto* from the *cahier* of the City of Paris. See Georges Picot and Paul Guérin, eds., *Documents relatifs aux Etats généraux de 1614* (n.p., n.d.), p. 51. This version of the first article agrees with the copy in A.D. Morbihan cited in footnote 1, with the exception of two further minor deletions.

[13] *Reg. délib. Paris*, XVI, 61.

[14] A.N. K 675, nos. 138, 142. The only source for the claim that the article was inspired by a suggestion in the box is the large pamphlet *Les résolutions et arrestéz de la chambre du Tiers Estat touchant le premier article de leur cahier* ... (Paris, 1615). The preface of the pamphlet implies that it was an official reply of the Third Estate to an earlier pamphlet (probably *Manifeste de ce qui se passé dernièrement aux Estats généraux entre le clergé et le tiers Estat* (n.p., 1615)). *Les résolutions* was most probably written by deputies of the Third Estate. But the fact remains that the records of the Hôtel de Ville do not support the claim that the inspiration for the article came first from the box at the Hôtel de Ville.

[15] Pierre Blet makes the connection much more definitely in 'L'Article du Tiers aux Etats généraux de 1614', *Revue d'histoire moderne et contemporaine*, II (1955), 81–106.

unwarranted. The *Parlement* of Paris was quite capable of fighting its own battles and in any event was disinclined to use the Estates General. The *Parlement* had even refused to allow its members to be chosen as deputies to the Estates General. If glory was to be gained the Judges would gain it for themselves. As for the deputies of the Third Estate they held themselves apart from the *Parlement* and resisted its attempts to impose its will on their *cahiers*.

On the afternoon of Monday December 15 the First Estate began to hear rumors about the action taken by the Third Estate that morning regarding the first article of its general *cahier*. On the grounds that it was not within the province of the Estates General to discuss the power of the Pope, the clergy decided to ask Marie de Médicis to suppress the article. But the clergy learned the specific details only gradually, and the full effects of what came to be known as the 'First Article of the Third' were not felt for another week.[16]

During that week the deputies continued their regular business. The Third Estate went on with the preparation of its general *cahier*. On the afternoon of December 15 Claude le Doux, president of the *gouvernement* of Normandy and author of one of the accounts of the Estates General, proposed a number of articles for the introduction of the general *cahier*. Two of them met opposition. The first expressed approval of the Spanish marriages. The second asked the King to answer the *cahiers* without modification by the *Parlement* and before the deputies left Paris. After a spirited debate a compromise proposed by the deputies from Orléanais was accepted. In the *cahier* the Queen was to be thanked in general terms for her efforts toward peace, and the King was to be asked in person to carry out the plans for the Spanish marriages. The second article was accepted, although the reference to the *Parlement* was deleted for fear of offending that body which, in spite of its hostility, many of the deputies thought could be helpful.[17]

The bargaining within the Estates General continued, with each order trying to secure support from the other orders for its particular requests in return for its promise of support. The Third Estate was still trying to gain a reduction of the *taille*. The clergy wanted reform of the royal council and new regulations for nominations to benefices. The nobles were still petitioning the King for the establishment of a chamber of finances.[18]

The deputies of all three estates continued to ask for a more detailed financial report to be given openly to the Estates General and negotiated to obtain their particular reforms in spite of their growing preoccupation with the debate over the First Article of the Third. As yet the other estates had not seen

[16] PV-1, pp. 239–240.
[17] PV-3, pp. 92–102. B.N. MS fr. 10876, fols. 45r–48r. B.N. MS fr. n.a. 1395, fols. 46v–57r.
[18] PV-1, pp. 233–261. PV-2, pp. 132–156. PV-3, pp. 92–102.

a copy of the article with which the Third Estate had agreed to begin its general *cahier*, but information about its wording and its implications had been spreading among the deputies. Although the deliberations of each order were supposedly private, information about the activities of each circulated rapidly by word of mouth, helped along by the multiple family relationships among the three estates. Tension was growing in the Estates General.[19]

On December 20 the Third Estate was officially informed for the first time of the displeasure of the clergy with their article by Archbishop Paul Hurault de l'Hôpital. The burden of the speech given by the Archbishop of Aix was that the Third Estate should confer with the First Estate before putting any article concerning religion in its *cahier*. In return, the clergy would confer with the Third Estate about any article in their *cahier* concerning justice. Miron replied that the Archbishop was speaking in generalities. If a specific problem arose he promised that the Third Estate would give the clergy a specific answer. That afternoon the deputies of the Third Estate, fully aware of the reason for the clergy's concern, decided that the first article of their *cahier* concerned the sovereignty of the King, not religion, and that the clergy should be so informed. As for the matter of communication in general, the Third Estate decided that it was considering only the external discipline of the Church and not its doctrine, and since conferences would take up too much time they would not be worth-while. The Third Estate would trust the clergy to formulate good articles on justice.[20]

This answer was returned to the First Estate by Pierre Marmiesse, capitoul of Toulouse, but his eloquence failed to satisfy the clergy. On the 23rd the Bishop of Montpellier, Pierre de Fenouillet, spoke to the Third Estate and was able to convince the deputies that a copy of the article should be sent to the clergy, who as yet knew the contents only by hearsay. Champagne and Picardy objected to sending a copy of the article, but Provence and Orléanais wanted the Third Estate to discuss all matters touching on religion with the clergy. The other *gouvernements* agreed to send the article without making any promises. Pierre Marmiesse took a copy of the article to the clergy. That a significant number of the deputies had no intention of giving up their article is evident in Rapine's worry that Marmiesse's flowery language might give the clergy the impression that the Third Estate would abide by the First Estate's decision about it.[21]

---

[19] PV-1, pp. 255–306. PV-2, pp. 156–168. PV-3, pp. 103–111. *Mercure françois*, III, part 2, 101–104.

[20] PV-3, pp. 102–104. B.N. MS fr. 18256, pp. 143–148. On December 22 the nobles agreed to an exchange of articles with the clergy on matters that affected their respective orders. PV-2, pp. 156–157.

[21] PV-1, pp. 276–286. PV-3, pp. 105–107. Rapine, pp. 260–271. Marmiesse, *Remonstrances*, pp. 30–37.

The Christmas recess interfered at this point. Edmondes and Ubaldini knew what was at stake in the developing debate, but the other diplomats in Paris were silent on the subject. Writing to the French representative in Germany on December 23, Pierre Brûlart's only reference to the Estates General was a laconic comment that the meeting was lasting too long. Malherbe wrote to a friend on December 26 that the belief was growing that nothing of importance would happen in the Estates General. The calm was misleading; the pressure was so great that the six-day Christmas vacation did not alleviate it.[22]

On December 29 a debate in the Third Estate found half of the *gouvernements* willing to take the first article out of their *cahier*. A number of deputies were worried about opposing the clergy in what might after all be a theological matter. But Ile de France continued to lead the battle to ignore any outside influence. At the end of the session it was decided to send a copy of the article to the Second Estate. The next morning the nobles took the article to the clergy, who then opened their official discussion of the article and continued it throughout the afternoon. The clergy concluded that the article approximated to a theory of the Jesuit Martin Becanus that had been condemned as heretical in 1613. Further, the protection of the King had already been provided for in the fifteenth century by the decrees of the Council of Constance against regicide. Finally, the King's power was too dangerous a subject to be discussed in the Estates General. Cardinal Du Perron was appointed to speak to the Third Estate. He at first declined because he said he was unworthy, but finally accepted. On December 31, the Second Estate announced that it would follow the clergy's lead in regard to the article if some provision for the King's safety were made in the *cahiers*. The clergy told them of a plan to republish either the decree of the Council of Constance or similar measures to protect the King, referring to the Pope's promise given during the controversy over Suarez's book. Since the Third Estate would not meet again until January 2, that day was chosen for Du Perron's speech.[23]

Ironically, the greatest debate of the Estates General broke out just at the time when a number of the members of the Third Estate were willing to withdraw. But once the conflict was brought out into the open and the lines of battle were drawn, not only the Third Estate but England and Rome as well became involved in a debate over the relative powers of Pope and King.

The Third Estate was working on its general *cahier* on January 2 when Cardinal Du Perron entered its chamber followed by a large number of deputies from the First and Second Estates, some of whom were official

---

[22] B.N. MS fr. 4121, fol. 112r (Brûlart's letter). Malherbe, *Lettres*, p. 426.
[23] PV-1, pp. 279–306. PV-2, pp. 166–168. PV-3, pp. 107–111. Rapine, pp. 266–271.

delegates, most of whom were curious spectators. The Cardinal was carried in on a chair because of illness, but in spite of his condition he spoke for more than two and a half hours. Du Perron began quite carefully, using references to ancient history and the customs of the Gauls as a vehicle for praising the deputies of the Third Estate as the guardians of justice. Underneath the careful rhetoric, however, was the refrain that matters of religion belonged to the clergy who were as zealous for the safety of the King as his audience. As he continued he insisted that three essential points of disagreement existed between the clergy and the deputies of the Third Estate in regard to the first article of their *cahier*. First, the clergy were not sure of the consequences of the article if the King should become a heretic and try to force his subjects to follow him in that heresy. Second, laymen did not have the power to make decisions concerning faith and to impose their decisions on the clergy. Third, the article's insistence on absolutism separated from even indirect control by the Church could be construed as schismatic since the Pope and the rest of Christendom held to another opinion. Regicide was a sin; the temporal sovereignty of French kings was only an historical fact. The Cardinal concluded that although the intent of the article, preservation of the lives of kings, was indeed laudable, there were too many questionable phrases included and thus it had to be suppressed.[24]

President Miron immediately answered that the Third Estate would be willing to change a few words in the article, but that it would not change the substance. Cardinal Du Perron retorted that he had the assurance of many notable persons in the chamber of the Third Estate that they did not want to advance a schism. He then lectured the deputies of the Third Estate for going beyond their field of competence. As soon as the Cardinal had left the chamber with his followers it was evident that he had won support in the Third Estate, even though he had not definitely said that the Third Estate would be guilty of schism. Actually he had hinted that the whole question of the power of the Pope had not really been settled. A number of the deputies were also incensed by Miron's speaking for the entire Third Estate without first conducting a debate. However, after a long discussion the Third Estate voted to support Miron's answer to the clergy. The Third Estate then recessed until January 5.[25]

This was not all that happened on January 2. The *Parlement* of Paris, which

[24] B.N. MS fr. 10879, fols. 17r–128r. Jacques Davy, Cardinal Du Perron, *Harangue faicte de la parte de la chambre ecclésiastique en celle du tiers Estat, sur l'article du serment par Monseigneur le Cardinal du Perron* (Paris, 1615), pp. 1–114. The first edition was published privately for friends and other interested people. The second edition was printed in June, 1615.

[25] PV-3, pp. 111–118. Miron's reply seems at first to be too well supplied with appropriate quotations to be extemporaneous. But he did have almost three hours to prepare it. See Rapine, pp. 323–336.

had been meeting since Christmas on the question of the suspension of the *paulette*, chose that date to give its public support to the provisions of the First Article of the Third and its public retort to the suspension of its *arrêt* against Suarez's book. Its decree of that day also renewed *arrêts* of 1561, 1594, 1595, 1610, and 1614, which attacked Jesuits and their books and lent support to ideas contained in the First Article of the Third. This decree was speedily published by Morel and Mettayer, a leading printing firm which usually handled the official publications of the King.[26]

On January 5 Gaspard Dinet, bishop of Mâcon, came to the Third Estate with the clergy's proposal that section fifteen of the decrees of the Council of Constance be officially renewed to ensure the protection of the King. The Third Estate was swayed by what he said but in the end decided to take no decision. The strongest argument against the clergy's plan was that the Council of Constance had dealt with the religious aspects of the question; what was needed now was a civil law. The Third Estate also decided against accepting the invitation to join the clergy and nobles in their complaint to the King about the *Parlement*'s decree of January 2 on the grounds that the matter did not concern the Estates General. When the Third's delegation arrived to inform the clergy of their decisions they found that the First and Second Estates, expecting a negative reply, had already made plans to send their delegation to the Louvre.[27]

The clergy had already complained to the King on the afternoon of January 3. On January 4 the King received members of the *Parlement* and the *Chambre des Comptes* who had come to protest against the suspension of the *paulette* and in the course of the meeting ordered them not to allow the *arrêt* of January 2 to be signed or put into effect. On January 5 Bishop Miron of Angers, President Miron's uncle, spoke to Council for the clergy and nobles against the *arrêt* of the *Parlement*. Finally, on January 6 a full scale meeting of the Council was held to discuss the whole matter. Bishop Miron had asked that silence be imposed on the *Parlement* in matters of faith and doctrine; that the *Parlement* not be given jurisdiction over affairs concerning the deputies of the Estates General; that no *Parlement* in France involve itself in affairs of state without

[26] A.N. XiA 1867, fols. 114v–115v. A.N. F 94, p. 401. A.N. AD iii 20, no. 70. *Arrest de la Cour de Parlement du 2 janvier.* B.N. Clairambault 364, fols. 465r–467v. B.N. Cinq Cents 17, fol. 72r. Molé, *Mémoires*, pp. 18–20. Perrens, *L'église et l'état*, ii, 291, footnote 1.

[27] PV-1, pp. 309–320. PV-3, pp. 119–124. B.N. MS fr. n.a. 7853, fol. 28r. *Article de l'église apporté au Tiers Estat par Monseigneur l'évesque de Mascon le matin 5 jour de janvier 1615* (n.p., n.d.). On January 5 the First Estate prepared a formal statement concerning the renewal of the decree of the Council of Constance. The wording was bound to upset the Third Estate with its references to the clergy's rights and duties in protecting the King. Nevertheless, the statement clearly condemned anyone who 'maintained that it was permissible to threaten the sacred persons of kings even those who it was claimed were tyrants. . . .' PV-1, p. 313.

the express command of the king; that the *avocat général* of the *Parlement* of Paris (who had been instrumental in arranging for the *arrêt*) not be allowed to involve himself in any way in ecclesiastical matters. The result of the Council meeting was that the decree of the *Parlement* of Paris was rescinded and the *Parlement* was forbidden to discuss the matter again.[28]

The Prince of Condé had not been idle while all of this was going on. At the January 6 meeting of Council he praised the *Parlement* and the Third Estate while recommending that the King stop the discussion between the clergy and the Third and permit each estate to include in its *cahiers* whatever articles it wished. He also recommended that the *Parlement*'s *arrêt* be revoked. On January 8 Bouillon and Condé attacked the idea that the Huguenots had been involved in the formulation of the First Article and exchanged rough words with Cardinals Du Perron and de Sourdis.[29] The attack of Condé on the leaders of the clergy may have resulted from their earlier efforts to prevent him from gaining a new benefice. The praise for the *Parlement*, which he was careful to emphasize in his remarks to Council, marked the beginning of new efforts to cultivate that body.[30]

The whole affair of the article and the decrees provoked a storm of pamphlets. The Third Estate published a pamphlet defending its action. The First Estate answered in a work entitled *Copie d'une lettre d'un prélat*. Jean Savaron wrote two treatises on behalf of the Third Estate; these were criticized in yet another pamphlet. This in turn was excoriated in a work of 278 pages by

[28] A.S.F. Arch. Med., Carte Strozz. I, 55, fols. 16v–17r (Luca della Asini to Dowager Grand Duchess Christine, January 14, 1615). B.N. MS fr. 18010, fols. 16r–16v (Tresnel to Louis XIII, January 24). A.S.V., Arm. XLV, 10, fols. 93r–93v (Paul V to Louis XIII, February 28). Isambert, *Recueil*, XVI, 60–61. PV-1, p. 317, On January 2 Cardinal de Sourdis had called a special meeting of the First Estate for the following day to prepare the clergy's strategy. B.N. MS fr. 4082, fol. 38v.

[29] There is some confusion in the dates for both Miron's and Condé's remarks. Bishop Miron's are cited as having been made on either January 5 or 6, Condé's on the 4th, 6th or 8th. The sequence given above straightens out the confusion. See Héroard, *Journal*, I, 172; B.M. Stowe MS 175, fols. 146v–151r (Edmondes to Winwood, December 30/January 9). Henri II de Bourbon, Prince de Condé, *Advis donné au roy en son conseil par Monsieur le Prince* (n.p., n.d.), pp. 3–9. Fontenay-Mareuil, *Mémoires*, p. 81, Estrées, *Mén .res*, p. 284. Condé as usual was caught off guard when the debate broke out. He quickly returned to Paris from his Christmas holidays on the advice of unnamed friends (probably Bouillon) and got himself involved. B.M. Stowe MS 175, fol. 148v (Edmondes to Winwood December 30/January 9) and B.N. MS ital, 38, fol. 199r (Ubaldini's newsletter of January 17, 1615).

[30] To counteract any growth in Condé's popularity within the Third Estate the government on January 19 worked to get into the Third's *cahier* an article calling for the return of the fortifications granted to Condé by the Treaty of Sainte Ménéhould. B.N. MS fr. 18256, pp. 289–291; B.N. MS fr. 10876, fols. 73v–74r. The First Estate's efforts to organize a protest against Condé's acquisition of the abbey of Coulamp are recorded in B.N. MS fr. n.a. 1395, fol. 45r.

Savaron published in 1616. The large number of pamphlets defending the Third Estate's article attacked the clergy on several major points. The clergy favored the Jesuits, who were not to be trusted; the Third Estate's article protected the sovereignty of the King better than the measures proposed by the clergy; and France, through the clergy, was bowing to the court of Rome which was not the Catholic Church. The supporters of the clergy, in answer, pointed to the duty of the First Estate to protect the Church. The *Parlement* overstepped its bounds in trying to act as a legislature, they said. What the Third Estate wanted was the doctrine of heretics like Luther, Melancthon, and Calvin while the clergy were loyal Frenchmen who were deeply concerned with protecting the sovereignty of the kings.[31]

There was one heretic yet to be heard from – King James I of England. Cardinal Du Perron was an old enemy of his. In 1612 they had engaged in a debate as to whether or not Anglicans were Catholics. Du Perron had made some disparaging references to James in his speech to the Third Estate and again on January 6. Word of this reached the English King quickly and James answered in a pamphlet of his own. The pamphlet, first published in French and later in English, dwelt on his friendship with Henry IV and his interest in the welfare of France in such a way that it must have caused Henry to turn over in his grave at least once. Though King James admitted Du Perron's learning, he called him 'the man to whome France is least obliged'. He accused him of interfering with the freedom of the Second Estate. James seized on the weak point in Du Perron's speech: his admission, though guarded, that the matter of the Pope's power over a King was problematical. The development of these arguments in the French version was far more civil than in the highly insulting English edition. In the latter version James harped on the contradictions in Du Perron's speech, a speech that was 'like a bladder full of wind, without any

---

[31] *Procèz verbal de tout ce qui s'est passé en la chambre du Tiers Estat touchant le premier article de leur cahyer presenté au Roy* (n.p., 1615); *Copie d'une lettre d'un prélat député du clergé à l'assemblée des Estats sur ce qui s'est passé touchant l'article contentieux employé pour le premier au cayer du Tiers Estat* (n.p., 1615); Jean Savaron, *Traicté de la souveraineté du Roy et de son royaume à messieurs les députéz de la noblesse*... (Paris, 1615). Jean Savaron, *Second traicté de la souveraineté du Roy*... (Paris, 1615). Jean Savaron, *Les erreurs et impostures de l'Examen du traicté de M Jean Savaron De la Souveraineté du roy*... (Paris, 1616). Representative of the pamphlets published on the 'First Article of the Third' controversy are: Viole d'Athys, *Réponse à la harangue fait par l'illustrisimé Cardinal Du Perron* (n.p., n.d.). Guillaùme Ribbier, *Apologie de l'article premier du Tiers Estat* (n.p., 1615). *Les canons des conciles de Tolède, de Meaux, d'Oxfort et de Constance* ... *par lesquels la doctrine de déposer et user les roys est condamné* (n.p., 1615). *Discours remarquable advenus à Paris, pendant des Estats* (n.p., 1615). *Manifeste de ce qui se passé dernièrement aux Estats généraux entre le clergé et le Tiers Estat* (n.p., 1615). *Raisons pour l'opposition de messieurs du clergé et de la noblesse à l'article proposé par aucuns en la chambre du Tiers Estat* (n.p., 1615). *Les resolutions et arrestéz de la chambre du Tiers Estat touchant le premier article de leur cahier presenté au Roy* (Paris, 1615).

soliditie of substantiall matter'. James directed many of his remarks to the nobles who, he said, should be the King's protectors and taunted the French, saying that they did not have a very powerful King if '. . . Popes may tosse the French King from his throne like a tennis ball'.[32]

In the meantime the clergy were insisting that the First Article of the Third be revoked by the King. On January 7 they informed the Chancellor that they would not carry on their work in the Estates General until their demands were met. When the Chancellor refused to act, the clergy went to the King on January 8. They persuaded the nobles to join forces with them but only at the price of including their demands for more information on finances. Louis told them to go back to work on their *cahiers*. The clergy spent the next two days in discussing what steps to take next and in venting their anger against the Huguenots on the Council whom they conveniently blamed for the King's refusal. The clergy were worried about the public misinterpretation of the affair and decided that prayer was necessary. On Monday and Tuesday of the next week the clergy refused to hold their sessions. Cardinal Joyeuse, dean of the College of Cardinals, came to court from Conflans in spite of his great age and illness to use his influence with the Queen Mother. He impressed upon her the gravity of the situation, emphasizing the danger of schism. The task of finding a solution was entrusted to Sillery, Jeannin, and Villeroy on January 14. Finally on January 16 the King sent word to the clergy that the First Article of the Third had been evoked the preceding day. The *Parlement*

---

[32] Edmondes reported the insults in his letter of December 30/Jan. 9, B.M. Stowe MS 175, fols. 150r–151v. Jacques Davy, Cardinal Du Perron, *Lettre de Monseigueur le Cardinal Du Perron envoyée au sieur Casaubon en Angleterre* (Paris, 1612). James I, *Déclaration du serenissime Roy Jacques I Roy de la Grand'Bretagne, etc. déffenseur de la foy. Pour le droict des rois et independance de leurs couronnes. Contre la harangue de l'illustrissime Cardinal du Perron* . . . (n.p., 1615). James I, *A Remonstrance of the Most Gratious King James I King of Great Britain, France and Ireland for the Right of Kings and the Independance of the Crownes against an Oration of the Most Illustrious Card. of Perron* . . . (Cambridge, 1616). James I was helped by the Huguenot minister, Pierre du Moulin, with the French version. An example of the difference in the two editions is in the titles, where the etc. of the French version is replaced by James's full title in the English edition. Another is the difference in phrasing of the last quotation cited in the text. The French version says simply 'que le roy puisse être deposé par le Pape.' Spain knew of the dispute by February 11. A.N. K 1454, no. 10 (letter of King Philip III to Cardenas). In June Thomas Edmondes would present the official complaint of James I on this matter to Marie de Médicis. [Thomas Edmondes] *Remonstrances faictes par l'ambassadeur de la Grande Bretagne au roy et à la royne sa mère, en juin 1615* (n.p., 1615). See also B.M. Stowe MS 175, fols. 167v, 170v, 171r, 198r. Edmondes was suspected of dealing with the discontented in the Estates General and Paris, to the prejudice of France, throughout the Estates General. The suspicion was well founded. See also Georges Ascoli, *La Grande Bretagne devant l'opinion française au XVIIe siècle* (Paris, 1930), I, 23; II, 196. For the English background see Thomas H. Clancy, S. J., *Papist Pamphleteers* (Chicago, 1964), pp. 73–100, 238ff. Du Perron wrote a reply to James I's attack of 1615, but it was never published. Pierre Feret, *Le Cardinal Du Perron* (Paris, 1877), pp. 321–347.

had been forbidden to discuss the matter further, and the printer responsible for publishing its decree had been jailed. However, the King stood firm on one point – only a small number of deputies would be permitted to hear the report on finances.[33]

The Queen Mother felt compelled to accede to the clergy's demand if the Estates General were ever to finish its work. But steps had to be taken to pacify the Third Estate and the *Parlement*. On January 19 she thanked the Third Estate through President Miron for its affection and informed them that, although the article had been evoked, they could consider it as having been presented to the King, and the King would answer it. However, the Third Estate was far from satisfied. The twelve *gouvernements* split evenly on the vote to take immediate action and the discussion was postponed until the following day.[34]

On January 20 Miron was the center of a storm that rocked the Third Estate. Deputy after deputy accused him of bowing to the King rather than supporting the interests of the Third Estate. There was an attempt by Picardy to force a vote by *bailliage* which in Rapine's opinion would have supported an effort to retain the article in the *cahier*. Miron ruled the attempt out of order since a vote by *gouvernement* had already begun. The result of the *gouvernement* vote was that Picardy and Orléanais wanted a strong protest made to the King, the Ile de France and Burgundy wanted a moderate protest. Normandy, Dauphiné and Provence agreed to accept the King's decision with reservations. Brittany, Champagne and Guyenne had no reservations in accepting the King's order. Lyonnais and Languedoc could not cast a vote since the *bailliages* were split. At this point, despite strong protests, Miron left the chamber and went to the Louvre to inform Marie de Médicis that the article would not be in the *cahier*. A means of circumventing Miron's action was proposed by Guillaume Ribier of Blois. He suggested presenting the article in the *cahier* in a roundabout way.[35]

---

[33] PV-I, pp. 320–355. A.S.F., Carte Strozz. I, 55, fols. 23r–23v (Asini to Grand Duchess Christine, January 27, 1615). Ironically Henri de Mesmes, as lieutenant civil of Paris, had to arrest the printer Pierre Mettayer. *Manifeste de ce qui se passa dernièrement aux Estats généraux* ... (n.p., 1615).

[34] Guyenne, Brittany, Languedoc. Dauphiné, Provence and Lyonnais wanted to handle the problem immediately. B.N. MS fr. 18256, pp. 294–295.

[35] B.N. MS fr. 18256, pp. 297–300. Rapine, pp. 362–365. Rapine, pp. 366–369 lists those deputies who in protest against Miron's action signed a statement that the article should be included in the *cahier*. About ninety-eight deputies signed and Rapine claimed that there were others who wanted to sign but for one reason or another did not do so. The delegations that gave the strongest support were Ile de France (all but Miron), Picardy (all deputies), Burgundy and Orléanais. The least support came from Guyenne, Dauphiné, Provence (none), Brittany (none) and Normandy (none). On the basis of the recorded names the vote requested by Picardy or a vote to retain the First Article would have lost 4 to 7 (Lyon tied).

On January 21 the fight to overrule Miron's actions was led by Jean Savaron. The Ile de France, Lyonnais and Orléanais supported Ribier's idea as newly proposed by François Lanier, lieutenant general of Angers. Guyenne opposed this; Picardy still held out for using the original article. Burgundy offered an alternative proposal, a formula referring to the original article without specifying its nature. Finally, by a seven-to-three vote this proposal was accepted.[36]

The first article placed in their *cahier* by the dissatisfied deputies of the Third Estate read: 'The first article taken from the procès-verbal of the Chamber of the Third Estate, and signed by its Secretary and Registrar, has been presented to the King in advance of the present *cahier* on the fifteenth day of January, 1615, by *Monsieur* the President of the Third Estate assisted by one deputy of each *gouvernement*, by the commandment of His Majesty, who has promised to respond to it with the articles of this present *cahier*, and to do this he is profusely entreated'.[37]

The court had not reacted kindly to all this pressure. Secretary of State Brûlart had complained to the *sieur* of Sainte Catherine on January 9 that the Estates General was asking embarrassing questions, always the case when such an assembly was called. But Rome was pleased. Pope Paul V reconfirmed the decrees of the Council of Constance on January 2 though he left it up to the King to decide when the confirmation should be published.[38] On January 31 the Pope wrote to the clergy and nobility praising them for protecting the authority of his office. He sent a personal letter to Cardinal de Sourdis with the same message. Cardinal Ubaldini, who had kept the Pope informed throughout the controversy, wrote to Cardinal Borghese in Rome assuring him that the *cahiers* of the clergy and nobles would not contain any articles against the Jesuits and that the Council would not look favorably on the anti-Jesuit articles in the *cahier* of the Third Estate. He announced his final success on February 14 in another letter to Borghese: after much hard work on his part, he claimed,

---

[36] Champagne and Languedoc were not present, Guyenne opposed the whole idea, Provence and Dauphiné skirted the issue. PV-3, pp. 145–153. B.N. MS fr. 18256, pp. 297–304. B.N. MS fr. 10876, fols. 73v–74r. At least one deputy who favored the article was not as enthusiastic as Rapine. Etienne de Lalain was sick and just wanted the Estates General to end as soon as possible. Bibl. Ars. MS 4225, fols. 38r–38v, 39v.

[37] Lalourcé and Duval, eds. *Recueil des cahiers généraux des trois ordres aux Etats Généraux* (Paris, 1789), IV, 273. Edmondes reported on January 12/22 that many of the deputies of the Third Estate said that if they did not receive satisfaction concerning the matter, at the end of the Estates General they would go to the *Parlement* and ask it to register the article (B.M. Stowe, MS 175, fols. 197v–198v).

[38] B.N. MS fr. 4121, fol. 113r (letter to Sainte Catherine). B.N. MS fr. 18010, fols 71r–73r (Tresnel to Louis XIII, March 26).

articles favoring the Jesuits would be given an important place in the *cahiers* of the clergy and nobles.[39]

While the clergy had been fighting their battle during the first two weeks of January, the Second and Third Estates had continued their work. The Third Estate was informed on January 7 of the King's desire that the Estates General be finished by the end of the month. The other estates received the same message. Work on the *cahiers* progressed. The Third Estate set up a committee of twelve to formulate all but the most important articles for the general *cahier*. However, the *cahier* of Paris and Ile de France was still to be read in its entirety in the general assembly. The nobles continued to press for both the reduction of the number of royal offices and an increase in the number of these offices available to nobles. They received the support of the other orders in petitioning the King to suppress all offices that had been vacated by death since the beginning of January, 1615. The Third Estate again petitioned the King on January 12 for the reduction of the *taille* and again failed. The deputies were beginning by now to lose hope that any good would come to the people from the Estates General. But this did not stop all three estates from exerting themselves to put together a program of reform.[40]

Throughout the month of January pamphleteers continued to pour out their condemnations and plans for reform supposedly for the benefit of the deputies. Gabriel le Bien-Venu, the *soi-disant* drunken author of *Foucade aux Etats*, writing, he claimed, on New Year's day 1615, mocked many of his fellows — Bonhomme Jacques, Mathault, the Gentilhomme Champestre. They spoke of reform, he said, but all they were doing was pleading for special interests.

---

[39] B.N. Cinq Cents 17, fols. 77r–77v. Jacques Davy Cardinal Du Perron, *Les Ambassades et négotiations du Cardinal Du Perron* (Paris, 1623), pp. 1288–1291. Du Perron received support from other bishops, whom he later thanked. B.N. MS fr. 6379, fol. 247r. On the same day that Pope Paul V wrote to the clergy, he wrote to Cardinal Joyeuse asking him to work for the acceptance of the Council of Trent in France. B.N. Cinq Cents 43, fols. 205v–207v. Some of Ubaldini's letters are in Jean-Marie Prat S.J., *Recherches historiques et critiques sur la Compagnie de Jésus en France au temps du P. Coton* (Lyon, 1876), III, 632–633, 640–641, V, 326–327, 340–342. See also A.S.V., Nunz, fr. 56, fols. 152v–157r, 163v–164v (Ubaldini to Borghese January 17 and 27). The letters to the clergy and the nobles were later published as pamphlets. Paul V, *Lettre de nostre S. père le Pape, escrite à messieurs de la noblesse députéz aux Estats généraux de ce royaume* (n.p., n.d.). *Lettre de nostre S. père le Pape escrite à messieurs du clergé députéz au Estats de ce royaume avec la réponce faicte par L.E.D.* (n.p., 1615). The response was by Du Perron. Ubaldini singled out twelve bishops for special praise: Joyeuse, Sourdis, Du Perron, Rochefoucault, Bonzy and Miron got the highest ratings, with Marquemont, Gondi, Berthier, Fenouillet, Richelieu and Aubespine placed in second rank. A.S.V. Nunz. fr. 56, fols. 157r–158v. Du Perron particularly thanked Bishop Miron for his support. Du Perron, *Ambassades*, p. 711 (letter of April 25, 1615). Letters of Paul V to Joyeuse, Sourdis, Du Perron, Rochefoucault and Bonzy are in A.S.V., Arm. XLV, 10, fols. 96r–99r.

[40] PV-2, pp. 174–200. PV-3, pp. 125–142. B.N. MS fr. n.a. 1395, fols. 58v–60r.

Everything and everyone from tax collectors to courtiers, from the bourgeois to the bishops, needed reform. As for the deputies of the Estates General, they were ruled, said Gabriel, by self interest just like the pamphleteers. As serious as ever and out of touch with events, Sully, on January 7, published a pamphlet that mourned the death of Henry IV and the Grand Design but which looked forward to the accomplishment of Henry IV's plans by his son.[41]

After displaying some interest in the First Article of the Third Estate, Parisian society paid little further attention to the Estates General. In his memoirs Bassompierre would describe the first two months of 1615 in two sentences. 'The year 1615 began with the argument over the Article of the Third Estate which caused a bit of a murmur within the Estates; finally it was settled. The fair of St Germain followed, then Mardi Gras, during which M. le Prince put on an excellent ballet; the next day the Estates were ended'.[42]

---

[41] *Foucade aux Estats* (n.p., 1615). *Paralleles de César et de Henri le Grand* (Paris, 1615). The author of *Foucade* remembered Henry IV as a great lover and predicted that Louis XIII would be as great as his father in that domain.

[42] *Journal de ma vie*, II, 1.

9

THE CLOSING OF THE ESTATES GENERAL: JANUARY 17 TO MARCH 24

As Lent neared the courtiers continued to seek diversion in ballets and other amusements. Marie de Médicis could not afford that luxury. She was caught in a three-way squeeze between the clergy and nobles, the Third Estate, and the *Parlement*. A compromise had been worked out that pleased the First and Second Estates. The Third Estate was still restive and therefore a concession concerning the revocation of extraordinary commissions would have to be made to it. The *Parlement* was still sulking; Condé was back in town and looking for trouble; Sillery and Concini were intriguing against Villeroy at court and in Spain. There was only one thing to do – minimize the opportunities for intrigue by ending the Estates General as quickly as possible.[1] The deputies aware that the end was near went doggedly on hammering out their program of reform, though old animosities and basic differences in attitude, not to mention the growing hostility of the government, still interfered with progress.

Between January 17 and 21 the three orders reached an understanding with Jeannin about the detailed report on finances. The court, hoping to end the meetings of the Estates General as soon as possible, announced unexpectedly that it would permit one deputy from each *gouvernement* in each estate to hear a detailed report on the finances of the Regency. That same week the First Estate finished drawing up a list of the most important articles to be included in its *cahier* and set out to persuade the other orders to place similar articles at the head of their *cahiers*. As a result of the ensuing negotiations and the difficulties raised by the other estates the clergy decided to ask for a conference with the King to draw up a formula precisely defining and limiting the liberties of the Gallican Church.[2]

---

[1] The best source for tracing these developments is the set of letters sent to Dowager Grand Duchess Christine of Tuscany in A.S.F., Carte Strozz., I, 55, fols. 15r–46v (January 14–February 24, 1615). See also A.S.V., Fond. Borgh. II, 244, fols. 7r–7v (Ubaldini to Cardinal Borghese January 27) and B.N. MS ital. 1767, pp. 245–247, 255–259, 271–273 (letters of Venetian ambassador, December 23, January 6, February 3). The growing power of Concini is reflected in the pamphlets opposing him which began to appear in early 1615. See for example *A messieurs des Estats* (n.p., n.d.) which describes him as 'ce monstre d'avarice et d'orgueil', p. 3.

[2] PV-1, pp. 356–373. PV-2, pp. 200–205. PV-3, pp. 142–153.

On Wednesday January 21 the University of Paris sent its representatives to each of the estates trying to obtain a hearing as it had done on numerous previous occasions during the meetings of the Estates General. This time the rector and eight members of the arts faculty appeared, stating that since the university was not allowed to have a seat in the Estates General, they wished to present its *cahier*. President Miron referred them, as clerics, to the First Estate. But the deputies of the Third Estate liked their article on the power of the King and several of their articles on universities so their *cahier* was given to Savaron, who was compiling the chapter on universities, for study. The nobles received the *cahier* with the vague promise that they would try to help the university, while the clergy merely promised to study it and let the university know their decision. But as soon as the rector and his committee had left their chamber, the clergy decided that since the whole university had not drawn up the *cahier* it was of little value. The Bishop of Paris, nevertheless, was appointed to study it.[3]

On January 22 the clergy announced to the nobles that they had decided to propose a plan permanently to suppress the *paulette* and venality of office and to give more offices to gentlemen. The nobles considered this plan but decided, in spite of the King's request that the *cahiers* be ready by February 3, to seek the support of the other orders for their own plan to suppress venality and the *paulette*. This plan had been presented to the nobles by Jean de Beaufort and was discussed by the nobles as early as December 22. The Third Estate at first refused to support this plan which they condemned as 'rotten at the core' because of Beaufort's prejudice against their estate. The nobles and clergy, however, went on debating the merits of the plan.[4]

The First and Second Estates finally agreed on January 29 to present Beaufort's plan to the King with some additions proposed by Samson de Saint Germain, *sieur* of Juvigny. Beaufort's plan, which had been championed by the Vidame of Chartres, called for the reduction of the number of officials of the *Parlement*, the abolition of the office of lieutenant general of presidial seats, the abolition of the *Cour des Aides* and the *Chambre des Comptes* of Rouen

---

[3] PV-1, pp. 366–367. PV-2, pp. 202–205. PV-3, pp. 151–152. The clergy were also putting pressure on the King to issue a new edict against dueling. The Bishop of Montpellier spoke to the King about this on January 26 after the nobles refused to involve themselves.

[4] PV-1, pp. 373–381. PV-2, pp. 205–208. PV-3, 153–156, 158–162. All three estates, but especially the nobles, had been approached by people with particular requests. Usually the requests were investigated. See Rapine, pp. 343–344, 358; B.N. MS Dupuy 209, fols. 183r–185v (speech of representative of Duke of Lorraine); B.N. MS Dupuy 91, fols. 142r–144v (request of the *Sieur* of Vertau). More general advice in the form of pamphlets continued to be addressed to the deputies. The best of the pamphlets of early 1615 which appeared in slightly different forms with separate titles was addressed to the King: *Le conseiller fidèle à son Roy* (n.p., n.d.) and *Libre et salutaire discours des affaires de France* (Paris, 1615). The latter was dated February 28, 1615.

and Blois, plus the reduction in number of other offices. The former office holders were to be reimbursed and nobles were to be given a substantial number of the remaining offices. Juvigny wanted the King to tighten up the collection of domain revenue and feudal dues. On the same day the Estates General heard from the deputies who had listened to Jeannin's financial report. This report had been detailed enough to make clear that the expenses of the Regency had risen greatly over those of Henry IV, especially in 1614. But the deputies were not permitted to examine the accounts closely themselves.[5]

During this period the meetings of the Third Estate were anything but peaceful. The deputies demurred at showing the First Estate the chapter of their *cahier* on the clergy, using the excuse that not enough time remained to carry on any more discussions. Violent arguments were provoked by the Second Estate's new plans for abolishing venality and offices. Tempers were also flaring over the Council's failure to enforce its *arrêt* of December 16 revoking a number of extraordinary commissions. On January 30 representatives of the Third Estate sought an audience with the King to protest against this failure but were unsuccessful because the King was out hunting. On January 31 they were asked to delay the audience until after the Feast of the Purification since the King was preparing to lay his hands on the sick. Marie de Médicis also was not available; she was preparing for the feast because she had a special devotion to the Blessed Virgin. The Third Estate chafed under the obvious evasion but had no choice except to wait. Finally on February 3 the Council did order the enforcement of the earlier decision. In general the revocations, including that of the commission established in 1606 for reformation of hospitals headed by Cardinal Du Perron, were to be effective until the *cahiers* were answered.[6]

---

[5] PV-1, pp. 381–408. PV-2, pp. 186–189, 208–218. PV-3, pp. 156–163. B.N. MS fr. 23195, fols. 201r–216r (original of Juvigny's plan). See also Juvigny, *Quatre Propositions* ... (Paris, 1618), pp. 3–6 in which he outlined his efforts to get his plans accepted between 1612 and 1617. For Beaufort see Mousnier, *Venalité*, pp. 583–585. Jeannin's second report delivered to the select committee was an adaptation of one of Sully's vague reports. The figures used do not apply to any actual year though analysis shows that the figures roughly match those for 1611–1612. Rapine, pp. 525–550 gives one version; a second is critically studied in Roger Doucet, 'Les finances de la France en 1614 d'après le Traicté du revenue et dépense des finances', *Revue d'histoire économique et sociale*, XVIII (1930), 133–163. The criticisms of the inaccuracies in the report by Doucet, Forbonnais and Clamageran miss the essential point. Jeannin, in his first report, gave an idea of the income and expenditure of the Regency government; in his second he gave the Estates General an impression of the workings of the financial system. The Regency government was not hiding its policy which was made clear by Jeannin. Rather the government did not consider it the business of the Estates General to meddle with the actual business of managing France. The only reason for the second report was to quieten the deputies so they would finish their *cahiers* and go home.

[6] Louis XIII, *Articles presentées au Roy par les députés de la chambre du Tiers Estat avec les responses de sa majesté* (Paris, 1615), pp. 1–15. See Chapter 10 below.

As work on the *cahiers* progressed and the pressure on the deputies increased, all three orders grew more fearful that the Estates General would be dismissed before the *cahiers* were answered. This they wanted to prevent at any cost since it would mean that their recommendations would be in danger of being ignored. At one point on January 20 a number of the deputies in the Third Estate wanted to suspend all further meetings in protest against such a contingency. Proposals and counterproposals followed in all three orders. Finally, on February 5, the Estates General received assurance from the court that some of their members would be permitted to sit on the commission that would answer the *cahiers*. The promise was not kept.[7]

The Queen Mother was greatly angered by these debates over the dismissal of the Estates General and by the deputies' agitation to gain a place on the committees that would answer the *cahiers*. She warned Cardinal de Sourdis that she wanted no innovations. If the deputies would only finish their *cahiers*, they would receive contentment before they were sent home. A sign of the growing tension between the court and the Estates General was the speech made on January 30 by Charles Miron, Bishop of Angers and uncle of the President of the Third Estate. This usually loyal member of both the Estates General and the royal council proclaimed that a clear protest must be made about the course of events, and since no one had paid any attention to what he had said up to this time, he was going to speak again. The two major aims of the Estates General must be reform of the royal council and regulation of the finances of the kingdom; these were the keys to the reform of France. The King should be pressed for a full financial report so the deputies would know what must be done. As for the Council the Chancellor was a good man, but he was not effective enough, especially against the Huguenots who had a voice in Council. Things would be even worse if Jeannin and Villeroy retired, as was rumored, because then jealousy would tear the Council apart.[8]

Although the three estates were in general agreement that they should remain in session until the *cahiers* were answered, they disagreed over such issues as Beaufort's plan, the establishment of institutions to make loans to the nobles, and the sharing of information among the estates about articles of mutual concern. The conflicting interests and antagonisms underlying these quarrels were about to be further aggravated by a personal incident involving members of the Second and Third Estates.

---

[7] PV-1, pp. 429–432. PV-2, pp. 218–238. PV-3, pp. 163–168. For the process developed by the Third Estate to complete work on its *cahier* see Rapine, pp. 276, 346, 348–349, 380, 397, 401, 403. The method was to delegate much of the work to committees.

[8] PV-1, pp. 412–416. This speech reflects also the growing problems within the government, brought about by the shifting loyalties of Sillery and Concini. Miron spoke of 'other powerful people, who, under the name of the King and Queen, his mother, dispose of all things as they please or as they are able ...'.

On February 3 the long-standing quarrel between Henri, *seigneur* of Bonneval, and Jacques Chavaille, *sieur* of Fougières, lieutenant general of the Sénéchaussée of Bas Limousin, exploded into open fighting. Bonneval, a deputy to the Second Estate from Haut Limousin, had opposed Chavaille's election to the Third Estate from Bas Limousin on technical grounds. His animosity increased as the Estates General continued, and he ended by breaking his cane over the Lieutenant General's head in the streets of Paris. When Chavaille reported the outrage to the Third Estate on February 4 the deputies clamored for redress. They decided that such an insult to the Estates General, to Paris, and to Chavaille's office could be dealt with only by the King. President Miron set out for the Louvre accompanied by such a crowd of furious deputies that the session had to be suspended until the afternoon. The King's answer when they finally found him, was to turn the case over to the *Parlement*.[9]

The next day, Wednesday, the clergy in a flurry of anxiety sent Claude Gélas, Bishop of Agen, to the Third Estate with an offer to mediate in the quarrel. But President Miron announced that this time the Third Estate had had enough. The Bishop left and the deputies again fell to discussing the insult to their honor. The deputies reached the decision that it was time to stop the clergy's attempts to control the Estates General through mediation of the disputes between the Second and Third Estates. At this point the Duke of Ventadour arrived from court to announce to all the estates that they were to have representatives on the commission set up to answer the *cahiers*, but that the King thought it a dangerous precedent to reply to the request to abolish venality of office permanently before the *cahiers* were presented. The King asked the deputies to concentrate on finishing their work soon. There were some protests at this, especially from the clergy, who blamed the Third Estate and its many petitions for the delay in their own work. However, the significance of Ventadour's remarks was lost in the tumult over the Bonneval affair.[10]

The nobles asked the clergy to join them in preventing the Bonneval case from going to the *Parlement* of Paris. They claimed that the Third Estate had already committed two offenses against them by asking the *Parlement* to intervene and by enlarging a particular offense into a general one. In spite of their protests the case was eventually tried before the *Parlement* and nothing was done to spare the nobles' feelings; the *Parlement* had a chance for revenge. The *Parlement* sent a crier to the vicinity of the Augustins to announce the coming trial and returned the verdict on March 11 that Bonneval was guilty of a crime of *lese majesté* in the city of Paris. He was to be beheaded and all his property confiscated. However, this sentence was carried out only in effigy

---

[9] PV-3, pp. 169–170. Rapine, p. 384. A.N. E 47B, fols. 114r–114v. Major, *Deputies*, pp. 101–102, B.N. MS fr. n.a. 1395, fol. 78r.

[10] PV-1, pp. 429–436. PV-2, pp. 236–238. PV-3, pp. 171–174. Rapine, pp. 384–395.

since Bonneval had fled. The Third Estate, for its part, seems to have relaxed once it became certain that the *Parlement* would try the case.[11]

The orders were drawn a little closer together by their common condemnation of Condé's behavior toward the Queen Mother on February 6. Condé was accused by Marie of complicity in an armed attack on an officer of the King's Guard on February 5. The group of horsemen involved had been led by one of Condé's followers. There was bad blood between Condé and the officer, Bertrand de Crugy, *seigneur* of Marcillac. Once a follower of Condé, he had revealed some of Condé's secrets to the Queen, been dismissed by Condé and rewarded by the Queen with a royal office. It was no secret that Condé wanted Marcillac punished. Condé admitted his responsibility but claimed that it was his business and no concern of the court. When reprimanded by the Queen Mother, Condé exchanged harsh words with her and stalked out of the room.[12]

There was more to the *affaire* than appeared on the surface. As early as January 21 the Secretary of State Brûlart had reported to the French representative in Germany that Condé and Bouillon were involved in some sort of intrigue. On January 26 the deputies were warned by the court not to receive Condé, who threatened to appear in all three chambers to express his grievances about the way in which the government was being run. The Queen had asked Bouillon to tell Condé not to take action against Marcillac, but Bouillon claimed that he never relayed her message because he was incapacitated by an attack of gout. After another attempt to gain favor with the Estates General by giving up his claims to Amboise, which he held in trust as a guarantee from Marie that the Estates General would meet (after it was apparent that the deputies would demand it), Condé began to direct more attention to the *Parlement*. His first move was to carry on a campaign in the *Parlement* to free his accomplice Rochefort, who had been imprisoned for leading the attack on Marcillac. On February 22 he presented a ballet before the Queen, which to many people seemed intended as a peace offering. However, only the younger members of the *Parlement* were asked to participate in the dancing, rather than the usual courtiers, and the performance was evidently meant to gratify the *Parlement* rather than the court.[13]

The Estates General, in the meantime, had again turned their attention to their major concerns. There was a dispute as to whether the King should be

[11] PV-2, pp. 234–236. PV-3, pp. 174–175. Rapine, p. 492. *Commission extraordinaire du Roy* ... (n.p., 1615). In spite of the hostility of the Third Estate the clergy were busy trying to restore harmony. B.N. MS fr. 4082, fols. 47v–48r, Bibl. Ars. MS 4255, fols. 43r.

[12] PV-1, pp. 440–444. PV-2, pp. 242–244. Rapine, pp. 395–400. Lalain claimed that the Third Estate wanted to be careful not to offend Condé. Bibl. Ars. MS 4255, fols. 43v–44v. According to Clapisson, only Lyonnais was worried about this. PV-3, pp. 178–179.

[13] B.N. MS fr. 4121, fols. 114r–114v. Rapine, pp. 178–179; B.N. MS fr. n.a. 1395, fols. 70r–71r. B.N. MS Dupuy 91, fols. 6v–9v, 14r, 15r–16r. Arnauld d'Andilly, *Journal*, pp. 42–54. Pontchartrain, *Mémoires*, pp. 339–340. Rohan, *Mémoires*, p. 504.

requested to provide more specific information concerning the commission which would answer the *cahiers*. On February 10 the Third Estate once again was ready to break off all communications with the clergy after Cardinal de Sourdis lashed out at one of their delegations for their preoccupation with their own particular program. But finally the Third Estate, in spite of reservations about setting bad precedents, joined the other estates in presenting a united petition to the King. On Saturday, February 14, representatives of the three orders went to the Louvre with petitions requesting the establishment of the chamber on finances, the acceptance of Beaufort's plan, and the continuation of the Estates General until the *cahiers* had been answered. As had happened so often in the past month, the King was not available. The Queen Mother informed them that she wanted the *cahiers* presented the following Thursday. The Council would then decide whether the Estates General was to continue in session until the *cahiers* were answered. But, she assured them, the committee that would study the *cahiers* would be so well chosen that the Estates General could have no complaints. She warned the delegation that no consideration would be given to any more new ideas or proposals.[14]

On February 17 the closing date for the Estates General was set for Monday February 23. On the same day the *Conseil d'Etat et des finances* agreed to place several more restrictions on extraordinary commissions in line with the decrees of December 16 and February 3.

Between February 16 and February 19 the nobles were called upon to defend their plans for financial reform. The nobles had arranged to have Beaufort's plan published as a book. On the pretext that it was inimical to the King's service, royal finance officials entered the printer's office and seized all the finished copies before they could be distributed. The Estates General protested against the seizure. Jeannin replied that he would read the book, *Le trésor des trésors de France*, and if it were a good work he would permit it to be distributed. In the meantime he had copies of it sent to the Estates General.

Several deputies reported at this time various intrigues to induce the Estates General to adopt programs inimical to the government. A member of the Second Estate, Théophile de Damas, Baron of Digoyne of the *bailliage* of Charolais and an officer of the Duke of Mayenne's troops, was accused of being involved in this. He demanded that anyone who had something to propose for the good of the country be permitted to speak without fear. But the Second Estate declined to make an issue of the matter. All of this served to confuse matters, but the Queen Mother kept the situation under control by insisting that the deputies finish their work.[15]

---

[14] PV-1, pp. 448–469, PV-2, pp. 244–264. PV-3, pp. 175–188. At this time there is some disagreement among the *procès-verbaux* on the exact sequence of events. The King had been practising his speech for the closing ceremony since February 11, Héroard, *Journal*, I, 173.

[15] PV-2, pp. 264–278. PV-3, pp. 188–193.

The clergy insisted that the most urgent work of the Estates General now was to draw up a separate, shorter common *cahier* containing all the most important articles. The nobles finally appointed a committee for this purpose on February 17. But the members of the Third Estate, although they could be persuaded to support the plan of the nobles to seek aid for disabled soldiers or the plan of the clergy to protest against the appointment of a Huguenot to a new office in the *Parlement*, would not agree to any form of common *cahier*. They used the excuse that not enough time remained, but the reason for refusal was much more fundamental. The Third Estate knew very well that the main concern of the clergy was unanimous support for the reception of the decrees of the Council of Trent; the Third Estate wanted no part of .his.[16]

Throughout the meetings of the Estates General the clergy had been working for the inclusion in all of the *cahiers* of an article calling for the admission by the King of the decrees of the Council of Trent into France. The arguments over the Council had been long and bitter. For many years the major opponent of the clergy in this matter had been the *Parlement* and the conflict, under the leadership of President de Thou and Antoine Arnauld, had become increasingly bitter since 1610. The issues of Gallicanism, the Jesuits, and related questions were again involved. In 1614 the situation differed from that which had prevailed at the Estates General of 1576. The clergy now solidly supported the admission of the decrees of the Council of Trent. But the *Parlement*, angered by the ecclesiastical condemnation of Edmund Richer's book in 1613 and by the clergy's hostile reaction to its censures of Jesuit works, was more adamant than ever. The Third Estate was in complete agreement with the *Parlement* on this issue. Neither Ubaldini nor anyone else could sway them.[17]

---

[16] PV-1, pp. 482–483, 492. PV-2, p. 273. PV-3, pp. 188–190. B.N. MS fr. 10876, fols. 256r–258v.

[17] Martin, *Gallicanisme et réforme catholique*, pp. 345–399. Michel François, 'La réception du Concile en France sous Henri III', *Il Concilio di Trento e la Riforme Tridentina* (Rome, 1965), I, 383–400. Many of the reforms of the council had been incorporated into the ordinances of Orléans and Blois. Though the decrees of the council were never formally accepted in France, the Assembly of the Clergy of 1615 accepted them on behalf of the clergy. See Blet, *Clergé* I, 125–129. The Council of Trent was a live subject for pamphleteers in 1614–1615. Some examples are: *Discours sur la réception du Concile de Trente en France* (n.p., 1615). *Extraict des registres des Estats sur la réception du concile de Trente au royaume de France* (n.p., n.d.). For other examples see Martin, *Gallicanisme et réforme catholique*, pp. xxv–xxvi. For the beginning of Ubaldini's campaign see A.S.V. Nunz. Fr. 56, fols. 143r–143v (December 20) and A.S.V. Fond. Borgh., II, 242, fols. 88r–88v (December 30). Edmondes in his letter of August 27/September 6, 1614 was suspicious that the reason so many bishops had been elected to the Estates General was a plan to get the decrees of the Council of Trent accepted. B.M. Stowe MS 175, fol. 31r. That was not the case, but Ubaldini was happy when he found out who had been elected, partly because he was sure that they would favor the acceptance of Trent, A.S.V. Fond. Borgh. II, 242, fol. 67r.

On February 19 René Potier, bishop of Beauvais, opened the last phase of the clergy's Trent campaign by trying to persuade the Third Estate to include an article in its *cahier* favoring the acceptance of the decrees of the Council. President Miron's reply expressed both the Third Estate's determination to maintain its Gallican position and the animosity that continued to separate the First and Third Estates. He told the bishop that unfortunately the Third Estate had already completed its *cahier*; this matter should have been brought to the deputies' attention earlier. 'The confused times . . . make it necessary to reject the publication of the Council of Trent. . . . Nevertheless the clergy could begin among themselves the execution and observation of the Council, taking it for the rule and model of customs and actions. . .'. Later he added '. . . that the company nevertheless embraces the faith it contains, but are not able to understand the administration of it, because it is prejudicial to the state; that the clergy can themselves guard and observe the Council and thus give the first example . . .'. The clergy's protests that the rights of the Gallican Church would be protected were to no avail. The Third Estate formally voted on the acceptance of the decrees of the Council of Trent on February 20; only Provence and Dauphiné voted for it. The clergy made another attempt to win the support of the Third Estate for those decrees of Trent which concerned faith and doctrine on the afternoon of February 21 but this, too, failed.[18]

Though they failed with the Third Estate, the deputies of the First Estate managed to complete their other work down to the minute instructions to the General Agents for storing the furniture and tapestries of their chamber until the approaching meeting of the Assembly of the Clergy. The deputies of the First Estate also agreed to remain in Paris to represent their areas in the Assembly. This idea was sold to the provinces on the grounds that the deputies would serve without charge and that the deputies could thus stay in Paris until the *cahiers* were answered.[19] They reached agreement on February 19 with the nobles concerning the articles to be emphasized in the *cahiers*, and the Second Estate gave its very reluctant approval to the acceptance of the Council of Trent.[20]

However, on February 20 eight of the nine Huguenot deputies of the Second Estate walked out of their chamber in protest against the article calling on the

[18] PV-3, pp. 194–201. Rapine, pp. 427–436. The Third Estate did not actually finish its *cahier* until February 21. PV-3, pp. 201–204.

[19] A.D. Aube, G 140, fols. 191r–198v (from letter of the General Agents of the Clergy, Behety and Breteville, to the Bishop of Troyes). Actually the deputies got the King to approve an additional tax on the clergy to pay for the Assembly, A.N. E 48A, fol. 323r (Council, March 5, 1615). The Third Estate was also busy with a series of last-minute details including providing money for missionaries planning to leave for Canada. B.N. MS fr. n.a. 1395, fol. 88r.

[20] A list of articles agreed on as the most important by the nobles and the clergy is to be found in B.N. MS fr. 3718, fols. 1r–9r. See Chapter 10 below.

King to preserve inviolably the Catholic religion. They refused to sign the *cahier* and on February 21 they signed a formal protest against the inclusion of this article in the *cahier* of the Second Estate. In hopes of smoothing over the difficulty Marie asked the Second Estate to modify the article to state that nothing should be done to violate the Edict of Nantes. The nobles refused to do this, saying that they had acted in accordance with their consciences. The nobles, however, were not willing to go too far in their opposition to Marie. On February 21 they sent unopened to the Queen Mother the letter from Pope Paul V given to President Senecey by Cardinal Ubaldini, which congratulated the nobles for opposing the First Article of the Third. Marie de Médicis returned the letter with thanks after reading it. During that final week the Estates General engaged in the usual exchange of formal courtesies and by the morning of February 23 all work was concluded.[21]

The formal closing of the Estates General on the afternoon of February 23 can only be described as farcical. Although the Queen Mother's desire for a speedy ending grew out of her fears concerning the trouble the requests of the deputies could cause, the growing struggles within the government, and Condé's newest offensive, the actual date for the closing was determined by the necessity of preparing the Hôtel de Bourbon, where the final ceremonies were to be held, for the ballet to be presented by the King's sister Elizabeth.[22] Condé, who just a year before had so confidently insisted that the Estates General be called, did not even appear at the closing. He pleaded fatigue, his highly successful ballet having been presented the night before, but it is probable that he had no desire to hear speeches which were certain not to be in his favor. Pleased with the success he was having with the *Parlement*, the value of the Estates General was now negligible to him. The deputies to the Estates General were receiving a minimum of consideration from any source. So many

---

[21] PV-1, pp. 495–545. PV-2, pp. 278–305. B.N. MS fr. n.a. 7254, fols. 187v–191r. B.N. MS Dupuy 323, fol. 192r (the signed original of the protest of the eight Huguenots). The King renewed the Edict of Nantes on March 12. The Huguenots were also promised that they could hold an assembly in 1615. B.N. Moreau 1427, fol. 82v. See also B.M. Stowe MS 175, fols. 235r–236v (Edmondes to Winwood, February 14/24) which blames the clergy for inflaming tempers by their agitation for the Council of Trent and their misrepresentation of an incident in Milhau where Huguenots attacked Catholics, while they ignored a Catholic attack on Huguenots, at a time when both incidents were under investigation. The one Huguenot noble who did not walk out, Odet de la Nouë, later defended his action on the grounds that he was at the Estates General as a deputy not only for the Huguenots, but also for the nobles of Poitou; that he had worked hard to defeat the article on the King's oath and the Council of Trent but had been outvoted. This had happened in other instances also and he had not walked out then. Finally he claimed that Bouillon and Condé were behind the agitation. B.N. Cinq Cents, 17, fols. 159r–163v.

[22] B.N. MS ital. 38, fols. 207r–209v. Malherbe contributed some verses for the ballet, see L. Maurice-Amour, 'Les poésies de Malherbe et les musiciens de son temps', *XVIIe siècle*, no. 31 (1956), pp. 317–318.

spectators were admitted to the closing ceremonies that the deputies had difficulty in finding seats.[23]

When the hall was finally quieted, the King appeared and the speakers appointed by the three orders presented their last official words. Richelieu, speaking first, traced the causes of the major problems of France to excessive expenses, to pensions, and to the selling of offices. Because the nobles did not hold the offices that should be theirs they were forced to depend on revenues that belonged to the Church. The clergy, too, should be given their rightful place in government and rendered all that was their due. Their rights should be respected without interference from laymen who should not exceed their own jurisdiction. The best remedy for the evils that troubled France was the enforcement of existing edicts, old and new, not just for a day but perpetually. Only the King could do this; only he had the power and grace to bring reform to France. Richelieu admitted that the clergy were guilty of abuses which they themselves must reform, but there were many evils in the Church that could be cured only by the King. The method he should choose was the enforcement of the decrees of the Council of Trent. Richelieu's speech praised Marie de Médicis for preserving peace and for arranging the Spanish marriages. He expressed the confidence of the deputies that the Queen Mother would bring the work of the Estates General to a fruitful conclusion. He suggested that one way of doing this was to allow the Estates General to remain in session until the *cahiers* were answered.[24]

The Baron of Senecey spoke for the Second Estate. He called the King the hope of France who alone could bring good out of the work of the Estates General. He praised Marie de Médicis for preserving peace at home and abroad. However, he did not pass up the opportunity to point out the excellence of the nobles. 'The nobles, more attached to Your Majesty than any of the other orders in quality, give way to none in affection...' He insisted that venality be done away with. Merit alone should determine appointment to the offices of the government; that is, the nobles should be given these positions. Pensions belonged to the nobles by right because of their wartime service. The *pauvre peuple* were the only other group mentioned – they needed protec-

---

[23] Arnauld d'Andilly, *Journal*, p. 58 (sketch of closing). Bassompierre, *Journal*, II, 1. B.N. MS fr. 4116, fol. 23r. Fontenay-Mareuil, *Mémoires*, p. 83. Even Guy Goualt, whose letters are usually matter of fact, was peeved at the time it took to hold the closing ceremonies. A.D. Morbihan 87 G 4 (letter of February 25).

[24] PV-1, pp. 545–547. PV-2, pp. 305–307. Armand Jean du Plessis, *Harangue prononcée en la salle du Petit Bourbon, le xxiii février par Armand Jean du Plessis de Richelieu, évesque de Luçon* (Paris, 1615), pp. 3–64. At Richelieu's request the clergy had given him an outline of the most important points to be covered in his talk on the morning of the 23rd. He was speaking for the clergy, not himself, in the body of the speech. But the introduction, conclusion and embellishments, undoubtedly carefully prepared long before, were his own. PV-1, pp. 525–527; the only accurate modern version is in Richelieu, *Mémoires*, I, 340–365.

tion from the tax collectors. The speech closed with a plea that the *cahiers* be answered and that the nobles be restored to their former greatness.[25]

Of the three speakers, only Miron followed the old custom of addressing the King from a kneeling position. Beneath the surface rhetoric of praise for the the King and Queen Mother and apology for the presumption of the Third Estate, his speech voiced a strong appeal for the program drawn up by that estate. Complaining that the ecclesiastics abused piety and the officials abused justice, he listed the faults of the clergy, nobles, and office-holders. He then summarized the *cahier* of the Third Estate. He dwelt on the need to abolish venality of office and the *paulette*. His speech returned to the abuses of the nobles and then he pleaded for the reduction of the *taille*. He ended with praise for the virtues of the Third Estate – especially its humility – and slipped in a reminder that the members of the Estates General wanted to remain in session until the *cahiers* were answered.[26]

When the speeches were over and the *cahiers* had been officially presented to the King, Louis, Marie, and their entourage rose and without ceremony left the hall. The Estates General of 1614 had officially ended.

On February 24 the deputies found that they had been locked out of the monastery of the Augustins. They were told that they could meet but only at the houses of their presidents. They were not to take up any new business. The three estates did hold some meetings, and the Third Estate, at least, continued its debates.[27] However, members of the Estates General were not permitted to sit on the committees discussing the *cahiers*. The Third Estate managed to present its ideas to Jeannin and other committee members but with little effect.[28] The Third Estate was especially worried about reports that new salt and wine taxes were to be devised to replace the *paulette* revenue and to pay the wages of the deputies of all three estates. Sixty-six members of the Third Estate protested against this on March 20. The King made his final

---

[25] Lalourcé and Duval, *Recueil de pièces*, VIII, 240–249. B.N. MS fr. 10879, fols. 230r–238v. Senecey's speech was the only closing speech that was not later reprinted as a pamphlet. His father's and grandfather's speeches at the Estates of 1588 and 1576 do exist, *Remerciement fait au nom de la noblesse* ... (Paris, 1588); *Proposition de la noblesse* (Paris, 1577).

[26] Robert Miron, *Harangue prononcée devant le roy et la reyne ... à la présentation du cahier de Tiers Estat* ... (n.p., n.d.), pp. 3–68. Richelieu and Miron each spoke for about an hour and a half, Senecey for an hour. B.N. MS fr. n.a. 7254, fol. 191r.

[27] The best account of the period February 25–March 24 is le Doux's, B.N. MS fr. n.a. 1395, fols. 97r–110v. Also see Rapine, pp. 476–505.

[28] Originally seven men from the *Parlement* and the Royal Council formed the committee. In early March five committees (church, nobles and royal household, finance, justice, administration and merchandise) were set up with 31 members of the royal council serving on them. B.N. MS ital. 38, fols. 204r–204v; A.S.F., Arch. Med., MS 4853, fols. 184r–185v; B.N. MS fr. n.a. 1395, fol. 98v.

ruling on March 26: Each order was to be taxed separately to support its own deputies.[29]

The final disbanding of the Estates General on March 24 gave little comfort to the deputies. After they had been ordered home the government sent letters throughout the kingdom announcing the closing of the Estates General and explaining the reasons for dismissing the deputies. The letters said that as soon as the five committees appointed to study the *cahiers* had begun their work, it had become evident that preparations of suitable answers would take a long time. The expense of keeping the deputies in Paris was exorbitant, so, at the request of some of the deputies, the leaders of the Estates General had been summoned to the Louvre on March 24 to hear the answers to the most important parts of the *cahiers*. The deputies were promised that the *paulette*, venality, and unnecessary offices would be abolished. A chamber of justice would be established to look into financial abuses. Pensions would be regulated and moderated. The other articles in the *cahiers* would be answered as soon as possible.[30]

The government was gratified by its success in dismissing the deputies without an uproar. A letter to the *Sieur* of Sainte Catherine on March 6, 1615, announced jubilantly that the Estates General had ended well, no matter what anyone said.[31] In general the deputies of the First and Second Estates accepted the end gracefully. The clergy planned to be in Paris for some time and still hoped for success. The Third Estate was least happy, though degrees of sadness varied. Florimond Rapine said 'Nevertheless they were not disposed to accord us what we asked; we received nothing but an equivocal and ambiguous response and were forced to leave without hope of coming near our design ...'.[32]. On the other hand Claude le Doux was pleased because the Queen gave him tickets to a ballet. He was mainly concerned with the outcome

[29] PV-1, pp. 547–554. Rapine, pp. 493–500. B.N. MS, fr. 18256, pp. 383–389. A. Miron de L'Espinay, *Robert Miron et l'administration municipale de Paris de 1614 à 1616* (Paris, 1922), p. 133. *Requeste presentée au roy par les députés du Tiers Estat* (n.p., 1615). B.N. MS fr. n.a. 7853, fols, 337r–340r. B.N. MS Dupuy 853, fols. 260r–260v (the signed decree of March 26 on payment of deputies). A.N. E 48A, fols. 415r–415v, 419r–419v. B.N. MS Dupuy 91, fols. 163r–164r (the signed complaint of the deputies of the Third Estate concerning payment; there are sixty-six signatures). The edict of December 1614, providing wage increases for certain officials from tax revenues, gave the deputies a precedent to worry about. See Chapter 7 above, footnote 28.

[30] Bibl. Ars. MS 4255, fol. 55r. B.N. MS fr. 18256, pp. 390–392. According to Hallé the Chancellor said that one person from each *gouvernement* could remain in Paris to wait for the answers to the rest of the *cahier*, B.N. MS fr. n.a. 7254, fols. 191v–192r. B.N. F 46927(8) *De par le roy* (notification to the Seneschal of Albret of the dismissal of the deputies). B.N. Moreau 1427, fols. 82r–82v, 84r–85r (letters of the King announcing the end of the Estates General). A.D. Somme 1 B 17, fols. 28r–29r.

[31] B.N. MS fr. 4121, fols. 119r–119v.

[32] Rapine, p. 505.

of Norman affairs and the way in which the deputies would be paid for their services.[33]

The court was busy with many other matters. On April 2 the first stone of the Palais de Luxembourg was laid. The University of Paris, against Ubaldini's protests, was demanding that the Jesuits should not be permitted to reopen their Collège de Clermont, across the street from the Sorbonne. The Huguenots had to be reassured by a formal reaffirmation of the Edict of Nantes. In May the recruiting of troops for Parma or Savoy within France had to be forbidden as part of an effort to bring peace between Spain and Savoy. On May 30 an edict exiling all Jews from France was published. But two matters of special importance absorbed the court and pushed the Estates General further into the background: preparations for the coming royal marriages, and the *Parlement*'s attempt to set itself up as a new Estates General.[34]

The committees were still working on the answers to the *cahiers* on April 3, but after that date no records of any further attempt to answer the grievances of the Estates General of 1614 is to be found for many years.[35] But this should be no surprise. The Estates General had not been called to bring reform to France, but to foil Condé and to gain the approval of the kingdom for the policies of the Regency. An analysis of the activities of the Royal Council and the *Parlement* of Paris in 1614 and 1615 shows how little attention the government actually paid to the wishes of the Estates General. The *Parlement* of Paris registered eight royal ordinances between January 1614 and the end of March 1615 that were in accord with the reforms requested by the deputies. On the other hand there were seventeen ordinances registered that were in direct opposition to the intent of the *cahiers*, including five that granted naturalization and privileges to foreigners and five that permitted violations of the water and forest reforms. The last five would hinder the rebuilding of the royal domain and thus make more difficult the reduction of the *taille*.[36]

The collections of printed royal edicts, declarations and *arrêts* for the period January 4, 1614 to May 23, 1615 contain five edicts that were in accord with

[33] B.N. MS fr. n.a. 1395, fols. 103v–105r, 110v–112v. Not even the loyal Le Doux was overly happy, however.

[34] A.N. AD + 158, no. 16 (edict against the Jews). See also B.N. MS ital. 1768, p. 3 (Venetian ambassador March 3, 1615). Fouqueray, *Compagnie*, 111, 352–353. Prat, *Compagnie de Jésus*, v, 350–351 (Ubaldini to Borghese, March 24, 1615). B.N. Cinq Cents 43, fols. 259v–292v. Pontchartrain, *Mémoires*, pp. 341–342. A.D. Somme I B 17, fols. 28r–32v (copies of all the edicts mentioned) and B.M. Stowe MS 175, fol. 253r (Edmondes to Winwood March 4/14, 1615).

[35] B.N. MS fr. 4121, fols. 121r–121v.

[36] A.N. X1A 8647, fols. 466r–511v; X1A 8648, fols. 1r–171r. It is interesting to note that during this period seven patents or monopolies for the use of new manufacturing processes were granted. A study of this aspect of royal power over a longer time could be fruitful.

the wishes of the three estates, while twelve were contrary, including three that created new offices and four that imposed new taxes. Clearly it was 'business as usual'.[37]

Nor did the deputies receive much credit for their endeavors and hardships from the rest of the country. The deputies had come from every part of France. Some had traveled for several weeks in order to reach the capital. For more than five months they had been absent from their homes and their own affairs. Those without connections in Paris had had to trust to the inns. All the deputies had to put up with the rise in prices in Paris during the meeting of the Estates General. The Florentine Ambassador gave a sigh of relief at the end of February 1615. With the deputies on their way, 'This city is beginning to find life less expensive.' And when they were finished many had great difficulty in collecting their wages.[38]

In 1614 French opinion no longer agreed with the author of Le réveille-matin des françois who in 1573 had stated '... that these three estates are as sovereign magistrates above the king in this area ...'. In fact the provincial estates had been held during 1614–1615 as if there had been no meeting of the Estates General. The Estates of Quercy met as they did each year. The Estates of Vivarais met twice in 1614 and again in February of 1615, with no deputy to the Estates General taking part in any of the meetings as was the rule throughout France. The Estates of Normandy met in September 1614 and proceeded to draw up their own cahier which they presented to the King on January 29, 1615. The provincial estates of Languedoc met on November 24, 1614 and took up the problems of that province. In June, 1615 the Estates of Provence met and unanimously supported the First Article of the Third Estate and rejected the proposal that the decrees of the Council of Trent should be accepted in France. It instructed the King to disregard, in so far as Provence was concerned, any statement to the contrary made by the deputies of Provence at the Estates General. The Huguenots, too, at their assembly in the summer of 1615 presented their own requests to Louis XIII. They supported the First Article of the Third, opposed the adoption of the decrees of the Council of

---

[37] A.N. AD+ 156, 157, 158. The records of the Council of State, A.N. E 43A–49, of which the Parlement records cited above serve as an excellent summary, reveal the same pattern. To cite one example: During the month of April, 1615, of the forty-four pieces of business recorded in the Council minutes, only one decision could be said to favor the requests of the Estates General. Some actions were neutral: but the spirit of most of the decisions was distinctly opposed to the wishes of the deputies. A.N. E 48B–49, fols. 1r–92v. Similarly A.N. AD IX 4, 416, 470, 490 (collections of edicts, declarations and arrêts concerning aides, gabelles, tailles and the treasurers general) contain only edicts opposed to the wishes of the Estates General during the period in question.

[38] A.S.F., Arch. Med. 4629 (Bartolini's report of February 24). For examples of the deputies' difficulties in collecting their wages see Major, Deputies, pp. 148–157.

Trent, and even asked the King to consider the latest claims made by Condé.[39]

But Frenchmen had expected more of the Estates General than it had accomplished, and the pamphleteers let the world know the disappointing results. As the author of *Le Patois Limosin*, addressing himself to Condé, expressed it:

And generally all three orders together produced only disorder and confusion. For have you seen, my prince, that they talked of finding out the truth about the murder of Henry the Great? Have you seen that they concerned themselves with hunting out the larceny of the most eminent people? Have you seen that they tried to banish the Spanish from the council of our king? Have you seen them taking offense at the transporting of our money to Italy? Have you seen them complaining about the tyrannical taking of the most important places for the preservation of France from our nobles and the giving of them to a harlequin who has never drawn a sword? No, my prince. They say that these are affairs too delicate, that this would be to wish to knock down the towers of Notre Dame by throwing boiled potatoes, or like giants to pile mountains one on top of the other to drive Jupiter from his throne and take the thunder from his hand. In brief (they say) they would have to attack a marquis, the Duc d'Epernon, the Chancellor, Villeroy, the greatest persons of the kingdom. O good God! Who should be seized other than those who are the cause of our troubles.[40]

The deputies were only too well aware of the failure of their efforts. They had drawn up a program of reform, but the court's summary dismissal of the petition that the *cahiers* be answered before the deputies were sent home held little hope for the future. Rapine said as much at the end of his account of the

---

[39] *Le réveille-matin des François et de leurs voisins, composé par Eusèbe Philadelphe Cosmopolite en forme de dialogues*, in Pierre Mesnard, *L'essor de la philosophie politique au XVIe siècle* (Paris, 1936), pp. 348, 352, R. Fage, ed., *Documents rélatifs aux Etats de la vicomté de Turenne* (Paris, 1894), I, 50–51, 62. Baudel, ed., *Notes pour servir à l'histoire des Etats provinciaux du Quercy* (Cahors, 1881), pp. 5–6, 41. A. Le Sourd, *Essai sur les Etats du Vivarais, 1601–1789*, (Paris, 1926), pp. 365–366. A. Le Sourd, *Le personnel des Etats du Vivarais, 1601–1789* (Lyon, 1923). Charles de Robillard de Beaurepaire ed., *Cahiers des Etats de Normandie sous le règne de Louis XIII et Louis XIV* (Paris, 1876), I, 93–121, 268–269. De Vic, *Histoire générale de Languedoc*, XI, pt 2, 919–920. *Resultat de l'assemblée des Estats de Provence tenus à Aix au mois de Juin* (n.p., 1615), pp. 3–7, in B.N. MS fr. 4131, fols. 106r–109r. Léonce Anquez, *Histoire des assemblées politiques des réformés de France, 1573–1622* (Paris, 1859), p. 267, footnote 1.

[40] *Le patois Limosin* (n.p., 1615). Some of the reprints of this pamphlet are entitled *Le matois Limosin*.

THE CLOSING OF THE ESTATES GENERAL

Estates General. In later years Richelieu summed up the end of the Estates General of 1614:

> Thus the Estates ended as they had begun. The proposition to hold them had been under specious pretext, without any intention of taking advantage of them for the service of the King and public, and the conclusion was without fruit, the whole assembly having no effect except to overburden the provinces with the tax they had to pay to their deputies, and to let the whole world see that it is not enough to know evils if one does not have the will to remedy them, which God grant when he desires to make the kingdom prosperous, and let not the great corruption of the centuries bring anything to stop it.[41]

Pierre Robert, lieutenant general of Dorat, who had been elected as a deputy from Basse Marche but was prevented by illness from coming to Paris, summed it up more succinctly. He was not sorry that he had not been able to attend, since '... the deputies did nothing in return for the great expense they had caused the whole province, for which they received only the maledictions of the people'.[42]

The government was aware that there would be a general outcry over the expense of holding the Estates General. It had tried to cloak its curt dismissal of the deputies under the pretext of preventing further expense for the people and by promising that the *cahiers* would soon be answered. The court had to turn its attention to the immediate problems posed by the *Parlement* and Condé. The need for this was made evident by the pamphlets that began to appear after the closing of the Estates General. There was far more interest in the policies of the government than in the failure of the Estates General.

If the government had planned to divert blame for the failure of the Estates General from itself to the deputies, the policy was not a complete success. Bouillon wrote to Jeannin on June 9, 1615, that he and Jeannin both knew that the Estates General had had little liberty and less satisfaction and that discontent was now spreading throughout the provinces.[43] He did not mention that most of the relatively few pamphlets that attacked the deputies came from his party rather than from supporters of the government.

The biggest complaint voiced by the pamphlets was that the Estates General had accomplished nothing lasting concerning venality, reduction of taxes,

---

[41] Richelieu, *Mémoires*, I, 367–368. Rapine, p. 505.
[42] Quoted in J. Russell Major, 'The Payment of the Deputies to the French National Assemblies, 1484–1627', *Journal of Modern History*, XXVIII (September, 1955), 229, and in Poulbrière, *Corrèze*, p. 307.
[43] B.N. MS fr. n.a. 7262, fol. 116v.

financial and judicial abuses, or the Council of Trent. In short, the Estates General had accomplished nothing. A pompous city official like Balthazar de Vias of Marseille might publish a speech he had made to the King, saying that all was well with the kindgom and going to be better. But the pamphleteers did not share his opinion. The Estates General had failed to remedy serious evils. The only reaction befitting such failure was scorn and satire.[44]

The deputies were mocked at for having come to Paris to learn the royal ballet. Taunted with their weakness and lack of authority they were laughed at for their petty haggling and their self-contradictions. They had come to Paris to restore peace to the kingdom, but had achieved only silence and everything would go on as it had before. All their oratory was only the singing of idle songs and the crying of women.[45]

The dismissal of the deputies to the Estates General at the end of March made life easier for the royal government. But that government was not making life easy for itself. The Chancellor Sillery, perhaps tired of being lost in the shadow of Villeroy, had allied himself with Concino Concini. The latter had satisfied his desire for wealth and was now anxious to attain political power. Together the Chancellor and the adventurer were able to make life difficult enough for Villeroy to cause him to leave court in anger at the end of December, 1614. At first Marie de Médicis was happy to get rid of the omniscient Villeroy, especially since he seemed to be procrastinating in arranging for the Spanish marriage. However, the confusion of the last days of the Estates General, the insistence of the Spanish that they wanted to deal with Villeroy, in spite of the efforts of Sillery's younger brother Noel Brûlart to turn them against him, and perhaps the insistence of Jeannin, made Marie realize that she could not get along without Villeroy. The newly-restored Villeroy was not as effective as he had formerly been; he had to keep an eye on his enemies. But the old triumvirate of Marie, Villeroy and Jeannin was able to restore

---

[44] *Discours sur la réception du Concile de Trente en France* (n.p., 1615). Loyac, *L'eupheme* (n.p., n.d.). Balthazar de Vias, *Harangue faicte au roy et la royne par Monsieur Balthazar de Vias, assesseur et député de la ville de Marseille aux Estats généraus de France* (Paris, 1615).

[45] *Le plaidoyer des préséances et difficultéz des Estats. Recueillis à l'hostel de Monseigneur le Prince, premier pair de France, reuniateur des subjects du roy. Lequel a authorisé l'esprit de Pierre des Vieltes d'y respondre, et des les rediger par escrit, estant à Paris le seizième mars* (n.p., n.d.), in B.N. MS fr. 10877, fols. 257r–260v. *Les articles des cayers généraux de France, presentées par Maistre Guillaume aux Estats* (n.p., n.d.). B.N. MS fr. 9225, fols. 74r–77v, 89r–91r; these are two poems in manuscript form, one on the bishops at the Estates General, one simply entitled 'Vers de médisance faicts durant les Estats généraux tenus à Paris 1614'. There was a pamphlet that praised the deputies, *Remerciement de la France à Messieurs les députéz* ... (Paris, 1615). The First Estate was described as 'les véritable Druydes de la France' and the nobles as 'le précieux diamant de la France'. The deputies of the Third Estate did not rate their own descriptive phrase, but all the deputies together were described as 'ces véritable Hercules, qui rapportans leurs labeurs à la conservation de l'Estat', pp. 10, 12, 7.

some order; Sillery on occasion helped. It was none too soon. The *Parlement* had opened a new offensive and Bouillon was eager to get involved in it.[46]

On March 28, four days after the dismissal of the deputies, and after almost a month of deliberation on the problems created by the revocation of the *paulette*, the *Parlement* of Paris, with all chambers assembled, invited the lay and ecclesiastical peers of France to join the regularly-sitting members so that together they could form the Court of Peers and advise the Chancellor what must be done to reform the government of France. This produced a new crisis. In spite of what Richelieu later said, Molé's account and the actions taken by Marie showed plainly that she was worried. It must be remembered that the *Parlement* had already received two rebuffs from the court. A third could dangerously antagonize a group of men whose support was essential for the maintenance of order. The *Parlement*'s importance to Marie was evident in the way she had cultivated it during Condé's rebellion in 1614. The court's anxiety was underlined by the nervous words of Pierre Brûlart to the French representative in Germany. The best he could manage as late as June 11 was a hope that the troubles with the *Parlement* would soon end.[47]

Marie and Louis summoned the leaders of the *Parlement* to the Louvre for a scolding on March 30. The leaders' reaction to this was a promise to confer with their colleagues about their action of March 28. Since nothing happened the whole *Parlement* was summoned on April 9 to face the King, the Queen Mother and the Chancellor. Those who came received orders to cease their plans for a plenary session and the formulation of remonstrances. The *Parlement* was not intimidated and continued to discuss its plans. On May 13 the Royal Council announced that the *paulette* would be extended until the

[46] Villeroy returned to court in early January, but he was unable to act with any freedom until sometime in March. B.N. MS ital. 1767, pp. 245–247, 255–259, 262–264, 271–273 (Contarini's reports of December 23–February 3). For the Spanish intrigue see B.M. Stowe MS 175, fol. 221r and B.N. MS fr. 16116, fols. 275r–312v (Vaucelas and Noel Brûlart to various, January–March 1615). Marie and Villeroy were fully reconciled by early April. B.M. Stowe MS 175, fol. 284v (Edmondes to Winwood March 31/April 9). Concini's rise to power did not go unnoticed in France and was the subject of several pamphlets. See for example *La chemise sanglante* (n.p., n.d.) which attacked not only Concini but also Sillery and the Jesuits while praising *les grands* and Villeroy. Other examples are *Le catholique christianizé* (n.p., 1615) and *Cassandre françoise* (n.p., n.d.). Concini found little support in the pamphlets. One weak example is *L'Espagnol françois* (n.p., n.d.), pp. 21–30, which tried to support Concini by saying that it was not unnatural for a king to love some of his subjects more than others. During the period from March to July 1615 the number of pamphlets attacking and supporting the government were roughly equal. But far more editions of those attacking the government were published, suggesting a strong anti-government campaign.

[47] Arnauld d'Andilly, *Journal*, pp. 60–62. Isambert, *Recueil*, XVI, 61. Molé, *Mémoires*, I, 20–28. B.N. MS fr. 4121, fol. 138r. In early April the *Chambre des Comptes* would add to the government's problems by asking for an investigation of finances. Boislisle, *Pièces justificatives*, pp. 303–304.

end of 1617. There was no doubt, despite the general terms of the declaration, that this was a concession to the *Parlement*.[48]

At first the *Parlement* seemed not to notice this major concession. The government at the time and most contemporaries who later wrote about the incident blamed Condé for encouraging the *Parlement* to persist in its plans. However, past frustration and the momentum of events were just as important in what followed.[49] On May 19 a list of grievances was drawn up by the *Chambre des Enquêtes*. This was accepted by the whole *Parlement* on the following day and was presented to the King on May 22.

The *Remonstrances* began defensively with a claim that the *Parlement* was acting in line with its historic rights in calling for a Court of Peers and asking for reforms. Then followed a list of grievances: The First Article of the Third Estates should be accepted; the alliances of Henry IV should be maintained; the Princes of the Blood and the former secretaries of state (read Sully) should be given a role in government; important government positions should not be given to foreigners (read Concini); and a strong plea was made for the preservation of the rights and privileges of the Gallican Church. The rest of the document read like a summary of the *cahier* of the Third Estate, though the financial policy of the Regency was more strongly attacked.[50]

Molé in his memoirs reported that the Queen Mother was so angry that she was forced to break off in the middle of her answer to the representatives of the *Parlement*. She asked Sillery to continue for her. He attacked each of the grievances and then summed up his attack with words that were reminiscent of the First Article that the *Remonstrances* was defending, 'France is a monarchy where the King alone commands. Holding his kingdom from God alone, he must govern it according to the laws and ordinances, without being held to render an account to anyone.' Jeannin then joined in to defend his financial policy. Nevertheless, Sillery promised that the Council would deliberate the matter raised by the *Parlement* and reply.[51]

The answer came quickly. On May 23 an *arrêt* of Council was published annulling the *Parlement*'s decree of March 28 and its *Remonstrances* of May 22.

[48] A.N. X1A 1868, fols. 1v–5r. A.N. AD + 158, no. 25. Molé, *Mémoires*, I, 21–26. *Discours véritable de ce qui s'est passé au Parlement, en suitte de l'arrest de la cour du 28. mars dernier, et des remonstrances* (n.p., n.d.).

[49] Thomas Edmondes, who was getting more and more involved, claimed that as late as early April Condé had nothing to do with the *Parlement* and that he lacked courage to take action. B.M. Stowe MS 175, fols. 278r–278v (Edmondes to Winwood March 22/April 1). James I railed at Condé's 'pusillanimnity and baseness of spirit', *ibid.*, fol. 290r (Winwood to Edmondes April 1/11 1615).

[50] A.N. X1A 1870, fols. 187v, 194r–197r. Isambert, *Recueil*, XVI, 64–75. *Remonstrances presentées au roi par nosseigneurs de Parlement le 21 mai 1615* (n.p., 1615).

[51] Molé, *Mémoires*, I, 27–52. *Discours de ce qui s'est passé en la présentation des remonstrances* ... (n.p., n.d.). Shennan, *Parlement*, pp. 244–246 greatly confuses the years in which these events took place.

When the *Parlement* received notice of the *arrêt* it began the preparation of a new remonstrance. On June 7 the King insisted that the *arrêt* of May 23 be registered. But the *Parlement* had already gained what it really wanted – the reinstatement of the *paulette* and tempers were beginning to cool. On the request of the *Parlement*, which stated in conciliatory terms that it had intended no offense by its action, the King announced that if the *Parlement* made no attempt to call together the peers, the Council would consider the reforms desired by the *Parlement*. Marie had won another battle by compromise and delay.[52]

Condé was not yet finished. Urged by Bouillon he had decided at the end of April to encourage the *Parlement* in its plans. Though the *Parlement* retreated, Condé, once started, did not stop.[53] He left court late in May, again protesting to Marie in a letter of June 5 that he had only the service of the King in mind. Bouillon wrote to Jeannin on June 9 from Sedan stating his and Condé's grievances, which straddled both sides of the issues: The *Remonstrances* of the *Parlement* was just and should be heeded; there was great worry throughout the provinces that the *cahiers* of the Estates General would not be answered; venality and the *paulette* should be abolished. Most of all the Spanish marriages were a matter of concern to Condé and Bouillon. Were they going to take place or not, and if so, when? Finally, they said, the Spanish alliance was not a wise step. France would lose its old allies and the balance of power in Europe would be ruined.[54]

The final stage of planning the royal marriages had begun with the dispatch of Noel Brûlart to Spain on January 20, 1615. The last details had been worked out by France's ambassador in Spain, Vaucelas. The French, faced with continuing opposition at home, did not commit themselves to an exact date until the last moment. The Spanish, eager for the marriages, nevertheless vacillated as they heard of the *Parlement*'s protest and then Condé's actions.[55] The great rallying point for the men who gathered around Condé in the summer of 1615 was the Spanish marriages. The southern Huguenot nobles and the English who had not supported Condé previously were now worried enough to get

---

[52] B.N. MS Moreau 1427, fol. 96r. Isambert, *Recueil*, XVI, 61–64. Molé, *Mémoires*, I, 52–57. Richelieu evidently kept a record of these events, see A.A.E, France 770, fols. 2r–40r. One pamphlet appeared that supported *Parlement*: *Le pacifique pour la défence de Parlement* (n.p., n.d.). The author, who claimed to be an old soldier, attacked Concini and warned that the government's refusal to listen to the grievances of the Estates General and *Parlement* could cause a strong reaction throughout France.

[53] B.M. Stowe MS 175, fols. 301r, 317r (Edmondes, letters of April 14/24 and May 1/11 1615).

[54] B.N. Dupuy 365, fol. 164r (original of Condé's letter); B.N. MS fr. n.a. 7262, fols. 116r–118r. Bouillon, *Lettre au président Jannin* ... (n.p., n.d.).

[55] Brûlart was also working for smoother relations between Savoy and Spain. B.N. MS fr. 16116, fols. 275r–416v (dispatches January 20–August 21, 1615).

involved. Thomas Edmondes was under orders to make a last-ditch effort to arrange a marriage alliance between France and England. But when that failed or rather as Villeroy continued to put him off, Edmondes received orders of a different nature. He was to try to convince the French government to stop the Spanish marriages for the sake of the Huguenots and for '. . . the preservation of the welfare of Christendom', to investigate the death of Henry IV, to accept the *Remonstrances* of the *Parlement*, to enforce the Edict of Nantes, and to repudiate the decrees of the Council of Trent. If these goals could not be obtained then Edmondes was enjoined 'not to suffer the PP. [Princes] to be ruined'. Edmondes was to provide direct help 'Unless you bee very well advised that the PP., joyned with the bodye of the Religion, are of themselves able, and sufficyent both to subsist, and to gayne their cause. Otherwise his Ma^ty is persuaded both they and theyr cause, without his intervention together will perish.'[56]

Condé gathered his allies and rejected any reconciliation despite the entreaties of Villeroy and Pontchartrain, who were sent to him with the promise that his complaints would be considered and to ask him to join the royal entourage for the trip to Guyenne for the marriage ceremonies. Bouillon for his part refused the entreaties of Jeannin. Negotiations were finally broken off on July 29 and once again all the towns in areas likely to be threatened by Condé were warned to be on their guard. On August 3 Condé issued letters calling for armed support. At first there was debate within the government whether Condé's forces in Champagne and the Ile de France should be attacked, but the decision was made to proceed under heavy guard to Bordeaux for the marriages.[57]

---

[56] B.M. Stowe MS 175, fols. 347r–350r (Winwood to Edmondes, September 5/15, 1615). Winwood was speaking of plans formulated much earlier. Edmondes made his appeal to Louis XIII in June. Edmondes, *Remonstrances*, pp. 3–11. In hopes of angering the Spanish the English were providing money for the Duke of Mayenne to raise troops in France to fight for the Duke of Savoy. But, partly through French efforts, a peace treaty was signed at Ast on June 21, 1615. Marie had already made arrangements to have six to seven thousand Spanish troops ready on the border of Sedan to distract Bouillon, Lonchay, *Correspondance*, I, 451–456 (Philip III to Archduke Albert, and Spinola to Philip III, June 4 to October 23, 1615).

[57] Louis XIII, *Lettre du Roy à Monseigneur Le Prince* (n.p., 1615). Pontchartrain, *Mémoires*, pp. 342–348. A.N. K 110, no. 36² (original of Condé's letter calling for troops). B.N. MS fr. 15582, fols. 18r–21v, 39r–39v, 40r–40v (Villeroy's attempts to settle the crisis). A pamphlet. that summed up Condé's complaints and tried to win noble support for his cause was *La noblesse françoise au Chancelier* (n.p., n.d.). The strongest attack on the government was *Le protecteur des Princes* (n.p., 1615). Of the political pamphlets that appeared in 1614–1615, 28% were published between July and December 1615. As in early 1614 a great majority favored the government. When directly threatened the government used all of its resources to protect itself.

On August 17 the court left Paris but a halt had to be called at Poitiers because Princess Elizabeth became ill. This gave Condé or rather Bouillon, who now stepped in as commander of Condé's forces, a chance to collect his troops near Rheims. Bouillon had an army of about 3,000 men, including some troops supplied by his brother-in-law, the Count of Nassau. Marshal Boisdauphin was sent with a numerically superior force to Meaux to keep Bouillon away from Paris, which he did. As a precaution extraordinary security measures were undertaken in Paris.[58]

There was another army to face however. After the appeal made by the Assembly of Huguenots meeting at Grenoble to defer the marriages was rejected, the Duke of Rohan and the Marquis of La Force organized a Huguenot army in Guyenne to halt the marriages through force. By September 25 Princess Elizabeth had recovered and after three days of indecision the royal party set out again, protected by all available troops. The court reached Bordeaux on October 7 without incident. Rohan and La Force had been unable to raise enough support within France; neither Lesdiguières nor the Protestant towns would join them. The Swiss and Dutch had refused to send aid, the attempts to win favor with the Venetians had failed, and the promised English help proved illusory. On October 18 the marriage ceremony for Elizabeth was performed at Bordeaux with the Duke of Guise serving as proxy for the Infante. A similar ceremony was performed at Burgos for the Infanta with the Duke of Lerma acting as proxy for Louis XIII. Though the insurgents were still in arms and Bouillon had managed to move his army into the West, the exchanges of Princesses was made on November 9 at the Spanish border without incident.[59]

Marie de Médicis had achieved her goal. The rebellion continued for a time, but by January 1, 1616, Condé was ready to negotiate. The marriages had taken place despite him and once again he found no widespread support in France. Largely through the efforts of Villeroy a peace was signed on May 3, 1616 at Loudun. Condé seemed to have gained many of his demands in the peace treaty. Louis XIII agreed to investigate further the death of his father,

[58] B.N. Dupuy 76, fols. 139r–147r. Pontchartrain, *Mémoires*, pp. 350–353. Prinsterer, *Archieves*, II, 457 reprints a letter from Bouillon to Count John of Nassau of September 23, 1615. Bouillon's other brother-in-law, the Prince of Orange, refused to help. *Lettre du Prince d'Orange en forme de remonstrance* ... (Paris, 1615), pp. 3–14. For the security precautions in Paris see A.N. H 1892 and *Reg. délib. Paris*, XVI, 234–244.

[59] *Première lettre de Messieurs de l'Assemblée de Grenoble ... au Roy ... et seconde au Roy et à la Royne* (n.p., 1615). B.N. MS fr. 16116, fols. 424r–461r (reports of Vaucelas and Senecey on the marriages). B.N. MS fr. n.a. 23369, pp. 415–434 (De Lomenie to La Force July 5–October 26, 1615). For the Swiss refusal to help see Rott, *Représentation,*, 111, 981, 983; for the United Provinces' refusal see Du Maurier, *Ouvré*, pp. 239–240 and *Refus faict à Monseigneur la Prince de Condé par le Sr de Bernaveld* .... (Paris, 1615). The last contact between Bouillon and the Venetian ambassador was on April 9, 1615. B.N. MS ital. 1768, fol. 27r.

to lift the suspension of *arrêt* of the *Parlement* supporting the First Article of the Third Estate, to nullify the *arrêt* of May 23, 1615, to continue to study the *cahiers* of the Estates General and particularly the First Article of the Third Estate, to maintain the *Parlement*'s authority, to abolish venality of royal household positions and to observe the terms of the the Edict of Nantes. In addition Condé and his followers were given large sums of money and a number of offices. Convinced of his success Condé entered Paris in triumph to take his place in Council. On September 1, 1616, he realized his mistake – Marie imprisoned him. His supporters tried to organize resistance, but once again the French refused to support *les grands*.[60]

The continuing failure of Condé to organize opposition cannot be viewed as another success for the government of Marie de Médicis. With the Estates General and the *Parlement* circumvented, with the marriages completed and with Condé in prison, Marie lost interest in the governing of France. Tired of trouble, weary of intrigue, and perhaps worn out by the constant demands for action from Villeroy, Marie looked the other way as Concini and his allies took power. After all he had supported her throughout the troubles of 1614–1616, perhaps not heroically, but he had not made continual demands like the troublesome French. He was an Italian, the husband of her dearest and perhaps only friend. Faced with the *fait accompli* the three aged advisers had to surrender. Sillery and Jeannin retired and finally Villeroy was forced out of office. Then as the government ceased to function Louis XIII proved that he was his father's son. On April 24, 1617, encouraged by his former falconer Luynes, Louis seized power, had Concini arrested and shot, and began the era of his personal rule.

Marie de Médicis would soon be in exile, her advisers dead, and her reign vilified. She deserved more from France. In spite of the mistake she made in permitting Concini's greed for power full sway in 1616, Marie had served France well. She was not a great ruler but supported by a loyal group of advisers she frequently performed better than expected. It was she who had chosen Villeroy, Jeannin and Sillery. Together these three had chosen the small group of perhaps ten men who attended most Council meetings, who negotiated with the Huguenots at Saumur in 1611, with the Princes at Soissons in 1614, who were on the commissions that analyzed the *cahiers* in 1615, and who negotiated at Loudun in 1616. Villeroy, Jeannin and Sillery died shortly after Marie lost power, though Villeroy was recalled by Louis and was still serving him when he died in the fall of 1617. The men of the second rank, Champigny, Bullion and the rest, remained in government and

---

[60] Birch, *Historical View*, pp. 389–390. Edmondes was involved in the negotiations at Loudun. Pontchartrain, *Mémoires*, pp. 419–446. Bouchitté, *Loudun*, *passim*, especially pp. 715–744.

continued to give their support to the King in his struggle against the nobles and Huguenots. Richelieu, who first met these men in 1614 and served with them for a short time in 1616, continued to use their abilities after he assumed power in 1624. Richelieu was able to move forward in the 1630s because Villeroy, Jeannin, and Sillery and the men they trained had preserved France. These men would not have had the opportunity to do so if Marie had not chosen and supported them.

Without Marie there could have been no successful financial and foreign policy. In the crisis of 1614–1615 it was Marie who had decided to take direct action against Condé, to postpone the final settlement until the most opportune time, to defeat the attempts during the summer of 1614 by the rebels to gain new support. It was Marie who had used her powers of patronage and the prestige of the monarchy to influence the elections to the Estates General. She had personally chosen the presidents of the three estates, had refused to act on the special requests of the deputies, and had sent them home burdened with the guilt of failure. The *Parlement*'s attempt to set itself up as a new Estates General had been thwarted by her decision to renew the *paulette*. And finally, after six years of effort, she had managed to accomplish the Spanish marriages despite the real danger of rebellion and possible death for herself.

Tactical errors had been made between 1610 and 1615. Villeroy at least, should have been better prepared for the demands made by the Estates General for reform. On occasion luck rather than skill had saved the Regency – if kings more forceful and shrewd than James I and Philip III had ruled England and Spain the problems of the Regency would have been more severe. And finally there was the collapse of late 1616, for which Marie must take full blame. But in the end it was she who had chosen the right men in 1610, it was she who had supported them and it was she who had first picked out Richelieu. She had preserved the throne and the power of her husband and had given her son a solid foundation to build on. She had served France well.

THE *CAHIERS*

The traditional and most important function of the Estates General was the presentation to the King of *cahiers de doléances* which embodied advice on the reforms that were needed in the kingdom. In fact, strictly speaking, the Estates General had met on only two occasions in 1614 and 1615: at the opening and closing ceremonies when the King had told the deputies what he wanted and when they had given their reply. In 1302 this process had taken only hours; in 1614–1615 it took months. In the final analysis the Estates General can best be judged on the results of its primary activity – the compilation of the *cahiers*. The details about the intervening sessions, the debates, the intrigues, while they reveal much about France, its people, and the reasons for the relative successes and failures of the Estates General, remain of secondary importance when an Estates General is being judged.

The general *cahiers* were the result of committee work and they show it. There seems to have been no attempt on the part of the deputies to provide for any logical progression in their requests nor any organization of them beyond a loose grouping in more or less traditional chapters. The main task of the deputies was to reflect accurately in their finished product the sense of the local *cahiers* that they had brought with them to Paris. Direct contradictions between articles were almost always avoided by voting on contentious issues and thus some deputies were bound to be unhappy. But, if at all possible, requests of minority groups were included somewhere in each of the three general *cahiers*.

To the twentieth-century reader the general *cahiers* present a mass of confusion. This chapter is in effect a highly compressed paraphrase of the three general *cahiers* presented to the King on February 23. Similar articles scattered throughout each chapter of the *cahiers* have been arbitrarily grouped together and many insignificant bits and pieces have been preserved only in spirit. It would be possible to concentrate only on the main themes to be found in each general *cahier* or to launch immediately into a comparison of the similarities and differences among the general *cahiers* of the three estates. But to do so would give the reader a false picture of the Estates General of 1614. To understand the work of the deputies it is necessary first to grasp the complexity of the issues that the deputies of each estate faced and the variety of responses that were given. Only then will it be possible to search out themes and finally, in the following chapter, to place the general *cahiers* of 1614 into context.

The First Estate presented the king with a *cahier* of 302 articles, to which were appended thirty-six articles dealing with church administration. The main body of the *cahier* was divided into eight chapters: 'On Religion and the Ecclesiastical Estate', 'On Religion and Monasteries', 'On Universities', 'On the State and the Administration of the Kingdom', 'On the Nobles', 'On the Third Estate', 'On Justice', and 'Infractions'. The last thirty-six articles were given the title 'Règlement Spirituel'.[1]

The *cahier* of the First Estate confirms the dominant position of the bishops in the meetings of the estates. The power of bishops is continually asserted. At the same time there is no mistaking that a major purpose of this insistence on episcopal jurisdiction was reform. Article 6 succinctly expressed the spirit of the French Catholic reform movement of the first half of the seventeenth century, 'the first and principal reformation of the Church consists in providing good and capable pastors and prelates . . . '. This reform of the Church was to be ultramontane and imposed from above, with little regard for privileges that had been amassed by individuals or communities in the course of the ages, even though the reformers, without admitting it, participated in abuses such as *in commendam* benefice-holding. At the same time it was just as certain that the leaders of the First Estate wanted to make sure that the King and his officials would not try to take reform matters into their own hands, as had been the case in the Ordinances of Blois and Orléans in the sixteenth century, though they wanted the government's help in insuring that bishops built seminaries and that benefice-holders contributed to church repairs. As a brake on the power of the reforming bishops the Gallicans (usually chapter members) were able to make their wishes felt. The devotion to Trent was continually modified by a respect for previous concordats.

All the clergy present, reformers or not, had a very strong sense of their own importance and their superiority over members of the other estates; nor were they reluctant to make detailed recommendations concerning reforms of the government and the part the clergy should be allowed to play in administering France. In their own eyes the First Estate was just that: the clergy saw themselves as the most important and best trained subjects of the

---

[1] In 1649 Mazarin wanted to study what had happened at the Estates General of 1614. However, no copy of the *procès-verbal* or *cahier* of the clergy could be found. After much searching one copy was found in a bookseller's shop. This was used as the text for a new printing. An example of the 1615 edition is in A.N. G8* 632A, pp. 1–216, 1–66; an example of the 1615 printing of the *cahier* alone is in B.N. MS fr. 10876, fols. 280r–312v. The *cahier* printed in Lalourcé and Duval, eds., *Recueil des cahiers généraux des trois ordres aux États généraux* (Paris, 1789), IV, 1–165, was checked with these, found accurate, and used since it is more readily available. This 1789 edition is also preferable because the editors corrected the misnumbering of the articles in the 1615 and 1649 editions (A.N. G8*632B). The abbreviation L & D will be used to designate Lalourcé's and Duval's work. The pamphlet *Cahiers généraux des articles resolus et accordéz entre les députéz des 3 estats* (Paris, 1615) is not an authentic representation of the requests of the three estates; too much is left out and the supposed answers of the King were never given.

King; subjects who because of their functions were not to be too closely regulated but permitted to take care of their own problems and be trusted to serve the King as they knew best that he should be served. They not only thought this; they said it to the King in Article 14 of their *cahier*. They noted that they rendered respect to the King voluntarily, not as the result of 'a right or duty appertaining to your crown . . .'.

Since the *cahier* of the clergy was even less coherently organized than those of the other two Estates its chapter organization will be partially ignored in this study and the recommendations of the clergy will be presented by drawing similar articles from various chapters of the *cahier*.

The first part of the chapter on the ecclesiastical estate, which contained ninety-eight articles, was concerned with the general religious reforms wanted by the clergy. Of primary importance were the official reception in France of the decrees of the Council of Trent, the re-establishment of *'la Religion Catholique, Apostolique & Romaine'* as the only religion in France, the papal renewal of the decree of the Council of Constance against regicide, and the protection of papal power.[2]

Specific reforms for the clergy were the concern of much of the rest of the chapter. Six articles dealt with the reform of the granting of benefices, including restrictions on the King's power of appointment and examinations for knowledge and behavior, and with the reform of episcopal and chapter elections to insure that capable men were chosen for these positions. Condemnation of *confidences* and simony was balanced by a tacit admission that the former would continue to exist. *In commendam* benefices were not specifically mentioned. Throughout, the power of the bishops in reform matters, even over exempt religious orders, was emphasized.[3]

---

[2] Arts, 1–5, L & D, pp. 2–6. (Articles cited specifically in the text will be noted in the footnotes in the order in which they are mentioned.)

[3] Arts. 6, 8–9, 13–15, 46; 11–12, 94–95, L & D, pp. 6–18, 35–36, 67. A benefice was *in commendam* when all of the revenues went to a non-resident ecclesiastic or a layman. *Confidence* described a benefice which had a titular ecclesiastic holder who split the revenues with a layman. *Confidence* was forbidden by an edict of 1610, registered by the *Parlement* in 1612. One of the requests of the clergy (Articles 46 and 47), was that hospitals and poorhouses be under ecclesiastical administration. In a series of edicts between 1561 and 1593 hospitals and charitable institutions had for the most part been placed under the control of city officials. The Council of Trent called for supervision of these institutions by the bishops. The kings from 1519 onwards had entrusted their power in this matter to their grand almoners. Beginning in early 1614 Cardinal Du Perron, who was grand almoner, had been attempting to reform charitable institutions. This caused opposition from laymen and also the clergy (article 42). Doucet, *Institutions*, 11, 807–810. B.N. MS fr. n.a. 7255, fol 174r. Jacques Davy, Cardinal Du Perron, *Règlemens fait par monsieur le Cardinal du Perron . . . et messieurs les juges ordonnéz par le roy pour la générale réformation des hospitaux, maladeries et autres lieux pitoyables de ce royaume* (Paris, 1614). See also the general *cahier* of the Third Estate, L & D, IV, 292–296.

The *Règlement Spirituel*, which began with the admission that the clergy needed reform, supplemented the first chapter. The keys to reform were frequent provincial assemblies and observance of the canons of the Council of Trent. Seventeen articles outlined the reform of the episcopate: the bishops were to live in their sees, carry out the prescribed visitations of their parishes, attend services as often as possible, introduce the reforms of Trent in their dioceses, ordain only those of canonical age who knew Latin and had means of support, and ensure that catechism and Christian doctrine were taught in all the parishes of their dioceses. At the least, benefice-holders were to be ordained at twenty-two, attend diocesan synods when required, and see to the spiritual and temporal upkeep of their benefices. *Curés* were to be 'gens de bien & sans scandale', who were well trained in administering the sacraments and who knew 'l'idiome du pays'. They were to reside in their parishes or, if dispensed, provide a competent vicar. Huguenots and those who died on the field while dueling were not to be buried in Catholic churches or cemeteries. On the whole the *Règlement Spirituel* was a summary of the decrees of the Council of Trent as modified by the rights of the Gallican Church.[4]

The First Estate's great concern for its privileges was evident in the chapter on the ecclesiastical estate. Sixteen articles supported clerical exemption from taxation. Two articles, one very lengthy, supported clerical rights to the tithe, and four supported the feudal rights of the clergy. Six articles concerned the return of clerical property to its original owners, especially that lost as a result of the Wars of Religion and through grants to Huguenots. Six articles called for the protection of the rights of benefice-holders. Twelve articles prohibited appeals by clerics to secular courts and supported the jurisdiction of the clerical courts against inroads by royal authority in property matters. One of the twelve articles was a petition that ecclesiastical courts be permitted to sentence clerics to the galleys for very serious crimes.[5] The rights of the ecclesiastical courts would also be stoutly defended in the chapter on justice.

The regular clergy received special attention in a chapter of nineteen articles. Again, reform was synonymous with the decrees of the Council of Trent. Again, the power of the bishops was emphasized. Royal officials were to assist visitators in their duties, but the *Parlements* were not to attempt to legislate ecclesiastical reform. Every monastery of twelve or more religious

---

[4] Arts. 1; 2–3, 4–6, 11, 22; 31, 8, 7, 10; 26, 27; 13. L & D, pp. 150–155, 158–161. The quoted words are on pp. 159–160.

[5] Arts. 58–64, 66, 70, 77–79, 83–86; 51–52; 55–57, 97; 53–54, 67–68, 80–81; 72–76, 88; 20–21, 24–30, 33–34, 92; L & D, pp. 23–30, 38–62, 66–68. In 1626 the King gave the clergy an extension of five years in which to buy back property sold or lost during the Wars of Religion. B.N. Cinq Cents 4, fol. 264r. In their *cahier* the nobles asked that this privilege not be extended and that they be given the same rights as the clergy. L & D, IV, 183, 197. The Third Estate was opposed to either the nobles or the clergy having this right. L & D, IV, 288.

should send one member each year to a university to study theology. The students were to be supported by those who held abbotships and priorships *in commendam*. Various rules were laid down for the filling of vacancies and for safeguarding elections from outside interference. Members of any monastery of a reformed religious order were to be eligible for election as superior of any of the monasteries of that order. The Pope was to be asked to insure that there would be no discrimination against Frenchmen in elections held in foreign countries. All religious houses were to be reformed, but the Benedictines and those nuns who escaped reformed convents by residing in royal hospitals were singled out for special attention as were the monasteries which did not have titular abbots in residence.[6] In the *Règlement Spirituel* a number of articles developed the same themes. Bishops were to work especially hard at reforming the Benedictines, Augustinians, and the various orders of nuns within their jurisdiction. Independent Benedictine houses were to join one of the three existing Benedictine congregations within six months or come under episcopal jurisdiction. The nuns were to be cloistered and provided with competent confessors. The bishops were to make sure that all girls who were to take vows were acting without constraint.[7]

The chapter on universities contained sixteen articles. The deputies of the First Estate wanted a general reformation of the universities. The tenor of the proposed reformation was the restriction of admission to only the most capable students and the elimination of abuses in granting degrees. Conditions were so bad, the clergy said, that to obtain a degree in law one had only to 'send money and his name'. Jesuits were to be readmitted to the faculty of the University of Paris, to be allowed to teach in their Collège de Clermont, and to receive protection and permission to carry out their work throughout the kingdom. Three articles in the university chapter were concerned with the prohibition of books against God, the King and the Pope. Only approved printers were to be allowed to exercise their craft. Again, the bishops were to play a paramount role in enforcing these regulations. University professors were to be required to teach at regular times, take fewer vacations, and account for their teaching time.[8]

---

[6] Arts. 105–106; 111, 108; 100–102, 117; 103, 104, 107, 114, 110. L & D, pp. 68–74.

[7] Arts. 32–33, 35–36. L & D, pp. 161–164. The question of episcopal jurisdiction over monasteries was a constant theme in French history from the Middle Ages to the late eighteenth century when the state began to impose its authority on religious orders.

[8] Arts. 118–126; 127, 129, 130; 123, 129, 130; 130. L & D, pp. 75–83. The quoted words are on page 79. The printing of breviaries had been a question that occurred a number of times in the deliberations of the First Estate. In article 132 the problem was resolved by asking that printers in cities other than Paris be permitted to print breviaries so that the cost would be lower.

The thirty articles on 'The State and Administration of the Kingdom' begin with a request that the double marriage arranged by the Kings of France and Spain be carried out since they were 'useful for the good of Christianity, the repose and tranquillity of your kingdoms, and of the estates of both'. Eight articles were concerned with the troubles of the royal government with the rebel nobles; all were a repudiation of Condé and his followers. No one was to be exempt from the King's justice, no one was to be permitted to have troops during peacetime except the King, the Queen Mother, and the King's brother. Leagues were to be forbidden, chatêaux and fortresses which were not necessary for defense or which were 'dangerous' were to be razed. No one was to have a position of authority in a place where he or a relative had attacked the King's sovereignty. Requests for reform of the administration of the kingdom were presented in ten articles. Experienced army officers were to be chosen for duty while the number of officers and soldiers was to be reduced. Money spent on roads and bridges was to be curtailed, as were unnecessary pensions. The Council of State was to be reduced in membership so that it would function better. The Council should concern itself only with administration, and the *Parlement* should concern itself only with justice. The Chamber on Finances was to be quickly constituted and members of the Estates General were to be given a place on it. Money for this project was to come from that saved by abolishing unnecessary offices. Tax collectors were also criticized in this chapter, especially those who collected special taxes.[9]

The nobles were the subject of a chapter of eighteen articles. Eleven of these articles called for the maintenance of noble privileges. Their tax exemptions were to be maintained; two Catholic nobles of the short robe should sit in each *parlement*; when the King filled a vacant benefice or judicial post he should appoint a noble if he had qualifications equal to the other applicants; and certain positions such as that of *bailli* and seneschal were to be reserved for the nobility. There was to be a severe fine for pretending to the noble rank, and the King was asked to ennoble only men who had given long and remarkable service. Several articles placed limitations on the nobility. No officer or pensioner of the King was to accept any money or position from a foreign ruler. No lord should usurp the rights of a vassal. All those who claimed the right to collect tolls had to post the rate of that toll and keep the roads and bridges in good repair. An article was included asking that the buying and selling of noble offices be forbidden; another called for the reduction of the number of marshals of France to four, the traditional number. More than two pages were devoted to an article against dueling. Anyone who participated

[9] Arts. 134; 136, 137, 145, 144; 146; 149, 159, 158, 157, 156, 154, 155. L & D, pp. 83–84, 86–89, 91–97. The quoted words are on page 83.

in a duel in any way was to lose all honors, offices, and property. There was to be no forgiveness by the King for this crime.[10]

Though there were forty articles in the chapter devoted to the Third Estate most of them dealt with that part of this order that the majority of the King's 'pauvre sujets' as the clergy liked to call them, hated as much as anyone else— tax collectors. Ten complaints were registered against tax farmers, extraordinary commissioners and partisans, asking for regulation of their salaries, prohibition against search by collectors of the *aides*, elimination of as many middlemen as possible and limitations on collections of arrears. Seventeen of the articles discussed taxation reduction. Four of these articles concerned the *taille*, asking that it be reduced to the rate of 1576 and that exemptions be limited. One of the means proposed for the reduction of the *taille* was the re-uniting (buying back) of that part of the domain of the King that had been alienated. Four other articles called for regulation of the *gabelle*, asking that the price of salt be reduced to the amount charged in 1588. Three of the articles on taxes asked for the abolition of temporary taxes whose time limit had expired. Clerical concern was shown in an article which called for the protection of widows and orphans from town councilmen and in two others against luxurious living, including one that called for restrictions on the number of people permitted to wear silk stockings.[11] In the chapter on justice the clergy asked the King not to listen to the Third Estate in matters concerning the reform of the clergy, since the deputies of the Third Estate had not conferred with them on this matter and since the introduction of the decrees of the Council of Trent into France would take care of reform.[12]

Seven of the articles in the chapter on the Third Estate were in support of what would later be called mercantilism. The export of money should be

[10] Arts. 172, 174, 177, 167, 168, 166, 165, 173, 171; 179–180; 169–170; 181. L & D, pp. 96–105. The provision concerning the marshals could have been a slap at Concini, Marechal d'Ancre, who had received his post in 1613 though similar requests are to be found in the *cahiers* of previous Estates General. The nobles and the Third Estate also wanted the same reduction. *Ibid.*, 199, 306–307. Cf. *Seianus françois au roy* (n.p., n.d.) attributed to 1615. The citation of the Ordinance of Blois was quite common in the First Estate's *cahier*. The other orders cited the other ordinances of the sixteenth century, especially that of Orléans, with much more regularity than the clergy, but they, too, often referred to Blois which was the most comprehensive ordinance of the century.

[11] Arts. 199, 213, 183, 188; 182, 184–185, 204–205, 214–217, 192–193, 206; 218; 221. L & D, pp. 105–117. The reason the King was called upon to buy back his domain, or feudal lands, was that the *taille* had originally been levied to make up for the money the King had lost through alienation of his domain. The *gabelle* too had supposedly been a temporary tax. Meuvret, 'L'Impôt', pp. 60–61. The Third Estate supported the clergy in this request. On the contrary, the nobles wanted those parts of the royal domain with little revenue to be given to nobles. L & D, IV, 227, 373–376.

[12] Art. 268, L & D, p. 136.

limited, French wool should be made into cloth within France, there should be no tariff between provinces and restrictions should be placed on the importation of precious stones by foreign merchants. The rights of towns were supported in three articles, and there was a request for a standard system of weights and measures throughout France. The development and protection of French maritime commerce was discussed in three articles in the same chapter. The clergy called for agreements with Spain and the Turks to protect French sailors, for regulations to prevent privateers from becoming pirates, and for investigation of an offer to provide France with armed and fitted vessels for three years' service.[13]

The clergy were particularly concerned with the administration of royal justice. Twenty-one of the forty-nine articles in the chapter on justice concerned its administration, including limitations on the jurisdiction of the royal council, the prohibition of courts half of whose members were Huguenots (*chambres miparties*) from trying cases involving ecclesiastical rights, protection of the rights of seigneurial and ecclesiastical courts, lowering taxes involved with judicial administration, and abolishing venality and unnecessary officials, as well as combining smaller royal jurisdictions. Three articles called for decent wages for judicial officials so that they would not charge money for carrying out their duties. Twenty articles were directed against the abuses of judicial officials, especially those brought about by close family relationships between judges or judges and plaintiffs. The clergy's reaction to the problems of the judicial process led them as far as a request that lawyers be required to 'plead modestly without injuring or offending' those involved in the case under pain of disbarment. No judicial official was to overcharge for services. Minor articles in this chapter included a statement that collectors of the *gabelle*, who were too numerous, should not have the right to search houses. The crime of forgery was to be curtailed by forbidding masters of penmanship to teach a standard form of writing.[14]

The clergy's feelings towards the Huguenots were expressed throughout the *cahier*. In the chapter on administration seven articles concerned relations between Huguenots and Catholics. One requested that Béarn and Navarre be made part of France and that Catholicism be re-established there. Another called upon the government to protect Catholics in Pau. The clergy asked for

[13] Arts. 203, 202, 207–208, 220; 197–199; 201; 152–153, 163. L & D, pp. 109–110, 116–117, 108–109, 90–91, 95. The last proposal may be connected with the plan presented to the Royal Council, the City of Paris and the Estates General by François du Noyer. *Proposition, advis et moyens* ... (Paris, 1614), *Ce sont icy partie des moyens* ... (Paris, 1614) see footnote 32 below. It might also be the result of the plan of one, Barillier. See Bibl. Ars., MS 4255, fols. 48r–49r.

[14] Arts. 222–224, 259; 246, 255; 257–258, 264; 225; 227; 228; 252; 233–235; 230–232; 238–242; 249–250; 270; 260–261. L & D, pp. 118–137. The quoted words are on page 125.

the suppression of the Huguenots' *villes de securité* because the time limitation stipulated in the Edict of Nantes had expired and because they were no longer necessary. All but two of the thirty-two articles of the chapter on infractions were devoted in some way to the Huguenots. Eighteen dealt with restrictions that the clergy wanted. Huguenots were not to be permitted to have any seminaries or colleges, no foreign Protestant teachers were to be allowed entry into France, Huguenots were not to possess or allocate benefices. Their courts were accused of being too lenient. Royal officials were to be permitted to attend the Huguenot political and religious assemblies. All preaching was to be in French and only in restricted areas. Huguenots were not to be buried in ordinary cemeteries. In fact, the clergy called for the banning of *La religion prétendue réformée* in France, and if this were not possible, as they seemed to realize, then the Huguenots were not to have any more rights than they had had at the death of Henry IV. Seven articles in the chapter on infractions were concerned with such matters as those who became Huguenots, especially those who did so for tax purposes or those clerics who became converts to escape ecclesiastical punishment. The King was asked to send commissioners to check into the many local complaints against Huguenots. Finally, the Huguenots were to return church property and rebuild the churches they had destroyed since 1598.[15]

The general *cahier* of the Second Estate was presented in 436 unnumbered paragraphs organized into four chapters, 'On the Church', 'On the Nobility', 'On Justice and Administration', 'On Administration'. At the end of the *cahier* particular requests of the nobles of nine of the *gouvernements* were added, which asked for maintenance of special privileges of certain areas and solutions of special problems. The first twenty paragraphs of the *cahier*, covering the equivalent of twelve quarto pages, presented a general program of reform. These pages were the result of the conference between the First and Second Estates to decide on what were the most important articles – a conference that the Third Estate had declined to attend.[16]

---

[15] Arts. 138–143, 147; 295, 281, 285, 294, 299; 287, 289, 278, 280, 283, 273; 271; 279, 286, 272, 300; 296. L & D, pp. 84–86, 88, 137–149. At least three bishops (Beraudière, Cornu de la Courbe and du Sault) had to rebuild cathedrals destroyed by the Huguenots during the Wars of Religion. Du Perron and Hurault de l'Hôpital had both been Huguenots in their early life.

[16] The original of the *cahier* of the First Estate evidently included a similar section; see A.D. Ile-et-Vilaine C 3793, fols. 1r–10r and B.N. MS fr. 3718, fols. 1r–9r. See also PV–1, pp. 530–543. Two signed contemporary copies of the *cahier* of the Second Estate exist, one made by Jean Hurault de l'Hôpital, the *seigneur* of Gommerville, who was the deputy from Nemours, B.N. MS fr. 3716, fols. 1r–63v, and one signed by the secretary of the Second Estate, Raymond de Montcasin, in A.A.E. France 769, fols. 230r–301v. The text in L & D is again used though it is incomplete, lacking most of the particular requests at the end. For these the copy of Montcasin preserved by Richelieu is used (A.A.E. France 769, fols. 286v–301v). The articles in the *cahier* of the Second and Third Estates are not numbered.

After a long section in praise of the King and Queen Mother and the Regency government and a protestation that they were presenting the *cahiers* only as counsels, remonstrances, and supplications, followed by a reminder of how loyal the nobility had always been and how well they had served the King, the reform program was presented. The Queen Mother should be kept as head of the Council. Regicide must be condemned by renewing the decree of the Council of Constance. The Catholic religion should be maintained and the decrees of the Council of Trent should be published and received in France (always preserving the rights and privileges of the Gallican Church). The Spanish marriages should be carried out and the present alliances maintained. The private and state councils should have sixty-four members with four ecclesiastics, eight nobles and four nobles of the long robe serving in each three-month period. There should be no selling of offices in the army or royal household, *survivances* should be abolished, as should the *paulette*. Judicial offices should be reduced to the number in existence during the reign of Francis I. The number of the treasurers of France should be reduced to two in each province because their wages were depleting the treasury. The job of the *élus*, collecting the *aides* and *taille*, should be performed by royal officials and ordinary judges. These men should be given sufficient wages and not permitted to accept any payments from those they dealt with. In providing for all this the nobles asked that the proposals of Claude Beaufort be considered. Extraordinary commissions should be revoked as well as new edicts. Provinces should be permitted to replace the *gabelle* by an annual payment to the King. Since the King had agreed to set up a chamber of justice to look into the abuses in the management of finances, this should be instituted immediately. Some of the members of this chamber should be from the Estates General. The money ordinarily given to the officials whose positions were to be abolished should be used to pay the expenses incurred in the investigation of the financiers. The expenses of the King's household were not to be increased. The companies of soldiers were to be reduced to the number that existed at the beginning of the year 1609. The officials that Louis XIII had as Dauphin should be given to his brothers and sisters. One-half of the money destined for roads and bridges should be set aside for unexpected projects; then ordinary and extraordinary *tailles* could be reduced by one-quarter. Pensions of ladies and gentlemen of merit should be equitably regulated and those given to officials of justice and finance should be suppressed for the benefit of the people. So that the nobles could serve the King, the *compagnies d'ordonnance*, which were the permanent part of the army, were to be maintained at the same strength as in the time of Henry II. Only officers or soldiers with the rank of captain were to be admitted to these companies, and they were to be supported by the *taillon*. One-third of the sovereign courts and other offices should be filled by gentlemen of extraction'. The Jesuits should be allowed to teach in their

183

Collège de Clermont and to build other colleges as long as they submitted to the laws and statutes of the universities and towns. Anyone who proposed new means to tax the people or to create new offices or edicts should be declared a criminal and punished as such. The nobles felt that one of the greatest evils in France was the diminished value of money. The clergy and nobility had been especially hurt by this because they possessed the right of quit-rent (censive). In the last two hundred to three hundred years, they said, their effective income from this right had diminished by one-fourth. The value of all money should be regulated and kept constant. All merchandise, wages, and rents should be priced in proportion to the écu, and quit-rent should be paid according to the new values.[17]

After this fine if somewhat jumbled summary the cahier of the nobles wandered around from subject to subject though the chapter divisions were more strictly adhered to than in the cahier of the First Estate. On the whole the cahier of the Second Estate was a fight for feudal privileges, conducted especially against the judicial power of the Third Estate. The nobles wanted the commoner judges and officials to be put in their proper place, far below the nobility. When the cahier of the Second Estate mentioned the salt-tax and the abuses of the collectors of this tax, the King was not simply asked to provide reform. The usual form of polite request was replaced by deeply felt pleading that the nobles be spared. There is no doubt that the lower ranks of the nobility, its majority, were speaking. All of the articles of the introduction were repeated in the other chapters, sometimes with a loss of force or with implicit modification, showing that the first section was grafted onto the cahier.

The first chapter of the main body of the cahier, 'On the Church', was much more critical of the clergy than was the introduction. The first of the fifty-two paragraphs was the one that had caused so much trouble for the Huguenot deputies in February. It asked the King to 'maintain and inviolably preserve in imitation of your predecessors, the very Christian Kings, the Catholic, Apostolic and Roman religion' as he swore to do at his coronation. Ten paragraphs concerned the abuses of holders of benefices. No one should hold more than one benefice with care of souls. Holders of benefices should see to the instruction of the people, and should make the necessary repairs of the buildings entrusted to them. Archbishops were to carry out ordinations on prescribed days and personally examine the candidates. Seminaries were to be established and supported by ecclesiastical benefice-holders. There should be no charge for the administration of sacraments. Other paragraphs asked that no mendicants be given benefices, that nuns be closely supervised, that all abbots live in their monasteries, and that the excess funds of the monasteries be assigned to the care of the poor. The Jesuits were to be permitted

[17] L & D, IV, 166–177. Money regulation was a major concern for the Second Estate in 1614.

to reopen their Collège de Clermont. A close accounting of the records of the receiver of tithes was to be maintained. Nine paragraphs in the first chapter were devoted to the rights of the nobles. Only nobles were to be admitted to royal foundations, one-third of all benefices in cathedral and collegiate churches were to go to noblemen, the poorer nobility were to be given oblate-ships in the monasteries, and nobles' prerogatives in parish churches were to be protected.[18]

The nobles used eighty-four paragraphs to discuss their own order. There was no self-criticism; rather, there was a sense of desperation in the twenty-eight requests that their privileges be maintained. They began the chapter by asking for the preservation of all their 'honors, rights, franchises, immuni-ties, prerogatives . . .'. The nobles were always to be first in honor. Those living in towns were not to be taxed as the inhabitants were. They should be given their rightful places in the King's household. One-third of all officials of justice and finance should be nobles, all *baillis* and seneschals were to be nobles, and, most importantly, the nobles should hold all significant military positions. The navy was to be enlarged and the officers drawn solely from the nobility. Eighteen paragraphs were devoted to the re-establishment of the power of the *baillis* and seneschals.

Seven paragraphs in the chapter on the nobility were directed against those who pretended to nobility, including those who bought land formerly belong-ing to nobles. All letters of ennoblement given less than 30 years before were to be revoked unless the holder had performed important military services. No one was to pretend to the title of *écuyer, chevalier, or messire*. Judicial and financial officials were not to be made nobles. Interestingly, another paragraph asked that appointive positions should not be passed from father to son because the son is not necessarily as good as the father. A long paragraph complained of the hunting rights pretended to by the inhabitants of the towns. The King was asked to pay no attention to what the Third Estate had to say about noble justice, because what the nobles possessed they had because of long service to the King and at the price of their blood.

On duels the Second Estate said that they needed some system of reparation and satisfaction for injuries to their honor. The marshals of France should devise the system, but even then dueling should be permitted when the offense to honor was very great. The King was also asked that the nobles be per-mitted to engage in large trading ventures without forfeiting their nobility.[19]

In the eighty paragraphs of the chapter entitled 'On Justice and Adminis-

---

[18] L & D, IV, 178–187. The quoted words are on page 178. The emphasis on the bishops found in the clergy's *cahier* is not to be found in that of the nobles.

[19] *Ibid.*, pp. 188–205. The quoted words are on page 188. The general *cahier* of the nobles took a more lenient stand on dueling than the extant local *cahiers*.

tration' the greatest emphasis was placed on the sums of money that the judges made from their cases, the violations of the edicts involved in some of their practices, such as hearing cases of near relatives or hearing cases without a full complement of judges present, and the length of the judicial process. The *Parlement* was to be forbidden to discuss the decisions of the King's Council without the permission of the Council. Two nobles of the sword were to be admitted to each *parlement*. The nobles seemed to trust the lower royal courts more than the *Parlement* and non-royal, non-noble courts, but royal judges were to be forbidden to interfere with the rights of nobles possessing 'high justice'; nor were judges to buy seigneurial land within their own jurisdictions. Officials' salaries in general were to be lowered, the number of offices diminished, extraordinary commissions abolished, and the *paulette* revoked. Limitations on the power of the procureurs, *advocats*, sergeants and other officials were detailed. Presidial seats were to be done away with because they had served no real function. The aim of these reforms was cheaper justice, simpler processes and protection of the nobles and peasants from arbitrary treatment. The nobles felt that the best means of saving the nobles and people from the money grabbing and tricks of the judicial officials was to appoint more nobles to these offices.[20]

The last chapter of 180 paragraphs entitled simply 'On Administration' was a vast hodgepodge of requests. Its primary aim was to encourage the government to protect all the privileges of the nobility, especially the feudal privileges. To this end the nobles requested a multitude of reforms of royal officials, protested excessive taxation, and attacked the 'pretended' privileges of the officials of the Third Estate. Various proposals for moral reform were interspersed. These included means for protecting the young from places of debauchery, enforcement of stringent rules on hostelries, and the putting of vagabonds to work in the royal galleys. Disabled veterans were to be given support and the poor were to be cared for. Feudal rights such as seigneurial justice, banalities, and rights over common land were supported. The nobles'

---

[20] *Ibid.*, pp. 205–222. A *procureur* was a prosecutor or plaintiff's lawyer; an *advocat* (*avocat*) was the defendant's lawyer; presidial seats (*siège presidial*) established in 1552 were organized in some of the *bailliages* and *sénéchaussées* and consisted of lieutenants general and particular, civil and criminal and seven councilors. These courts could handle small civil cases and the same criminal cases as a *bailliage* court. They also could receive appeal cases from inferior tribunals and the *bailliages*. The purpose of their existence was to serve as a step between the *bailliage* and the *parlement*, to cut down the number of appeals to the latter body, and to limit the intervention of the sovereign courts. Because of the limitations of these courts, for example they could not try questions of feudal law, and because appeal was often possible from them, they did not work as had been hoped, but often simply added another part to an already complex judicial system. Doucet, *Institutions*, 1, 264–267, 11, 529–530, 537. There are frequent requests for their suppression in local *cahiers* in 1614 and in the *cahiers* of previous Estates General.

rights to such positions as *bailli* were again emphasized. Royal officials were not to have exemption from the *taille* though the *metayers* of the nobles were to be free of it in personal *taille* areas with regard to the noble land they farmed, as were nobles who bought common land. Officials were to be qualified for their positions, the number of offices reduced, fees for services lowered. Anything of recent origin that harmed the nobles was an abuse, but any privilege, exemption, or right that the nobles had held for thirty years was to be incontestable.

The nobles were interested in plans that would aid internal commerce such as free trade within France and the use of boats on all navigable rivers. But with the exception of the Normans they were not interested in foreign commerce. For example the *cahier* asked for more galleys along the coasts of Provence but the reason cited was to add to the grandeur of the King and to protect the commerce of Provence.

Taxation, especially the *gabelle*, to which the noble deputies devoted twenty paragraphs detailing abuses in the various parts of France, was the source of much complaint. The nobles' attitude toward taxation and to the whole state of affairs which they found confronting them was summed up in a long dirge addressed to the King. 'It is a strange thing to your nobles, Sire, to be called before commissioners like criminals to render account under constraint of the number of children and servants they have, the pigs that they have killed each year ... and to have to take salt from storehouses in whatever quantity it pleases the commissioners. Your nobles were not treated in this manner under Clovis, Philip Augustus, and Louis XII.' The best way of keeping the loyalty of the nobility, the deputies said, was 'to let us live in our old liberties or at least let us not be reduced to wearing a yoke ... to enrich certain harpies, partisans and enemies of this state and those that favor and support them'.[21]

The large, very detailed *cahier* of the Third Estate contained 609 unnumbered paragraphs divided into eight chapters: 'On the Estate of the Church', 'On Hospitals', 'On the University', 'On the Nobility', 'On Justice', 'On Finances and Domain', 'On Suppressions and Revocations', 'On Administration and Commodities'.[22]

The Third Estate in its *cahier* consistently favored the jurisdiction of royal officials to ecclesiastical and seigneurial officials. The deputies accepted the prerogatives of the first two estates but wished to prevent both the abuses of these rights and the extension of them beyond what they considered to be

---

[21] L & D, IV, 222–260. The quoted words are to be found on pp. 248–249. The pamphlet *La noblesse françoise au chancelier* (n.p., n.d.), despite its pretensions, does not represent the views of the noble deputies in 1614.

[22] The best MS copy of the *cahier* of the Third Estate is one made and signed by Hallé, the secretary of the Third Estate. A.N. K 674, no. 15, fols. 1r–118r. L & D was found accurate and is cited below.

187

an acceptable limit; though the definition of that limit would be hard to express precisely. The deputies of the Third Estate, like the clergy and nobles, favored themselves in their *cahier*. But the charge of historians that the *cahier* of the Third Estate overly favored royal office-holders is not true. The peasants and town workers got little attention but the views of the merchants and town officials were distinctly represented in most chapters. In addition, the royal government was severely taken to task in a complicated series of articles that ranged from requests for minute adjustments to blanket condemnations of the judicial and financial procedures. The refusal of the Third Estate to be dictated to was evident even in the introduction to the *cahier*. The Queen Mother received the usual praise but the deputies immediately pointed out that there were troubles in the kingdom and that it had been thirty years since the Estates General had last met to reform the country. The deputies of the Third Estate asked forgiveness if they spoke somewhat boldly, but felt that the situation demanded it. Only then was support given to Marie's policy for the Spanish marriages and foreign alliances and that in weak terms.[23]

The Third Estate set aside the first five of the paragraphs of its *cahier* as 'fundamental laws'. The first of these was the article on the authority of the King, which in accord with the King's command, was not included. But it was noted that the King had already received the article and that he had promised a reply when he answered the other articles of the *cahier*. The Third Estate asked for a meeting of the Estates General every ten years. All leagues and associations with foreign princes or lords without the consent of the King were to be forbidden, and there was to be no forgiveness for joining such a league. No one was to hold a pension from a foreign prince under pain of *lèse majesté*, and none of the King's domestics or officers were to receive pensions from any prince, *seigneur*, or community. Finally, there was to be no levying of troops or gathering of arms without the King's permission under pain of *lèse majesté*. This section ended with a request that the King 'respond to and decide on [answers to] the *cahiers* ... before the deputies of these estates depart'.[24]

In the chapter on the Church, the Third Estate agreed fully with the First Estate that there was need for reform of the clergy. But the Third Estate in its seventy-two paragraphs relied on its own experience and the provisions of

---

[23] L & D, IV, 270–273. The other orders supported both the marriages and the alliances more wholeheartedly in their general *cahiers* though not in the local ones.

[24] *Ibid.*, 273–274. The last request is a continuing theme in the *cahiers* of all estates on all levels. The other requests in this section with the exception of the first are found in a number of local and governmental *cahiers* of both the clergy and nobles. If comparisons were to be made to the requests of bodies similar to the Estates General in other countries these fundamental laws would serve as a prime example of a major difference – in France royal power, not the rights of individuals, groups or localities, receives the major emphasis.

the Ordinances of Orléans and Blois rather than the decrees of the Council of Trent, with the same general results. For example, seminaries should be built (article twenty-four of the Ordinance of Blois), and clandestine marriages prohibited (article forty of Blois). The major difference between the ecclesiastical reforms proposed by the First and Third Estates was that the Third Estate put more emphasis on reform of the *curés*, their education, payment and their attention to the education and care of the people. Another difference, in emphasis rather than intent, was the frequent request that benefice-holders, abbots and priors, be French. Complaints of the parishioners about their *curés* were to be addressed to royal judges rather than to ecclesiastical courts; it was felt that the latter were failing to do their job well. The Jesuits were mentioned, but in a different context, 'Jesuits are bound by the same civil and political laws as are other religious living in France.' The clergy were to be reminded that hunting, business, tax collecting, and law, other than canon law, were not their concerns. Nor were the clergy to be permitted to buy back church property that had been alienated. Better church records were to be kept, business was to be forbidden on Sundays, and several marriage regulations were to be instituted.[25]

The thirteen paragraphs that the Third Estate provided in its chapter on hospitals supported control and administration of these institutions by local judges and officials except where royal foundations were concerned. The power of the King's grand almoner was to be restricted. The sick and poor were to return to their place of origin where they were either to support themselves by work or, if this were impossible, be taken care of by local officials. Benefice-holders were also to pay what was required of them for the maintenance of these people. Oblateships in monasteries were to be given to poor gentlemen, captains, and wounded solders without their having to live in the monasteries.[26]

When the Third Estate turned its attention to the universities in a chapter of thirty-two paragraphs, its main complaints centered around the re-estab-

[25] *Ibid.*, 274–292. The quoted words are on page 283. The Third Estate was as interested in marriage regulations as the Second Estate was in inheritance laws. More articles on this subject were in the chapter on justice. The greatest concern was marriage without parental consent. *Ibid.*, 284–285. See the decree of the *Parlement* of January 29, 1615, on this matter in A.N. AD+158, no. 7. The nobles agreed with the clergy concerning the Jesuits and to a limited extent concerning Trent. The Second Estate also emphasized the nobles' rights to ecclesiastical positions. Otherwise they agreed with the reforms and the spirit of the reforms of the Third Estate. Perhaps the reference to clerics and law was based on the fact that so many clerical deputies in 1614 had law degrees.

[26] L & D, IV, 292–296. The nobles would completely endorse this chapter. The great objection of all three estates was to the *Chambre de la Charité* established in 1606 which gave the power for reform of hospitals to royal officials and the Grand Almoner of France. The *Chambre* existed from 1607 to 1673. See footnote 3 above.

lishment of the laws of good order, administration, and teaching (fourteen paragraphs). Professors were to retire after twenty years of public teaching, but they were to retain their privileges and be given a benefice for their support so that they could turn their attention to public administration or writing. The eternal complaint of the bourgeoisie about the rowdiness of students was repeated in this chapter. Most of the trouble, the deputies thought, came during the election of student officers which should be forbidden. The students were to be formally registered, take regular examinations, and be forbidden to carry swords, guns, or knives. The Third Estate also called for preliminary education in the humanities before admission to the faculties of law, medicine, theology, or arts. No minors were to be permitted to study outside of France without the permission of the King. Four articles were included on regulations for printing books, including the necessity of *imprimaturs* by royal and ecclesiastical officials and the inclusion of the name and location of the publisher. Magicians and astrologers were to be punished and the King's first doctor was to be shorn of his power to appoint a barber surgeon in each town of the kingdom.[27]

Sixty paragraphs were devoted to the nobility. The Third Estate was willing that the rights and privileges of the nobility be maintained, even their feudal rights, as long as these were not abused, since the 'estate of the nobles is that among the orders to which has been committed power and management of arms for the protection and defense of the kingdom. . .'. But a noble had to be able to prove his rights, he had to follow all the edicts limiting these rights, and no noble (or royal official) was to be permitted to enter business. The deputies of the Third Estate also proposed four regulations directed against those who pretended to noble rank. Their concern in this matter was at least partly motivated by fear of a proportionately increased tax burden on the non-noble population. The chapter listed seventeen limitations that should be imposed on the nobility, including nine very strict ones concerning dueling. Illegal *corvées*, hunting on sown land, and the keeping of gypsies to frighten the people were among the abuses of the nobility singled out. The King was asked to reduce the expenses of his household, keep stricter accounts, and abolish a number of posts held by the nobles, including the governors and captains of non-frontier towns that had been established since the beginning of the Wars of Religion. Nine paragraphs were devoted to administrative regulations, mostly with regard to governors and their lieutenants general. For example, these men were to live in their jurisdictions, they were not to try to

[27] *Ibid.*, 296–304. These concerns were in general shared by the First Estate. The nobles had only one article on universities, asking that their privileges be maintained. In local *cahiers* universities were a concern only to the inhabitants of university towns, though concern for better education in general was fairly widespread. The barber surgeon concern was evident in a number of towns.

impose a *corvée*, requisition supplies, nor allow gold and silver to leave the kingdom when prohibited by edict. There were six military regulations, which included raising the number of troops to the prescribed levels to take care of nobles and old soldiers. Troops were to be taken into the field only at the King's command and they were to be kept moving from place to place. Four articles called for the destruction of châteaux and fortresses not on the frontiers. The King was also asked to take back the garrisons and territory given to the rebels by the treaty of Sainte Ménehould.[28]

After those fairly homogeneous chapters, the Third Estate came into its own, spending two-thirds of its *cahier* in a meticulous discussion of the administrative, financial and judicial faults of the government. The main burden of the chapter on justice which contained 167 paragraphs was that the jurisdiction of the lower or ordinary and local judges should be respected and that local authorities should be allowed a distinct degree of autonomy. In all cases the edicts and provincial customs were to be followed. All abuses, especially recent ones, were to be abolished. Since there was such confusion in these matters, the deputies said, a committee composed of the King's Council, members of the sovereign courts, and other judges and officials should be established to settle the conflicts and codify in one volume the most necessary and useful laws. The same should be done for customary law.

The various offices, from the Council (five paragraphs) through the sovereign courts (twenty paragraphs) and all the way down to the lowly, hated sergeant, were brought under scrutiny and reforms proposed for each. The membership of the royal council should be reduced and each of the twelve *gouvernements* should be represented. The Council was not to interfere in the judicial process. The King himself was to attend the Council meetings and grant a public audience twice weekly, as Louis IX had done. The sovereign courts' right to confirm royal edicts was affirmed and the King's officials were admonished not to interfere in the proceedings of these bodies. The sovereign courts were to speed up their work, make clear statements, and respect local judges and laws. Relatives were not to serve in the same court.

Seigneurial justice was also to be reformed. Most important, the nobles were to be required to prove their rights to exercise such justice. But the Third Estate did not take up the fight against seigneurial justice with the same

---

[28] *Ibid.*, 305–322. The quoted words are on page 305. All the estates wanted soldiers in the field to keep on the move. Dueling was a serious matter to all three estates. Cf. Jean Savaron, *Traicté contre les duels, avec les ordonnances et arrests du roy sainct Loys* ... (Paris, 1614). Jean Savaron, *Discours abrégé avec l'ordonnance entière du roy sainct Loys contre les duels* ... (Paris, 1614). The request concerning châteaux and fortresses occurs in several local and governmental *cahiers* of the First and Second Estates as well as in their general *cahiers*. All three estates were also concerned about royal officials entering business.

191

determination and at such length as the nobles had in trying to protect it. The deputies also condemned the abuses perpetrated by members of their own estate. The number of judicial offices was to be reduced, venality was to be abolished, and there were to be provisions for sufficient wages and freedom from taxation with all other forms of income limited. The relative ranking and functions of judicial, financial and local officials was to be determined once and for all.

Many unrelated articles were strewn through the chapter on justice. Arrears in feudal dues were to be absolved after ten years, as were most other debts. Vagabonds and pickpockets were to be condemned to flogging, branding and six years' servitude in the galleys for their first offense. A second offense was to be punished by hanging. Those who robbed at night, stole from churches, or picked pockets in churches or courts were to be punished by death. Even the number of syllables-per-line and the number of lines-per-page that registrars were to use in certain documents were provided for. More important, all mortemain and serfdom were to be abolished. Compensation was to be given to the nobles involved by the people freed.[29]

The Third Estate needed 183 paragraphs to treat the royal domain and finances. The subject of the royal domain was quickly dismissed. The King should do all in his power to retrieve all of his domain lost during the troubles of the sixteenth century so that taxes could be reduced. In addition Navarre and Béarn were to be declared to have been part of France since the time of Henry IV. However, no one was to try to unite to the royal domain any land that had always been allodial. Any former royal land held by a noble could be bought from him by the people living on that land for the price the noble had paid to obtain it. If the inhabitants did not have enough money, the King was asked to give them half of the sum needed. Restrictions were placed on the selling of wood from royal forests. Several articles were added on other land problems. The most important concerned the payment of the *franc-fief* which was to be greatly restricted.[30]

The theme of the rest of the chapter was that taxes and the wages of the important officials should be reduced to the level of 1576. The number of office-holders should be reduced and those left, particularly on the lower

[29] L & D, IV, 323–373. The complexity of the judicial system of France illustrated by this chapter helps to explain the frustration of the untrained nobles who had to face it. Even the lawyers of the Third Estate were appalled by it. A concrete example of the complexity of the judicial system is to be found in *Police général du royaume de France avec la façon de procéder en toutes sortes de jurisdiction* (Paris, 1617), in Cimber and Danjou, *Archives*, 2nd series, III, 225–258.

[30] *Ibid.*, pp. 373–382. Except for insistence on their own land rights the clergy and nobles would basically agree with this section of the *cahier*. The concern about royal forests is a constant theme in the local *cahiers* of all three estates.

level, should be carefully controlled. To prepare for the new era a thorough
and continuing investigation of all aspects of royal finance and tax collection
was to be initiated. There should be closer supervision at all levels from the
Council on Finances down to the partisans who, all three estates agreed, were
the real villains. No minister of state, councilor, or member of the sovereign
courts was to be permitted to receive any gift or pension from a tax farmer or
partisan. Only native-born Frenchmen were to be officials, and since all in
France were *concitoyens*, there should be no tariffs between parts of France.

The two most important sections of the chapter on finance concerned the
paulette and the *taille*. The King was asked to revoke the *paulette*. Those pre-
sently holding office were to remain exempt from the law of forty days and
were to be permitted to resign their offices to capable persons. However, when
offices became vacant elections should be held to fill them according to the
ordinances of Orléans and Blois. As for the *taille*, it was to be reduced to the
level of 1576 along with the *aides*, *gabelles*, and many other taxes. Means for
making up the money lost to the government because of these reforms were
proposed. Exemptions from the *taille* should be rescinded. The 'great and
excessive' pensions and gifts should be abolished. The number of governors
should be reduced to the traditional level. There should be fewer soldiers
and generally all 'superfluous and extraordinary' expenses should be abolished.
When pensions were given they should be granted only at the end of the year
after all other expenses were paid, and only to those who had earned them.
There was a complaint that the exemptions of certain towns and villages from
the *taille* put a burden on the rest of the country. Further on the Third Estate
partially contradicted itself by asking that these privileges be maintained,
but that people who moved to these towns were not to have the exemption until
they had lived in that town for ten years. Though the *taille* was the most
hated tax, the *aides*, *gabelles* and customs taxes also bothered the Third Estate
greatly. Salt was to be sold in smaller lots for the sake of the poor. The power
of the townsmen in the meetings of the Third Estate is exemplified in the
request that all residents of cities, including nobles and clergy who were
exempt from the *taille*, should be taxed for fortifications, bridge and street
repairs, and the maintenance of colleges and hospitals.[31]

---

[31] *Ibid*, 382–438. The Third Estate specifically called for the dismissal of Denis Feydeau
from his post as farmer general of *Aides*; however, he had passed this office on to his brother
Antoine in 1611. Heumann, 'Antoine Feydeau', p. 183. The word *partisan* was equivalent to
traitant and meant a person who held one of the tax farms of the king. Meuvret, 'L'Impôt',
p. 75. In 1614–1615 the word *partisan* was applied to the lower-echelon tax farmers – those
closely connected with the actual collecting of taxes. In a letter Jules Gassot, the King's
secretary, has preserved a maxim that was applied to the treasurers of the early seventeenth century, *Reçoy avant que tu escrive,/Escry avant que tu délivre,/A recevoir fais diligence/Et fais
tardive délivrance*. Gassot, *Sommaire memorial*, p. xv.

The chapter entitled 'On Suppressions and Revocations', complemented the two preceding chapters and was in effect a list, composed of fifty paragraphs asking for suppression of offices. The list started with certain officials in the King's household such as secretaries of the King's chamber, and went from there to the sovereign courts, whose officers were to be reduced to the number called for in the Ordinance of Blois, to the chancellery, and on through the ranks to the registrars and notaries. The offices of provosts of marshals, assistant *baillis* and assistant seneschals as well as all the offices in their jurisdictions were to be abolished. Provisions of the edict of July 1610 which abolished certain offices were to be enforced. Finally, in desperation, the Third Estate said that it could not possibly name all the offices that should be suppressed. The King was simply asked to abolish all new offices. And all those who tried to establish new offices or re-establish ones that the Third Estate had mentioned were to be put to death as 'enemies and disturbers of the general peace of all your subjects'.[32]

The last chapter of the *cahier* of the Third Estate contained sixty-seven paragraphs. Its title was 'On Administration and Commodities', but it was really a collection of leftovers that can be discussed under five headings: local government, moral regulations, sumptuary laws, money regulations and foreign and domestic trade. The major point concerning town officials was that they were to reside in the towns in which they served and that they were to be elected. There was a whole series of moral regulations centering on gambling and the frequenting of taverns. It is tempting to think that this reflected the experience of the deputies in Paris, but in fact this concern was expressed in the local *cahiers* as well, including the request 'that all inhabitants of cities, towns and villages be forbidden to drink or eat in taverns and cabarets'. Sumptuary laws were to be enforced to limit the wearing of silk, gold cloth, pearls and diamonds. Such regulations stemmed both from moral concern and mercantile interest. The deputies of the Third Estate had less to say than the nobles concerning money regulation but they emphasized that money was to continue at the same value and that exchange rates were to be standardized. This same concern for standardization was to be seen in the wish for uniform weights, measures, and sizes and quality of cloth.

Most of the last chapter was taken up with the problems of the merchants. There were to be limitations on the guilds, fair privileges were to be protected, and the activity of foreign merchants was to be restricted. French commerce and merchants were to be protected. Foreign glassmakers in France were to take French apprentices. French ambassadors were to seek the same privileges for French merchants as foreign merchants had in France. The French merchants were to have more protection at sea, especially against Mediterranean

---

[32] L & D, IV, 438–454. The words quoted are on p. 454.

and English pirates. The Mediterranean galleys particularly were to be more active. All French merchants were to have the right to trade throughout France, in Canada, and elsewhere inside and outside the kingdom. Within France roads and navigation were to be improved. The import of merchandise made of gold, silver, or cloth was to be forbidden. Blasphemers, pickpockets, and vagabonds were to be put to work in French mines. Many of the regulations were minute in their prescriptions. For example the materials to be used to dye wool black and the conditions under which a butcher could sell his meat within a city were set down.[33]

At first reading, the *cahiers* of the three estates seem to be a vast confused mass of requests. Not even within any one chapter is there a logical order. But it soon becomes evident that there are underlying themes in the *cahier* of each estate.[34] Upon close comparison a program supported by all three estates emerges. It is true that the First Estate was convinced of the necessity of accepting the decrees of the Council of Trent and of giving a free hand to the Jesuits and that it was opposed in this by the Third Estate. The clergy saw the Third Estate primarily as the King's *pauvre sujets*, and the nobles did not even deign to grant them a separate chapter in their *cahier*. The First Estate wanted to protect its benefices and tax privileges and the Second Estate wanted to reassert its feudal, honorary, and official rights. The Third Estate wanted to maintain its place in royal and local government and to be freed of part of its

[33] *Ibid.*, 454–475. The quoted words are on page 458. The demands for what became known as mercantilism, evidence of which is found especially in the *cahiers* of the First and Third Estates, received some attention from royal officials. In 1613 restrictions were placed on the import of spices and drugs from the Levant and Spain. *Arrest du conseil d'estat du roy partant règlement pour les espiceries et drogueries qui sont transportées par mer de la Rochelle à Rouen, du quatorzième mars 1613* (n.p., n.d.). *Extraict des registres du conseil d'estat* (n.p., n.d.), both in A.N. AD IX 473, nos. 29, 30. On August 3, 1614, the King named three commissioners to visit the ports and harbors of the kingdom to re-establish the navy. *Lettres patentes du Roy Louis XIII donnée à Paris le 3 Août 1614* (n.p., n.d.) in A.N. K 110, no. 46². Jacques Fresneau and François Du Noyer had tried to interest the Second Estate in schemes for the betterment of sea trading but with no success. Each printed some of his suggestions. Jacques Fresneau, *A messieurs des Estats en la chambre de la noblesse* (n.p., 1615). François Du Noyer, *Ce sont ici autres parties de plusiers autres moyens...* (Paris, 1614). See also L. A. Boiteaux, 'Un économiste méconnu du Noyer de Saint Martin et ses projets, 1608–1639', *Revue d'histoire des colonies*, XLIV (1957) 5–68. Sumptuary laws and regulations on morality were to be found in all three estates. Another example of the type of advice available to the deputies on these general problems is *Advis du Roy* in Cimber and Danjou, *Archives*, series 2, Vol. I, 431–462. For a discussion of this pamphlet, perhaps by Montchretien, see Lionel Rothkrug, *Opposition to Louis XIV: The Political and Social Origins of the Enlightenment* (New York, 1965).

[34] A partially successful attempt to compare the reform program of the Third Estate in 1614 with the other two estates is Benjamin Rivière, 'Le tiers aux Etats généraux de 1614', *Mémoires de la Société d'agriculture, sciences et arts du Departement du Nord*, series 3, V (1893–1894), 227–339. See also Picot, *Etats Généraux*, IV, 173–251.

tax burden at the expense of the other estates. Yet despite all the disagreement coming from these contrary aims, despite all the quarrels, the deputies to the Estates General of 1614 were agreed upon many things. Further, when the local *cahiers* are considered in the next chapter it will be seen that the deputies in Paris preserved the tenor of the complaints and desires of their constituents. The preponderance of bishops in the First Estate and of royal officials in the Third Estate had an effect on the *cahiers*, but not an overwhelming one. Most evident in the general *cahiers* is the support that the royal government won in its opposition to Condé. The final statements of all three estates show absolutely no sympathy for Condé or for rebellion by any group. Pensions were decried, despite some reservations on the part of the nobles, the destruction of châteaux and fortresses not on the borders was advocated, and Condé was to be required to return the territory given him as security until the Estates General should meet. Most important, the Spanish marriages and the alliances formed by Marie de Médicis were explicitly approved by all three estates as was her Regency. Even the somewhat reluctant Third Estate supported the government's policies.

Marie de Médicis and her advisers had been successful in their gamble to defeat Condé by giving him what he wanted. They had anticipated his request for an Estates General, had manipulated the elections, and had arranged to put the Estates General under the control of the Queen's picked leaders: De Sourdis, Senecey, and Miron. But beyond this repudiation of Condé the deputies had other ideas. They went beyond what the government wanted of them. The kingdom needed reform, and it had needed reform, so the deputies felt, ever since the Wars of Religion had begun, even since the death of good King Louis XII. They were determined to provide the basis for that reform.[35]

All three estates were convinced that the Church needed reforms. Despite the Third Estate's rejection of the proposal that the decrees of the Council of Trent be accepted in France all the estates wanted better-trained clergy. They wanted worthy holders of benefices who were clerics, who saw to the education and care of the people, and who were French. The parish clergy were to be paid a decent wage and live celibately and soberly. It was agreed that the charitable institutions needed better management, and that this management could best be accomplished at the local level, though there was disagreement as to who should arrange this. All agreed that life should be simpler and that gambling,

---

[35] J. Russell Major is right when he says that in distinction to other meetings of the Estates General since 1558 the government managed to secure an Estates General favorable to the government in 1614. Major, 'Royal Initiative', pp. 253–255. Yet 1614 was a part of the longer process in that the deputies produced reform *cahiers* despite the government.

drinking and unnecessary personal expense should be curtailed.[36] The clergy and Third Estate saw the need for reform in education and the regulation of universities, and the nobles proposed nothing to oppose this. Some of the local *cahiers* of the Second Estate supported these educational reforms. That the rights and privileges of the nobles should be protected was agreed upon, though there was a difference of opinion as to the extent of these rights and privileges. All the estates called for the abolition of extraordinary commissions and a statute of limitations on debt payment and tax arrears. The *paulette* and venality of office in general, especially the selling of judicial offices, met with universal condemnation. All three estates held that justice should cost less and that judicial procedures should be less complicated and less open to corruption. The Third Estate insisted throughout the meeting of the Estates General that abolition of venality of office should be accompanied by abolition or reduction of pensions, which in the end was agreed upon by the other estates. The second measure proposed by the Third Estate was lowering of taxes, which the other two estates also accepted, especially as regarded the *taille* and the *gabelle*. The three orders even agreed in general on an elaborate plan that should be followed to make tax reduction possible. Pensions were to be reduced, the royal domain was to be re-established, unnecessary offices were to be abolished, the treasury officials and tax collectors were to be investigated and compelled to be honest, and as many middlemen as possible were to be removed from the tax-collection hierarchy.

The deputies of the Estates General of 1614 wanted a better organized state, a centralized state with clearly defined organs of government led by a strong monarchy. The privileges of its component parts should be respected, but the state was to take active measures against its internal and external enemies and against wrongdoers. The deputies wanted a state that regulated trade and that protected the rights of Frenchmen. They wanted a more effective army and they wanted peace. Above all they wanted their reform program to be enacted and to remain in force. To accomplish this old laws and procedures should be codified and simplified. In the future better records should be kept at all levels of government and provincial or national assemblies of some sort should meet regularly to review progress.

[36] For connections between sumptuary laws and mercantilism, see Paul Lacroix, *XVIIe siècle: Institutions, usages et coutumes* (Paris, 1880), p. 539 and Cornelius Sippel III, 'The *Noblesse de la Robe* in Early Seventeenth Century France: A Study in Social Mobility' (unpublished doctoral dissertation, University of Michigan, 1963), 236, 245–256. For sixteenth-century attempts to develop mercantilism see Daniel Hickey, 'Politics and Commerce in Renaissance France, The Evolution of Trade along the Routes of Dauphiné,' *Canadian Journal of History/ Annales canadiennes d'histoire*, VI (1971), 133–151.

THE *CAHIERS* IN CONTEXT

The local *cahiers de doléances* prepared for the Estates General of the sixteenth and seventeenth centuries are a most valuable source for the study of French social history between 1560 and 1615. An exhaustive, comparative study of these documents has not yet been made, but it could reveal a fund of information on the state of French society; specifically the evolving attitudes of Frenchmen toward and dissatisfaction with social organization, the judicial and financial procedures of the various levels of government, education, religion, and the economy. The problem would be to use these documents properly. To do so would require a large group of trained researchers and the sophisticated application of computer methods of information retrieval and classification. The purpose of such research would be to identify the basic problems facing the society of the *Ancien Régime* and to trace the variations in response to these problems at different times, localities and levels of society. This information, when combined with the findings of French economic and social historians who depend on other sources of information, could greatly increase our understanding of French society.[1]

This chapter will use the twenty governmental *cahiers*, the 117 *bailliage* and town *cahiers*, the fifty-one guild *cahiers*, the 163 statements of Parisians and thirteen other fragments of local *cahiers* that have been unearthed for 1614, as well as the general *cahiers* of the Estates General of 1484, 1560, 1576 and 1588, the *cahiers* of the Assemblies of Notables of 1617 and 1626, five Ordinances of the second half of the sixteenth century, and the Edicts of 1618 and 1629, to discover to what extent the Estates General of 1614 responded to the complaints of Frenchmen in that year, to what extent the grievances of the general *cahiers* had been modified in the course of a century and to what extent the program of 1614 had been translated into law by 1630. In contrast to the preceding chapter the purpose here is to present only an impression rather than a detailed analysis of the contents of the documents. Any other approach would have entailed writing another book.

---

[1] It is to be hoped that Yves Durand and his colleagues will continue to publish the *cahiers* of 1614, and that he will extend his project to include earlier Estates General. Unfortunately the latest *cahiers* to be published, 'Cahiers de doléances de la noblesse des gouvernements d'Orléanais, Normandie et Bretagne pour les Etats Généraux de 1614', *Enquêtes et Documents* (Nantes, 1971) I, 53–134, were taken from a defective manuscript. The Brittany *cahier* is particularly confused and incomplete.

THE *CAHIERS* IN CONTEXT

The parish, town, *bailliage*, diocesan and provincial *cahiers* for each estate were drawn up in the summer and early fall of 1614. The governmental *cahiers* were assembled by the deputies to the Estates General of each *gouvernement* during November and December as part of their work in Paris. The number of local and governmental *cahiers* that have been found for this study is not enough to permit fully developed answers to the relevant questions; nor have these *cahiers* been compared with the local and governmental *cahiers* of preceding years. No one even knows how many of those exist. But enough can be learned to present several conclusions.

One area in which the record-keeping propensities of the clergy seem to have broken down is in the matter of preserving *cahiers*. Perhaps this was because these documents could not be cited in court cases to maintain their privileges or because the clergy knew only too well that the *cahiers* had little effect on the King. Whatever the reason there are only a few local and governmental *cahiers* for six of the twelve *gouvernements*: Ile de France, Orléanais, Champagne, Guyenne, Lyonnais and especially Burgundy. In two *gouvernements*, Brittany and Dauphiné, all three estates drew up a single *cahier*. For the other four nothing remains.[2]

The concern of the general *cahiers* of the First Estate for the implementation of the decrees of the Council of Trent, reduction of offices, abolition of venality, lowering of taxes, limitation of the Huguenots, resistance to the inroads of royal officials especially in judicial matters, and maintenance or re-establishment of clerical prerogatives was mirrored in these *cahiers*. The local *cahiers* also revealed a basic loyalty to the Regency government.

The *cahiers* of each *bailliage* and particularly of each *gouvernement* leave a separate impression but together they present a clearer picture of the problems of *l'église Catholique, Apostolique et Romaine* in France than can be gained from the general *cahier*. The picture is one of the churches and monasteries damaged or ruined during the Wars of Religion and still unrepaired because

---

[2] Ile de France: *Prevoté* and *vicomté* of Paris in AN G8, no. 635. Orléans: *Bailliage* of Orléans in B.Mun. Orléans MS 541 (427), fols. 46v–52v; *Bailliage* of Poitou in A.A.E. Fr. 769, fols. 180r–190r; Diocese of Angers, *ibid.*, fols. 191r–198v (the last two were evidently preserved by Richelieu who was involved in drawing up the *cahier* of Poitou); the three chapters of Saumur in A.D. Maine-et-Loire, IBG no. 4. Champagne: governmental *cahier* in A.D. Aube G 140 and the *cahier* of the *bailliage* of Troyes, *ibid.*, partially reprinted in Durand, *Cahiers Troyes*, pp. 312–317. Guyenne: *Sénéchaussée* of Bordeaux in *Archives historiques de la Gironde*, x, 7 (1868), pp. 16–24. Lyonnais: Diocese of Clermont in A.D. Puy-de Dôme 2G 746. Burgundy: governmental *cahier* in A.D. Saône-et-Loire C 505, no. 16; *bailliages* of Mâcon, Beaujolais, Bresse and Bar-sur-Seine, *ibid.*, nos. 17, 20, 30, 31 (no. 14 is an imperfect copy of the Mâcon *cahier* despite its title). At the end of the governmental *cahier* of Burgundy there are short excerpts from the *cahiers* of all nine *bailliages*. Unlike the situation in the other two estates the *cahier* of the clergy of the Ile de France did not serve as the model for the general *cahier* of the First Estate.

the benefice-holders, often laymen or even Huguenots (especially in Burgundy and Poitou), used the revenues for themselves. At the same time there was a curious counter-claim that lay officials were trying to charge benefice-holders too much for repairs rather than taking care of the repairs from their own funds. The country clergy were presented as poorly educated and poorly paid, sometimes leading immoral lives, at the mercy of the nobles who disrupted services with disputes over precedence and in general interfered with clerical duties. The monasteries seem to have been underpopulated and in need of repairs, the monks poorly educated and in general need of reform, particularly in the case of the Benedictines and Augustinians, a number of whose houses were independent of any centralized authority.

Emphasis on the power of the bishops was found only in the *cahiers* of the *sénéchaussée* of Bordeaux, the diocese of Clermont and the *gouvernement* of Champagne. The reform of bishops was emphasized in Orléanais and Champagne. The Council of Trent was given much less emphasis in the *cahiers* of Burgundy and Clermont than elsewhere. Monastic reform was particularly emphasized in the *prévôté* of Paris, the *bailliages* of Bresse and Orléans, the diocese of Clermont and in Champagne; reform of canons was singled out in Champagne and in Poitou; Huguenots were most feared in the *sénéchaussée* of Bordeaux, the *bailliages* of Orléans and Poitou and throughout Burgundy. Vagabonds were a special worry of the clergy of Champagne and Burgundy; the nobles seem to have caused the most problems for the clergy of the same two *gouvernements*. The poverty of the Church was apparent in the *cahiers* of the *gouvernements* of Orléanais and Burgundy and in Basse Auvergne (Clermont). All in all, the Church seemed to be most in need of spiritual and physical rebuilding in Burgundy, with Poitou, Basse Auvergne and Champagne running a close second. There is a world of difference between the concern about superstition in the *cahiers* of Burgundy and the sophisticated proposals for reform of Church and State in Angers. The *cahier* of Angers, undoubtedly influenced by the active royal councilor Bishop Miron, seems to have served as the model for the general *cahier* of the clergy in matters of office reform and mercantilism. Concern for the reform of monetary policy came from Bresse, Troyes and Paris. The proposal to demolish fortified châteaux not situated on borders appeared in Mâcon and Champagne.

Throughout all these *cahiers* of the First Estate from the rhetorical 'Ô grand malheur' of Bresse to the reasoned proposals of Angers there was a nostalgia for the good old days. The recent past was continually identified as the time of civil war and heresy. The era of Louis XII and Francis I was regarded as a time when all had been well. There was also a sense of concern best voiced by the clergy of Troyes: 'That most of this which we have presented above and asked the King to rule on has already been ordered by former Kings ... '. The only recourse the authors of the *cahiers* had was to ask again and plead that this time the laws that resulted from their complaints should be enforced.

The governmental *cahiers* drawn up by the noble deputies during the Estates General to represent the sense of the *bailliage cahiers* have been preserved for all the *gouvernements* except those where the three estates drew up a common *cahier*. This was evidently the result of an order from the king.[3] Below the governmental level there are two local *cahiers* from both Orléanais and Burgundy and one each from Lyonnais, Guyenne, Ile de France, Champagne and Languedoc.[4]

What is most obvious about all of these *cahiers* is that the general *cahier* was an accurate reflection of the desires of the nobles from all areas of France who participated in the *cahier* formation process. As was the case in the Third Estate the *cahier* of the Ile de France was used as the basis for the general *cahier* with modifications and additions from the other governmental *cahiers*. But it is rare to find an article in a governmental *cahier* whose sense was rejected in the general *cahier*. The most significant omission was the article

---

[3] B.N. MS fr. 4083, fol. 40r. Note of Senecey of August 6, 1615 to the effect that he was ordered by the King to submit the original signed copy of the *cahier* of Lyonnais on that date.

[4] Ile de France: governmental *cahier* in A.N. H, no. 747[2] and in B.N. MS fr. 4083, fols. 44r–61v; Beauvais in B.N. MS Clairambault 742, pp. 17–39. Burgundy: governmental *cahier* in A.D. Côte d'Or 3473 and B.N. MS 4083, fols. 66r–76r; *Bailliage* of Bresse in A.D. Saône-et-Loire C 505, no. 29; Mâcon, *ibid.*, no. 22 and A.C. Mâcon AA 10, no. 38. Normandy: governmental *cahier* in B.N. MS fr. 11916, fols. 6r–29r and B.N. MS fr. 4083, fols. 78r–101v. Guyenne: governmental *cahier* in B.N. MS fr. 4083, fols. 104r–147v; *Sénéchaussée* of Guyenne in *Archives historiques de la Gironde*, X, (1868), 468–484; Champagne: governmental *cahier* in B.N. MS fr. 4782, fols. 46r–72r; Chaumont-en-Bassigny in B.N. MS fr. n.a. 2080, fols. 1r–10r. Languedoc: governmental *cahier* in B.N. MS fr. 4782, fols. 73r–79r, printed in de Vic, *Languedoc*, cols. 1638–1649; *Sénéchaussée* of Lauragais in B.N. MS Dupuy 658, fols. 197r–203v. Picardy: governmental *cahier* in B.N. MS fr. 4782, fols. 84r–92r. Provence: governmental *cahier* in B.N. MS fr. n.a. 5174, fols. 90r–100v. Lyonnais: governmental *cahier* in B.N. MS fr. 4083, fols. 1r–2v and MS fr. 4782, fols. 1r–29r; Haute Auvergne in *Revue de Haute Auvergne* (1947–1949), pp. 117–121. Orléanais: governmental *cahier* in B.N. MS Clairambault 742, pp. 49–114 and B.N. MS fr. 11976, fols. 1r–19v; Angers in A.D. Maine-et-Loire 1 Mi 11 (R1), printed in *Mémoires de l'academie des Sciences, Belles Lettres et Arts d'Angers* Series 8, I (1957), 89–90; Berry in B.N. MS fr. 3328, fols. 38r–55r. There is another *cahier* in *Archives historiques de la Gironde*, Series 1, XIX, 434–440, supposedly from the *noblesse* of Guyenne given to their deputy Bernard de Cazilis. Who he was or which part of Guyenne he represented cannot be discovered. However the *cahier* has no unusual characteristics. The *cahier* was either for a different Estates General or Cazilis did not make it to Paris in 1614. The *cahiers* of Burgundy, Normandy, Guyenne, Champagne, Languedoc, Picardy, Lyon, and Berry are summarized in a seventeenth-century manuscript now in the Saltykov-Shchedrin State Public Library in Leningrad (Fr. II 79/1–2). This manuscript also includes a number of other *cahiers* for the period 1560–1626. The MS could well have been produced to aid deputies preparing for the proposed Estates General of 1649 or 1651 as were the works of Rapine and Quinet. Of all the noble *cahiers* of 1614 that of Berry is the most often found in various manuscripts.

in the *cahier* of the *gouvernement* of Paris and the Ile de France that corresponded to the First Article of the Third Estate.[5] The practice of the nobles of adding particular requests at the end of the general *cahier* ensured that many local problems would be brought to the attention of the King. An interesting example of this is the request of the nobles of the *bailliage* of Dourdan in the Ile de France that manufacturers of silk stockings in the area be prohibited from hiring able-bodied men since this seriously interfered with the labor supply available for farming.[6] This request was appended to both the governmental *cahier* of the Ile de France and the general *cahier*. When a request was made in only one governmental *cahier* that referred to a concern of the nobles of the whole *gouvernement* or a significant part of it, the article in question was often made a part of the body of the general *cahier* rather than being added at the end. The best example of this is the request from the Second Estate of Normandy that nobles be allowed to engage in large-scale foreign commerce without losing their status as nobles. It is interesting to note that the only other support for this proposal in an extant *cahier* came from the clergy of Angers.

The governmental *cahiers* of the Second Estate all demonstrate a basic loyalty to the monarchy. The only modification of what was evidently a general feeling of the nobles elected to the Estates General, and it was slight, was to be found in the *cahiers* of Champagne and Guyenne. This provides further proof of the success of the royal government's election efforts. On the other hand specific endorsement of the Spanish marriages was rarely expressed in the governmental or local *cahiers* and when ecclesiastical reform was discussed the King was asked to enforce the ordinances of Orléans and Blois rather than to accept the decrees of the Council of Trent. The influence of the royal government and the bishops on the noble deputies in Paris is again evident.

There were significant differences in the attitudes of the nobles of various parts of France toward new nobles, peasants and town dwellers. The only two areas where no strong resentment was shown toward new nobles were Guyenne and Languedoc. The rights of the nobles below the rank of baron were particularly emphasized in the *cahiers* of the *gouvernements* of Orléanais and Languedoc and in those of Beauvais, Chaumont-en-Bassigny and the *sénéchaussée* of Guyenne. The greatest concern for the peasants was shown throughout the *gouvernement* of Orléanais, in Beauvais and particularly in Haute Auvergne which was suffering from famine. A corresponding disdain for townsmen

[5] No evidence of an article of the same tenor but differently phrased that was supposedly in the *bailliage cahier* of Dourdan has been found. See Malingre, *Histoire du règne de Louys XIII*, pp. 458–459.

[6] On the question raised by this article see Miron de l'Espinay, *François Miron*, pp. 135–143, 352–356.

was expressed in the *cahiers* of Beauvais and Haute Auvergne and was also present in the governmental *cahier* of Lyonnais. The nobles of Picardy, Guyenne and Languedoc do not seem to have been particularly concerned about the problems of the peasants. Of all the *gouvernements*, that of Normandy would seem to have had the most homogeneous population, though even here the rights of the old families were emphasized.

None of the noble *cahiers* exhibited any doubt about where the Second Estate stood in the scheme of things, whatever their differences in attitude toward the society around them. The expression of this certainty varied from the relatively modest statement of the deputies of Provence that they were 'plus grandes que les autres Estatz' to the historical survey of the *cahier* of Orléanais, which upheld the position of the nobles as the warriors and law-givers of France since late Roman times. The nobles of Beauvais did not hesitate to use the phrase, 'La noblesse qui est une pureté de sang et comme la quinte essence du genre humain. . .'. The nobles of the *sénéchaussée* of Guyenne warned that unless the nobles' privileges were restored France would be ruined, despite the opinions of some political theorists who did not understand the constitution of France. All the nobles were sure that they had been mistreated and that conditions had been better in the time of Louis XII. The fault lay with the members of the Third Estate who were encroaching on their seigneurial rights and with the royal officials who were stealing their judicial power and attempting to use the fact that many noble records had been destroyed during the Wars of Religion to impose unfair taxation. The final blows suffered by the Second Estate were the lack of sufficient military positions, particularly for the poorer nobles, and venality of office and the *paulette* which made it impossible for the nobles to compete for government positions. There was some realization that nobles needed better formal training to prepare themselves for governmental office but this was tempered by the realization that it would still be very difficult to break into the lines of succession established within families who controlled the important positions. The nobles realized that a related problem was that too few people held too many positions. They repeatedly asked that no one should be permitted to hold more than one charge so that, as the nobles of the *sénéchaussée* of Guyenne put it, 'le gasteau soict plus générallement desparty. . .'.

Not only did the authors of the *cahiers* of the Second Estate know where they should stand in French society and what had happened to them but they agreed on what should be done to restore proper order. There should be a clear definition of who was a nobleman. This could be accomplished by drawing up local lists of those who had possessed noble privileges for at least thirty or forty years and preferably for three generations. New grants of nobility were to be severely restricted. The nobles should be provided with more employment, allowed to live a simpler, less expensive life and severe restrictions should be placed on dueling. Finally the nobles should be protected from royal officials. The noble *cahiers* agreed on a plan for the reform of the general problems of France. There should be no venality of office, lower taxes, far fewer pensions, reforms of the Church based on the edicts of the sixteenth century and freer trade.[7]

There are far more *cahiers* available on all levels (except the governmental) for the Third Estate than for the other two Estates.[8] The framers of the *cahiers* of the Third Estate were a far more diverse group. In the First Estate bishops and chapter members dominated, and in the Second Estate the lower nobles controlled the process. The authors of the local *cahiers* of the Third Estate

---

[7] Davis Bitton's work, *The French Nobility* is too general in scope and too limited in sources to provide sure answers. The book particularly reflects the ideas of the newer, educated nobles. The *cahiers* of 1614 for reasons described in Chapter 3 above represent the views of the older 'ordinary' nobles. The history of the French nobles in the sixteenth and seventeenth centuries has yet to be written, though Labrousse et al., *Histoire économique et sociale de la France*, II (Paris, 1970), has good material for the period after 1660. Further information can be gathered from Jean-Dominique Lassaigne, 'Les revendications de la noblesse de France pendant la Fronde,' *Album Helen Maude Cam*, 1, 267–275. The first half of the seventeenth century especially needs work. When the history is written care will have to be taken to distinguish between the different areas within France and the different levels of the nobility.

[8] Paris and Ile de France: governmental *cahier* in A.D. Morbihan 27 G 4; City of Paris in A.N. K 674, no. 13 published in Picot and Guérin, *Documents rélatifs aux Etats généraux de 1614*, pp. 50–87; a slightly different version is in Guérin and le Grand, *Reg. délib. Paris*, XVI, pp. 99–136; guilds of Paris in A.N. K 675, nos. 7–43, 49, 134, 136, 144, 160–161, 173, 197, 203; individuals in Paris, *ibid.*, nos. 1–6, 46–47, 50–133, 135, 137–143, 145–159, 162–172, 174–196, 198–202, 204–207, 209–211, 213, 215; a number of these are printed in Picot and Guérin, *Documents*, pp. 88–196; *Prévoté* and *vicomté* of Paris, *bailliage* of Ferté-Alais in A.D. Yvelines 6 B 304; *Prévoté* and *vicomté* of Paris, parish of Colombes in Archives de Paris D. 2 B², printed in Georges Grassoreille (ed.), 'Les cahiers de doléances de la paroisse de Colombes aux Etats généraux de 1614', *Bulletin de la Société de l'histoire de Paris et l'Ile de France*, XV (1888), 14–21; *Bailliage* of Vermandois in Bibl. Ars. MS 4255, fols. 60bisr–76r; *Bailliage* of Vermandois, town of Rheims in B. Mun. Reims, MS 1700, fols. 1r–25v; area around Rheims, *ibid.*, fols. 27r–29r; *Bailliage* of Vermandois, secondary *bailliage* of Marle in A.D. Aisne B 503; *Bailliage* and town of Beauvais, originally in A. Mun. Beauvais AA 12 (destroyed during World War II), the two *cahiers* exist in a copy in B. Mun. Beauvais *Collection Bucquet Aux Cousteaux*, LXXXVI, 665–668, 669–688; the two *cahiers* were studied in detail but not printed in G. Monbeig, 'Notes relatives aux Etats généraux de 1614. Analyse des doléances de la ville de Beauvais et des cahiers d'aucune du Tiers-Etat du bailliage de Beauvais', *Bulletin de la Société d'études historiques et scientifiques de l'Oise*, IV (1908), 1–32. Burgundy: governmental *cahier* in B.N. MS fr. n.a. 7255, fols. 165r–200r; *Bailliage* of Mâcon in A.D. Saône-et-Loire BB 78 (an imperfect copy is *ibid.*, C 505, no. 24). The towns of Mâcon, Tournus, Cluny and Saint-Gengoux-le-Royal for the Estates of Mâconnais, *ibid.*, BB 78; city of Auxonne in A.D. Côte d'Or C 3473. The existence of the *cahiers* for Mâcon and Maconnais was brought to my attention by Professor J. Russell Major. Normandy: *Bailliage* of Cotantin, a *cahier* supposed to be in A.D. La Manche but which evidently no longer exists is described in P. Blaizot, 'Jacques Germain', pp. 12–14. Guyenne: *Sénéchaussée* of Périgord, town of St Cyprien in A.D. Dordogne

were peasants and merchants, leaders of the guilds and members of the royal household, local lawyers and important royal officials. This diversity at least partially explains differences in attitude on specific questions. Yet such differences are few and far between. The overwhelming impression gained from reading all of the local and governmental *cahiers* of the Third Estate is one of uniformity. The concerns of the general *cahier* were constantly present: opposition to the *taille* and the *gabelle*, too many royal officials, a too complicated and venal system of justice, a respect for the decisions of previous Estates General, loyalty to the crown, abhorrence of the human failings of the clergy and of their failure to carry out their duties, worry that the nobles asked too much and gave too little or rather that they returned violence. As would be expected the peasants were most worried about poor crops, ruined roads and bridges and about the unavailability of the clergy. Interestingly it is not they but the townsmen who were most upset by the actions of the nobles. This confirms the impression gained from the noble *cahiers*; the real hostility in the

6 C 1; *Sénéchaussée* of Agenois in A.D. Lot-et-Garonne AA 45, printed in Georges Tholin, ed., *Cahiers de doléances du Tiers Etat du Pays d'Agenais aux Etats généraux, 1588, 1614, 1789* (Paris, 1885), pp. 14–53; *Sénéchaussée* of Lannes in A.D. Landes H 23, nos. 87–89. Champagne: preparatory notes for the governmental *cahier* in Yves Durand, *Cahiers Troyes*, pp. 297–300; *cahiers* of the guilds of Troyes, *ibid.*, pp. 291–296; 54 *cahiers* of the *châtellenies* and *seigneuries* of the *Bailliage* of Troyes, *ibid.*, pp. 77–289. Durand did not publish the *cahier* of one village, that of Lévigny, which can be found in B. Mun. Troyes BB 16, no. 2 along with the *cahiers* he did publish. Languedoc: governmental *cahier* in A.D. Herault C 7673, fols. 178r–195r; City of Toulouse, *ibid.*, fols. 168r–174v (also in A. Mun. Toulouse AA 22, no. 58; this copy has two articles added at the end concerning the cloth industry). Provence: governmental *cahier* in A.D. Bouches-du-Rhone C 2068. Lyonnais: governmental *cahier* in A. Mun. Lyon AA 146, fols. 33r–96r; *Sénéchaussée* of Lyon, City of Lyon, *ibid.*, fols. 1r–22v; Bas Pays of Auvergne in A.D. Puy-de-Dôme 5 C Aa 3rr; *cahiers* of thirteen towns of Basse Auvergne, *ibid.*; *Bailliage* of Saint Flour and Haute-Auvergne in A.C. Saint Flour, Chap. V, art. 1, no. 25. Orléanais: *Sénéchaussée* of Anjou in B. Mun. Angers, MS 911 (820), fols. 1r–65v, printed in Albert Meynier, ed., *Cahiers des gens du Tiers Etat au pays et duché d'Anjou en 1614* (Angers, 1905), pp. 27–120; *Sénéchaussée* of Anjou, secondary *sénéchaussée* of Saumur, originally but not now in A.D. Maine-et-Loire, printed in Celestin Port, ed., 'Cahier du Tiers Etat de la sénéchaussée de Saumur aux Etats généraux de 1614', *Revue historique, littéraire et archéologique d'Anjou*, I (1867), 206–210; *Bailliage* of Touraine in Charles de Grandmaison, ed., *Plaintes et doléances de la province de Touraine aux Etats généraux*, pp. 120–157; *cahiers* of 12 towns in Touraine described in Charles de Grandmaison, 'Doléances du Tiers-Etat de Touraine aux Etats généraux de Paris, 1614', *Bulletin de la Société archéologique de Touraine*, VIII (1889–1891), pp. 40–42. (these *cahiers* were originally in A. Mun. Tours AA 6, but they are evidently no longer there or in A.D. Indre-et-Loire); *Bailliage* of Berry, extract in Lalourcé et Duval, eds., *Forme générale et particulière*, II, 184–187; *Bailliage* of Blois in B. Mun. Blois BB18; *Bailliage* of Vendôme in A.N. K 674, no. 18, printed in C. Bouchet ed., 'Cahier du Tiers-Etat Vendômois', *Bulletin de la Sociéte archéologique, scientifique et littéraire du Vendômois*, XI, (1872), 3–44; *Bailliage* of Nivernois in A.C. Nevers BB 21, fols. 133r–140r, described in François Boutillier, 'Documents relatifs aux Etats généraux de 1560 à 1651 et conservés aux archives communales de Nevers', *Bulletin de la Société Nivernaise des sciences, lettres et arts*, series 3, I (1883), 234–235.

provinces was between town and country rather than estates. The same hatred for the town is found in many village *cahiers*; townsmen were buying up all the village property. There was also a hostility directed toward royal officials, but this was shared by all three estates, urban and rural. There were conflicts between local and royal officials, between individual guilds, and between the guilds and other town dwellers; but these conflicts were not serious enough to prevent a fairly united front in favor of a better organized and less corrupt bureaucracy. The specific complaints of the peasants got left behind as the *cahiers* were refined and as their real concerns about poverty were replaced by supposed complaints of the peasants about the nobles. On the other hand the peasants' major complaints about taxation were fairly represented at all levels and if, as a result of the Estates General, taxes had been lowered they would have been happy. The ordinary worker of the town is heard from least often in the *cahiers* of the Third Estate, but the conflicting requests of the members of the various guilds were answered by the local and royal officials joining together to ask for abolition of much of the restraining structure of the guild system.[9] If these latter requests had been heeded the ordinary worker and the more prosperous merchants, especially those involved in inter-city trade, would have been pleased. All in all, the majority of the members of the Third Estate and the majority of the groups that made up the Third Estate would have quite content with the reforms proposed in Paris both by their own estate and by the general program of all three estates.

If one is looking for striking departures from the norm the local *cahiers* of the Third Estate can provide a number of examples especially in questions of an ecclesiastical nature. The only extant *cahier* of the Third Estate which called for an acceptance of the decrees of the Council of Trent in France came from the small town of Billom in Basse Auvergne. The *cahier* of the *bailliage* of Vendôme foreshadowed the French Revolution or reflected the *cahiers* of the sixteenth century when it asked for the election of *curés* by parishioners. If Blaizot is correct, and the document he found is actually the *cahier* of Cotantin, then the Third Estate there called for confiscation of all the temporal revenue of the Church for six years or longer to provide funds to buy back the royal domain and provide for the needs of the people. The *cahiers* from

---

[9] On the question of the *cahiers* of the guilds of Paris see the excellent article of Henri Hauser in *Vierteljahrschrift für Sozial- und Wirtschaftsgeschichte*, I (1903), 372–396. Also see Miron de L'Espinay, *François Miron*, pp. 108–134, 342–351. Though economic questions dominated these *cahiers*, two guilds, the *Bonnetiers* and the *Drapiers* (K 675, nos. 9, 20) presented fully-developed programs of reform. The only other city for which guild *cahiers* have been preserved is Troyes. These were much shorter and only show concern for a few problems of their specific trade, except for an article in the *cahier* of the *marchands*; in the three cases where the same guilds are represented by *cahiers* (*Drapiers, Tanneurs, Tourneurs*) the problems discussed are quite different, but no pattern can be established.

Huguenot areas have little if anything to say about the Catholic Church, but the others, the vast majority, are completely predictable in what they say about ecclesiastical matters.

The memory of the miseries of the Wars of Religion, regional problems (failures of the wheat crop in Basse Auvergne, wine-growing troubles in Champagne), and the need for specific minor reforms are stronger on the local level, but the intent of all the *cahiers* is basically the same. From a desire for uniform weights and measures to a reluctance to spend too much for the support of the clergy; from a fascination with the details of the administration of justice to a desire to go back to the good old days of Louis XII (or the days of Henry II for the more realistic), the *cahiers* of the Third Estate were of one mind.

Three *cahiers* have not been discussed, those of the three estates acting together in Brittany, Dauphiné and the city of Rouen.[10] The effect of the three estates working together to draw up a single *cahier* was to blunt the criticism of each order for the other two The end results were *cahiers* that supported the basic reform programs of the three estates and supported the actions of the royal government.

When the *cahiers* from the parish to the governmental level are compared without making any distinction between the three estates a few patterns become evident. The inhabitants of the eastern and southern border areas of France were naturally the most concerned about securing freedom of foreign trade for Frenchmen, while the Third Estate of these areas from Champagne to Guyenne was also interested in limiting the freedom of foreign merchants coming into France. The areas where there had been troop movements during the early part of 1614 were those most upset about the abuses committed by soldiers.

There is enough material available to make some general statements about conditions and attitudes in seven of the twelve *gouvernements*. For two of these, Languedoc and Provence, there is limited material for the Second and Third Estates only. About Languedoc it can be said that a definite loyalty to the royal government was exhibited in the *cahiers* while there was little concern about new nobles. A bit more can be said about Provence. Loyalty was stronger here, especially on the part of the nobility, who said that anyone who threatened the life of the King through word or deed should be executed along with his father, mother, brothers and sisters, while the rest of his relatives were to be banished. The Third Estate of Provence would have been satisfied if only the guilty

<hr>

[10] Brittany: B.N. MS fr. 4782, fols. 31r–43v. Dauphiné: B.N. MS fr. 3718, fols. 101r–110r. Rouen: A. Mun. Rouen A 22, fols. 422v–433v. For evidence of how the three estates of Brittany worked together see the letters of Guy Goualt to his brother in Rennes in A.D. Morbihan 87 G 4, for example the letter of October 25, 1614.

person were executed, his possessions confiscated and his relatives banished. The two estates of Provence were united in opposition to new nobles and to venality of office. There are some *cahiers* for all three estates in Champagne but the only thing that stands out in all three estates beyond the expected is a concern that the members of each estate should fulfil their functions and stay in their proper place in society. However, this unity is modified by the overlapping claims of the individual estates. All three estates of the Ile de France seemed to have been strongly Catholic and very interested in Church reform. They were especially concerned with monastic reform. There is also no doubt of their loyalty to the Crown. The Third Estate showed no interest in abolishing venality of office. It is tempting to say that the *cahiers* of the Ile de France were more sophisticated in approach and understanding than those of other areas. But when this statement is considered more carefully it is found that the bourgeois of Lyon and the clergy of Angers, to cite only two examples, were every bit as sophisticated as the deputies from the vicinity of Paris. Further, men of learning and talent like Jean Savaron and Florimond Rapine came from the most backward part of France while the individual requests of the citizens of Paris put into the box in front of the Hôtel de Ville were often naive in the extreme. It would be far more accurate to say that men who governed other men were more likely to have a broader view of the problems facing France than ordinary citizens. Further, on the whole, the higher a man was in the hierarchy of either the Church or the secular government the broader his view. Perhaps only in the case of the nobility were those from around Paris more sophisticated than their provincial brethren. A probable reason for this is that the noble delegation from the Ile de France had a higher proportion of the upper nobility and more important officials than the noble delegations from most areas. Those deputies would also have had a greater day-to-day contact with the royal government than the provincial nobles.

For only three *gouvernements* are there enough *cahiers* extant to make it possible to speak with some measure of certainty about conditions and attitudes. In Orléanais the deputies of all three estates showed a distinct concern for reform of the Catholic Church and in the case of at least the first two estates there was distinct hostility shown toward the Huguenots. The *cahiers* from this area also showed a marked concern for the malfunctioning of the royal government though there is no evidence of disloyalty to the crown itself. The *cahiers* of Burgundy in addition to showing the expected concern for the problems of border dwellers confirm that the Catholic Church of Burgundy was in need of both reform and rebuilding and that the Huguenots were a strong force in a number of areas particularly around Mâcon, where the nobles asked that the Edict of Nantes be made a Fundamental Law of France. On the whole Burgundy seems to have been a poorer province than Champagne, but the inhabitants were not in as desperate a position as those of Auvergne in

Lyonnais. Though the Burgundian *cahiers* were concerned with high taxation, on the whole there does not seem to have been as much concern with the royal government as was to be found in most other areas. All of Lyonnais was concerned with the *gabelle*, particularly with the fact that the collection arrangements of this tax forced its inhabitants to pay great sums of money to Languedoc.[11] The Languedoc *cahiers* were almost as insistent that this system continue. Beyond the *gabelle* problem the existing *cahiers* from Lyonnais were split. In the city of Lyon the concern of both the Second and Third Estates was the royal government; specifically, the authors of the *cahiers* complained that their distance from Paris made it difficult to get good government positions. In both Haute and Basse Auvergne on the other hand the overriding issue was poverty; a poverty caused by nature for which no one saw a cure. The result of this poverty was emigration by many, despair for those who remained.[12]

The France of 1614 was large and sprawling; it lacked homogeneity in population, law systems, administrative procedures, tax collection and just about everything else. The rich burghers of the North with their concern for sending the wandering poor back to their place of origin had no understanding of the plight of the farmers of the Auvergne or southern Champagne, nor did the *capitouls* of Toulouse who wanted to condemn the poor to the galleys. There was little love lost between many, if not most, Huguenots and Catholics. The nobles felt that they were under attack from the royal officials and bourgeoisie; the bourgeoisie in turn felt that they were the ones who were suffering – at the hands of the nobility. If the one group in French society whose voice was not heard, the rural *curés* and vicars, had been able to speak through the *cahiers* they would most probably have said that no one understood the strain that poverty and isolation put upon them; drinking, concubinage, disregard for duty were only symptoms of their basic problems. And yet in spite of all the differences of problems, opinions and emphases that have been described in this chapter the three estates of France in 1614 had produced a unified program of reform for France; a program that had the support of the majority of the population of France.

If the major reforms proposed by all three estates in 1614 are compared with the *cahiers* of the Estates General since 1560 and with the major ordinances and edicts since 1561 the immediate reaction is that there is nothing new under the sun. All of the major reforms except a statute of limitations on debt and repeal of the *paulette* had been requested by previous Estates

[11] The *cahiers* contradict the discussion of the *gabelle* in Doucet, *Institutions*, II, 577–587, particularly in the case of the Haute Auvergne.
[12] The emigration from Auvergne to Languedoc is confirmed by Ladurie, *Paysans de Languedoc*, I, 96–97.

General. One other request of the three estates in 1614 had rarely been asked for – abolition of venality of financial offices.[13] What stands out in the reform proposal of 1614 is not its novelty but its inclusiveness and its expertise. No other single Estates General or ordinance had presented such a coherent or well developed program and no previous Estates General had been so unanimous in presenting its program. Thus the major criticism levelled at the Estates General of 1614 by historians is not substantiated by a reading of the *cahiers* and ordinances. The program of reform proposed by the Estates General of 1614 was actually more unified in its requests, despite all the wrangling that went on during the meetings, than that of any preceding Estates General.

If one goes further back in time and reads the *cahiers* of the Estates General of 1484 more light is shed on 1614. Though many of the reforms requested in the *cahiers* of 1614 had been proposed at the end of the fifteenth century the spirit of the single *cahier* produced in 1484 is completely different. The good old days then were the time of Louis IX, the major problem for the clergy was the preservation of the 'rights' of the clergy from the growing control of Rome over Church affairs. Reform was rarely discussed. The nobles were trying to protect their local privileges from the King and limit their military service. The Third Estate was most worried about roving bands of soldiers. Reflections of some of these desires can be found in the *cahiers* of 1614 but they are a pale shadow. In the intervening years France had become more peaceful and centralized. The organs of central government were more fully developed. The change can be traced in the *cahiers* from 1560 onwards. France had already entered into a new period of its existence by 1560 as was shown, for example, by the concern for codification of provincial laws in the *cahiers* of that year. That problem had been largely solved by the beginning of the seventeenth century and was only a minor issue in the *cahiers* of 1614.

The deputies in 1560 began the struggle to understand the new state, but the problems raised by the existence of the Huguenots and the insistence of many deputies on remaining firmly rooted in the past prevented any possibility of unity even within a single estate. More often than not the *cahiers* of 1560 reflect 1484 rather than prefigure 1614.

In 1576 the Third Estate had a somewhat clearer conception of the sources of the problems facing France – the changes in the nature of government,

[13] Some idea of the age and complexity of the problems that faced the Estates General of 1614 solely in the matter of taxation can be seen in Rothkrug, *Opposition to Louis XIV*, pp. 135–144; Jean Meuvret, 'Comment les Français voyaient l'impôt', *XVIIᵉ Siècle*, nos. 25–26 (1955), pp. 59–82; Lublinskaya, *Frantsiya*, pp. 148–156. J. B. Maurice Vignes, *Histoire des doctrines sur l'impôt en France* (2nd ed., Padua, 1961), pp. 148–161, and David Parker, 'The Social Foundation of French Absolutism, 1610–1630', *Past and Present*, no. 53 (Nov. 1971), pp. 67–89.

TABLE 7 *Relationship of the major unanimous requests of the Estates General of 1614 to the requests of other Estates General and Assemblies of Notables and provisions of Royal Ordinances*[a]

	1614	Estates General										Assemblies				Ordinances				
		1484	1560			1576			1588			1617	1626	1561	1563	1566	1579	1597	1618	1629
		1	1	2	3	1	2	3	1	2	3									
Church																				
trained, capable clergy			X	X		X	X		X					X		X		X	X	X
seminaries						X			X											
anti-plurality					X	X	X		X	X	X						X	X	X	X
benefice-holders – clerics		X			X	X	X	X	X	X	X						X	X	X	X
benefice-holders – reside		X			X	X	X	X	X	X	X			X			X	X	X	X
anti-simony			X		X	X	X	X	X	X	X						X	X	X	X
anti-*confidence*					X		X		X	X	X			X			X	X	X	X
anti-*in commendam*[b]								X												
anti-'selling' sacraments		X	X		X	X			X	X	X			X			X	X	X	X
more pay for curés		X	X			X	X		X	X	X			X			X	X	X	X
theological education in parishes									X	X	X									X
elect bishops and abbés		X			X	X			X	X	X			X	X		X	X	X	
bishops and abbés to be French							X		X	X	X						X	X		
visitation by bishops				X		X			X	X				X	X		X	X	X	
monastic reform by bishops		X		X			X		X					X	X				X	X
Hospitals																				
better management		X	X			X	X		X	X						X	X		X	X
poor problems		X	X			X	X		X	X				X		X	X	X	X	X
Universities																				
better regulations		X	X			X	X		X	X				X			X	X	X	X
especially law schools					X		X			X							X			

211

TABLE 7 (*continued*)

	Estates General					Assemblies			Ordinances					
	1614	1484	1560	1576	1588	1617	1626	1561	1563	1566	1579	1597	1618	1629
Nobles														
protect privileges	X	X	X	X	X			X			X	X	X	X
provide royal offices	X	X	X	X	X			X		X	X	X	X	X
provide army positions			X	X	X		X			X	X		X	X
oppose violations committed by nobles		X	X	X	X	X		X			X			
restrict new nobles		X	X	X	X	X		X			X			X
Administration														
Council reform	X	X	X	X	X	X	X						X	
reduce number of offices	X	X	X	X	X	X		X		X	X		X	X
abolish extraordinary commissions	X	X	X	X	X		X	X	X		X		X	
statute of limitations (debt, tax)									X				X	
anti-venality – judicial	X	X	X	X	X	X		X		X	X		X	
anti-venality – financial			X		X	X					X			
anti-*survivance*				X	X									
anti-*paulette*						X								
anti-close relationship	X	X	X	X	X	X		X		X	X	X		X
épices regulation			X	X	X				X		X	X	X	X
cheaper justice	X	X	X	X	X				X		X			X
simpler procedure	X	X	X	X	X			X	X	X	X		X	X
investigate financial officials			X	X	X									
enforce edicts	X	X	X	X	X					X	X		X	X
more Estates General[c]	X	X	X	X	X									X
Finance														
taille lowered	X	X	X	X	X		X						X	
gabelle lowered	X	X	X	X	X									
aides moderated			X	X	X								X	
pensions and gifts reduced	X	X	X	X	X	X	X					X	X	X

taille exemptions reduced
preserve and re-buy
royal domain

Trade
pro-mercantilism
freer internal trade
unity of weights and measures
monetary reform
restrict guilds

Morality
anti-gambling
anti-taverns
simpler life
anti-blasphemy
anti-usury
anti-duels

Other
anti leagues, associations
no business for nobles
sea trade for nobles[d]

[a] Estates General of 1484: Jean Masselin, *Journal … 1484*, A. Bernier (ed.), (Paris, 1835), pp. 661–703. Estates General of 1560: Lalourcé and Duval, *Recueil des cahiers généraux des trois ordres aux Etats Généraux* (Paris, 1789), I; 1576: *Ibid.*, II; 1588: *Ibid.*, III. Ordinance of Orléans (1561): Lalourcé and Duval, eds., *Recueil de pièces originales et authentiques concernant la tenue des Etats généraux* (Paris, 1789), I, 287–329; analyzed in Georges Picot, *Histoire des Etats généraux considérés au point de leur influence sur le gouvernement de la France de 1355 à 1614*, 2nd ed. (Paris, 1888), II, 432–436. Ordinance of Roussillon (1563): François Isambert, ed., *Recueil général des anciennes lois françaises* (Paris, 1829), XIV, 160–169. Ordinance of Moulins (1566): *Ibid.*, 189–212. Ordinance of Blois (1579): *Ibid.*, 380–463, analyzed in Picot, *Etats généraux*, III, 351–365. Edict of 1597: Isambert, *Recueil général*, XV, 120–128, analyzed in Picot, *Etats généraux*, IV, 135; Assembly of Notables of 1617: Charles Joseph Mayer, ed., *Des Etats généraux et autres assemblées nationales* (The Hague, 1788–1789), XVIII, 53–113. Assembly of Notables of 1626: *Ibid.*, 299–312, analyzed in Picot, *Etats généraux*, IV, 273–292 and in Jeanne Petit, *L'assemblée des notables de 1626–1627* (Paris, 1937). Edict of 1618: B.N. Ms fr. 23396, fols. 295r–350r. Ordinance of 1629 (Code Michaud): Isambert, *Recueil général*, XVI, 223–342, analyzed in Picot, *Etats généraux*, V, 118–136. Picot accurately summarizes the ordinances but his tables do not give full expression to the work of the Estates General since he lists only those articles that were actually transformed into law.

[b] Not mentioned by the First Estate in 1614.

[c] Mentioned only by the Third Estate in 1614.

[d] Mentioned only by the Second Estate in 1614.

religion and social and economic structures – and some of the means that could be used to deal with these problems. The deputies of the Third Estate were able to build upon what had already been established by the Estates General of 1560. The nobles of 1576 were more united than they had been in 1560. However, they had little realistic appreciation of the necessary remedies beyond the confines of their own estate. They saw clearly that noble titles were being recklessly inflated and that too many merchants and officials were being allowed to buy their way into the nobility. Caught in the middle were the older rural and military gentlemen. But when it came to the central government they naively proposed the total abolition of the entire financial bureaucracy. The clergy in 1576 were still very bothered by the Huguenots, and though they asked for the enforcement of the reforms of Trent they spent much of their time opposing the application of those reforms by the royal government and insisting on the preservation of their privileges.

By 1588 the First and Second Estates had also begun to work within the context of past Estates General and ordinances. The nobles and clergy were slowly progressing toward a better harmony between the old and new in France. But the immediate pressures of the Wars of Religion and particularly the threat to the old order posed by Henry of Navarre distracted all three estates. Also the clergy and the nobles were still greatly interested in the preservation of local and provincial government. The Third Estate concentrated on the organization of the central government. For example, it maintained the earlier desire of all three estates to have regular meetings of the Estates General while the other two estates regressed to requests for more frequent provincial and *bailliage* estates.

By 1614 the deputies of the three estates were calmer in assessing the problems that faced France and proposed more realistic reforms than had been the case in the sixteenth century. Henry IV must be given credit for lowering the fever of Frenchmen and the Regency government for maintaining this state of health. A sign of the change was the relatively minor role that anti-Huguenot feeling played in the *cahiers* of 1614. The deputies in 1614 were readier to live with the central government and far less concerned with local and provincial rights than deputies had been in the past, though there was general agreement that extraordinary impositions of governmental authority, especially in matters of taxation, had to be resisted. The deputies were more prepared to let each estate lead its own life within the kingdom in spite of the urban–rural hostility that existed and the members of each estate showed less animosity toward other members of their own estate than had been the case in the sixteenth century.

France was changing. The change had begun in the first part of the sixteenth century, was interrupted during the second half of that century, and finally was entering a new phase in the early seventeenth century. But the deputies

214

in 1614 had to look backward in an attempt to take care of the problems of
the France that had been created in the first half of the sixteenth century.
These problems came from bureaucratic abuses that were a natural result of
centralization and from social dislocations that stemmed from economic and
religious changes that affected all of Europe. Extraordinary commissioners
were an example of the first type of problem; the place of the nobility in
society was an example of the second type. What influence did the Estates
General of 1614 have on the future, on the settling of the problems that had
to be taken care of to make a strong central government function well? It had
proposed a comprehensive program of reform and most of that program, with
the important exceptions of reduction of the *taille* and abolition of venality
of office, was included in the Edict of 1618. But interestingly enough the edict
was never registered by the *Parlement* and the King did not force the issue.
In 1629, influenced too much by the Assembly of Notables of 1626 and the
immediate concerns of Richelieu, the Code Michaud ignored most of the
administrative and financial reforms proposed in 1614 to concentrate on
justice, the nobles, the army, the navy and commercial problems.[14] But even
this partial enactment of the program of 1614 fell foul of the intrigues of
government and the resistance of provincial *parlements* and it failed ever to
reach even a minimum observance. Despite this many of the reforms proposed
in 1614 to handle bureaucratic abuse and social dislocation became part of
the program of Richelieu and later of Colbert. Any effort to show that these
men and other reformers were directly influenced by the Estates General of
1614 is probably fruitless, even though Richelieu was part of 1614 and Colbert
made a special study of the Estates General.

Richelieu's *Political Testament* was written in the spirit of the *cahiers* of
1614. There were distinct modifications of the program put forward in the
cahiers that came for the most part from Richelieu's experiences as chief
minister. Thus he defended venality of office as a regrettable necessity. There
were also differences in emphasis. Richelieu, revealing his episcopal background, directed most of his attention to bishops and sovereign courts in
ecclesiastical and judicial matters; *curés*, local officers and peasants were
rarely mentioned in the *Political Testament*. However, when Richelieu turned

[14] The Estates General of 1614 had a measure of influence on the Assemblies of Notables
of 1617 and 1626. Twelve of the deputies in 1617 (23% of the assembly) and eight of the
deputies in 1626 (14%) had been deputies in 1614. The method of selection of the members
of the Assemblies worked against the Third Estate since only representatives of the sovereign
courts were chosen for the Third Estate. Henry de Mesmes, who was at Rouen in 1617 was the
only deputy of the Third Estate in either assembly. The only man to serve in 1614 and in both
assemblies was Bishop Miron of Angers. Three noble deputies of 1614 were at the meeting of
1617 and three others at the meeting of 1626. Thus the clerical deputies of 1614 had
the greatest opportunity to influence subsequent assemblies.

to a discussion of financial abuses he shared the desire of the three estates to reform the system at all levels. Despite the changes and the modifications, to a large measure Richelieu's program was 1614's program. Colbert was further removed from the events of 1614. From a table of past ordinances that he drew up, probably before 1661, it would seem that he was most influenced by the attempts of Barnabé Brisson and Michel de Marillac to draw up comprehensive law codes. Whatever the source of his inspiration many of his reforms were in the spirit of 1614.[15] It is more reasonable to say that the reforms proposed in 1614 were proposed by men who had lived with a system long enough to be able to see what its merits and faults were, and that these men, loyal to the system, had produced a sensible reform program whose merit was obvious to anyone sufficiently instructed in public affairs.

From the moment the Estates General of 1614 ended, criticism was heaped upon the deputies and this criticism has remained accepted dogma. The deputies were accused of failure because they wasted time with ceremonies and arguments over precedence and with fighting among themselves. But such problems were the natural outgrowth of the society of early seventeenth-century France and in the end the deputies overcame these problems. More recent attacks hold that they failed because they did not unite to put pressure on the government during the meetings and thus surrendered France to overbearing absolutism. These charges ignore two facts. The deputies had no experience of overbearing absolutism and did unite on a number of occasions to present special requests to the government, but with no positive result. They had no means to impose their will successfully on a government that chose not to listen. But their major task had been to produce *cahiers* and this they accomplished. The deputies of 1614, looking back over a hundred years of French history defined in their *cahiers* the reforms that France needed: abolition of clerical abuses, restrictions on the unfounded claims of the nobility, rejection of venality of office, reduction in the number of officials, close scrutiny of the remaining officials, and tax reduction. The deputies pinpointed the major areas of concern for a developing strong government: disloyal elements within the state, a poorly organized system of administration, lack of free trade within France, and a confused policy on foreign trade.

They produced an excellent program of reform but the government did not listen. Marie de Médicis' advisers were also looking back and in the light of

<hr/>

[15] Richelieu, *Testament Politique*, ed. Louis André, (Paris, 1948), *passim.*, especially pp. 93–317, 415–449. Colbert, *Lettres, Instructions et Mémoires de Colbert*, ed. Pierre Clément (Paris, 1869), IV, 361–367. Other examples of reforms proposed by Colbert that were in line with the program of 1614 can be easily cited; for example on financial reform see the letter of Colbert to Mazarin of October 1, 1659, *ibid.*, VII, 164–183 or his proposals of 1661 for a Chamber of Justice to investigate financiers, *ibid.*, 195–197, 198–201. Bossuet studied the Estates General of 1614 and was quite probably influenced by it. Fénelon and Malesherbes, opponents of absolutism, both called for another meeting of the Estates General as a check on royal authority.

their long experience they sacrificed the reforms proposed by the Estates General of 1614 in order to concentrate on maintaining the sovereignty of the King and the strength of France against the threats posed by overmighty subjects: Condé, the Huguenots and the *Parlement*. Villeroy, Jeannin and Sillery were successful. But the problems that the reforms were designed to to solve did not go away.

They produced an excellent program of reform but the important provincials did not listen. The members of the provincial estates that still existed were too interested in their own local problems and privileges. The members of the provincial *parlements* did not deign to involve themselves. The clergy were primarily interested in other matters. The local bureaucrats who had not attended the Estates General were too involved in the abuses under attack. The provincials were successful in ignoring the Estates General but the problems that the reforms were designed to solve did not go away.

In later years Richelieu and Colbert were too busy with their own plans for strengthening the government to bother with an Estates General. Besides 1614 had taught a lesson – an Estates General could prove embarrassing to the government. It served to focus the complaints of the people. The Estates General of 1614 failed because it had no means of imposing its will on the government and because the unity of its *cahiers* frightened the upper-echelon bureaucrats. For the first time sensible men from the provinces had united and shown the way to reform, but the reform seemed too dangerous. That could not be permitted to happen again. If it did the bureaucrats might lose control of the situation. They might be forced to try reform which if it worked would lessen their growing power and if it did not might plunge France into civil war. The continuation of the process of strengthening the central government and of ignoring abuses that could not be easily uprooted seemed to be the only sensible choice. When the system of government perfected by Richelieu and Colbert began to fall apart under the double stress of fully developed absolutism and the Enlightenment and when not enough was done to curb bureaucratic abuses or to mitigate the problems of growing social dislocation, the more radical ideas of reform that can be found in a few local *cahiers* in 1614, but which had been fairly common in the chaos of the second half of the sixteenth century, began to receive more support. The end result was the French Revolution. This is not to say that the enforcement of the program of 1614 would have prevented the French Revolution. Too much happened in the 175 years after 1614 for any one event to have had a preponderant influence. But it is at least tempting to say that if the program of 1614 had been enacted the history of France would have been different. Absolutism of some variety would still have come to France. Eventually absolutism would have passed from France. But the change might well have come less violently.

But all that happened in a world that the deputies of 1614 could not have understood. Descartes was only eighteen in 1614. None of the deputies knew what Galileo was doing; few if any of them had read Copernicus. Newton, Bayle, Montesquieu, Voltaire and Rousseau had not yet been born. Bacon was just an English politician, Hobbes an unknown twenty-six-year-old tutor. The world was about to change in 1614, but it had not yet. Neither absolutism nor rationalism, neither deism nor empiricism meant anything to the deputies. Skepticism, yes. They knew Montaigne. But Montaigne was their contemporary; he had lived through the same chaos. Montaigne reacted in disgust; they reacted in hope, hope that reform could save what existed. The deputies and the advisers of Marie de Médicis all remembered the chaos. The deputies used their knowledge of the past in an attempt to reform the confusion of the present, to regain the days of Henry IV or Henry II. The advisers used their knowledge of the past to enable them to preserve the monarchy until better days, days like those of Henry IV or Henry II. The end result was to be Louis XIV and Louis XVI.

Frenchmen in the early seventeenth century felt that they had a clear understanding of where they stood in relation to the past and they wanted to regain that past. The future was seen only in relation to the past. The deputies of 1614 knew what was wrong with their country and if their reforms had been enacted the future of France would have been different. But that could not be. It could not be because the very abuses of the past they wanted to root out had too strong a hold on France. France was too divided and France and the world were about to change beyond all recognition. The men of 1614 were not equipped to understand either the Age of Louis XIV or the Enlightenment. They were limited by their past, they were limited by their assigned role and they were limited by lack of effective support from the important inhabitants of the provinces. But within their limitations they performed magnificently.

218

APPENDIX I

ROYAL INCOME AND EXPENSE
1600–1630[a]

TABLE I *Ordinary income*

Year	Bois	Aides	Gabelles	Other fermes[b]	Parties casuelles	Recettes générales[c]
1600	33,651	408,398	1,676,318	1,012,628	1,644,046	11,433,782
1601	166,880	195,529	1,466,894	891,945	625,006	11,769,213
1602	241,730	554,400	1,923,485	1,019,771	1,314,312	11,140,828
1603	123,285	578,555	2,190,253	1,171,571	1,967,530	11,443,627
1604	108,550	565,442	2,087,894	793,582	1,551,674	11,569,331
1605	160,115	1,062,402	2,239,601	1,516,062	2,324,394	11,683,851
1606	162,600	1,273,431	3,027,788	1,804,459	1,918,067	11,604,326
1607	447,955	1,034,429	3,026,739	1,528,543	1,842,638	11,305,283
1608	278,636	948,940	3,382,375	1,756,787	3,479,592	10,875,301
1609	282,271	1,000,815	3,442,019	1,695,557	2,263,751	10,692,161
1610	267,533	1,060,547	2,991,644	1,472,007	1,668,108	10,364,489
1611	308,144	1,180,104	3,262,726	2,026,911	1,868,082	10,112,643
1612	402,717	1,199,946	3,204,260	2,060,286	2,421,746	10,269,129
1613	342,414	1,207,173	3,042,636	2,374,166	4,797,286	10,396,888
1614	335,209	1,166,455	3,842,930	2,044,994	3,766,285	10,656,733
1615	615,963	1,468,607	3,687,738	2,111,868	2,183,795	10,850,718
1616	277,130	702,831	4,274,795	1,698,909	10,717,400	11,388,551
1617	403,476	1,773,214	4,167,673	1,714,243	6,067,975	10,492,527
1618	342,064	1,114,727	3,833,573	1,778,648	2,569,016	10,544,545
1619	351,806	3,334,888	7,129,782	2,417,798	3,771,836	10,420,201
1620	415,659	733,686	4,290,322	1,989,293	13,267,639	11,446,586
1621	501,364	1,253,418	2,561,199	2,728,853	14,295,607	10,323,760
1622	447,912	1,105,485	5,496,260	1,543,876	20,052,155	9,872,625
1623	388,378	1,040,061	1,987,051	2,187,831	17,419,025	10,021,066
1624	447,252	1,518,702	2,829,385	1,394,820	10,260,198	10,511,524
1625	377,104	1,864,037	1,927,706	2,267,352	16,264,263	6,600,347
1626	637,168	2,020,709	2,150,494	3,345,147	15,692,951	10,090,277
1627	184,965	2,023,442	2,053,611	2,572,881	17,329,473	6,451,240
1628	366,248	2,037,888	4,252,315	3,534,039	11,303,490	7,252,977
1629	515,933	2,251,307	2,336,846	3,484,820	17,090,690	10,212,762
1630	551,791	1,864,610	1,598,662	3,050,107	18,917,005	11,217,606

[a] Derived from Mallet, *Comptes rendus*, pp. 184–185, 190–195, 198–199, 208–211, 218–223. In Appendix I, Table III Mallet's figures are compared with those of Buisseret for 1600–1610 and those in A.A.E. Fr. 768–770 for the years 1611–1616. All sums are in *livres tournois*.

[b] Includes domain revenue, a significant proportion of which, despite its origins, was now farmed out. The other *fermes* were customs duties.

[c] Mainly the *taille*, but includes the *taillon* – Mallet lists this separately; Buisseret erroneously includes *taillons* with *dernières extraordinaires*.

TABLE II *Ordinary expense*

Year	Pensions and gifts[a]	Household[b]	Other[c]	War[d]
1600	2,283,942	2,368,899	2,454,079	6,568,235
1601	2,326,920	2,440,740	3,783,619	3,791,838
1602	2,318,683	2,260,517	3,702,760	4,001,164
1603	2,689,543	2,242,961	3,162,228	3,802,086
1604	2,645,659	2,211,189	3,393,625	1,898,942
1605	3,281,340	2,154,171	3,018,800	4,805,018
1606	3,549,717	2,743,793	2,972,309	5,106,956
1607	3,019,746	2,184,188	5,042,627[e]	4,148,434
1608	3,323,534	2,598,154	3,601,399	4,966,329
1609	3,869,282	2,563,623	3,411,079	4,332,469
1610	4,690,829	3,850,862	3,243,814	8,974,025
1611	6,739,904	2,331,860	3,083,534	4,065,559
1612	7,216,881	3,080,752	3,037,504	5,089,865
1613	7,313,040	2,830,354	3,002,203	5,765,139
1614	6,808,341	4,551,660	3,054,547	7,550,224
1615	5,224,231	3,992,731	3,255,311	8,923,336
1616	5,959,643	4,423,074	1,442,846[f]	11,759,252
1617	6,137,238	4,887,289	2,023,920	12,544,791
1618	6,770,765	4,518,272	2,549,084	8,017,934
1619	7,289,781	7,229,031	2,395,330	11,209,791
1620	6,431,475	5,927,444	2,637,760	12,972,380
1621	6,693,806	5,413,648	2,149,250	18,842,672
1622	5,182,246	4,630,959	1,449,377	22,433,466
1623	3,614,945	4,197,358	1,369,248	11,891,393
1624	4,631,512	5,734,028	2,666,523	11,483,683
1625	1,903,891	5,090,871	3,746,166	17,167,279
1626	5,104,756	6,232,849	3,807,448	12,082,122
1627	3,989,551	5,551,669	1,863,246	14,136,955
1628	4,655,401	5,065,973	1,721,283	19,368,753
1629	4,171,052	5,494,241	2,216,770	18,324,513
1630	3,267,054	4,616,369	2,414,715	22,977,243

[a] Includes: Pensions and *acquits patents* (*dons par acquits*).

[b] Includes: *Maison du Roi, chambre aux deniers, argenterie, menus, écuires, offrandes et aumônes, troupes de la maison du Roi, prévoté de l'hôtel, cents suisses, venerie et fauconnerie, maison de la Reine* (1600–1610, 1616–1630), *maison de la Reine mère* (1611–1630), *maison de Monseigneur* (1615–1630).

[c] Includes: *Ambassades, Ligues Suisses, menus dons et voyages, batiments, ponts et chaussées.*

[d] Includes: *Ordinaire et extraordinaire des guerres, artillerie, fortifications, marine et galères.*

[e] The great rise in other expense is explained by an unusually large expenditure for the *Ligues-Suisses*. For the problems involved in assessing the true nature of the *Ligues-Suisses* payments see Albert Chamberland, 'La compatibilité imaginaire des deniers des coffres du roi et les dettes Suisses', *Revue Henri IV*, II (1908), 50–64.

[f] The great drop in other expense came from a greatly decreased payment for the *Ligues-Suisses*.

TABLE III   *Totals: A – Income*

Year	Total ordinary^a	Total ordinary minus parties casuelles	Extraordinary^j	Total ordinary plus extraordinary^k	Total ordinary plus extraordinary^l
1600	16,208,823	14,564,777	4,333,994	20,542,817	20,542,817
1601	15,115,467	14,490,461	1,003,059	16,118,526	16,118,526
1602	16,194,526^b	14,880,214	3,370,903	19,565,429	19,565,429
1603	17,474,821	15,507,291	3,566,519	21,041,340	21,041,340
1604	16,676,473	15,124,799	4,897,987	21,574,460	21,574,460
1605	18,986,425	16,662,031	7,892,643	26,879,068	26,879,068
1606	19,790,671	17,872,604	8,587,688	28,378,359	28,378,359
1607	19,185,587	17,342,949	10,656,470	29,842,057	29,842,059^m
1608	20,721,631	17,242,039	12,065,665	32,787,296	32,787,296
1609	19,376,574	17,112,823	13,086,864	32,463,438	32,463,438
1610	17,824,328	16,156,220	15,515,008	33,339,336	33,655,821^n
1611	18,758,610	16,890,528	8,877,398	26,636,008	27,622,004^o
1612	19,558,084	17,136,338	7,188,716	26,746,800	26,951,471
1613	22,160,563	17,363,277	6,023,934	28,184,497	28,761,027
1614	21,812,606	18,046,321	7,641,693	29,454,299	29,423,740
1615	20,918,689	18,734,894	3,380,865	24,299,554	24,551,600
1616	29,059,616	18,342,216	4,013,579	33,073,195	34,487,159^o
1617	24,619,108^c	18,551,133	9,465,552	34,084,660	
1618	20,182,573	17,613,557	7,455,239	27,637,812	
1619	27,426,311	23,654,475^e	11,862,414	38,288,725	
1620	32,143,185	18,875,546	6,812,593	38,955,778	
1621	31,664,201	17,368,594	11,146,918	32,811,119	
1622	38,518,313	18,466,158	11,415,506	49,933,819	
1623	33,043,412	15,624,387^f	4,260,733	37,304,145	
1624	29,961,881	16,701,683	7,087,534	34,049,415	
1625	29,300,809	13,036,456^g	21,715,302	51,016,111	
1626	33,936,746^d	18,243,795	10,194,620	44,131,366	
1627	30,615,612	13,286,139^h	8,773,237	39,388,849	
1628	28,746,957	17,443,467^i	12,969,026	41,715,983	
1629	35,892,358	18,801,668	19,527,404	55,419,762	
1630	37,199,781	18,282,776	5,606,147	42,805,928	

^{a} Mallet counts income from *parties casuelles* as ordinary income only for the period 1600–1610. In this column it is counted as ordinary income for the whole period. Therefore to check Mallet's figures from 1610 it is first necessary to add the sum he gives for *parties casuelles* to his total.

^{b} Mallet's figure 15,994,526 *livres* is wrong because of a copying error in transferring the total income of *fermes* from p. 184 to p. 191.

^{c} Mallet's figure 24,619,088 *livres* is wrong because of a copying error in transferring the total income of *fermes* from p. 199 to p. 211.

^{d} Mallet's figure 33,935,996 *livres* is wrong because of an adding error in the total income of *fermes* on p. 199.

^{e} The large increase came from a general rise in *fermes*, especially *gabelles*, *aides*, *cinq grosses fermes*.

Footnotes to Table III (*continued*)

f The decrease came from a decline in the revenue of the *gabelles de France* (i.e. the *gabelle* in the *pays d'election*).

g The decrease came from a decline in *recettes générales*, especially in the *pays d'election*.

h The large decrease came from a decline in *recettes générales* in both the *pays d'état* and *pays d'election*.

i The increase came from a rise in revenue from the *gabelles* and *cinq grosses fermes*.

j These sums are as given by Mallet; they differ from those in Buisseret, *Sully*, p. 77, because he included the *taillon* in his figures. In these tables the *taillon* is included with the *recettes générales*, as was the custom at the time. Without an itemized breakdown over a long period, which is impossible given the state of the records, these figures are of little help, especially since both in extraordinary income and extraordinary expense sums on hand and paid to the treasurer of the Bastille are included.

k According to Mallet.

l According to Buisseret and A.A.E. Fr. 768–770.

m The difference between Buisseret's and Mallet's figures arises from the difference in *bois* income.

n The difference between Buisseret's and Mallet's figures arises from the difference in *taillon* income.

o The great difference between Mallet and A.A.E. documents is undoubtedly because of the attempt of the author of the A.A.E. account to make his budget balance, which it did not in 1611 and 1616.

TABLE III   *Totals: B – Expense*

Year	Total ordinary	Extraordinary[c]	Total: ordinary plus extraordinary[d]	Total: ordinary plus extraordinary[g]
1600	13,675,155	7,067,685	20,742,840	20,446,819[h]
1601	12,343,117	3,940,935	16,284,052	16,189,333
1602	12,283,124	7,688,426	19,971,550	20,011,606
1603	11,896,818	9,144,529	21,041,347	21,041,347
1604	10,149,415	11,331,207	21,480,622	21,474,462
1605	13,259,329	13,614,346	26,873,675	26,873,375
1606	14,372,775	13,960,894	28,333,669	28,434,556
1607	14,394,995	15,551,230	29,946,225[e]	29,930,018
1608	14,489,416	18,383,208	32,872,624	32,172,624
1609	14,176,453	18,396,956	32,573,409	32,573,449
1610	20,759,530	12,814,536	33,574,066	33,580,066
1611	16,220,857[a]	10,400,401	26,621,258[f]	27,612,573
1612	18,425,002	8,731,806	27,156,808	26,915,002
1613	18,910,736	9,849,933	28,760,699	28,760,674
1614	21,764,772	7,660,295	29,425,067	29,423,740
1615	21,395,609	3,197,281	24,592,890	24,572,901
1616	23,584,815	10,751,335	34,336,150	34,388,039
1617	25,593,436	8,704,677	34,297,915	
1618	21,856,055	5,958,158	27,814,213	
1619	28,123,933	11,552,567	39,676,500	
1620	27,969,059	8,758,566	36,727,625	
1621	33,099,376	10,053,341	43,152,717	
1622	33,696,068	15,601,079	49,297,147	
1623	21,072,944	11,523,382	32,596,326	
1624	24,515,746[b]	8,920,122	33,435,868[f]	
1625	27,908,207	21,616,350	49,524,557	
1626	27,254,175	17,402,986	44,656,161	
1627	25,541,421	12,935,056	38,476,477	
1628	30,811,410	11,040,220	41,851,630	
1629	30,206,576	24,434,778	54,641,354	
1630	33,275,381	8,637,296	41,912,677	

[a] Mallet's figure for 1611: 16,230,857 *livres* comes from his error in adding.

[b] Mallet's figure for 1624: 24,415,746 *livres* comes from his error in adding.

[c] As with extraordinary income this figure is of little help because of the lack of breakdown for a long enough period and because of the book-keeping methods.

[d] According to Mallet.

[e] The totals for Mallet given in Albert Chamberland, 'Le Bu___ __ de l'Epargne en 1607 d'après des documents inédits', *Revue Henri IV*, II (1907–1908), 324–325, are inaccurate, turning a deficit into a surplus.

[f] Modified to correct Mallet's error.

[g] According to Buisseret and A.A.E. Fr. 768–770.

[h] Buisseret's figures which, as in the preceding table, cover the years 1600–1610 differ from Mallet's because of the information he gathered from Sully's accounts. Evidently Sully did the same thing as Jeannin did in 1611 and 1616—juggled the accounts to make things look better.

APPENDIX 2
PRICES OF CEREALS, OIL AND WINE, 1590–1630[a]

TABLE I   *Année Civile*

A. Averages

Year	Wheat	Wheat, rye, oats, wine	Barley, oil, millet	Average of all prices
1590	17·62	10·57	8·07	9·50
1591	20·97	13·39	8·59	11·33
1592	20·99	13·87	8·44	11·54
1593	21·06	12·81	7·98	10·74
1594	11·45	7·13	5·50	6·43
1595	13·63	9·04	7·88	8·55
1596	14·06	8·78	6·83	8·13
1597	15·13	9·71	7·28	8·67
1598	13·16	8·96	7·43	8·30
1599	10·47	7·11	5·87	6·58
1600	9·57	6·67	4·11	5·57
1601	8·18	5·51	3·93	4·83
1602	7·73	5·50	2·80	4·34
1603	9·83	6·78	5·42	6·20
1604	10·72	6·98	5·03	6·15
1605	10·99	7·04	5·24	6·25
1606	10·48	6·96	4·31	5·82
1607	10·75	7·30	5·15	6·38
1608	11·10	7·28	5·02	6·31
1609	9·77	6·47	4·89	5·79
1610	8·53	6·09	4·13	5·25
1611	8·88	6·35	4·02	5·35
1612	10·73	7·48	5·03	6·43
1613	10·09	6·85	4·59	5·87
1614	10·99	7·53	5·78	6·78
1615	8·27	5·93	4·30	5·23
1616	8·93	6·00	4·43	5·33
1617	9·67	6·44	4·31	5·53
1618	11·52	7·67	4·89	6·47
1619	12·02	7·86	5·46	6·83
1620	9·80	6·59	4·93	5·88
1621	10·57	6·57	4·44	5·66
1622	13·53	8·81	5·69	7·49
1623	11·72	7·42	5·22	6·48
1624	10·25	6·58	4·66	5·76
1625	9·83	6·65	4·18	5·59

224

Year	Wheat	Wheat, rye, oats, wine	Barley, oil, millet	Average of all prices
1626	12·40	7·63	5·69	6·80
1627	12·07	7·72	5·40	6·73
1628	12·41	8·22	5·55	7·07
1629	11·65	7·03	5·35	6·31
1630	16·38	10·34	7·52	9·13

^a The numbers in the columns on this and the following pages represent *livres tournois* and decimal fractions of *livres* per Paris *setier* (156 *litres* for all grains except 273 *litres* for oats) except wine where the *muid* of Béziers (660 *litres*) is used and oil where the *charge* of Béziers (182 litres) is used. For purposes of graphing and averaging, the wine and oil prices have been reduced by 90 per cent to bring them in line with other prices. In the other parts of the appendix, however, their true price is given. The sources used for the prices were René Baehrel, *Une Croissance: La Basse Provence Rurale* (Paris, 1961), pp. 535, 559, 560; Micheline Baulant et Jean Meuvret, *Prix des céréales extraits de la mercuriale de Paris, 1520–1698* (Paris, 1962), I, 65–81, 152–153, 243–246; II, 4–8, 135–138; Pierre Deyon, *Amiens, capitale provinciale* (Paris, 1967), pp. 50, 504–505; G. & G. Frêche, *Les prix des grains, des vins et des légumes à Toulouse* (Paris, 1967), pp. 48–53, 87, 92, 93, 119–120; Pierre Goubert, *Beauvais et le Beauvaisis de 1600 à 1730*, pp. 400–402; Emmanuel Le Roy Ladurie, *Les paysans de Languedoc* (Paris, 1966), II, 821, 823, 950–956. The conversion factors used to align the non-Parisian measures and prices in the sources cited with those of Paris to produce the figures in the appendix are as follows – Wheat, barley, rye, millet: Paris as is, Beauvais × 4·72 ÷ 20; Toulouse × 1·67, Béziers × 2·36, Aix × 0·96 (rye only × ·96 ÷ 20) – Oats: Paris as is, Beauvais × 5·46 ÷ 20, Toulouse × 2·45 ÷ 20, Aix 1·05 ÷ 20 – Wine: Béziers as is, Toulouse × 1·73, Aix × 11·43 ÷ 20 – Oil: Béziers as is. Where necessary the Paris prices were changed from *année recolte* to *année civile* and the Toulouse prices from *année civile* to *année recolte*. Micheline Baulant has provided figures for Paris wheat prices by *année civile* based on the average of four seasons in an article subsequent to her book. These figures differ somewhat from the ones printed on the following pages, which are based on twelve-month averages in all cases, but the same pattern is to be found in her set of figures and the ones derived for use here; 'Le prix de grains à Paris de 1431 à 1788', *Annales*, XXIII, 3 (1968), 520–540. The wheat and rye prices of Paris in all cases are averages of maximum prices, as are the averages used by Mme. Baulant. For the Toulouse *année civile* prices the yearly averages given by the Frêches on pp. 87, 119–120 have been used as the basis for conversion even though they rounded their averages off to the first decimal place. The differences that would result from rounding off to the second place as has been my practice may be illustrated for the years 1590–1593 (9·03, 7·97, 14·46, 14·97). These differences are not enough significantly to alter the average.

B. Wheat

Year	Paris	Toulouse	Aix	Average
1590	29·55	9·02	14·30	17·62
1591	32·04	8·02	22·85	20·97
1592	19·17	14·53	29·28	20·99
1593	19·35	15·03	28·80	21·06
1594	15·13	8·68	10·54	11·45
1595	17·80	12·19	10·90	13·63
1596	18·24	8·02	15·93	14·06
1597	18·25	10·02	17·11	15·13
1598	14·77	13·86	10·84	13·16
1599	9·82	12·36	9·22	10·47
1600	8·51	6·85	13·36	9·57
1601	7·96	5·01	11·56	8·18
1602	7·73	4·84	10·61	7·73
1603	10·00	6·18	13·31	9·83
1604	9·05	8·35	14·76	10·72
1605	8·51	10·86	13·60	10·99
1606	8·52	8·68	14·23	10·48
1607	8·90	9·69	13·65	10·75
1608	12·31	7·35	13·63	11·10
1609	11·16	6·68	11·47	9·77
1610	9·48	5·18	10·94	8·53
1611	9·81	5·51	11·32	8·88
1612	9·75	8·52	13·91	10·73
1613	8·92	8·85	12·51	10·09
1614	9·68	11·02	12·27	10·99
1615	9·23	5·51	10·08	8·27
1616	8·99	6·18	11·62	8·93
1617	11·27	6·35	11·38	9·67
1618	14·22	7·68	12·67	11·52
1619	10·18	8·85	17·02	12·02
1620	9·39	9·02	10·98	9·80
1621	10·47	8·68	12·57	10·57
1622	13·34	10·19	17·07	13·53
1623	13·66	7·68	13·82	11·72
1624	11·56	6·51	12·67	10·25
1625	12·28	5·68	11·52	9·83
1626	18·96	5·85	12·38	12·40
1627	16·02	7·52	12·67	12·07
1628	12·17	10·52	14·54	12·41
1629	11·18	9·19	14·59	11·65
1630	13·87	15·70	19·58	16·38

C. Rye

Year	Paris	Toulouse	Aix	Average
1590	17·90	6·18	11·23	11·77
1591	20·05	5·34	17·28	14·22
1592	11·08	10·02	21·60	14·23
1593	11·80	10·86	24·00	15·55
1594	8·56	5·51	7·10	7·06
1595	11·96	8·02	8·06	9·35
1596	10·79	5·68	11·62	9·36
1597	11·23	6·68	14·40	10·77
1598	9·10	10·02	8·35	9·16
1599	4·25	9·52	6·48	6·75
1600	4·08	4·01	9·79	5·96
1601	4·07	3·01	8·40	5·16
1602	3·73	3·01	7·49	4·74
1603	5·48	4·18	9·89	6·52
1604	4·59	5·68	11·04	7·10
1605	3·45	7·35	10·18	6·99
1606	3·68	5·68	11·57	6·98
1607	4·49	6·51	9·98	6·99
1608	6·87	4·68	11·42	7·66
1609	6·00	4·51	7·92	6·14
1610	4·51	3·34	7·20	5·02
1611	5·13	3·51	6·62	5·09
1612	5·05	5·34	9·70	6·70
1613	4·49	6·01	7·54	6·01
1614	5·35	7·52	8·06	6·98
1615	5·47	3·51	6·43	5·14
1616	4·79	3·34	7·30	5·14
1617	5·19	3·67	6·91	5·26
1618	7·55	5·34	8·02	6·97
1619	5·57	6·51	13·82	8·63
1620	4·10	6·51	7·78	6·13
1621	5·19	5·34	7·87	6·13
1622	6·70	6·35	14·11	9·05
1623	7·16	5·18	9·79	7·38
1624	5·66	4·51	8·54	6·24
1625	6·45	4·01	7·49	5·98
1626	10·74	4·01	7·68	7·48
1627	8·92	4·68	8·74	7·45
1628	6·63	6·35	10·99	7·99
1629	6·16	5·34	—	5·75
1630	8·33	11·86	14·40	11·53

D. Oats

Year	Paris	Toulouse	Aix	Average
1590	11·00	6·37	10·08	9·15
1591	17·90	6·37	14·07	12·78
1592	9·20	9·31	17·59	12·03
1593	9·83	9·80	—	9·82
1594	7·67	5·88	8·24	7·26
1595	8·96	11·03	10·29	10·09
1596	8·69	7·11	9·82	8·54
1597	9·73	7·60	9·66	9·00
1598	7·62	10·29	7·72	8·54
1599	5·22	8·58	6·93	6·91
1600	5·88	5·88	14·07	8·61
1601	5·71	4·66	9·45	6·61
1602	4·45	4·90	8·56	5·97
1603	6·22	5·64	8·72	6·86
1604	6·12	6·86	9·45	7·48
1605	4·83	6·62	9·98	7·14
1606	4·17	5·64	7·93	5·91
1607	4·02	6·62	8·51	6·38
1608	4·90	4·41	7·35	5·55
1609	5·55	4·66	9·40	6·54
1610	6·73	4·90	8·82	6·82
1611	7·30	5·15	9·24	7·23
1612	7·30	6·62	10·82	8·25
1613	6·50	6·37	7·51	6·79
1614	5·68	7·35	8·30	7·11
1615	7·41	4·41	9·03	6·95
1616	6·59	4·90	9·61	7·03
1617	5·29	4·66	8·03	5·99
1618	6·92	5·39	8·56	6·96
1619	6·15	6·37	9·50	7·34
1620	6·05	6·13	8·40	6·86
1621	5·98	5·39	8·09	6·49
1622	6·90	5·64	12·65	8·40
1623	6·36	5·15	10·40	7·30
1624	6·64	6·13	10·40	7·72
1625	7·49	6·13	10·92	8·18
1626	11·08	5·39	8·61	8·36
1627	9·67	5·64	10·71	8·67
1628	8·31	6·86	12·08	9·08
1629	7·01	5·39	—	6·20
1630	8·76	9·07	13·23	10·35

E. Wine

Year	Toulouse clair de marque	Toulouse clair de pays	Béziers old	Béziers new	Aix	Average
1590	53·63	31·14	48	20	34·29	37·41
1591	60·55	48·44	49	39	82·30	55·86
1592	88·23	70·93	90	60	102·87	82·41
1593	72·66	48·44	30	—	41·15	48·06
1594	34·60	27·68	—	—	20·57	27·62
1595	43·25	22·49	37	25	27·43	31·03
1596	44·98	22·49	—	—	27·43	31·63
1597	58·82	34·60	34	36	34·29	39·54
1598	84·77	51·90	50	18	44·58	49·85
1599	64·01	39·79	38	33	41·15	43·19
1600	38·06	20·76	43	12	13·72	25·51
1601	34·60	15·57	15	12	25·15	20·46
1602	48·44	27·68	—	30	—	35·37
1603	46·71	34·60	47	—	28·58	39·22
1604	36·33	24·22	33	12	27·43	26·20
1605	39·79	24·22	18	16	48·01	29·20
1606	50·17	32·87	47	—	48·01	44·51
1607	60·55	34·60	60	—	48·01	50·79
1608	58·82	29·41	69	—	34·29	47·88
1609	62·28	34·60	25	12	37·72	34·32
1610	53·63	32·87	32	—	41·15	39·91
1611	44·98	24·22	54	45	41·15	41·87
1612	41·52	31·14	42	—	54·86	42·38
1613	57·09	39·79	44	25	54·86	44·15
1614	89·96	48·44	36	36	41·15	50·31
1615	51·90	36·33	45	8	27·43	33·73
1616	32·87	24·22	34	30	22·86	28·79
1617	43·25	25·95	60	57	54·86	48·21
1618	86·50	32·87	56	30	54·86	52·05
1619	55·36	27·68	40	15	34·29	34·47
1620	65·74	32·87	20	20	37·72	35·67
1621	69·20	38·06	24	8	15·43	30·94
1622	79·58	38·06	45	30	20·57	42·64
1623	58·82	32·87	40	18	13·72	32·68
1624	—	—	30	15	18·29	21·10
1625	—	—	33	18	27·43	26·15
1626	—	—	27	18	22·86	22·62
1627	—	—	37	30	13·72	26·91
1628	—	—	44	30	27·43	33·81
1629	—	—	45	—	—	45
1630	—	—	38	24	—	31

	F. Barley	**G. Oil**	**H. Millet**
Year	Paris	Béziers	Toulouse
1590	14·67	42	5·34
1591	16·96	33	5·51
1592	8·40	49	12·02
1593	9·04	37	11·19
1594	5·90	51	5·51
1595	9·50	58	8·35
1596	8·15	—	5·51
1597	8·33	65	7·01
1598	6·63	58	9·85
1599	3·60	55	8·52
1600	3·48	45	4·34
1601	3·62	50	3·17
1602	3·12	21	3·17
1603	4·86	74	4·01
1604	3·89	57	5·51
1605	3·26	46	7·85
1606	2·92	45	5·51
1607	3·27	55	6·68
1608	5·14	49	5·01
1609	4·57	56	4·51
1610	3·74	53	3·34
1611	4·14	44	3·51
1612	4·48	46	6·01
1613	3·77	45	5·51
1614	4·52	43	8·52
1615	5·24	40	3·67
1616	4·56	54	3·34
1617	3·37	59	3·67
1618	5·02	48	4·84
1619	3·69	70	5·68
1620	3·46	60	5·34
1621	3·63	40	5·68
1622	4·95	56	6·51
1623	5·31	55	4·84
1624	4·84	48	4·34
1625	4·60	46	3·34
1626	8·34	54	3·34
1627	6·43	46	5·18
1628	5·49	53	5·85
1629	4·88	50	6·18
1630	5·86	60	10·69

TABLE II   *Année Récolte*

A. Averages

Year	Wheat	Oats	Average
1590–91	20·42	10·50	15·46
1591–92	14·06	8·77	11·42
1592–93	16·52	7·95	12·24
1593–94	12·17	6·45	9·31
1594–95	13·14	7·78	10·46
1595–96	13·92	8·56	11·24
1596–97	16·88	7·95	12·42
1597–98	14·45	9·22	11·84
1598–99	10·52	6·73	8·63
1599–1600	8·88	5·52	7·20
1600–01	8·63	5·62	7·13
1601–02	7·80	4·44	6·12
1602–03	8·92	4·60	6·76
1603–04	9·58	6·62	8·10
1604–05	9·83	5·71	7·77
1605–06	9·62	4·32	6·97
1606–07	10·00	4·95	7·48
1607–08	10·92	4·48	7·70
1608–09	11·33	4·65	7·99
1609–10	8·83	5·33	7·08
1610–11	9·20	6·28	7·74
1611–12	9·73	7·18	8·46
1612–13	10·04	6·47	8·26
1613–14	9·65	5·95	7·80
1614–15	8·63	5·59	7·11
1615–16	8·15	6·12	7·14
1616–17	9·03	4·96	7·00
1617–18	12·25	5·99	9·12
1618–19	11·04	6·08	8·56
1619–20	9·58	5·74	7·66
1620–21	9·82	5·13	7·48
1621–22	11·64	5·86	8·75
1622–23	13·13	5·68	9·42
1623–24	11·25	5·59	8·42
1624–25	10·26	6·24	8·25
1625–26	13·23	7·19	10·21
1626–27	14·05	8·01	11·03
1627–28	11·97	7·67	9·82
1628–29	11·00	6·14	8·57
1629–30	11·22	6·64	8·93
1630–31	18·27	11·36	14·82

231

B. Wheat

Year	Paris	Béziers	Beauvais	Average
1590–91	39·91	12·32	9·04	20·42
1591–92	21·42	12·77	7·98	14·06
1592–93	20·00	20·06	9·51	16·52
1593–94	16·40	10·55	9·56	12·17
1594–95	16·56	8·71	14·16	13·14
1595–96	17·29	9·61	14·87	13·92
1596–97	19·10	15·84	15·69	16·88
1597–98	16·29	13·55	13·50	14·45
1598–99	11·69	10·83	9·04	10·52
1599–1600	8·76	10·55	7·32	8·88
1600–01	8·06	10·62	7·20	8·63
1601–02	7·51	10·15	5·73	7·80
1602–03	9·20	10·01	7·55	8·92
1603–04	9·87	11·80	7·08	9·58
1604–05	8·40	14·68	6·42	9·83
1605–06	8·49	13·88	6·49	9·62
1606–07	8·82	14·21	6·96	10·00
1607–08	10·16	12·98	9·61	10·92
1608–09	12·94	11·85	9·20	11·33
1609–10	9·45	10·43	6·61	8·83
1610–11	9·84	10·43	7·32	9·20
1611–12	9·82	11·97	7·39	9·73
1612–13	9·13	14·16	6·84	10·04
1613–14	9·41	12·22	7·32	9·65
1614–15	9·19	9·63	7·08	8·63
1615–16	9·28	8·33	6·84	8·15
1616–17	9·76	9·49	7·84	9·03
1617–18	14·02	10·93	11·80	12·25
1618–19	11·87	12·58	8·66	11·04
1619–20	8·98	13·10	6·66	9·58
1620–21	9·88	11·33	8·26	9·82
1621–22	12·43	12·81	9·68	11·64
1622–23	14·09	14·44	10·86	13·13
1623–24	12·27	11·80	9·68	11·25
1624–25	11·14	11·14	8·50	10·26
1625–26	16·88	10·55	12·27	13·23
1626–27	17·72	11·45	12·98	14·05
1627–28	13·25	12·98	9·68	11·97
1628–29	11·51	12·81	8·68	11·00
1629–30	11·63	12·98	9·04	11·22
1630–31	19·54	19·82	15·46	18·27

C. Oats

Year	Paris	Beauvais	Toulouse	Average
1590–91	18·69	6·69	6·13	10·50
1591–92	11·42	6·63	8·27	8·77
1592–93	9·40	3·88	10·56	7·95
1593–94	8·71	4·10	6·55	6·45
1594–95	8·02	6·36	8·96	7·78
1595–96	9·35	7·37	8·96	8·56
1596–97	8·58	8·05	7·23	7·95
1597–98	9·29	8·60	9·76	9·22
1598–99	5·66	5·24	9·29	6·73
1599–1600	5·15	4·37	7·04	5·52
1600–01	6·52	5·73	4·61	5·62
1601–02	4·53	3·55	5·25	4·44
1602–03	4·85	4·50	4·45	4·60
1603–04	7·21	5·73	6·92	6·62
1604–05	5·09	4·91	7·13	5·71
1605–06	4·38	3·60	4·98	4·32
1606–07	4·06	3·47	7·33	4·95
1607–08	4·41	4·37	4·65	4·48
1608–09	5·45	4·42	4·08	4·65
1609–10	5·89	5·00	5·10	5·33
1610–11	7·45	6·28	5·10	6·28
1611–12	7·23	8·11	6·21	7·18
1612–13	7·22	6·14	6·06	6·47
1613–14	5·51	4·10	8·23	5·95
1614–15	6·33	5·73	4·72	5·59
1615–16	8·05	6·01	4·31	6·12
1616–17	5·10	4·64	5·15	4·96
1617–18	6·47	6·61	4·88	5·99
1618–19	6·41	5·46	6·37	6·08
1619–20	6·15	4·50	6·57	5·74
1620–21	5·72	4·64	5·04	5·13
1621–22	6·83	4·50	6·25	5·86
1622–23	6.52	5·18	5·35	5·68
1623–24	6·38	4·72	5·68	5·59
1624–25	7·02	4·91	6·80	6·24
1625–26	10·23	5·87	5·47	7·19
1626–27	10·23	8·46	5·33	8·01
1627–28	8·94	7·23	6·84	7·67
1628–29	7·14	5·19	6·08	6·14
1629–30	7·12	5·73	7·06	6·64
1630–31	11·54	9·01	13·54	11·36

APPENDIX 3
DEPUTIES

The twelve *gouvernements* of France, arranged in the order of precedence proclaimed by Louis XIII on November 15, 1614, were: (1) Paris and Ile de France, (2) Burgundy, (3) Normandy, (4) Guyenne, (5) Brittany, (6) Champagne and Brie, (7) Languedoc, (8) Picardy, (9) Dauphiné (10) Provence, (11) Lyonnais, and (12) Orléanais.

The order of the *bailliages* and *sénéchaussées* presents a much greater problem. The source that has the most information on the deputies, that published by Quinet, uses a very original and very confusing arrangement, one that defies all logic. The other sources do not solve the question because they fail to agree. After a comparison of the various lists it has been decided to use the *gouvernement* and *bailliage* order followed by the Second and Third Estates in voting, in so far as this can determined.[1] In the spirit of 1614 it should be added that this is by way of provision and expediency alone.

A. THE DEPUTIES TO THE FIRST ESTATE[2]

PARIS AND ILE DE FRANCE

Provostship, Town and Viscounty of Paris

Henri de Gondi (d. 1622): Bishop of Paris (1597); Councilor of the King (State and Private); Master of Oratory of the King (1610); J.U.L.

J. de. M., no. 17800; Gulik, p.270; Gauchat, pp. 13, 30, 271, 241.

---

[1] Sources used to determine the order include B.N. *Collection Dupuy* 684, fols. 3r–9r; A. De Landine, *Des Etats généraux ou histoire des assemblées nationales en France* (Paris, 1788), pp. 254–269; Henri Grelin, *Livre contenant l'ordre tenue par messieurs de la noblesse aux Estats généraux de France . . . avec leurs noms, surmons, et qualitéz* (Paris, 1615), pp. 3–20 in A.N. K 674, no. 16; Lalourcéz and Duval, *Recueil de pièces*, v, 141–143; *Ordre des bailliages observé en la convocation des Estats généraux . . .* (Paris: Saugrain, 1615), pp. 98–104 (cited as Saugrain); Toussaint Quinet, *Recueil générale des Estats sous les rois Charles V, Charles VIII, Charles IX, Henri III et Louis XIII* (Paris, 1651), pp. 221–283; Rapine, *Recueil*, pp. 506–508.

[2] The list of deputies and their offices for all three estates was compiled by comparing B.N. MS fr. 4131, fols. 82r–105v; MS fr. 18513, fol. 157r; *Collection des procès verbaux des assemblées générales du clergé de France depuis l'année 1560 . . .* (Paris, 1768), II, 58–65; De Landine, *Des Etats généraux*, pp. 254–269; Grelin, *Livre contenant l'ordre*, pp. 3–20. Henri Grelin, *Ordre*

234

Louis Dreux: Canon and Grand Archdeacon of the Church of Paris (1583–1620).
J. de M., no. 13257; *Reg. délib. Paris*, XVI, i, 35.
Charles Faye: Councilor of the King in the Parlement (1577); Prior of Gournai (1601); Canon in the Church of Paris. J.U.D.
C.D., VII, cols. 840–841; G.C., X, col. 1306(?); Maugis, III, 859.

observé en la convocation et assemblée des Estats généraux de France ... avec les noms, surnoms et qualitéz des députéz des trois ordres ... (Paris, 1615); Lalourcé and Duval, *Recueil de pièces*, V, 2–52; Further information about the deputies was gained from Bernard Barbiche (ed.), *Correspondance du nonce en France Innocenzo del Bufalo* (Paris, 1964); Pierre Blet, S. J., *Assemblées*, François Bluche, Pierre Durye, *Les Honneurs de la Cour*, 2 vols. (Paris, 1957); Bluche and Durye, *L'Anoblissement par charges avant 1789*, 2 vols. (n.p., 1962); M. Bouchitté, *Négociations*; Pierre Broutin, *La réforme pastorale*; De la Chenaye-Desbois et Badier, *Dictionnaire de la Noblesse*, 19 vols., 3rd ed. (Paris, 1863–1876) (cited as C.D.); Marius Clairefond, 'Notice sur les députations de la Province de Bourbonnais et du départment de l'Allier aux grandes assemblées nationales depuis 1413 jusqu'en 1848', *Société d'Emulation du départment de l'Allier* (1850), pp. 242–263; J. Balteau, *et al.*, *Dictionnaire de Biographie Français*, vols. I–XII (Paris, 1932–); Henri Faure, *Histoire de Moulins*, vol. I (n.p., 1900); Henri de Frondeville, *Les Conseillers du Parlement de Normandie*, 2 vols. (Paris, 1960–1964); Henri de Frondeville, *Les Présidents du Parlement de Normandie* (Rouen, 1953); *Gallia Christiana*, 16 vols. (Paris, 1715–1865), cited as G.C. For bishops this work has been superseded by Gauchat and Gulik and is not listed in their entries; P. Gauchat, *Hierarchia Catholica Medii et Recentoris Aevi*, vol. IV (Munster, 1935); E. Griselle, *Etat de la maison du roi Louis XIII* (Paris, 1912); E. Griselle, *Supplement à la maison du roi Louis XIII* (Paris, 1912); G. van Gulik, *Hierarchia Catholica Medii et Recentoris Aevi*, vol. III (Munster, 1923); Emile and Eugène Haag, *La France Protestante*, 10 vols. (Paris, 1846–1859); Jean Héroard, *Journal*; Henri Jougla de Morenas, *Grand Armorial de France*, 7 vols. (Paris, 1934–1952), cited as J. de M.; *Lettres Missives de Henri IV*; D. Luttin, *Recherches historiques sur la ville d'Orléans*, (Orléans, 1837); Major, *deputies*; E. Maugis, *Parlement*; Yves Durand, *Troyes*; R. Mousnier, *Stratification sociale* (Paris, 1965); R. Mousnier, *Venalité*; Jeanne Petit, *L'assemblée des notables*; J.B. Poulbrière, 'Les deputés du Limousin et de la Marche aux divers Etats généraux de France', *Bulletin de la Société scientifique, historique et archéologique de la Corrèze* (1890), pp. 293–321; *Registres des déliberations de la ville de Paris*, vols. XV and XVI (Paris, 1921–1927); *Mémoires du cardinal de Richelieu*, vol. I; P. Thomas-Lacroix, 'Les Bretons aux Etats généraux de 1614', *Mémoires de la Sociéte d'histoire et de archéologie de Bretagne*, XV (1934), 1–14; Regis Valette, *Catalogue de la Noblesse Française contemporaine* (Paris, 1959). Other works that pertain to only one deputy are cited in full after that deputy's entry. English has been used for titles and occupations whenever common usage or common sense dictated this. When possible place names have been modernized. French words have not been italicized. Dates placed after names indicate life span, placed after offices they indicate when the office was assumed and, if there are two, when it was given up. Words in parentheses are variants found in some sources. Abbreviations used include: O. Chart. – Carthusian; O. Cist – Cistercian; O.F.M., Cap. – Capuchin; O.F.M. (Cord) – Cordelier; O. Min – Minims; O.S.A. – Augustinians; Can. Reg. OSA – Canons Regular of Saint Augustine; O.S.B. – Benedictines; O.Trin. – Trinitarians; Th.D. – Doctor of Theology; Th.M. – Master of Theology; Th.B. – Bachelor of Theology; J.U.D. – Doctor of Canon and Civil Law; J.U.L. – Licenciate of Canon and Civil Law; J.U.Dip – Diplôme in Canon and Civil Law; J.C.L. – Licenciate in Canon Law; J.D. – Doctor of Law; J.L. – Licenciate in Law; Dec. D. – Doctor of Decretals; Dec. L. – Licenciate in Decretals; Dec. B. – Bachelor of Decretals; J. de M. – Jougla de Morenas, *Grand Armorial*; C.D. – Chenaye-Desbois, *Dictionnaire*; D.B.F. – *Dictionnaire de Biographie Français*; G.C. – *Gallia Christiana*.

235

Denis (Coulon) Colom (1548–1626): Prior and Vicar of the Abbey of St Victor in Paris (1603) and General of the Canons and Religious of the Augustinians of Saint Victor. Can. Reg. O.S.A.

G.C., VII, cols. 697–698; *Reg. délib. Paris*, XVI, I.

Adam Oger: Prior of the Chartreux of Paris; O. Chart.

Antoine Fayet: Canon of the Church of Paris; Curé of Saint-Paul of Paris.

Roland Hébert: Penententiary of the Church of Paris; Curé of Saint-Cosme of Paris. Th.D.

Bailliage of Vermandois

Benjamin de Brichanteau (1585–1619): Councilor of the King (State and Private); Bishop and Duke of Laon (1612); Peer of France and Count of Anisi. Can. Reg. O.S.A.; J.C.D.

D.B.F., VII, Gauchat, p. 216.

Jean Aubert (d. 1626): Grand Archdeacon of Rheims; Councilor, Almoner, and Preacher Ordinary of the King; Abbot of Saint-Jean-de-Laon (1607). Th.D.

D.B.F., IV, col. 34.

Bailliage of Senlis

François Cardinal de la Rochefoucault (1558–1645): Councilor of State (1585); Bishop of Senlis (1610); (Bp. Clermont 1585–1610; Cardinal 1607). J. de M., no. 29505; C.D., XVII, col. 367; Gulik, p. 170; Gauchat, pp. 10, 316; G. de La Rochefoucauld, *Le Cardinal François de la Rochefoucauld* (Paris, 1926).

Bailliage of Clermont en Beauvoisis

Etienne de Ruptis: Monastic Prior of the Church and Abbey of Notre-Dame-de-Froidmont. O. Cist. Th.D.

Bailliage of Chaumont en Vexin

Jacques Jacart: Prior of Magny.

Bailliage of Valois

Jean Berthier (chose to sit with Toulouse).

Pierre Habert (d. 1636): Councilor of the King; Councilor in the Parlement (1611); Master of Requests of the King's House (1611); Abbot of La Roche; Prior of Saint-Arnould-de-Crespy-en-Valois.

C.D., X, col. 187; Gauchat, pp. 142, 315; G.C., X, col. 1492; Maugis, III, 315.

Bailliage of Melun

Antoine Chauveau: Councilor of the King in the Bailliage; Canon and Chanter of Notre-Dame-de-Melun; Prior of Châtillon. J.L.

Bailliage of Nemours

François Le Charron: Pronotary of the Holy See; Abbot *in commendam* of Notre-Dame-de-Cercanceau.
G.C., VII, col. 275.

Bailliage of Montfort-Lamaury

Philippe Hurault (1579–1620): Councilor of the King (State and Private); Bishop of Chartres (1608); Grand Almoner of Marie de Médicis (1615–1629). J.U.L.
C.D., X, col. 895; Gulik, p. 153; Gauchat, p. 135; *LMHIV*, VII, 402.
Jean Le Roy: Curé of Montfort. Dec. B.

Bailliage of Mantes and Meulan

The Bishop of Chartres

Bailliage of Dourdan

Jacques du Lac: Councilor of the King; Almoner Ordinary of the King; Prior of Notre-Dame-de-Louye.

Bailliage of Beauvais

René Potier (1576–1616): Councilor of the King (State and Private); Bishop and Count of Beauvais (1596); Peer of France; Vidame of Gerbroy.
J. de M., no. 27448; C.D., XVI, col. 231; Gulik, p. 131; Gauchat, p. 113.

Bailliage of Soissons

Dreux Hennequin (1575–1651): Sieur of Villenoze; Councilor of the King in the Parlement (1598); Canon and Treasurer of the Cathedral Church of Soissons.
C.D., X, col. 545; Gauchat, pp. 153, 324; G.C., XI, col. 834, Maugis, III, 314.

Bailliage of Dreux

Félix Vialart: Prior of Beu; Canon in the Cathedral of Chartres.
C.D., XIX, cols. 663–665 (?).

Bailliage of Magny

Charles des Boues: Sieur of Rauces; Protonotary of the Holy See; Councilor and Almoner of the King; Grand Vicar of Pontoise and Vexin-le-François.

GOUVERNEMENT OF BURGUNDY

Bailliage of Dijon

Nicolas Boucherat (d. 1625): Abbot of Citeaux (1601); Master General of the Cistercians; Councilor of the King in the Parlement of Dijon. O. Cist.; Th.D.

C.D., III. cols. 655–656.

Bailliage of Autun

André Venot: Canon and Chanter of the Church of Autun; Official and Syndic of the clergy of the diocese of Autun.

Bailliage of Châlons-sur-Saône

Cyrus de Tyard (1563–1624): Councilor of the King (State and Private); Bishop of Châlons (1594). Th.B.

J. de M., 32735; C.D., XVIII, col. 927; Gulik, p. 144; Gauchat, p. 125.

Bailliage of la Montagne

Robert Corderam: Curé of Buncey.

Bailliage of Mâcon

Gaspard Dinet (1569–1619): Councilor of the King; Bishop of Mâcon (1600). O. Min.

D.B.F., XI, 374; Gulik, p. 238; Gauchat, p. 202, 235; Whitmore, *The Order of Minims in Seventeenth Century France* (The Hague, 1967), pp. 70, 290.

Bailliage of Auxois

Lazare Morot: Abbot of Saint-Pierre of Châlon; Dean of Avalon.

Bailliage of Auxerre

François de Donadieu (1560–1640): Councilor of the King (State and Private); Bishop of Auxerre (1599–1623). Th.D.

D.B.F., XI, col. 503; Gulik, p. 125; Gauchat, pp. 87, 273.

Herard de Rochefort: Abbot of Vezelay; Dean of the Cathedral of Auxerre (1610–1622).

C.D., XVII, cols. 319–320; G.C. XII, cols. 355–356.

Bailliage of Bar-sur-Seine

Guillaume Minet: Minister of the Maison-Dieu of Bar-sur-Seine. O. Trin.

Bailliage of Charolais

Legier des Molins: Curé and Theologal in the Church of Notre-Dame of Paroi. O.F.M. (Cord.); Th.D.

Bailliage of Bugey-en-Bresse

Jean Pierre Camus (1584?–1652): Councilor of the King; Bishop and Seigneur of Bellay (1609). J.C.L.
C.D., IV, col. 636; D.B.F., VII, vols. 1013–1014; Gulik, p. 131; Gauchat, p. 112; Popkin, *History of Scepticism* (New York, 1968), pp. 63–65; Albert Garreau, *Jean Pierre Camus* (Paris, 1968); Jean Pierre Camus, *Homélies de Etats Généraux*, 1614–1615, ed. Jean Descrains (Geneva 1970).

Bailliage of Gex

Maximian de Molins: Superior of the Capuchins of the Mission of Gex for the conversion of the Huguenots. O.F.M. Cap.

Bailliage of Bresse

Albert de Grillet: Abbot of la Chassaigne; Prior of Ompsierre.

GOUVERNEMENT OF NORMANDY

Bailliage of Rouen

François Cardinal de Joyeuse (1562–1615): Dean of the College of Cardinals; Archbishop of Rouen (1604); Primate of Normandy (Bishop of Narbonne, 1575–1588; Archbishop of Toulouse, 1588–1604; Cardinal 1583).
J. de M., no. 8768; C.D., XI, col. 134; Gulik, pp. 47, 253, 315; Gauchat, p. 298; Blet, I, 15–16.
Antoine de Breteville: Official of Rouen; Canon and Chancellor of the Metropolitan Church of Rouen; Prior of Saint-Blaise-de-l'Huy; Syndic General of the clergy of the province of Normandy.
D.B.F., VII, col. 253.

Bailliage of Caen

Jacques d'Angennes (1574–1647): Councilor of the King (State and Private); Bishop of Bayeux (1607).
C.D., I, col. 510; D.B.F. II, 1095–1096; Gauchat, p. 108.

Bailliage of Caux

Antoine de Banastre: Seigneur and curé of Arcenville and sieur of Saint-Sul-pice.

C.D., II, col. 268.

Guillaume Helie (d. 1640?): of the Abbey of Sainte-Cathérine-du-Mont of Rouen; Almoner Ordinary of the King; Prior and Seigneur of Cléville. O.S.B.; Th.D.

G.C., XI, col. 280.

Bailliage of Cotantin

François de Péricard (1559–1639): Councilor of the King (State and Private); Bishop of Avranches (1588).

Gulik, p. 91; Gauchat, p. 65; Frondeville, I, 565, 583–584.

Bailliage of Evreux

François de Péricard (d. 1646): Councilor of the King; Bishop of Evreux (1613). Gauchat, pp. 179, 328; Frondeville, I, 501.

Bailliage of Gisors

Claude de Bauquemare: Prior of Sausseuze (1575–1629) and of Crasville; Canon of Rouen (1572).

J. de M., no 3479; C.D., II, cols. 569–570; D.B.F., V, cols. 942–943. Frondeville, *Présidents*, pp. 63–64.

Bailliage of Alençon

François de Rouxel de Medavi (1577–1617): Councilor of the King (State and Private); Bishop and Count of Lisieux (1599).

J. de M., no. 30331; C.D., XVII, col. 879; Gulik, p. 224; Gauchat, pp. 220, 299; *Le Tou-Beau Feu* (Paris, 1614), app.

Jacques Camus de Pontcarré (1584–1650): Councilor of the King (State and Private); Bishop of Séez (August, 1614).

C.D., IV, cols. 636–637. J. de M., no. 7582; D.B.F., VII, cols. 1017–1018; Gauchat, p. 299.

GOUVERNEMENT OF GUYENNE

City of Bordeaux and Sénéchaussée of Guyenne

François d'Escoubleau Cardinal de Sourdis (1575–1628): Archbishop of Bordeaux (1599); Primate of Aquitaine.

J. de M., no 14147; C.D., VII, cols. 344–345; Gauchat, pp. 6, 48, 123, 229; L. W. Ravenez, *Histoire du Cardinal de Sourdis* (Bordeaux, 1867).

Pierre de Perissac: Canon and sub-Dean of the Metropolitan Church of Bordeaux.

Sénéchaussée of Bazadois

Jean Jaubert de Barrault (1584–1643): Councilor of the King (State and Private); Bishop of Bazas (1611–1631). Th.B.; J.U.L.
C.D., XI, cols. 42–43; Gauchat, pp. 92, 359; *Arch. Hist. Gironde* X (1868), 552–555.

Sénéchaussée of Périgord

François de la Berauderière (Beraudière) (d. 1646): Councilor of the King; Bishop of Périgueux (July, 1614). J.U.L.
J. de M., no. 4179; Gauchat, p. 277.
Jean de Carbonières de Jayac: Dean and Canon of the Cathedral Church of Sarlat; Councilor and Almoner Ordinary of the King.
C.D., IV, col. 692; G.C., II, col. 1531; D.B.F., VII, col. 1112.
Jean Tricard: Canon and School Master of the Church of Périgueux.

Sénéchaussée of Rouergue

François de la Vallette Cornusson (d. 1622): Councilor of the King (State and Private); Bishop of Vabres (1600).
J. de M., no. 33995; C.D., XIX, col. 427; Gauchat, pp. 355–356.

Sénéchaussée of Saintonge

Nicolas le Cornu de la Courbe (d. 1617): Councilor of the King (State and Private); Bishop of Saintes (1576).
Gulik, p. 338; Gauchat, p. 304; Griselle, p. 229.
Michel Raoul (1570?–1631?): Dean and Canon of the Cathedral Church of Saintes (1598–1617). J.U.L.
Gauchat, p. 304; G.C., II, col. 1092; Griselle, p. 7.

Sénéchaussée of Agenois

Claude Gélas (1564–1630): Councilor of the King (State and Private); Bishop of Agen (1609). J.C.D.
Gauchat, p. 72; Héroard, II, 275.

Pays and County of Comminges

Octave de (Saint Lary de) Bellegarde (1587–1646): Councilor of the King; Bishop of Couserans (1613–1623); Deputy of the Estate of Comminges. J.U.L.

241

C.D., XVIII, cols. 117–118; D.B.F., V, cols. 1331–1332; Gauchat, pp. 160, 313; Petit, p. 234.

Gilles Souvré (d. 1631): Bishop of Comminges (1614 [1617] – 1625); deputy for the clergy of the pays.

J. de M., no. 32174; C.D., XVIII, col. 670; Gulik, p. 177; Gauchat, pp. 87, 163; Broutin, I, 159–160.

Jugerie of Rivière-Verdun

The Bishop of Comminges.

Sénéchaussée of Lannes and Saint Sever

Bertrand D'Echaux (1556?–1641): Councilor of the King (State and Private); First Almoner of the King (1611); Bishop of Bayonne (1599–1618). D.B.F., XII, 1109–1110; Gulik, p. 128; Gauchat, pp. 108, 350. Réné Veillet, *Recherches sur la ville et sur l'église de Bayonne* (Bayonne, 1910), pp. 189–203.

Jean Jacques du Sault (1570–1623): Councilor of the King (State and Private); Bishop of Dax (1598); Dean of the Collegial Church of Saint-Severin in Bordeaux; First Almoner of Queen Marguerite. J.D. D.B.F., XII, cols. 845–846; Gulik, p. 113; Gauchat, p. 89.

Sénéchaussée of Albret

[No deputy for the clergy.]

Sénéchaussée of Armagnac

Léonard de Trapes (d. 1629): Councilor of the King; Archbishop of Auch (1599). O.F.M., Cap. Gulik, p. 126; Gauchat, p. 105.

Jean de Tresses (1582–1646): Councilor of the King; Bishop of Laodicia; Co-adjutor Bishop of Lectoure (1609). Th.M. Gauchat, pp. 214, 218.

Sénéchaussée of Condomois and Gascogne

Antoine de Caux (1569–1648): Councilor of the King; Coadjutor Bishop of Condom (1604). J.U.L. Gulik, p. 175; Gauchat, pp. 103, 159.

Sénéchaussée of Haut Limousin and Town of Limoges

Henri de Lamartonie (d. 1618): Councilor of the King (State and Private); Bishop of Limoges (1587). J. de M., no. 23063; C.D., XIII col. 314; Gulik. p. 222.

Sénéchaussée of Bas Limousin

Jean de Genouillac de Vaillac (1575?–1652): Councilor of the King; Bishop, Viscount, and Seigneur of the town of Tulles (1599, consec. 1608). C.D., IX, cols. 537–538; Gulik, p. 322; Gauchat, p. 351; Gustave Clement-Simon, *Archives historiques de la Corrèze* (Paris, 1903–1905), I, 581; II, 366–370.

Sénéchaussée of Quercy

Claude Antoine d'Ebrard de Saint Sulpice: Abbot of la Garde-Dieu; Grand Archdeacon and Canon in the Cathedral Church of Cahors. J. de M., no. 13893; C.D., VII, cols. 173–175; D.B.F., XII, 1099–1100; G.C., I, cols. 187–188.

Pays and County of Bigorre

Saluat d'Iharce (d. 1648): Councilor of the King; Bishop of Tarbes (1602). Gulik, p. 309; Gauchat, p. 326.

Gratian d'Iharce: Canon and Archdeacon in the Cathedral Church of Tarbes; Grand Vicar of the Bishop of Tarbes.

GOUVERNEMENT OF BRITTANY

Deputies of the Estates of Brittany

François Laihnier (l'Archiver) (d. 1619?): Councilor of the King; Bishop of Rennes (1602).
Gauchat, p. 293.

Guillaume le Gouverneur (d. 1631?): Councilor of the King; Bishop of Saint-Malo (1610). Dec. L.
Gauchat, p. 227.

Artus d'Espinay (1589?–1621?): Abbot of Rhédon; Councilor of the King (State and Private).
C.D., VII, col. 422; Gauchat, p. 234.

Pierre de Cornulier (1575–1639): Councilor of the King in the Parlement of Brittany; Abbot of Saint-Méen. J.U.L.
J. de M., no. 11225; G.C., XIV, col. 1024; D.B.F., IX, col. 712; Gauchat, pp. 293, 342.

Sébastien de Rosmadec (1586–1646): Abbot of Peimpont (1608). J.U.L.
Gauchat, p. 362; G.C., XIV, col. 1036.

Claude de Goualt: Archdeacon of the Cathedral Church of Vannes.
G.C., XIV, col. 940; Thomas-Lacroix, pp. 2–3.

Bailliage of Troyes

René de Breslay (1588–1641): Councilor of the King; Bishop of Troyes (1605). D.B.F., VII, cols. 219–220; Gauchat, p. 342; Durand, pp. 57–58.
Michel Roté: Doctor of the Faculty of Theology and Canon of the Collegiate Church of Saint-Etienne of Troyes. Th.D. Durand, p. 312.

Bailliage of Chaumont en Bassigny

Denis Largentier (1557–1624): Abbot of Clairvaux (1596). O. Cist. Th.D. G.C., IV, cols. 812–813; Louis Lekai, *The Rise of the Cistercian Strict Observance in Seventeenth Century France* (Washington, 1968), pp. 27–46.
Pierre Pietrequin: Dean of Chaumont; Dec. L. C.D., XV, col. 850.

Bailliage of Meaux

Jean de Vieux-Pont: Councilor of the King (State and Private); Bishop of Meaux (1602). C.D., XIX, col. 730; Gulik, p. 240; Gauchat, p. 237.

Bailliage of Provins

Charles Moissy: Doyen de la Chrétienté in Provins; Canon of Notre-Dame-du-Vale; Curé of Saint-Ayoul.

Bailliage of Sézannes

Hierémie le Mère (d. Dec. 8, 1614): Doyen de la Chrétienté of Sézannes. Th.D.

Bailliage of Sens

Jacques Cardinal Du Perron (1556–1618): Grand Almoner of France (1610); Archbishop of Sens (1606); Primate of the Gauls and Germany; (Bishop of Evreux, 1592–1606). C.D., VI, col. 795; D.B.F., XII, cols. 339–341; Gulik, p. 190; Gauchat, pp. 7, 179, 313; Haag, IV, 217–220.
Sébastien Zamet (1588–1655): Abbot of Juilly; Duke Bishop designate of Langres and Peer of France; Count of Monthageon; almoner. Th. L. J. de M., no. 35412; Gulik, pp. 226, 274; Gauchat, p. 221; Louis Prunel, *Sebastien Zamet* (Paris, 1912).

Bailliage of Vitry-le-François

François le Picart: Councilor and Almoner Ordinary of the Queen; Abbot *in*

commendam of Notre-Dame-de-Chartreuve Prior of Notre-Dame-Chastel
-en-Porcien.
G.C., ix, col. 485.

Bailliage of Château-Thierry

François Palmarot: Curé of Dormans-sur-Marne. Th.D.

GOUVERNEMENT OF LANGUEDOC

Sénéchaussée and town of Toulouse

Jean Cardinal de Bonzy (1560–1621); Bishop of Béziers (1598); Grand
Almoner of Marie de Médicis (1601–1615). J.D.
Gulik, p. 135; Gauchat, pp. 11, 116; Madame Bellaud Dessalles, *Les
évêques Italiens de l'ancien diocèse de Béziers, 1547–1669* (Paris, 1901),
pp. 215–368.
Louis de la Valette (1583–1639): Archbishop of Toulouse (1613–1627).
J. de M., no. 25036; Gulik, p. 315; Gauchat, pp. 14, 340; Petit p. 233.
Jean Berthier (Bertier) (d. 1620): Councilor of the King (State and Private);
Bishop of Rieux (1602): Chancellor of Queen Marguerite.
C.D., iii, cols. 42–43; Gauchat, pp. 103, 296; Jean Mariéjol, *La vie de
Marguerite de Valois* (Paris, 1928), p. 337.
Alphonse d'Elbene (1580–1651): Councilor of the King (State and Private);
Bishop of Albi (1608–1634).
C.D., vii, col. 200; D.B.F., xii, cols. 1181–1182; Gauchat, p. 75.

Sénéchaussée of Carcassonne and Béziers

Christolphe de l'Estaing (d. 1621): Councilor of the King (State and Private);
Bishop of Carcassonne (1603); Chapel Master of the Music of the King
(Bishop of Lodève 1580–1603).
Gulik, pp. 191, 227; Gauchat, pp. 134, 181; *LMHIV*, vii, 361.

Sénéchaussée of Beaucaire and Nîmes

Charles de Rousseau (1569–1623): Councilor of the King; Bishop and Seigneur
of Mende (1609); Count of Gevaudan. Dec. D.
Gulik, p. 244; Gauchat, p. 242.
Paul Antoine (de Fay) de Perault (1583–1633): Councilor of the King; Coad-
jutor bishop of Uzès (July, 1614). Th. M.
J. de M., no. 14951; C.D., vii, col. 811; Gauchat, p. 354.

Sénéchaussée of Puy-en-Vellay

[No deputy for the First Estate.]

245

Town, Gouvernement, and Sénéchaussée of Montpellier

Pierre de Fenouillet (1578–1652): Councilor of the King (State and Private); Bishop of Montpellier (1608). Th.D.
Gauchat, p. 248; Petit, p. 235.

Sénéchaussée of Lauragais

[No deputy for the First Estate]

Sénéchaussée, Pays, and County of Foix

Joseph d'Esparbes Lussan (d. 1625): Councilor of the King (State and Private); Bishop of Pamiers (1605). Th.L.
J. de M., no. 14217; C.D., VII, col. 390; Gulik, p. 111; Gauchat, p. 88.

GOUVERNEMENT OF PICARDY

Bailliage of Amiens

Prince Louis de Lorraine (1585?–1621): Archbishop and Duke of Rheims (1605); First Peer of France.
C.D., XII, col. 413; Gauchat, pp. 12, 91, 295; Barbiche, p. 201.
Raymond de Lamartonie (de la Marthonie) (1581–1627): Prior *in commendam* of Saint-Jean-de-Colle; Provost and Canon of the Church of Notre-Dame of Amiens.
C.D., XIII, col. 314; Gauchat, pp. 147, 219; G. C., X, col. 1209.

Sénéchaussée of Ponthieu

Jacques Saumont: Canon of the Church of Saint-Vulfran; Prior of Sainte-Croix; Curé of the Church of Saint-Gilles in Ponthieu. Th.D.

Sénéchaussée of Boulonnais

Antoine Clugnet (d. Nov. 30, 1614): Canon, Archdeacon, and Official of the Church of Notre-Dame of Boulogne. J.U.L.

Calais and Pays Réconquis

[No deputy for the First Estate.]

Provostship of Péronne

Antoine Thuet: Doctor of Theology in the University of Paris. Th.D.

Provostship of Montdidier

Raymond de Lamartonie of Amiens.

Provostship of Roye

Antoine Thuet of Péronne

GOUVERNEMENT OF DAUPHINÉ

Jean de la Croix (de Chevrières) (d. 1619): Councilor of the King (State and Private); Prince Bishop of Grenoble (1607); President of the Estates of Dauphiné. J.U.D.
  J. de M., no. 11919; C.D., VI, cols. 544–545; Gauchat, pp. 147, 197.
François Armuet (d. 1649?): Dean of the Church of Notre-Dame of Grenoble; Prior of Renesty.
  C.D., I, cols. 802–803; G.C., XVI, col. 263.

GOUVERNEMENT OF PROVENCE

Estates of Provence

Paul Hurault de l'Hôpital (d. 1624): Councilor of the King; Archbishop of Aix (1599).
  C.D., X, col. 901; Gauchat, p. 89; Haag, pp. 15–17.
Toussaint de Glandèsves (1579–1647?): Councilor of the King; Bishop of Cisteron (1606).
  J. De M., no. 17660; C.D., IX, col. 336; Gauchat, p. 318.

Town of Marseille

[The same deputies as the Estates of Provence.]

Town of Arles

[The same deputies as the Estates of Provence.]

GOUVERNEMENT OF LYONNAIS

Sénéchaussée of Lyon

Denis Simon de Marquemont (1572–1626): Councilor of the King (State and Private); Count Archbishop of Lyon (1612); Primate of France. J.U.D.
  Gauchat, pp. 19, 226.
Antoine de Gilbertès (d. 1639): Canon (1574) and Archdeacon in the Church of Lyon.
  J. de M., no. 17451; C.D., IX, col. 223.

247

Sénéchaussée of Forez

[The same deputies as Lyon.]

Sénéchaussée of Beaujolais

[The same deputies as Lyon.]

Bays Pays of Auvergne

Joachim d'Estaing (1590–1650): Bishop designate of Clermont. Dec.D.
J. de M., no. 14324; C. D., VII, col. 466; Gauchat, p. 153.
Gabriel du Croc: Provost of the Church of Clermont.

Bailliage of Saint-Flour and Haute Auvergne

André Pons de la Grange: Archdeacon of the Cathedral of Saint-Flour (1594).
J. de M., no. 27199; G.C., II, cols. 435–436.
Christophle Verdier (d. 1621): Seigneur and Abbot of Saint-Pibrac and of Saint-Rozi.
G.C., II, 465.
Jean d'Apchier: Sieur and Prior of la Volte.

Sénéchaussée of Bourbonnais

Pierre du Lyon: Councilor of the King (State and Private); Sieur of la Cane; Abbot of Saint-Melene and Menat; Dean of the Church of Saint-Nicolas of Mont Lusson.
Antoine Aubery: Canon of the Church of the Notre-Dame of Moulins.
Faure, I, 131; Clairefond, p. 246.
Nicolas Doutré: Curé of Yssure-les-Moulins. Th.D.

Sénéchaussée of the Haute Marche

[No deputy for the First Estate.]

Sénéchaussée of the Basse Marche

Gabriel Marand: Abbot of the Secular and Collegiate Church of Saint-Pierre of Dorat (? – 1631).
G.C., II, col. 551; Poulbrière, p. 307.

Bailliage of Saint-Pierre-le-Moutier

Eustache de Chery (1590?–1669): Treasurer and Canon of the Cathedral Church of Nevers.[3]
D.B.F., VIII, cols. 1035–1036; Gauchat, pp. 260, 279.

[3] Eustache de Chery was the only deputy honored with the title *noble et scientifique personne*.

GOUVERNEMENT OF ORLEANAIS

Sénéchaussée of Poitou (Fontenay and Nyort)

Armand Jean du Plessis (1585–1642): Bishop of Luçon (1606–1624); Councilor of the King (State and Private). Th.B.

> C.D., XV, cols. 948–949; Gulik, p. 230; Gauchat, p. 225.

Philippe Cacand: Dean and Canon of Saint-Hiliare-le-Grand of Poitiers.

Sénéchaussée of Anjou

Charles Miron (1570–1628): Councilor of the King (State and Private); Bishop of Angers (1588–1616, 1622–1626).

> C.D., XIII, col. 881; Gulik, p. 108; Gauchat, pp. 82, 226; Petit, p. 234.

Léonor d'Estampes de Vallancay (1588–1651): Councilor and Almoner of the King; Abbot and Baron of Saint-Pierre-de-Borgueil-en-Vallée.

> J. de M., no. 14325; C.D., VII, col. 482; Gauchat, pp. 135, 295; Petit, pp. 235–236; G.C., XIV, col. 666.

Louis de la Grésille: Canon of the Church of Angers; Sieur of Neliampart.

René Ponthery: Claustral Prior of the Abbey of Saint-Aubin of Angers. O.S.B.

Bailliage of Touraine and Amboise

François de la Guesle (1562–Oct. 30, 1614): Councilor of the King (State and Private); Archbishop of Tours (1597). J.U.D.

> C.D., X, col. 63; Gulik, p. 321; Gauchat, p. 350.

Amanion le Houx: Canon of the Church of Tours; Secretary Ordinary of the Archbishop.

Jean Chatard: Canon of Saint-Martin of Tours (elected to replace de la Guesle).

Sénéchaussée of Loudunois

The Bishop of Luçon.

Gouvernement of la Rochelle and Pays Aunis

[No deputy for the clergy.]

Sénéchaussée of Angoulême

Antoine de la Rochefoucault (1575–1634): Councilor of the King; Bishop of Angoulême (1607). Dec. L.

> J. de M., no. 29505; C.D., XVII, col. 370; Gauchat, p. 183.

Sénéchaussée of Maine

Charles de Beaumanoir (de Lavardin) (1585–1637): Councilor of the King (State and Private); Bishop of Mans (1610). J.U.D.

> J. de M., no 3666; C.D., II, cols. 655–659; Gauchat, p. 145.

Guillaume Richer: Abbot of the Monastery of Saint-Vincent of the Congregation of Chesau-Benoît (1614–1619). O.S.B.

G.C., xiv., cols. 466–467.

Claude Lefevre: Chanter and Canon of the Church of Mans.

Bailliage of Berry

André Frémiot (1573–1641): Councilor of the King (State and Private); Councilor in the Parlement; Patriarch Archbishop of Bourges (1604–1622).

Gauchat, p. 116; Major, p. 189; Petit, p. 234.

Guillaume Foucault (d. Nov. 1614): Abbot of Chalivri (Chalivoy); Canon and Grand Archdeacon in the Church of Bourges.

J. de M., no. 15926; C.D., viii, col. 446; G.C., ii, col. 194.

Bailliage of Chartres

Philippe Hurault: Councilor of the King (State and Private); Bishop of Chartres. (See Paris and Ile de France.)

Bailliage of Orléans

Gabriel de l'Aubespine (1579–1630): Councilor of the King (State and Private); Bishop of Orléans (1604). Th. B.

C.D., i, cols. 903–906; Gauchat, p. 102; LMHIV, vii, 677.

Charles de la Saussaye (1565–1621): Doctor in the Faculty of Theology and in the Laws; Councilor and Almoner of the King; Dean of the Church of Orléans. Th.D.; J.U.D.

G.C., viii, cols. 1510–1511; Major, p. 189.

Charles Fougeu (1568–1630): Councilor and Almoner of the King; Abbot in commendam of the Abbey of Saint-Euverte of Orléans (1609).

G.C., viii, col. 1578; Luttin, p. 153.

Bailliage of Blois

The Bishop of Chartres.

Bailliage of Étampes

Guy de Verembroys: Doyen de la Chrétienté and of the Church of Sainte-Croix of Etampes.

Bailliage and County of Gien

Melchior Sonnet: Curé of the Town of Ozoer. Th.D.

Bailliage of Montargis

Daniel Bonnet: Prior and Curé of Montargis. O.S.A., Th.D.

Duchy and Bailliage of Vendôme

Michel Sublet (d. 1649): Cardinal Abbot of the Abbey of Sainte-Trinité of Vendôme.
C.D., XVIII, col. 696 (?); G.C., VIII, col. 1379.
François Gérard: Curé of Saint-Amand.

Bailliage of Perche

François le Moine: Promoter in the Officiality of Séez at the seat of Mortagne; Provost of the Church of Mortagne; Curé of Saint-Céronne.

Bailliage of Nivernois

Jean Genest: Pronotary of the Holy See; Grand Archdeacon and Official of the Church of Nevers. Th.D.

Bailliage of Chatellerault

[No deputy for the First Estate.]

Bailliage of Château-Neuf-en-Thimerais

[No deputy for the First Estate.]

General Agents of the Clergy

Martin de Racine de Villegamblain: Abbot of la Vernusse; Treasurer of the Sainte-Chapelle of Bourges (1595–1626).
J. de M., no. 28103; G.C., II, col. 117.
Pierre de Behety: Abbot of Saint-Grace; Canon, Grand Archdeacon, Vicar General and Official of Couserans. J.U.D.

B. THE DEPUTIES TO THE SECOND ESTATE

PARIS AND ILE DE FRANCE

Provostship, Town and Viscounty of Paris

Henri de Vaudetar: Chevalier; Baron of Persen; Councilor of the King (State and Private); Deputy for the Viscounty.
J. de M., no. 34226.

Bailliage of Vermandois

Eustache de Conflans (d. 1628): Chevalier of the Two Orders of the King; Viscount of Auchy; Captain of Fifty Men of Arms of the ordonnances of the King; Councilor of State.
J. de M., no. 11001; C.D., IV, cols. 147–148.

Bailliage of Senlis

Louis de Montmorency (1565–1615): Chevalier; Seigneur of Bouteville; Bailly and Governor of Senlis; Vice-Admiral of France; Councilor of State.
J. de M., no. 24378; C.D., XIV, col. 389.

Bailliage of Clermont-en-Beauvoisis

Jacques de Longueval: Chevalier; Seigneur of Haraucourt; Bailly and Governor of Clermont-en-Beauvoisis; Councilor of the King (State and Private); Cornet of the Light Horse of the Queen.
J. de M., no. 21992; C.D., XII, col. 317.

Bailliage of Chaumont-en-Vexin

Pierre de Roncherolle (d. 1627): Chevalier; Seigneur and Baron of Pont-Saint-Pierre; Gentleman Ordinary of the Chamber of the King; Seneschal of Ponthieu.
J. de M., no. 29747; C.D., XVII, cols. 591–592; Richelieu, I, 302.

Bailliage of Valois

René Potier (1579–1670): Chevalier; Seigneur and Count of Tresme; Captain of the Body Guard of the King; Bailly of Valois; Captain Ensign of the Duke of Vendôme.
J. de M., no. 27448; C.D., XVI, col. 239.

Bailliage of Melun

Antoine de Brichanteau (1552–1617): Chevalier of the Two Orders of the King; Councilor of State; Captain of Fifty Men of Arms of the ordonnances of the King; Seigneur and Marquis of Nangis; Millan, and Ligueres.
C.D., IV, cols. 105–106; D.B.F., V, cols. 1191–1192.

Bailliage of Nemours

Jean Hurault de l'Hôpital: Chevalier; Seigneur of Gommerville and Fay; Gentleman Ordinary of the Chamber of the King.
C.D., X, col. 901; Haag, VI, 15–17.

Bailliage of Montfort-Lamaury

Charles de Cocherel (d. 1657?): Chevalier; Seigneur of le Parc; Bailly of Montfort and Houdan.
J. de M., no. 10526; D.B.F., IX, col. 68.

Bailliage of Mantes and Meulan

Louis de Tilly (d. 1635): Chevalier; Seigneur of Blaru; Lieutenant of One

Hundred Gentlemen of the Household of the King.
J. de M., no. 33024; C.D., XIX, col. 10.

Bailliage of Dourdan

Anne de l'Hôpital (d. 1620): Chevalier; Seigneur of Sainte-Mesine (Mesmé); Bailly of Dourdan.
J. de M., no. 19535; C.D., X, col. 722.

Bailliage of Beauvais

François de Boufflers (1583?–1670): Chevalier; Seigneur of Boufflers; Viscount of Ponche; Bailly of Beauvais.
J. de M., no. 6078; C.D., III, col. 691.

Bailliage of Soissons

Henri de la Marque: Chevalier; Seigneur and Count of la Marque; Colonel of One Hundred Swiss of the Guard of the King.

Bailliage of Dreux

Henri de Balsac: Chevalier; Councilor of the King in his Councils; Gentleman Ordinary of the Chamber of the King; Baron of Clermont d'Antragues; Seigneur of Messière.
J. de M., no. 2626; C.D., II, col. 254; D.B.F., IV, cols. 1519–1520.

Bailliage of Magny

[No deputy for the Second Estate.]

GOUVERNEMENT OF BURGUNDY

Bailliage of Dijon

Claude de Saulx (d. 1638): Chevalier; Seigneur and Count of Tavannes; Bailly of Dijon.
J. de M., no. 31397; C.D., XVIII, col. 313.

Bailliage of Autun

Léonor de Rabutin: Chevalier and Baron of Piry and Bussy; Gentleman Ordinary of the Chamber of the King.
J. de M., no. 28090.

Bailliage of Chalôns-sur-Saône

Henri de Bauffremont (1578–1622): Chevalier; Seigneur and Baron of Senecey; Captain of Fifty Men of Arms of the King; Governor of the Town and

253

Château of Ausonne; Bailly of Châlons; Lieutenant for the King in the Pays and County of Mâconnais.

J. de M., no. 3451; C.D., II, col. 519; D.B.F., V, cols. 918–919.

Bailliage of la Montagne

Hercules de Villars la Faye: Chevalier; Seigneur of Villeneuve.
J. de M., no. 34949; C.D., XIX, col. 820.

Bailliage of Mâcon

Léonard de Scemur: Chevalier; Seigneur of Tremont; Lieutenant of the Company of Men of Arms of Monsieur le Grand (Roger de Bellegarde, grand écuyer).

Bailliage of Auxois

Louis Danlezi: Chevalier; Seigneur of Chazelle.

Bailliage of Auxerre

Aymar de Prix (Prie): Chevalier; Baron of Toney (Toucy); Captain of Fifty Men of the ordonnances of the King.
C.D., XVI, cols. 419–420; *Tou-Beau Feu*, app.
Olivier de Chasteleu: Chevalier; Seigneur of Coulange and Val de Mercie.
C.D., V, cols. 312–317.

Bailliage of Bar-sur-Seine

Antoine de Lenoncourt: Chevalier; Seigneur of Marolle; Councilor of the King in his Councils; Gentleman of the Chamber of the King; Bailly of Bar-sur-Seine.
J. de M. no. 21533; C.D., XI, col. 863.

Bailliage of Charolais

Théophile de Damas (d. 1617): Chevalier; Seigneur and Baron of Digoyne; Ensign of One Hundred Men of Arms under the Duke of Mayenne.
J. de M., no. 12964; C.D., VI, cols. 720–721; D.B.E. X, col. 21.

Bailliage of Bugey en Bresse

Antoine de Champier: Chevalier of the Order of the King; Gentleman Ordinary of the Chamber of the King; Seigneur of Fauverge, Feilleve, and Mantueram.

Bailliage of Gex

Pierre Chevalier: Seigneur of Fernaix.
J. de M., no. 9073.

Bailliage of Bresse

Clériadus de Colligny: Chevalier; Seigneur of Cressia.
J. de M., no. 10728.

GOUVERNEMENT OF NORMANDY

Bailliage of Rouen

Louis de Mouy (Moy) (d. 1637): Chevalier; Seigneur of Maillerais (la Meilleraye).
J. de M., no. 24706; C.D., XIV, col. 720.

Bailliage of Caen

Jean de Longaunay: Chevalier; Seigneur of Damigny and Sainte Marie du Mont; Gentleman of the Chamber of the King; Captain of Fifty Men of Arms; Governor of Carantan.
C.D., XII, col. 281.

Bailliage of Caux

Samuel de Boullinvilliers (Boulainvilliers): Chevalier; Seigneur of Saint-Cère (Saire).
J. de M., no. 6120; C.D., III, cols. 712–713.

Bailliage of Cotantin

Henri Anquetil: Chevalier; Seigneur of Saint-Vast.
J. de M., no. 947; C.D., I, col. 599.

Bailliage of Evreux

Adrian de Breauté (d. 1658): Chevalier; Seigneur of Breauté.
C.D., IV, cols. 36–37; D.B.F., VII, cols. 184–185.

Bailliage of Gisors

Philippe de Fouilleuze: Chevalier; Seigneur of Flavacourt; Bailly of Gisors.
J. de M., no. 15965; C.D., VIII, col. 484; Mousnier, pp. 536–537.

Bailliage of Alençon

François de Vauquelin: Chevalier; Seigneur of Bazoches; Bailly of Alençon.
J. de M., no. 34274; Frondeville, I, 581–582.
François Anzeray: Chevalier; Seigneur of Fonteville; Gentleman Ordinary of the Chamber of the King.
J. de M., no. 1030; C.D., I, cols. 627–628; D.B.F., III, cols. 86–87; Frondeville, *Présidents*, p. 261.

GOUVERNEMENT OF GUYENNE

Town of Bordeaux and Sénéchaussée of Guyenne

Charles de Durefort: Chevalier; Seigneur of Castel-Bayart (Castelbajac); Baron of Cuzagues.

J. de M., no. 13783; C.D., VII, col. 129.

Sénéchaussée of Bazadois

Antoine Jaubert de Barrault: Count of Blaignac; Councilor of State; Seneschal and Governor of Bazadois; Vice-Admiral in Guyenne.

J. de M., no. 20031; C.D., XI, cols. 42–43; *LMHIV*, V, 640.

Sénéchaussée of Périgord

Armand de Hédie: Chevalier; Seigneur and Count of Riberac; Councilor of the King (State and Private).

Hector de Pont-Brian (Pontbriand): Siegneur of Montréal; Councilor of the King in his Councils.

J. de M., no. 27251.

Sénéchaussée of Rouergue

François de Nouaille (Noailles) (1584–1645): Chevalier; Seigneur and Count of Ayen.

J. de M., no. 24998; C.D., XIV, cols. 977–978; André Delmas, *Le Pays de Terrasson* (n.p., 1965), app. VIII.

François de Buissé (Buisson): Chevalier; Seigneur of Bournazel.

J. de M., no. 7227.

Sénéchaussée of Saintonge

François de Sainte More (Maure): Chevalier; Seigneur of Monac (Mosnac); Councilor of State.[4]

C.D., XVIII, col. 199.

Sénéchaussée of Agenois

François de Nompart (Nompar) de Caumont: Ecuyer; Seigneur and Count of l'Auzon (Lauzun); Councilor of the King (State and Private); Captain of Fifty Men of Arms of the ordonnances of the King.

J. de M., no. 7987; C.D., IV, col. 876; Bouchitté, p. 494.

François de la Goute: Baron of le Buisson; Chevalier; Seigneur of Cours, Prast and Pujade.

J. de M., no. 18028.

---

[4] According to C.D., XVIII, col. 199 his Christian name was Geoffroy.

APPENDIX 3

Pays and County of Comminges

Jean Denis: Chevalier; Seigneur of la Hilierre; Gentleman of the Chamber of the King.

Jugerie of Rivière-Verdun

[No deputy for the Second Estate.]

Sénéchaussée of Lannes and Saint-Sever

Antoine de Gramont (d. 1644): Chevalier; Seigneur and Count of Gramont; Councilor of State; Seneschal and Governor of Bayonne.
J. de M., nos. 18110–18111; C.D., IX, col. 641.

Sénéchaussée of Albret

Remond de Montcasin: Chevalier; Seigneur of Montcasin.
Jean de Chastillon: Chevalier; Baron of Mauvoizin.
J. de M., no. 8734 (?).

Sénéchaussée of Armagnac

Giles de Léaumont: Chevalier; Seigneur and Baron of Puygailliard; Captain of Fifty Men of Arms of the ordonnances of the King.
J. de M., no. 21396; C.D., XI, col. 820.

Sénéchaussée of Condomois and Gascogne

Jean de Buzet: Chevalier; Seigneur and Baron of Poudenas; Gentleman Ordinary of the Chamber of the King.
Jean Pol de Moulezin: Chevalier; Seigneur and Baron of Meillan.[5]

Sénéchaussée of Haut Limousin and Town of Limoges

Henri de Bonneval (d. 1642): Chevalier; Seigneur of Bonneval.
J. de M., no. 5655; C.D., III, cols. 507–508; Poulbrière, p. 306; Richelieu, I, 332, Héroard, II, 173.

Sénéchaussée of Bas Limousin

Charles de Saint Marceau: Chevalier; Seigneur of Courson; Viscount of Verdier.
Archives Corrèze, II, 577–578, Poulbrière, p. 306.

Sénéchaussée of Quercy

Antoine de Loisière (Lauzières) (d. 1621): Chevalier; Seigneur and Marquis of Themines; Seneschal and Governor of Quercy.

[5] Grelin, though agreeing on the title of *Meillan (Melien)*, uses the name Regnault Dansan instead of Jean Pol de Moulezin.

J. de M., no. 21335; C.D., XI, cols. 795–796.

Pays and County of Bigorre

Henri de Prez (Des Prez) (d. 1619): Marquis of Montpezat; Viscount of Aste; Baron of les Anges and Pinedor; Councilor of State; Captain of Fifty Men at Arms; Governor of the towns of Muret and Grenadec. J. de M., no. 12835; C.D., XVI, col. 408; D.B.F., XI, col. 39.

GOUVERNEMENT OF BRITTANY

Deputies of the Estates of Brittany

François de Cossé (1585–1651): Chevalier; Seigneur and Count of Brissac; Councilor of the King (State and Private); Lieutenant General for the King in Brittany.
J. de M., no. 11289; C.D., VI, col. 239; D.B.F., IX, col. 766.

Tomas de Gaymaduc (Guemadeuc): Chevalier; Baron of Gaymaduc and of Blossac; Governor of Fougères; Grand Hereditary Equerry of Brittany.
C.D., IV, cols. 577–578; Thomas-Lacroix, p. 2.

Jean du Mas (du Matz): Chevalier; Seigneur of Monmartin; Captain of Fifty Men of Arms; Marshal of Camp; Governor of Vitray.
J. de M., no. 23186; Thomas-Lacroix, p. 2.

Artus de Caydeu (Cahideuc) (1562–1630): Chevalier; Seigneur of Caydeu; Captain of Fifty Men of Arms of the ordonnances of the King.
C.D., IV, cols. 577–578; Thomas-Lacroix, p. 2.

François de la Piguelaye: Chevalier; Seigneur and Viscount of Chainait (Chesnay); Captain of Fifty Men of Arms of the ordonnances of the King.
J. de M., no. 26639; Thomas-Lacroix, p. 2.

Jean de Gegado: Chevalier; Seigneur of Querholin; Guardian of the Coast of the Bishopric of Cornuaille; Master of Camp of a Regiment of French Foot Soldiers; Captain of Fifty Men of Arms of the ordonnances of the King.
Thomas-Lacroix, p. 2.

GOUVERNEMENT OF CHAMPAGNE

Bailliage of Troyes

Jacques de Brouillart (d. 1631): Chevalier; Seigneur and Baron of Coursan, Racine, and Saint-Cire; Gentleman Ordinary of the Chamber of the King.
C.D., VI, col. 709; Mousnier, Labatut, Durand, pp. 124–5.

Bailliage of Chaumont-en-Bassigny

Juste de Pontalier: Chevalier; Seigneur and Baron of Pleurs.
J. de M., no. 27238; C.D., XVI, col. 123.

Bailliage of Meaux

Michel de Reillac: Chevalier; Seigneur of Lignere, of Mareul and of la-Grand-du-Mont-Magnis and Saint-Loup.
J. de M., no. 28590 (?).

Bailliage of Provins

Jacques de l'Hôpital: Chevalier of the Two Orders of the King; Captain of Fifty Men of the ordonnances of the King; Councilor of the King (State and Private); Marquis of Choisy.
J. de M., no. 19535; C.D., X, col. 718.

Bailliage of Sézannes

Claude Dansienville: Chevalier and Baron of Reuillon.

Bailliage of Sens

Charles de Seneton: Chevalier; Seigneur of la Verrière; Bailly of Sens.
J. de M., no. 31715.

Bailliage of Vitry-le-François

Charles d'Amboise: Chevalier; Seigneur and Baron of Bussy-en-Champagne; Marquis of Renel; Baron of Sexefontaine.
J. de M., no. 10465; D.B.F., II, cols. 506–507; Haag, III, 501–502.

Bailliage of Chateau-Thierry

Emanuel d'Anglebermer: Chevalier; Seigneur of Lagny; Gentleman Ordinary of the Chamber of the King.
C.D., I, col. 539.

GOUVERNEMENT OF LANGUEDOC

Sénéchaussée and Town of Toulouse

Jean de la Valette: Chevalier; Sieur of Cornuson and other places; Councilor of the King (State and Private); Captain of Fifty Men of Arms; Seneschal and Governor of the Town and Sénéchausée of Toulouse.
J. de M., no. 33955; C.D., XIX, col. 428.

Sénéchaussée of Carcassonne and Béziers

François de la Jugerie: Chevalier; Seigneur and Count of Rieux.

Sénéchaussée of Beaucaire and Nîmes

Antoine Hercules de Budes: Chevalier; Seigneur and Marquis of Portes; Councilor of the King (State and Private).

René de la Tour de Gouvernet (1545–1617): Chevalier; Baron of Chambaut; Viscount of Prinast; Councilor of the King (State and Private); Master of Camp of a Regiment of Foot Soldiers.
J. de M., no. 33227; C.D., XIX, col. 97; Haag, VI, 406–410.

Sénéchaussée of Puy-en-Vellay

Gaspard Armand (de Polignac): Chevalier; Seigneur and Viscount of Polignac.
J. de M., no. 27076.

Town, Gouvernement, and Sénéchaussée of Montpellier

François de Monlore (Montlaur): Chevalier; Seigneur of Meurles and Precor; Councilor of the King (State and Private); Captain of Fifty Men of Arms; Governor and Seneschal of the Town of Montpellier.
J. de M., no. 24361.

Jean Degardieu: Seigneur of Saint André; Gentleman Ordinary of the Chamber of the King; Captain of One Hundred Light Horse; Governor for the King in the Town of Montpellier.
Haag, IV, 464.

Sénéchaussée of Lauragais

François de Roger: Chevalier; Baron of Fairail; Seneschal of Lauragais; Superintendent General of the Affairs of Queen Marguerite in her County; First Equerry of Her Household.

Marc-Antoine d'Avessens: Chevalier; Seigneur of Saint Romme.
J. de M., no. 2137; C.D., II, col. 122; Haag, I, 200–201.

Sénéchaussée, Pays, and County of Foix

Jacques de Lordat: Chevalier; Seigneur of Castagnac.
J. de M., no. 22001; C.D., XII, col. 366.

GOUVERNEMENT OF PICARDY

Bailliage of Amiens

Charles de Haluin (Hallwin): Seigneur of Mailly; Councilor of the King (State and Private); Governor of the towns and citadels of Ruë; Captain of the Body Guard of the Brother of the King.
J. de M., no. 18959; C.D., X, cols. 226–229.

Sénéchaussée of Ponthieu

Charles de Rambures (d. 1633): Chevalier; Seigneur of Rambures; Councilor of State; Captain of Fifty Men of Arms of the ordonnances of the King; Governor of the Towns and Châteaux of Dourlans and Corotoy.
J. de M., no. 28203; C.D., xvi, col. 763; *LMHIV*, vii, 358–359.

Sénéchaussée of Boulonnais

Jean de Monchy (d. 1638): Chevalier; Seigneur of Moncaverel; Governor of Ardres.
J. de M., no. 24114; C.D., xiii, col. 930; Frondeville, i, 486.
Charles de Belloy: Chevalier; Seigneur of Landretum (Landrethun).
C.D., ii, 884.

Calais and Pays Reconquis

Marc (de) Foucault: Seigneur of Foucault.
C.D., viii, cols. 446–448.

Provostship of Peronne

Charles d'Estourmel (d. 1617): Chevalier; Seigneur of Plainville; Captain of the Bodyguard of the Scots Guard.
C.D., vii, cols. 555–558; Richelieu, i, 227.

Provostship of Montdidier

Charles d'Estmourmel

Provostship of Roye

Charles d'Estmourmel

GOUVERNEMENT OF DAUPHINÉ

Estates of Dauphiné

(Charles-) Henri de Clermont: Chevalier; Seigneur and Count of Tonnerre; Councilor of the King (State and Private).
J. de M., no. 10470; C.D., v, col. 866; D.B.F., viii, col. 1487.
Jean de Puy (1567–1658?): Seigneur of Montbrun; Councilor of the King (State and Private); Captain of Fifty Men of Arms of the ordonnances of the King.
J. de M., no. 27914; C.D. xvi, col. 527; D.B.F., xii, cols. 610–611; Haag, iv, 457–465.
Laurens de Plovier: Seigneur of Plovier and of Quaiz; Baron of Assieu and Surieu; Gentleman Ordinary of the Chamber of the King.
Jean de Murines: Chevalier; Seigneur of Bozancier.

GOUVERNEMENT OF PROVENCE

Estates of Provence

Arnault de Villeneufe (d. Dec. 14, 1614): Chevalier; Seigneur and Marquis of les Arts (Arcs).
J. de M., no. 34929; C.D., XIX, cols. 795–796.
André d'Oraison: Chevalier; Seigneur and Count of Boulbon.
J. de M., no. 25283; C.D., XV, col. 182; Haag, VIII, 51.
Roland de Castellanne: Chevalier; Seigneur of Monmejen.
C.D., IV, cols. 797–811; D.B.F. VII, col. 1359.
François de Vins: Chevalier; Seigneur of Vins.
J. de M., no. 35054; C.D., XIX, col. 856.
Jean de Castellanne: Chevalier; Seigneur of la Verdière.
C.D., IV, cols. 805–806; D.B.F., VII, col. 1359.
Palamedes Fabry: Chevalier; Seigneur of Valavés; Baron of Rians.
J. de M., no. 14581.

Town of Marseille

Théocrenes de Glandèves: Chevalier; Seigneur of Cuges.
J. de M., no. 17660; C.D., IX, cols. 335–336.
Léon de Valbelle: Ecuyer.
J. de M., no. 33915; C.D., XIX, col. 373.

Town of Arles

Gabriel de Varadier: Chevalier; Seigneur of Saint André (Andiol).
J. de M., no. 34086; C.D., XIX, col. 482.

GOUVERNEMENT OF LYONNAIS

Sénéchaussée of Lyon

Claude de Cremiaux (Crémeaux): Chevalier; Seigneur of Cremiaux and of Chemousset (Chamosset); Baron d'Antragues (Entraigues).
J. de M., no. 11806; C.D., VI, col. 461.

Sénéchaussée of Forèz

Jacques Paillard d'Urfé: Chevalier; Seigneur and Marquis of Bauge; Count of Urfé; Councilor of the King (State and Private); Seneschal of Forèz.
J. de M., no. 33778; C.D., XIX, cols. 293–294.

Sénéchaussée of Beaujolais

Philibert de Serpent: Baron of Goudras (Gondras), Lourdes, and Saint-Saturnin.
J. de M., no. 31772; C.D., XVIII, col. 541.

Bas Pays of Auvergne

Jean de la Guelle: Chevalier; Seigneur of la Chault; Baron of Nesle.
Claude de Chauvigny: Chevalier; Seigneur of Belot (Blot) l'Eglise.
J. de M., no. 8885; C.D., V, cols. 542–543; D.B.F., VIII, col. 920.

Bailliage of Saint Flour and Haute Auvergne

Jacques d'Apchon: Chevalier; Seigneur of Apchon and of Joille.
J. de M., no. 1038; C.D., I, 630–631.
Jacques de la Rocque: Chevalier; Seigneur of la Rocque.
J. ae M., no. 29789 (?).

Sénéchaussée of Bourbonnais

Gaspard de Coligny (d. 1629): Chevalier; Baron of Saligny; Gentleman Ordinary of the Chamber of the King.
J. de M., no. 10728; C.D., VI, col. 46; D.B.F., IX, col. 227.
Jean d'Apchon (d. c. 1620): Chevalier; Seigneur of Erezat (Serezat); Governor for the King in the Town of Cuset.
J. de M., no. 1039; C.D., I, 631–632.

Sénéchaussée of the Haute Marche

Geoffroy de la Roche Aymont: Chevalier; Seigneur of Saint Messan; Seneschal of Haute Marche.
J. de M., no. 29470; C.D., XVII, cols. 248–249.
Gabriel de Malice (Malesc): Chevalier; Seigneur of Malice and of Chastelu (Châtelus-Malvaleix).
Poulbrière, p. 307.

Sénéchaussée of the Basse Marche

Henri Poussart: Chevalier; Seigneur and Baron of Fors and le Vigéan.
J. de M., no. 27549; Haag, VIII, 312–314.
Gaspart Frottier: Chevalier; Seigneur of la Messelière. Master of Camp of Infantry.
J. de M., no. 16416; C.D., VIII, col. 699; *LMHIV*, IV, 946.

Bailliage of Saint-Pierre-le-Moutier

Florimont de Dormes: Chevalier of the Order of the King; Bailly of Saint-Pierre-le-Moutier.
Thomas de Bonnay: Chevalier; Seigneur of Bessay.
J. de M., no. 5586; C.D., III, cols. 478–481.

GOUVERNEMENT OF ORLEANAIS

Sénéchaussée of Poitou (Fontenay and Nyort)

Charles de Vivonne: Chevalier; Seigneur of la Chateigneraye.
J. de M., no. 35156; C.D., XIX, col. 911.
Odet de la Noüe: Chevalier; Councilor of State.
C.D., XV, col. 74; Haag, VI, 296–304.

Sénéchaussée of Anjou

Martin du Bellay: Chevalier; Seigneur of Bellay; Prince of Yvetot; Councilor of the King (State and Private); Marquis of Touarsay (Thouarcé); Baron of Commequiers; Captain of Fifty Men of Arms of the ordonnances of the King.
J. de M., no. 3938; C.D. II, 854–855.

Bailliage of Touraine and Amboise

René d'Argy: Chevalier; Seigneur of Pons.
C.D., I, col. 766; D.B.F., III, col. 611.

Sénéchaussée of Loudunois

[No deputy for the Second Estate.]

Gouvernement of la Rochelle and Pays Aunis

René de Tallansac (Talensac) (d. 1628): Chevalier; Seigneur of Loudrière; Governor and Seneschal of the Town of La Rochelle and Pays Aunis; Councilor of the King (State and Private).
Haag, IX, 337.

Sénéchaussée of Angoulême

Jacques de Bremont (1561–1651): Chevalier; Seigneur of Ars; Councilor of State.
J. de M., no. 6663; D.B.F., VII, cols. 205–208.

Sénéchaussée of Maine

René de Bouillay (Bouillé): Chevalier; Seigneur and Count of Créance; Councilor of State; Captain of Fifty Men of Arms of the ordonnances of the King.
C.D., III, col. 704.
Jean de Vaussay: Chevalier; Seigneur of Rocheux.

Bailliage of Berry

Guillaume Pot (d. 1616): Chevalier of the Orders of the King; Councilor in in the King's Councils; Grand Master of Ceremonies of France; First Carver and Crown Bearer of the King; Seigneur of Rhodes.

J. de M., no. 27427; C.D., XVI, col. 211.

Henri de la Chastre (b. 1574): Chevalier; Seigneur and Count of Nancey; Councilor of the King (State and Private); Bailly of Gien.
J. de M., no. 8804; C.D., V, cols. 343–344.

Bailliage of Chartres

Charles d'Angennes: Chevalier; Seigneur of Maintenon; Councilor of State.
C.D., I, col. 510; D.B.F., II, cols. 1089, 1097.

Bailliage of Orléans

François de l'Hôpital (1583–1660): Chevalier; Seigneur of le Hallier; Councilor of State; Ensign of the Company of the King; Captain and Governor of Fontainbleau.
C.D., X, cols. 726–727, Héroard, II, 179; Charmiel, *Trésorier*, p. 449; Petit, p. 238.

Bailliage of Blois

François de Racines: Chevalier; Seigneur of Villegomblain.
J. de M., no. 28103.

Bailliage of Étampes

Paul de Cugnac (d. Dec. 30, 1614): Chevalier; Seigneur of Inmouville (Imonville).
J. de M., no. 12062; C.D., VI, 634–642.

Bailliage and County of Gien

Henri de Postel: Chevalier; Seigneur of Ormois, Couberon, Corvoz, Escriuiders; Gentleman Ordinary of the Chamber of the Prince of Condé.
J. de M., no. 27422.

Bailliage of Montargis

Antoine des Hayes (1571?–1637): Chevalier; Seigneur of Cornemin and Courtoin; Bailly and Governor of Montargis.
D.B.F., X, cols. 1380–1381.

Duchy and Bailliage of Vendôme

Elisée d'Illiers: Chevalier; Seigneur of les Radraits (Radrets); Baron of Bourdoeil; Gentleman Ordinary of the Chamber of the King.
J. de M., no. 19761; C.D., X, cols. 924–928.

Bailliage of Perche

Etienne l'Hermite: Chevalier; Seigneur of la Salle Rougeris; Councilor of the King; Gentleman Ordinary of the Chamber of the King; Bailly of Perche.

Bailly of Nivernois

Jean Andrault de Langeron: Chevalier; Seigneur of Langeron; Bailly of Nivernois and Donziers; Gentleman Ordinary of the Chamber of the King.
J. de M., no. 772; C.D., I, cols. 481–482, XI, col. 417; D.B.F., II, cols. 879–880.

Adrian de Blanchefort (b. 1552?): Chevalier; Seigneur of Blanchefort; Baron of Anois (Asnois).
J. de M., no. 4986; C.D., III, col. 330.

Bailliage of Châtellerault

Emanuel Philibert de la Braudière: Chevalier; Seigneur; Baron of l'Isle and of Rouet; Councilor of the King (State and Private); Captain of Fifty men of Arms.

Bailliage of Châteauneuf-en-Thimerais

Prejen de la Fin (Prégent de Lafin) (d. 1625): Chevalier; Vidame of Chartres; Councilor of the King (State and Private); Captain of Fifty Men of Arms of the ordonnances of the King; Marshal of Camp in the Army of the King; Seigneur of Beaussac-la-Ferté-de-Beauvoir.
Haag, VI, 200–208.

C. THE DEPUTIES TO THE THIRD ESTATE

PARIS AND ILE DE FRANCE

Town of Paris

Messire Robert Miron (1569–1641): Councilor of the King (State and Private); President of Requests in the Parlement (1601); Provost of Merchants of Paris.
J. de M., no. 24003; C.D. XIII, col. 881; A. Miron de l'Espinay, *Robert Miron et l'administration de Paris* (Paris, 1922); Maugis, III, 309–310.

Noble Homme Israel Desneux: Grenitier of the salt stores of Paris; Sieur of Menières; Echevin of Paris.
J. de M., no. 12801.

Noble Homme Pierre Clappisson: Councilor of the King at the Chatelet of Paris; Echevin of Paris.

Noble Homme Pierre Sainctot: Seigneur of Vemars; Councilor of the City of Paris.
Reg. délib. Paris, XV, 494.

Noble Homme Jean Perrot: Seigneur of Chesnart; Councilor of the City of Paris. *Reg. délib. Paris*, XV, 481.

Nicolas de Paris: Bourgeois of Paris.
Reg. délib. Paris, XV, 19, 477.

Provostship and Viscounty of Paris

Messire Henri de Mesmes (d. 1650): Seigneur of Irval; Councilor of the King (State and Private); Lieutenant Civil of the Provostship and Viscounty of Paris.
J. de M., no. 23734; C.D., XIII, col. 754; *Reg. délib. Paris*, XVI, 1, 73.

Bailliage of Vermandois

Maître Etienne de Lalain: Sieur Despuissar, Roquincourt and la Suze; Avocat in the Bailliage of Vermandois and Presidial Seat of Laon.

Bailliage of Senlis

Philippe Loisel: Ecuyer; Councilor of the King; President, Lieutenant General, Civil and Criminal of the Bailliage and Presidial Seat of Senlis.
C.D., XII, col. 226; *Reg. délib. Paris*, XV, 5.

Gabriel de Montierre: Ecuyer; Sieur of Saint Martin; Councilor of the King; Lieutenant of the Bailly of Senlis at Pontoise.

Bailliage of Clermont-en-Beauvoisis

Noble Homme Pierre le Mercier: Councilor of the King; Lieutenant General of Bailliage of Clermont.

Noble Homme Simon Vigneron: Sieur of Monceau; Councilor of the King; Lieutenant Particular, Civil and Criminal of the Bailliage of Clermont.

Bailliage of Chaumont-en-Vexin

Maître Louis le Porguier: Provost Forain and Lieutenant General of the Bailliage of Chaumont (and Magny).

André Jorel: Ecuyer; Sieur of Saint Brice; Councilor of the King; Lieutenant General, Civil and Criminal of Magny.

Bailliage of Valois

Messire Charles Therault (Thibault): Seigneur of Vuaremal and Sery; Councilor and Master of Ordinary Requests of Queen Marguerite, Duchess of Valois; Lieutenant Particular of Crespy and Pierre-Fond.

Bailliage of Melun

Pierre de Jau: Ecuyer; Sieur of Giroles; Councilor of the King; Lieutenant General of the Bailliage and Presidial Seat of Melun.

Bailliage of Nemours

Noble Homme Maître Jean de Beau: Councilor of the King; Lieutenant General, Civil and Criminal of the Bailliage and Duchy of Nemours.

Noble Homme Guillaume le Gris: Captain of the Château of Nemours.

Bailliage of Montfort-Lamaury

Noble Homme Noël Rafron: Councilor of the King; Procureur of the King in the Bailliage and County of Montfort.

Nicolas Philippes: Justice in Eyre of Waters and Forests of Neufle-le-Chatel; Receveur of the Land and Seigneurie of Pontchartrain.

Bailliage of Mantes and Meulan

Maître Jean le Couturier: Councilor of the King; Lieutenant General, Civil and Criminal of the Bailliage and Presidial Seat of Mantes.

Antoine de Viot (Vion): Ecuyer; Councilor of the King; Lieutenant Civil and Criminal of the Royal Seat of Meulan.

C.D., XIX, cols. 862–872 (?).

Bailliage of Dourdan

Maître Pierre Boudet: Avocat in the Bailliage

Bailliage of Beauvais

Robert Darry (b. 1557): Sieur of la Roche and Ernemont; Councilor of the King; Lieutenant General, Civil and Criminal in the Bailliage and Presidial Seat of Beauvais.

C.D., VI, cols. 761–762.

Bailliage of Soissons

Pierre de Chezelles: Ecuyer; Sieur of la Forest and Grizolles; Councilor of the King; President and Lieutenant General of the Bailliage and Presidial Seat of Soissons.

Bailliage of Dreux

Maître Thibault Couppé: Sieur of la Plaine; Avocat in the Ballage of Dreux. J.U.L.

Bailliage of Magny

No independent representative in the third estate. Jorel, the deputy of Magny, was added to the Chaumont delegation.

Major, p. 29.

GOUVERNEMENT OF BURGUNDY

Bailliage of Dijon

Maître Claude Mochet: Seigneur of Azu; Avocat in the Parlement of Dijon and Council of the Three Estates of the pays.

Messire René Gervais: Councilor of the King; Lieutenant General of the Bailliage of Dijon.

Maître Antoine Jolly: Councilor of the King; Recorder of the Parlement and Estates of Burgundy.

Bailliage of Autun

Maître Philibert Venot (b. 1567): Avocat in the Bailliage of Autun. Major, *Deputies*, p. 73

Maître Simon de Montaigu: Lieutenant General in the Chancellery of Autun; Virq of Autun.

Bailliage of Châlons-sur-Saône

Maître Guillaume Prisque: Sieur of Serville; Lieutenant Criminal of the Bailliage of Châlons.

Maître Abraham Perrault: Councilor of the Bailliage; Mayor of the Town of Châlons.

Bailliage of La Montagne

Noble Claude François le Sain: Councilor of the King; Lieutenant General of the Bailliage of La Montagne at the principal seat of Chatillon-sur-Seine.

Maître François de Gissey: Councilor of the King; Lieutenant General in the Chancellery of Chatillon-sur-Seine.[6]

Bailliage of Mâcon

Messire Hugues Fouillard: Councilor of the King; Lieutenant General of Mâcon.

Bailliage of Auxois

Noble Homme Claude Espiart: Councilor and Secretary of the King; Court Crier of the Chancellery of Burgundy.

Noble Homme Jacques de Cluny: Councilor of the King; Provostship Judge in the town of Avalon.

---

[6] Gissey is listed only in Saugrain.

Bailliage of Auxerre

Noble Homme Maître Claude Chevalier: Councilor of the King; Lieutenant General of the Bailliage and Presidial Seat of Auxerre.
Guillaume Berault: Sieur of le Sablon; Juge-Consul-Echevin of the town of Auxerre.

Bailliage of Bar-sur-Seine

Noble Homme Lazare Coqueley: Master Particular of Waters and Forests; Mayor of Bar-sur-Seine.

Bailliage of Charolais

Maître Claude Maleteste: Avocat in the Bailliage of Charolais.
Maître Claude de Ganay (d. 1633): Sieur of Monté-guillon (Montaguillon); Lieutenant in the Bailliage of Charolais.
C.D., VIII, cols. 903–904.

Bailliage of Bugey-en-Bresse

Maître Charles Monin: Avocat in the Bailliage of Bugey.
Maître Pierre Passerat: Castelan of Stillon de Michailhe.

Bailliage of Gex

Maître Jacques Tombel: Bourgeois of Gex

Bailliage of Bresse

Maître Charles Chambard: Avocat of the Presidial Seat of Bourg; Syndic of the pays.

GOUVERNEMENT OF NORMANDY

Town of Rouen

Noble Jacques Hallé (d. 1632): Seigneur of Cantelou; Councilor and Secretary of the King, Household, and Crown of France; Ancien Conseiller and Second Echevin of Rouen.
Frondeville, *Présidents*, 413; Mousnier, 523–524.
Noble Homme Michel Mariage: Sieur of Montgrimont; Councilor and Secretary of the King; Comptroller in the Chancellery of Normandy; Councilor and Echevin Moderne of Rouen.
A.C. Rouen A 22, fols. 399v–400r.

Bailliage of Rouen

Honorable Homme Jacques Campion, of Anzouville-sur-Ry: Bourgeois.
D.B.F., VII, cols. 999–1000; A.C. Rouen A 22, fols. 399v–400r.

Bailliage of Caen

Guillaume Vauquelin (c. 1562–c. 1627): Ecuyer; Seigneur of la Fresnaye; Councilor of the King; President and Lieutenant General in the Bailliage and Presidial Seat; Master of Ordinary Requests of the Hôtel of the Queen; Deputy for the town of Caen.

J. de M., no. 34274; C.D., XIX, col. 552; Mousnier, pp. 61–62, 530.

Maître Abel Olivier: Sieur of la Fontaine; Syndic of Falaize; Deputy of the Bailliage.

Bailliage of Caux

Constantin Housset, of the Parish of Flamamville.

Bailliage of Cotantin

Maître Jacques Germain (1568–1620) of Arcanville: Avocat in Carentan; Seigneur of la Conte. J.L.

P. Blaizot, *Jacques Germain* (Poitiers, 1906).

Bailliage of Evreux

Maître Claude le Doux (1576–1641): Ecuyer; Sieur of Melleville; Councilor of the King; Master of Ordinary Requests of the Queen; President and Lieutenant General, Civil and Criminal of the Bailliage and Presidial Seat of Evreux.

Frondeville, I, 650–651; Mousnier, p. 521. Charles Molle, ed., 'Journal de ce qui s'est passé en la chambre du tiers Etats...', *Recueil des travaux de la société libre d'agriculture, sciences, arts et belles lettres de l'Eure*, VIII (1890), 495–499.

Bailliage of Gisors

Noble Homme Julian le Bret: Councilor of the King; Viscount of Gisors.

Bailliage of Alençon

Noble Homme Pierre le Rouillé: Councilor of the King; Avocat of the King in the Bailliage and Presidial Seat of Alençon.

C.D., XVII, col. 795.

GOUVERNEMENT OF GUYENNE

Town of Bordeaux and Sénéchaussée of Guyenne

Noble Homme Isaac de Boucaud: Councilor of the King in the Sénéchaussée and Procureur Général; Avocat in the Parlement; Jurat of Bordeaux.

Noble Homme Isaac de Boucaud: Councilor of the King in the Sénéchaussée and Presidial Seat of Guyenne.

Sénéchaussée of Bazadois

Maître André de Lauvergne: Councilor of the King; Lieutenant General of the Sénéchaussée of Bazadois.

Sénéchaussée of Perigord

Maître Pierre de la Brousse: Councilor of the King; Lieutenant General and Criminal at the Seat of Sarlat.

Maître Nicolas Alexandre: Avocat at the Presidial Seat of Perigueux.

Maître André (le) Charron: Councilor of the King; Lieutenant General of the Presidial Seat of Bergerac.

Sénéchaussée of Rouergue

Maître Jean Julles Fabry: First Consul of Rodez; Judge of Concoures. J.D.

Antoine de Bandinel: Seigneur of la Roquette; First Consul of the town and bourg of Rodez.

Foulcrand (de) Coulonges: Consul of Villefranche.

Maître Jean Guérin: Lieutenant in the Royal Magistracy of Creissel; Consul of Milhau. J.D.

Haag, v, 381.

Noble Homme Jacques de Fleires: Sieur and Baron of Boason; Syndic General in the Sénéchaussée of Rouergue. J.D.

Sénéchaussée of Saintonge

Raymond de Montagne (1568–1637): Seigneur of Saint Genes, Combrac, la Vallée, and other places; Councilor of the King; Lieutenant General in the Sénéchaussée of Saintonge.

Charles Dangibeaud, *Le présidial de Saintes, Raimond de Montagne* (Paris, 1881).

Sénéchaussée of Agenois

Maître Jean Villemon: Councilor and Procureur of the King in the Sénéchaussee of Agenois.

Julien de Cambefort: Ecuyer; Sieur of Selves; First Consul of the town of Agen. C.D., IV, col. 608; D.B.F., VII, col. 952.

Maître Jean de Sabaros: Sieur of la Motherouge; avocat in the Parlement of Bordeaux; Syndic of the pays.

Pays and County of Comminges

François de Combis: Ecuyer; Sieur of Combis and of la Mothe.

Jugerie of Rivière-Verdun

Maître Louis de Long: Councilor of the King; Judge General of the pays.

Sénéchaussée of Lannes and Saint-Sever

Maître Daniel de Barry: Councilor of the King; Lieutenant of the Sénéchaussée of Lannes at the Seat of Saint-Sever.
Maître Arnaul de Coisl: Syndic General of the pays and Seat of Saint-Sever.[7]

Sénéchaussée of Albret

Maître Pierre du Roy: Councilor of the King; Lieutenant Civil and Criminal in the Sénéchaussée of Albret.
Maître Jean (du) Broca: Consul of the town of Nerac; Avocat in the Parlement of Bordeaux and Chamber of Guyenne.

Sénéchaussée of Armagnac

Maître Samuel de Long: Councilor of the King; Lieutenant General and Chief Justice in the Sénéchaussée of Armagnac.

Sénéchaussée of Condomois and Gascogne

Noble Homme Guillaume Pouchalan: First Consul of Condom; Sieur of La Tour.
Noble Homme Raimond de Goujon: Bourgeois and Jurat of Condom.

Sénéchaussée of Haut Limousin and Town of Limoges

Léonard de Chastenet: Sieur and Baron of le Murat; Councilor of the King; Lieutenant General of the Sénéchaussée of Limousin and Presidial Seat of Limoges and other towns of the plat pays.
Grégoire de Cordes (Descordes): Sieur of Saint Ligourde (Haut Ligoure); Bourgeois of Limoges.[8]
Poulbrière, p. 306.

Sénéchaussée of Bas Limousin

Maître François du Mas (Dumas): Sieur of the noble house of la Chapoulie and in the dependencies of Pradel la Gane and la Gauterie; Councilor of the King; Lieutenant General in the Sénéchaussée of Bas Limousin and the Presidial Seat of Brives la Galliarde.
Poulbrière, p. 306.
Maître Pierre de Fenis: Sieur of le Theil; Councilor of the King; Lieutenant General in the Sénéchaussée of Bas Limousin.
C.D., VII, col. 902. Poulbrière, p. 306.
Maître Jacques de Chavaille (1593–1670): Sieur of Fougières (Faugeras) and le

---

[7] Elected as a substitute for Barry in case of necessity.
[8] Elected as a substitute for Chastenet in case of necessity.

Pouget; Lieutenant General, Criminal Assessor, and Commissaire examinateur in the Sénéchaussée of Bas Limousin, at the seat of Uzerches.[9] D.B.F., VIII, cols. 937–938; Poulbrière, p. 306.

Sénéchaussée of Quercy

Maître Pierre de la Fage: Avocat at the Presidial Seat of Cahors; First Consul of Cahors. J.U.D.

Maître Paul de la Croix, Syndic of the pays of Quercy. J.U.D.[10]

Pays and County of Bigorre

[No deputy for the Third Estate.]

GOUVERNEMENT OF BRITTANY

Deputies of the Estates of Brittany

Guy Goualt: Ecuyer; Sieur of Sénégrand; Councilor of the King; Provost and Judge Ordindary of Rennes.
Thomas-Lacroix, pp. 2–3.

Noble Homme Julien Salmon: Sieur of Querbloye; Councilor of the King; Procureur of the King at the Presidial Seat of Rennes.

Noble Homme Raoul Marot (d. 1627): Sieur of la Garraye; Councilor of the King; Seneschal of Dinan.
J. de M., no. 23000; C.D., XIII, col. 290; Thomas-Lacroix, pp. 2–3.

Noble Homme Jean Perret: Sieur of Pas-aux-Biches; Councilor of the King; Lieutenant in the Jurisdiction of Ploërmel.
J. de M., no. 26201.

Noble Homme Jean Picot: Sieur of la Giclaye.
Thomas-Lacroix, pp. 2–3.

Noble Homme Mathurin Rouxel: Sieur of Beauvais; Procureur-Syndic of the inhabitants of Saint Brieux.

Noble Homme Jean de Harouys: Sieur of Lespinay; Procureur-Syndic of the Estates of Brittany.

GOUVERNEMENT OF CHAMPAGNE

Bailliage of Troyes

Maître Pierre le Noble: Councilor of the King; President and Lieutenant General of the Bailliage and Presidial of Troyes.

---

[9] Saugrain lists his *qualité* as Doctor of Laws, avocat in the Parlements of Toulouse and Bordeaux.

[10] De la Croix is listed only in Saugrain.

Jean Bazin: Ecuyer; Sieur de Bouilly and Besenes; Mayor of Troyes.
J. de M., no. 3555; D.B.F., v, col. 1030; Bluche, H.C., I, 101, An.E 48B–49, fol. 31r.

Bailliage of Chaumont-en-Bassigny

Maître François de Grand: Councilor of the King; Lieutenant Criminal of the Bailliage of Chaumont.
Maître François Julliot: Councilor of the King at the Presidial of Chaumont; Mayor of Chaumont.

Bailliage of Meaux

Maître Louis Barré: Avocat in the Bailliage and Presidial seat of Meaux.
Maître Jacques Chalemont (Chalemot): Ancien Avocat and Echevin of Meaux.

Bailliage of Provins

Maître Pierre Retel: Councilor of the King; Lieutenant Particular Assessor of the Bailliage and Presidial Seat of Provins.

Bailliage of Sézannes

Maître Jacques Champion (Champy) (d. 1614–1615): Procureur of the King in the Bailliage of Sézannes.[11]

Bailliage of Sens

Maître Bernard Angenoust: Ecuyer; Sieur of Trencault; Councilor of the King; Lieutenant General of the Bailliage and Presidial of Sens.
J. de M., no. 855; D.B.F. II, cols. 1103–1105.

Bailliage of Vitry-le-François

Maître Jacques Rolet: Sieur of les Brestans; Councilor of the King; Provost and Judge Ordinary of Vitry-le-François.
Maître François Rouyer: Avocat in the Parlement of Paris; Resident of Saint Ménehould.

Bailliage of Chateau-Thierry

Claude de Vertu: Ecuyer; Sieur of Macongny; Councilor of the King; President and Lieutenant Criminal of the Bailliage and Presidial Seat of Chateau-Thierry.

---

[11] Died during the meeting of the Estates General.

GOUVERNEMENT OF LANGUEDOC

Sénéchaussée and Town of Toulouse

Maître Jean de Louppes: Councilor of the King; Criminal Judge of the King in the Sénéchaussée of Toulouse.

Noble Homme Maître Pierre Marmiesse: Lawyer in the Parlement of Toulouse; Capitoul of Toulouse. J.U.D.
J. de M., no. 22991.

Maître François de Boriez: Avocat in the Parlement of Toulouse; Capitoul and Head of the Consistory of the Hotel de Ville of Toulouse. J.D.

Sénéchaussée of Carcassonne and Béziers

Maître Philippe le Roux: Seigneur of Alzonne; Councilor of the King; President, Juge-Mage, Lieutenant né and General in the Sénéchaussée of Carcassonne and Béziers.[12]

David de l'Epinasse: Ecuyer: First Consul of the town of Castres and its deputy.

Sénéchaussée of Beaucaire and Nîmes

Maître François de Rochemore: Councilor of the King; Lieutenant General of the Sénéchaussée of Beaucaire and Nîmes.
C.D., XVII, col. 413 (?); Haag, VIII, 459–460.
Noble Louis de Gondin: Consul of the town of Uzès.
Haag, V, 301–302.

Sénéchaussée of Puy-en-Vellay

Maître Hugues de Filère: Councilor of the King and Principal Lieutenant in the Sénéchaussée of Puy.
Maître Jean Vitalis: First Consul of Puy. M.D.

Town, Gouvernement, and Sénéchaussée of Montpellier

Daniel de Gallière: Councilor of the King; Treasurer General of France; First Consul and Viguier of Montpellier.
A.N. E 47B, fols. 504r–505r.

Sénéchaussée of Lauragais

Maître Raimond de Cup: Councilor of the King; Juge-Mage of Castelnaudary.

Sénéchaussée, Pays, and County of Foix

Maître Bernard Meric: Avocat in the Sénéchaussée; Procureur of the King in the town of Foix. J.D.

---

[12] Saugrain lists him as *lieutenant né et Sénéchal*.

GOUVERNEMENT OF PICARDY

Bailliage of Amiens

Noble Homme Messire Pierre Pingré: Councilor of the King; Lieutenant General of the Bailliage and Presidial Seat of Amiens.
Deyon, *Amiens*, pp. 554–555.

Sénéchaussée of Ponthieu

Philippe de la Vernot Paschal: Ecuyer; President; Lieutenant General and Criminal in the Sénéchaussée and Presidial Seat of Ponthieu.

Sénéchaussée of Boulonnais

Messire Pierre de Vuillecot: Sieur of les Priez and of le Faux; Avocat of the King in the Sénéchaussée and County of Boulonnais.

Calais and Pays Reconquis

Louis le Beaucler: Ecuyer; Councilor of the King; President and Judge General of Calais and Pays Reconquis.

Provostship of Péronne[13]

Messire Robert Choquel: Councilor of the King; Procureur General in the Government and Provostship of Péronne; Mayor of Péronne.
Jules Dourmel, *Histoire général de Péronne* (Paris, 1879), p. 376.

Provosthip of Montdidier

Antoine de Berthin: Ecuyer; Lieutenant General, Civil and Criminal in the Government of Péronne, Montdidier, and Roye.

Provosthip of Roye

Maître Jacques de Neufville: Ecuyer; Sieur of Fontaines; Councilor of the King; Lieutenant General, Civil and Criminal of the Government of Roye.

GOUVERNEMENT OF DAUPHINÉ

Estates of Dauphiné

Noble Homme Louis Masson: Avocat in the Parlement; First Consul of the town of Vienne. J.D.
Noble Homme Etienne (de) Gilbert: Avocat in the Parlement.
C.D., IX, col. 251.
Noble Homme Gaspard de Ceressault: First Consul of Ambrun.

[13] The three provostships of Péronne, Montdidier, and Roye were given only one vote among them. A.N. E46B-47A, fol. 173r.

Noble Homme Claude Brosse (1570?–1643): Seigneur of Seritin (Sérezin); Syndic of the villages of Dauphiné.
D.B.F., VII, col. 429.
Maître Antoine Basset: Secretary of the Estates of the pays of Dauphiné.
D.B.F., V, cols. 751–754.

GOUVERNEMENT OF PROVENCE

Estates of Provence

Noble Homme Jean Louis de Mathaon (Matheron): Sieur of Salignac and Entrepierre; Avocat in the Court; Assessor in the town of Aix; Procureur of the pays.
C.D., XIII, cols. 371–372.
Maître Thomas de Feraporte: Avocat in the Court of the Parlement of Provence; Syndic of the Third Estate of the pays.
François de Sebolin: Sieur of la Mothe; First Consul of the town of Hières.
Maître Antoine Achard: Recorder of the Estates of Provence.

Town of Marseille

Maître Baltazard Vias: Avocat in the Court of the Parlement of Provence; Assessor of the Town of Marseille. J.U.D.

Town of Arles

Maître Pierre d'Augières: Avocat in the Parlement of Provence; Assessor of the Consuls and Communities of the town of Arles.
D.B.F., IV, col. 554.

GOUVERNEMENT OF LYONNAIS

Sénéchaussée of Lyon

Noble Homme Pierre Austrein (d. 1616): Seigneur of Jarnosse; President of the Parlement of Dombes (1601); Lieutenant in the Sénéchaussée and Presidial Seat of Lyon; Auditor of Camp of the Gouvernement of Lyon, pays of Lyonnais, Forèz and Beaujolais; Provost of Merchants of Lyon (1614–1615).
J. de M., no. 1978; D.B.F., IV, cols. 713–714.
Maître Charles Grollier: Ecuyer; Seigneur of les Couvires (de Servières); Avocat and Procureur General of Lyon.
J. de M., no. 18342; C.D., IX, cols. 912–913.
Maître Jean de Moulceau: Avocat in the Private Council of the King.
Maître Jean Goujon: Avocat in the Sénéchaussée and Presidial Seat of Lyon.
Maître Philippe Tixier: Captain and Castelan of Dargoire; Syndic of the plat pays of Lyonnais; Deputy for the plat pays.

Sénéchaussée of Forèz

Maître Pierre Rival: Assesseur in the Provostship and First Echevin of the town of Montbrisson.

Maître Claude Greysolon: Syndic of the pays of Forèz.

Sénéchaussée of Beaujolais

Noble Homme Claude Charreton: Seigneur of la Terrière; Councilor of the King; Lieutenant General, Civil and Criminal of the Sénéchaussée of Beaujolais.

Bas Pays of Auvergne

Messire Antoine de Murat: Councilor of the King (State and Private); Lieutenant General in the Sénéchaussée and Presidial Seat of Riom.

Maître Jean Savaron (1566–1622): Sieur of Villars; Councilor of the King; President and Lieutenant General in the Sénéchaussée and Presidial Seat of Clermont. Intendant for Marie de Médicis in Auvergne. J.U.Dip.

J. Mayniel, *Le Président Jean Savaron, ses théories, ses ouvrages* (Paris, 1906).

Guillaume Maritan: Echevin of the town of Clermont.

Bailliage of Saint-Flour and Haute Auvergne

Maître Pierre Chabot: Councilor of the King; Lieutenant General, Civil and Criminal in the Bailliage of the Haut Pays of Auvergne, established at Saint-Flour.

Pierre de Sauret: Second Consul of the town of Saint-Flour.
A.C. St. Flour, v, i, no. 24.

Maître Jean Monteil: Avocat in the Bailliage of Saint-Flour.
A.C. St. Flour, v, i, no. 24.

Maître Jean Sauret: Avocat in the Parlement of Paris and living there.[14]

Sénéchaussée of Bourbonnais

Jean de Champfeu: Seigneur of Garannes; Councilor of the King; President of the Bureau of Finances at Moulins; Mayor of Moulins.
Faure, i, 130.

Jean de l'Aubespin: Ecuyer; Bailly and Governor of Montaigu-les-Combrailles; Treasurer General of France at Moulins.

Maître Gilbert Balle: Sieur of Petit-bois; Avocat in the Sénéchaussée of Bourbonnais.[15]

Maître Jean Berauld: Lieutenant General, Civil and Criminal in the Chatellenie of Ainay.

---

[14] Jean Sauret was elected to fill the place of his brother Pierre if he should be absent.
[15] Balle's and Berauld's *qualités* are reported differently in Quinet, Saugrain, and De Landine.

Sénéchaussée of the Haute Marche

Maître Jean Vallenet: Sieur of la Ribière (Masière): Councilor of the King; Lieutenant Particular in the Seat of Gueret.

Sénéchaussée of the Basse Marche

Maître François Reymond: Sieur of Cluseau; Councilor of the King; Lieutenant General of the Sénéchaussée of the Basse Marche in the town of Bellac. Poulbrière, p. 307.

Bailliage of Saint-Pierre-le-Moutier

Noble Homme Maître Etienne Gascoing: Councilor of the King; Lieutenant General in the Bailliage and Presidial Seat of Saint-Pierre-le-Moutier.
Noble Homme Florimond Rapine (1580–1646): Sieur of Semxi; Councilor of the King; Avocat General of the King in the Seat of Saint-Pierre-le-Moutier.

GOUVERNEMENT OF ORLÉANAIS

Sénéchaussée of Poitou (Fontenay and Nyort)

René Brochard: Ecuyer; Sieur of les Fontaines; Councilor of the King in the Presidial Seat of Poitiers.
Maître François Brisson: Ecuyer; Sieur of le Palais; Councilor of the King; Seneschal of Fontenay.
D.B.F., VII, cols. 363–364.
Sire Coste Arnaut: Merchant of Poitiers.

Sénéchaussée of Anjou

Maître François Lanier: Sieur of Saint Jame; Councilor of the King; Lieutenant General of Anjou.
Albert Meynier, *Cahier des gens du tiers Etat du pays et duché d'Anjou en 1614* (Angers, 1905), pp. 11–12.
Maître Etienne du Mesnil: Ancien Avocat of the King at the Seat of Anjou; former Mayor and Captain of the town of Angers.
Meynier, *Cahier*, pp. 11–12.

Bailliage of Touraine

Maître Jacques Gautier: Councilor of the King in the Parlement of Brittany; President of the Presidial of Tours.
Maître René Sain (d. 1650): Councilor of the King; Treasurer General of France; Mayor of the town of Tours.
J. de M. no. 30698; C.D., XVIII, cols. 49–50; Charmeil, *Trésoriers*, p. 479.

Bailliage of Amboise

Noble Homme Maître Jean Dodeau: Councilor of the King; Lieutenant General in the Bailliage of Amboise.

Noble Homme Claude Rousseau: Procureur of the King in the Election and Ancien Echevin of Amboise.

Sénéchaussée of Loudunois

Maître Louis Trincaut (Trincant): Procureur of the King in the Sénéchaussée of Loudunois.

Maître Barthelemy de Burges: Receiver of Aides and Tailles in the Election of Loudun.

Gouvernement of La Rochelle and Pays Aunis

Maître Daniel de la Goutte: Councilor and Avocat of the King at the Presidial Seat of La Rochelle; one of the Peers of that town, a deputy of municipal officials of La Rochelle.

Noble Homme Maître Gabriel de Bourdigalle: Sieur of la Chabossière; Councilor of the King; Procureur of the King in the Presidial Seat and other jurisdictions of that town and Government of Aunis and La Rochelle.[16] Haag, II, 480.

Jean Tharay: Merchant; Bourgeois, Procureur-Syndic of the Bourgeois and inhabitants of La Rochelle; Deputy of the Bourgeois and inhabitants of La Rochelle.

Sénéchaussée of Angoulême

Philippe de Nemond: Ecuyer; Sieur of Brie; Councilor of the King; Lieutenant General in the Sénéchaussée and Presidial Seat of Angoulême; Master of Request of the Queen.

Sénéchaussée of Maine

Maître Michel Vasse (d. 1614–15): Lieutenant General and Criminal of the Sénéchaussée of Maine.[17]

Maître Julien Gaucher: Premier and Ancien Avocat of the King in the Sénéchaussée of Maine.

Bailliage of Berry

Louis Foucat (Foucault): Ecuyer; Sieur of Chamfort; Councilor of the King;

[16] Bourdigalle and Tharay were not given a seat in the Estates General until February 3, 1615. A.N. E 48A, fols. 204r–204v.
[17] Died during the meeting of the Estates General.

President of the Presidial Seat of Berry; Mayor of Bourges.
C.D., VIII, col. 446.

Noble Homme Philippe le Bègue: Avocat of the King; Councilor at the Presidial Seat of Berry.

Noble Homme François Carcat: Councilor of the King; Procureur of the King at the Royal Seat of Issoudun.

Noble Homme Paul Ragneau: Councilor the King; Lieutenant General, Civil and Criminal in the Bailliage and Royal Seat of Mehun-sur-Eure.

Bailliage of Chartres

Maître François Chavayne: Councilor of the King; President at the Bailliage and Presidial Seat of Chartres.

Maître Jacques de Essarts: Councilor at the Presidial Seat of Chartres; Councilor of State.

Bailliage of Orléans

Messire François de Beauharnois (d. 1651): Councilor of the King; President and Lieutenant General in the Bailliage and Presidial Seat of Orléans (1598); Deputy for the Castellenies Royal and non-Royal of the Bailliage.
J. de M. no. 3642; C.D., II, cols. 631–636.

Guillaume Rousselet: Bourgeois of the town of Orléans.

Maître Augustin de l'Isle: Councilor of the King; Lieutenant of the Bailly of Orléans at the Seat of Château-Regnard.[18]

Bailliage of Blois

Guillaume Ribier (1578–1663): Ecuyer; Sieur of le Hauvignon (Hautvignon); Councilor of the King; President and Lieutenant General in the Bailliage and Presidial Seat of Blois.
Richelieu, I, 380; A. Dupré, 'Notice sur Guillaume Ribier, Magistrat Blésois', *Mémoires de la Société des Sciences et Lettres de Loire-et-Cher*, IX, (1874–1875).

Noble Homme Jean Courtin: Sieur of Nantheuil.
J. de M., no. 11638. C.D., VI, col. 387. Dupré, 'Ribier', p. 12.

Bailliage of Étampes

Noble Homme Maître Jacques Petau: Councilor of the King; Lieutenant General, Civil and Criminal of the Bailliage and Duchy of Étampes; Mayor of Étampes.

---

[18] L'Isle was elected to take a place in the Estates General if Beauharnois were absent or sick. He participated in the meetings but was not given voice or vote. Rapine, p. 144.

Bailliage and County of Gien

Maître Daniel Chaseray: Sieur of Beauxnoirs; Councilor of the King; Lieutenant General, Civil and Criminal in the Bailliage and County of Gien.
Maître Pierre le Piat: Councilor of the King; Provost and Judge Ordinary, Lieutenant Civil, Assessor and Criminal of the town, county, provostship, and jurisdiction of Gien.

Bailliage of Montargis

Noble Homme Maître René Ravault: Sieur of Monceau; Ancien Avocat in the Bailliage of Montargis-le-Franc.
J. de M., no. 28352.

Duchy and Bailliage of Vendôme

Maître Jean Bautru: Sieur of les Matrats; Bailly of the pays and Duchy of Vendôme.
Maître Mathurin Rateau: Recorder of the Bailliage of Vendôme; Echevin of the town of Vendôme.

Bailliage of Perche

Noble Homme Maître Isaye Petigars: Seigneur of la Garenne; President in the Election of Perche.

Bailliage of Nivernois

Maître Henri Bolarie (Bolacre): Lieutenant General in the Bailliage and Peerage of Nivernois.
Maître Guillaume Salonnier: Councilor and Master of Accounts of the Duke of Nivernois.

Bailliage of Châtellerault

Maître François Ferand: Councilor of the King; Procureur of the King in the Bailliage of Châtellerault.

Bailliage of Château-Neuf-en-Thimerais

[No deputy for the Third Estate.]

BIBLIOGRAPHY OF SOURCES CITED

A. MANUSCRIPT SOURCES

A. CORRESPONDENCE AND PERSONAL PAPERS

Archives des Affaires Étrangères

Correspondance Politique

Allemagne 5 (1603–1617)   Hollande 7 (1608–1616)
Angleterre 26 (1612–1624)   Rome 23 (1601–1620)
Autriche 10 (1601–1625)   Sardaigne 3 (1613–1623)
Espagne 12 (1600–1620)   Venise 42 (1607–1623)
Mémoires et Documents, France
767 (1613), 768 (1614), 769 (1615), 770 (1616)

Archives Nationales

Series K
1428 (21 Mi 32) (consultas of Spanish government, 1613–1614)
1429 (21 Mi 33) (consultas of Spanish government, 1614–1615)
1453 (21 Mi 56) (Dispatches of Spanish King and Ministers, 1612–1614)
1454 (21 Mi 57) (Dispatches of Spanish King and Ministers, 1615–1616)
1469 (21 Mi 73) (Letters of Spanish Ambassador in France, 1614)
1610 (21 Mi 192) (Spanish State Council, 1614)
1611 (21 Mi 192) (Spanish State Council, 1615)
1634 (21 Mi 213) (Treaties and agreements between France and Spain, 1611–1626)
1635 (21 Mi 21) (Treaties and agreements between France and Spain)

Archives Privés
120 AP 28 (Sully's budget records, 1610–1611)

Archivio di Stato, Florence

Archivio Medicei
4629 (Letters of Tuscan Ambassador, 1613–1615)
4853 (News from France 1600–1619)
4867 (Letters of Tuscan Ambassador, 1614–1616)

Carte Strozziane
I, 55 (Minutes of letters to Grand Duchess Christine, 1614–1617)

Archivio Segreto Vaticano

Armadio LXV
  10 (Register of letters of Paul V, 1614–1615)
Fondo Borghese
  II, 242 (Letters of Papal Nuncio in France, 1614–1615)
  II, 244 (Letters of Papal Nuncio in France, 1614–1615)
Nunziatura di Francia
  56 (Letters of Papal Nuncio, 1614–1616)
  296 (Minutes of the Secretariat, 1615–1619)

British Museum

Stowe Manuscripts
  173 (Edmondes's Papers, Vol. VIII)
  174 (Edmondes's Papers, Vol. IX)
  175 (Edmondes's Papers, Vol. X)

Bibliothèque Nationale

Manuscrits français
  3654 (Letters to French Ambassador in Rome, 1610–1614)
  3712 (Papers of Jeannin)
  3713 (Copies of negotiation instructions, February, 1614)
  3788 (Letters of various including Marie de Médicis)
  3795 (Letters of various including Sully)
  3797 (Various letters)
  3799 (Government negotiations, internal, 1614–1616)
  3800 (Various letters)
  4067 (Copies of letters to Marquis de Coeuvres, 1614–1615)
  4112 (Diplomatic instructions, 1604–1622)
  4116 (Letters to French resident in Germany, 1612–1624)
  4121 (Letters to French resident in Germany, 1612–1621)
  6379 (Letters to Cardinal de Sourdis (1598–1616)
  7095 (Letters concerning French mission in Constantinople, 1611–1619)
  15581 (Letters to Villeroy, 1612–1614)
  15582 (Letters to Villeroy, 1615–1616)
  15644 (Various, 1606–1643)
  15986 (Copies of letters to and from French Ambassador in London, 1611)
  15987 (Letters to and from French Ambassador in London, 1613–1614)
  15988 (Letters to and from French Ambassador in London, 1615)
  16116 (Letters from French Ambassador in Madrid, 1614–1616)
  18009 (Letters from French Ambassador in Rome, 1614)
  18010 (Letters from French Ambassador in Rome, 1615)

Manuscrits français, nouvelles acquisitions
7260 (Copies of letters and statements of Villeroy)
7261 (Instructions for Ambassadors to Germany and Switzerland)
7262 (Copies of letters and statements of Jeannin)
23369 (Copies of letters to Duke of La Force, 1595–1631)
Cinq Cents de Colbert
1 (Letters and memoirs on the history of France, 1278–1616)
12 (Memoirs for the History of France, 1600–1616)
17 (Letters, etc., concerning France, 1609–1628)
43 (Prince of Condé, 1614–1615)
88 (Register of letters of Marie de Médicis, 1610–1614)
89 (Register of letters of Marie de Médicis, 1612–1617)
102 (Instructions and memoirs for Ambassadors)
Collection Clairambault
364 (Bossuet's historical collection, Vol. LIV, 1614)
365 (Bossuet's historical collection, Vol. LV, 1615)
Manuscrits italiens
38 (Ubaldini's Newsletters, 1610–1616)
1200 (Copies of letters of Papal Nuncio in France, 1608–1616)
1334 (Copies of letters of Papal Nuncio in France, 1607–1616)
1767 (Letters of Venetian Ambassador to France, 1614–1615)
1768 (Letters of Venetian Ambassador to France, 1615–1616)

B. GOVERNMENT RECORDS

Archives Nationales

Series A D +
156–158 (Edicts, Declarations, *Arrêts*, 1614–1615)
Series A D
III 20 (Book condemnations, 1406–1699)
IX 4 (*Arrêts*, Declarations, Edicts concerning *Aides*, 1600–1620)
IX 416 (*Gabelles*, 1577–1632)
IX 470 (*Tailles*, 1400–1789)
IX 473 (*Traités*, 1577–1659)
IX 490 (*Trésoriers généraux*, 1418–1709)
Series E
43A–49A (*Conseil d'Etat et de Finances*, 1614–1615, 8 vols.)
Series F
94 (Assemblies of *Chambres* of *Parlement*)
Series H
1796–1798 (Register of Hôtel de Ville of Paris, 1614–1616)
1892 (Minutes, Hôtel de Ville, 1614)

Series K
  109–111 (Louis XIII, 1610–1624)
  539 (Royal Household, 1594–1636)
Series V6
  1196–1199 (Register of *arrêts* of *Conseil Privé*, 1614–1615)
  1223 (*Resultats* of *Conseil Privé*, 1609–1614)
Series X1A
  1867–1870 (*Registre du conseil . . . Parlement*, 1614–1615)
  8647–8648 (Ordinances of Louis XIII, 1610–1617)

Bibliothèque Nationale

Manuscrits français
  3711 (Treaties, 1614–1629)
Cinq Cents de Colbert
  91–92 (*Registres Administratives* of Marie de Médicis, 1611–1619)
Collection Dupuy
  824–827 (Expense records, Treasury, 1611–1615)

C. ELECTION RECORDS AND 'CAHIERS'

(For description of sources see chapters 4, 5, 10, 11)

Archives des Affaires Etrangères

Mémoires et Documents, France
  769

Archives communales

Mâcon AA 10
Marseille AA 118
Nevers BB 21
Saint Flour, Chapter V, art. 1

Archives Départementales

Aisne B 503	Loire C 32
Paris D 2B²	Lot-et-Garonne AA 45
Ariège A 12	Maine-et-Loire 1 Mi 11 (R1)
Aube G 140	Maine-et-Loire 1, B G, nos. 1–3
Bouche-du-Rhone C 2068	Morbihan 87 G 4
Calvados series F	Puy-de-Dôme 2 G 746
Charente-Maritime,	Puy-de-Dôme 5 C Aa 3rr
Minutes de Masset, 1614	Saone-et-Loire BB 78
Côte d'Or C 3473	Saone-et-Loire C 505
Dordogne 6 C 1	Seine Maritime A 22

Hérault C 7673
Ile-et-Vilaine C 2648
Ile-et-Vilaine C 3793
Lannes H 23

Seine Maritime D 110
Somme 1 B 17
Yvelines 6 B 304
Yvelines 47 J 4

Archives Municipales

Lyon AA 146
Rouen A 22
Toulouse AA 22

Archives Nationales

Series G8
  87
Series G8*
  632A, 632B, 635
Series H
  747²
Series K
  674, 675

Bibliothèques Municipales

Angers MS 911 (820)
Beauvais *Collection Bucquet sur Cousteau* Vol. LXXXVI
Blois BB18
Orléans MS 541 (427)
Reims MS 1700
Troyes BB 16

Bibliothèque Nationale

Manuscrits français
  3328, 3716, 4083, 4131, 4782, 11916, 11976, 18513
Manuscrits français, nouvelles acquisitions
  2080, 5174, 7255
Collection Clairambault
  742
Collection Dupuy
  658
Collection Moreau
  1427

Saltykov-Shchedrin State Public Library

Fr. II 79/1–2

D. 'PROCÈS-VERBAUX' AND PROCEEDINGS OF THE ESTATES GENERAL

(For description of sources see Chapters 6–9)

Archives Départementales

Morbihan 87 G 4

Bibliothèque de l'Arsenal

MS 4255

Bibliothèque Nationale

Manuscrits français
  3715, 3718, 4082, 10876, 18256, 10879
Manuscrits français, nouvelles acquisitions
  1395, 7254
Cinq Cents de Colbert
  139
Collection Clairambault
  1129
Collection Dupuy
  323, 950

E. MISCELLANEOUS

Bibliothèques Municipales

Amiens BB 59 (City Council, 1610–1615)

Bibliothèque Nationale

Manuscrits français
  4310 (*chambres de justice*)
  6557 (Imperial negotiations)
  7794 (copies of letters and pamphlets)
  9225 (Verses)
  10877 (Noble *cahier* and pamphlets)
  20154 (Collection of historical documents, 1593–1644)
  23159 (Collection of historical documents)
  23396 (Assembly of Notables 1617, Edict of 1618)
Manuscrits français, nouvelles acquisitions
  7853 (Pamphlet collection)
Cinq Cents de Colbert
  4 (clerical records)

Collection Dupuy

76 (*Lits de justice* and royal marriages, 1378–1630)
91 (various documents, 1614–1615)
209 (pieces on Barrois)
684 (various pieces 1614)
744 (*Titres et actes* concerning history of France)
853 (*dons, capanages, contrats*, 1548–1617)

Mèlanges de Colbert

83 (Colbert's memoirs on Estates General)

B. PRINTED SOURCES

A. MEMOIRS, LETTERS, PROCÈS-VERBAUX, ETC

Arnauld d'Andilly, Robert, *Journal inédit d'Arnauld d'Andilly, 1614–1620*, ed. Achille Halphen, Paris, 1857.

Ballesteros Beretta, Antonio, ed., *Documentos ineditos para la historia de España*, new series, Vols. III–IV, Madrid, 1936–1944.

Barbiche, Bernard, ed., *Correspondance du nonce en France Innocenzo del Bufalo*, Paris, 1964.

Barbier, Pierre and Vermillet, France, eds., *Histoire de France par les chansons*, Vol. I, Paris, 1956.

Bassompierre, François de, *Journal de ma vie*, ed. M. de Chanterac, Vols. I–II, Paris, 1870.

Baudel, ed., *Notes pour servir à l'histoire des Etats provinciaux du Quercy*, Cahors, 1881.

Baulant, Micheline, and Meuvret, Jean, *Prix des céréales extraits de la mercuriale de Paris 1520–1698*, 2 vols., Paris, 1962.

Bernard, Jacques, *Recueil des traitéz*, Vol. III, Amsterdam, 1700.

Birch, Thomas, ed., *An Historical View of the Negotiations between the Courts of England, France, and Brussels, from the Year 1592 to 1617...*, London, 1749.

Boderie, Antoine Le Fèvre, Sieur de la, *Ambassades de Monsieur de la Boderie en Angleterre ... depuis les années 1606 jusqu'en 1611*, 4 vols., n.p., 1750.

Boislisle, A. de, *Chambre des comptes de Paris. Pièces justicatives, 1566–1701*, Nogent-le-Rotrou, 1873.

Boitel, P., *Histoire des choses plus memorables ... depuis ... 1610 ... jusques à ... 1617 ...*, Rouen, 1618.

Calendar of State Papers Domestic, Series of the Reign of James I, ed. Mary Green, Vols. VIII–IX, London, 1858.

Calendar of the Manuscripts of the Marquis of Bath, Vol. II, Dublin, 1907.

Camus, Jean Pierre, *Homélies des Etats Généraux, 1614–1615*, ed. Jean Descrains, Geneva, 1970.

Cimber, L. and Danjou, F., eds., *Archives curieuses de l'histoire de France,* series 2, Vols. I, III, Paris, 1837.

Colbert, Jean Baptiste, *Lettres, Instructions et Mémoires de Colbert,* ed. Pierre Clément, Vols. VI, VII, Paris, 1869.

Collection des procès verbaux des assemblées générales du clergé de France depuis l'année 1560 . . . , Paris, 1768.

Collin, ed., *Relation imprimée par un contemporain de tout ce qui s'est passé aux Etats généraux convoqués en 1614,* Paris, 1789.

D'Autreville, *Estat général des affaires de France,* Paris, 1617.

Desjardins, Abel, ed., *Négociations diplomatiques de la France avec la Toscane pendant le XVIᵉ siècle,* Vol. V, Paris, 1886.

Du Perron, Jacques Davy, Cardinal, *Les ambassades et négotiations du Cardinal Du Perron,* Paris, 1623.

Dupin, L. E., ed., *Recueil de pièces concernant l'histoire de Louis XIII,* Vol. I, Paris, 1716.

Estrées, François Annibal, duc d', *Mémoires du Maréchal d'Estrées sur le régence de Marie de Médicis (1610–1616), et sur celle de Anne d'Autriche (1643–1650),* ed. Paul Bonnefon, Paris, 1910.

Fage, R., ed., *Documents rélatifs aux Etats de la vicomté de Turenne,* Vol. I, Paris, 1894.

Fiefbrun, René de Cumont, sieur de, *Véritable discours de la naissance et vie de Monseigneur le Prince de Condé jusqu'à présent,* ed. E. Halphen, Paris, 1861.

Fontenay-Mareuil, François Duval, Marquis de, *Mémoires . . .* in Michaud and Poujoulat eds., *Nouvelle Collection,* Vol. XIX.

Frêche, G. and G., *Les prix des grains, des vins et des légumes à Toulouse,* Paris, 1967.

Gardiner, S. R., ed., *Narrative of the Spanish Marriage Treaty,* London, 1869.

Gassot, Jules, *Sommaire mémorial de Jules Gassot, secrétaire du roi,* ed. Pierre Champion, Paris, 1934.

Grelin, Henri, *Livre contenant l'ordre tenue par messieurs de la noblesse au Estats généraux de France . . . avec leurs noms, surnoms, et qualitéz* Paris, 1615.

Grelin, Henri, *Ordre observé en la convocation et assemblée des Estats généraux de France . . . avec les noms, surnoms et qualitéz des députéz des trois ordres . . .* , Paris, 1615.

Griffiths, G., ed., *Representative Government in Western Europe in the Sixteenth Century,* Oxford, 1968.

Griselle, E. ed., *Documents d'Histoire,* Vols. II–III, Paris, 1901–1912.

Henri IV, *Lettres Missives de Henri IV,* ed. Berger de Xivery, 9 vols., Paris, 1843–1876.

Herelle, Georges, ed., *Documents inédits sur le protestantisme à Vitry-le-François, Epense, Heilly-le-Maurupt, Nettancourt et Vassy*, Paris, 1880.

Héroard, Jean, *Journal de Héroard*, ed. E. Soulié and E. de Barthélemy, 2 vols., Paris, 1868.

Isambert, François, ed., *Recueil général des anciennes lois françaises* Vols. XIV–XVI, Paris, 1829.

Jeannin, Pierre, *Les négociations de monsieur le président Jeannin* in Michaud and Poujoulat, eds., *Nouvelle collection*, XVIII.

Journal de ce qui s'est passé aux Etats généraux de 1614 . . ., Paris, 1789.

Lacroix, Paul, ed., *Ballets et mascarades de cour de Henri III à Louis XIV, 1581–1652*, Vol. II. Geneva, 1869.

La Force, Duc de, *Mémoires authentiques de Jacques Nompar de Caumont Duc de la Force Maréchal de France*, ed. Marquis de la Grange, Vols. I–II, Paris, 1843.

Lalourcé and Duval, eds., *Forme générale et particulière de la convocation et de la tenue des assemblées nationales ou Etats généraux de France, justifiée par pièces authentiques*, 3 vols., Paris, 1789.

Lalourcé and Duval, eds., *Recueil de pièces originales et authentiques concernant la tenue des Etats généraux*, 9 vols., Paris, 1789.

Lalourcé and Duval, eds., *Recueil des cahiers généraux des trois ordres aux Etats Généraux*, 4 vols., Paris, 1789.

Lesdiguières, François de Bonne, duc de, *Actes et correspondance du connétable de Lesdiguières*, ed. Douglas and Roman, Vol. II, Paris, 1878.

L'Estoile, Pierre de, *Mémoires-Journaux*, ed. G. Brunet *et al.*, Vols. X–XII, Paris, 1889–1896.

Lonchay, Henri and Cuvelier, Joseph, eds., *Correspondance de la cour d'Espagne sur les affaires des Pays-Bas au XVIIᵉ siècle*, Vol. I, Brussels, 1923.

Malherbe, François de, *Lettres de Malherbe*, Paris, 1822.

Malherbe, François de, *Lettres inédites de Malherbe*, Paris, 1841.

Malherbe, François de, *Oeuvres de Malherbe, poésies et correspondance*, Paris, 1865.

Malingre, Claude, *Histoire du règne de Louys XIII*, Paris, 1646.

[Malingre, Claude], *Remarques d'histoire . . . depuis l'an 1600 . . .* Paris, 1632.

Mallet, Jean, *Comptes rendues de l'administration de finances du royaume de France, pendant les onze dernières années du règne de Henri IV, le règne de Louis XIII et soixante-cinq années de celui de Louis XIV . . .*, London and Paris, 1789.

Masselin, Jean, *Journal . . . 1484*, ed. A. Bernier, Paris, 1835.

Mayer, Charles Joseph, ed., *Das Etats généraux et autres assemblées nationales*, Vol. XVIII, The Hague, 1788–1789.

Mercure François, Vols. I–III, Paris, 1611–1617.

Michaud and Poujoulat, eds., *Nouvelle Collection des Mémoires relatifs à l'histoire de France depuis le XIIIᵉ siècle jusqu'à la fin du XVIIIᵉ siècle*, Vols. XVII–XIX, Paris, 1854.

Minge, Abbé, ed., *Collection intégral et universelle des orateurs sacrées*, Vol. I, Paris, 1844.

Molé, Mathieu, *Mémoires* ..., ed. Aimé Champallion-Figeac, Vol. I, Paris, 1855.

Mornay, Philippe de, seigneur de Plessis-Marly, *Mémoires et Correspondance de Duplessis-Mornay*, ed. Pierre René, Vol. XII, Paris, 1825.

Nouillac, J., ed., 'Avis de Villeroy à la Reine Marie de Médicis, 10 mars, 1614', *Revue Henri IV*, II, 1908, 79–81.

Ordre des bailliages observé en la convocation des Estats généraux, Paris: Saugrain, 1615.

Picot, Georges and Guérin, Paul, eds., *Documents rélatifs aux Etats généraux de 1614*, n.p., n.d.

Pontchartrain, Paul Phelypeaux de, *Mémoires concernant les affaires de France sous la régence de Marie de Médicis* ... in Michaud and Poujoulat, eds., *Nouvelle Collection*, Vol. XIX.

Pradel, Charles, ed., *Mémoires de J. de Bouffard-Madiane sur les guerres civiles du Duc de Rohan, 1610–1629*, Paris, 1897.

Prinsterer, G., Groen van, *Archives ou correspondance inédite de la maison d'Orange-Nassau*, series 2, Vols. I–II, Utrecht, 1858.

Quinet, Toussaint, *Recueil générale des Estats sous les rois Charles V, Charles VIII, Charles IX, Henri III et Louis XIII*, Paris, 1651.

Rapine, Florimond, *Recueil très-exact et curieux de tout ce qui s'est fait et passé de singulier et memorable en l'assemblée des Estats, tenus à Paris en l'année 1614 et particulièrement en chaque séance du tiers ordre*, Paris, 1651.

Régistre des délibérations du Bureau de la ville de Paris, ed. Paul Guérin and Jean le Grand, Vols. XIV–XVI, Paris, 1921–1927.

Richelieu, Armand Jean du Plessis, Cardinal, *Mémoires du Cardinal de Richelieu*, Vols. I–II, Paris, 1907.

Richelieu, Armand Jean du Plessis, Cardinal, *Testament Politique*, ed. Louis André, Paris, 1948.

Rohan, Henri, duc de, *Mémoires du duc de Rohan* in Michaud and Poujoulat, *Nouvelle Collection*, XIX.

Salva, M. and Lainez de Barada, P., eds., *Coleccion de Documentos ineditos para la historia de España*, Vol. V, Madrid, 1844.

Sully, Maximilien de Bethune, duc de, *Economies royales* in Michaud and Poujoulat, eds., *Nouvelle Collection*, XVII.

Thierry, Augustin, ed., *Recueil des monuments inédits de l'histoire du tiers état*, Vol. III, Paris, 1856.

Third Report of the Royal Commission on Historical Manuscripts, London, 1872.

Thwaites, Reuben, ed., *Jesuit Relations and Allied Documents*, Vol. II, Cleveland, 1896.

B. EDICTS, ARRÊTS, LETTERS PATENTES

Arrest de la Cour des Monnoyes portât defféces d'exposer prêdre & recevoir en payement les pièces estrangères . . . , Paris, 1617.

Arrest du conseil d'estat du roy partant règlement pour les espiceries et drogueries qui sont transportées par mer de la Rochelle à Rouen, de quatorzième mars 1613, n.p., n.d.

Arrest du conseil d'estat du Roy sur le règlement général des tailles . . . , Paris, 1613.

Bibliothèque Nationale
F 25926
F 46927 (8)

Commission extraordinaire du Roy, portant attribution de jurisdiction à la Cour de Parlement . . . Henri de Bonneval . . . , n.p., 1615.

Déclaration du roy sur l'édict de création & restablissement des officiers de finance triannaux, n.p., 1616.

Edict du roy portant révocation de la chambre de justice . . . , Paris, 1625.

Edict du Roy pour la levée des droicts d'entrée modéréz . . . , Paris, 1597.

Edict du roy pour la révocation de la chambre royale . . . , Paris, 1605.

Edict du Roy sur le faict et règlement général de ses monnoyes, Paris, 1602.

Edict du Roy sur le règlement et retranchement des exemptes des tailles . . . , Paris, 1615.

Extraict des registres du conseil d'estat, n.p., n.d.

Lettres patentes de commission du roy . . . pour la recherche des financiers . . . , Paris, 1605.

Lettres patentes du Roy Louis XIII donneé à Paris le 3 Août 1614, n.p., n.d.

Lettres patentes du roy . . . portant révocation de plusiers édicts et commissions extraordinaires . . . , Paris, 1610.

Lettres patentes du Roy . . . pour le révente en heredité de tous les offices de commissaires à faire les rooles des tailles . . . , Paris, 1631.

Ordonnance du Roy sur le faict et règlement général de ses monnoyes, Paris, 1615.

C. CAHIERS, ETC.

Archives Historiques de la Gironde, X, 1868.

Beaurepaire, Charles de Robillard de, ed., *Cahiers des Etats de Normandie sous le règne de Louis XIII et Louis XIV,* Vol. I, Paris, 1876.

Bouchet, C., ed., 'Cahier du Tiers-Etat Vendômois', *Bulletin de la Société archéologique, scientifique et littéraire du Vendômois,* XI, 1872, 3–44.

Boutillier, François, 'Documents relatifs aux Etats généraux de 1560 à 1651 et conservés aux archives communales de Nevers', *Bulletin de la Société Nivernaise des sciences, lettres et arts*, series 3, 1, 1883, 234–235.

Clairefond, Marius, 'Notice sur les députations de la province de Bourbonnais et du département de l'Allier aux grandes assemblées nationales depuis 1413 jusqu'en 1848', *Société d'émulation du département de l'Allier*, 1850, pp. 242–263.

Durand, Yves, ed., 'Cahiers de doléances de la noblesse des gouvernements d'Orléanais, Normandie et Bretagne pour les Etats Généraux de 1614', *Enquêtes et Documents*, Nantes, 1971, I, 53–134.

Durand, Yves, ed., *Cahiers de doléances des paroisses du bailliage de Troyes pour les Etats généraux de 1614*, Paris, 1966.

Grassoreille, Georges, ed., 'Les cahiers de doléances de la paroisse de Colombes aux Etats généraux de 1614', *Bulletin de la Société de l'histoire de Paris et l'Ile de France*, XV, 1888, 14–21.

Grandmaison, Charles de, 'Doléances du Tiers-Etat de Touraine aux Etats généraux de Paris, 1614', *Bulletin de la Société archéologique de Touraine*, VIII, 1889–1891, 40–42.

Grandmaison, Georges, ed., *Plaintes et doléances de la province de Touraine aux Etats généraux du royaume*, Tours, 1890.

Louvet, Jean, 'Récit véritable de tout ce qui est advenue de memoire, tout en la ville d'Angers, pais d'Anjou et autres lieux avec un journal allant de 1583 à 1634', *Revue d'Anjou et de Maine-et-Loire*, I, 1855, 17–18, 50–65, 129–143.

Mémoires de l'académie des Sciences, Belles Lettres et Arts d'Angers, series 8, I, 1957, 89–90.

Meynier, Albert, ed., *Cahiers des gens du Tiers Etat au pays et duché d'Anjou en 1614*, Angers, 1905.

Molle, Charles, ed., 'Journal de ce qui s'est passé en la chambre du tiers état aux Etats généraux de 1614', *Recueil des travaux de la société libre d'agriculture, sciences, arts et belles lettres de l'Eure*, VIII, 1889–1890, 495–597.

Monbeig, G., 'Notes relatives aux Etats généraux de 1614. Analyse des doléances de la ville de Beauvais et des Cahiers d'aucune du Tiers-Etat du bailliage de Beauvais', *Bulletin de la Société d'études historiques et scientifique de l'Oise*, IV, 1908, 1–32.

Port, Celestin, ed., 'Cahier du Tiers Etat de la sénéchaussée de Saumur aux Etats généraux de 1614', *Revue historique, littéraire et archéologique d'Anjou*, I, 1867, 206–210.

Revue de Haute Auvergne (1947–1949), pp. 117–121.

Tholin, Georges, ed. *Cahiers de doléances du Tiers Etat du pays d'Angenais aux Etats généraux, 1558, 1614, 1789*, Paris, 1885.

D. PAMPHLETS

Advis à messieurs des Estats sur la réformation et le retranchement des abus et criminels de l'estat, n.p., 1588.

Advis à Monseigneur le Prince, n.p., 1614.

Advis au Roy, n.p., 1588.

Advis au Roy, sur la réformation générale des abus ... en son royaume, n.p., 1614.

Advis d'un bon senateur sur la rupture du droit annuel, n.p., n.d.

Advis, remonstrances et requestes aux Estats généraux tenus à Paris, 1614 par six paysans, n.p., n.d.

Anatomie des trois ordres de la France sur le sujet des estats, n.p., 1615.

L'anti-Mauregard ou le fantosme du bien public, n.p., 1614.

L'anti-Morgard sur ses prédictions de la présente année mil six cens quatorze, Paris, 1614.

Article de l'église apporté au Tiers Estat par Monseigneur l'évesque de Mascon le matin 5 jour de janvier 1615, n.p., n.d.

Articles de la paix, Paris, 1614.

Les articles des cayers généraux de France, présentées par Maistre Guillaume aux Estats, n.p., n.d.

Articles présentées au roy par les députés de la chambre du tiers Estat de France avec les responses de sa Majesté, Paris, 1615.

Articles présentées au Roy par les députés du Tiers Estat en attendant la résolution du cahier général ..., n.p., n.d.

Athys, Viole d', *Response à la harangue fait par l'Illustrisime Cardinal du Perron*, n.p., n.d.

Beaunis de Chanterain, Pierre, sieur des Viettes, *Le Hola des gens de guerre ...*, Paris, 1614.

[Beaunis de Chanterain], Pierre, *Le lourdaut vagabond rencontré par l'esprit de la cour ...* Paris, 1614.

[Beaunis de Chanterain], Pierre, *Le plaidoyer des préséances et difficultéz des Estats. Recueillis à l'hostel de Monseigneur le Prince, premier pair de France, réuniateur des subjects du roy. Lequel a authorisé l'esprit de Pierre des Viettes d'y respondre, et des les rediger par escrit, estant à Paris le seizième mars*, n.p., n.d.

Beaunis de Chanterain, Pierre, *Prédiction du soleil memorable ...*, n.p., n.d.

Beaunis de Chanterain, Pierre, *Sapience manifestée ...*, Paris, 1614.

Beaunis de Chanterain, Pierre, *Le Tou-Beau Feu de la mémoire du seigneur Maréchal de Farvaques ...*, Rouen, 1614.

Bernaveld, *Refus faict à Monseigneur la Prince de Condé par le Sr. de Bernaveld ...*, Paris, 1615.

B.L.D., *Franc et libre discours ou advis aux députés des trois estats pour la réformation d'iceuy*, Paris, 1614.

Bernard, Charles, *Discours sur l'Estat des Finances du Roy*, Paris, 1614.

Le bon françois, n.p., 1614.

Bouillon, Henri de la Tour d'Auvergne, duc de, *Lettre au président Jannin* ..., n.p., n.d.

Bouillon, Henri de la Tour d'Auvergne, duc de, *Lettre de M. de Bouillon à M. le Prince sur l'affaire de Poitiers*, n.p., 1614.

Le cabinet de Vulcan, n.p., n.d.

Cahiers généraux des articles résolus et accordéz entre les députéz des 3 estats, Paris, 1615.

Camus, Jean Pierre, *Homélie des disordres des trois ordres de cette monarchie*, Paris, 1615.

Camus, Jean Pierre, *Homélie des trois fleaux des trois estats de France*, Paris, 1615.

Camus, Jean Pierre, *Homélie des trois simonies ecclésiastique, militaire et judicielle*, Paris, 1615.

Les canons des conciles de Tolède, de Meaux, d'Oxfort et de Constance: par lesquels le doctrine de deposer et user les roys est condamné n.p., 1615.

Cassandre françoise, n.p., 1615.

Le catholique christianizé, n.p., 1615.

Cauvigny, François de, *Réfutation de l'astrologie judiciare* ..., Paris, 1614.

Le certification de la paix ..., Paris, 1614.

La chemise sanglante, n.p., n.d.

Au clergé, n.p., n.d.

Le colonel de la milice de Paris, Paris, 1614.

Condé, Henri II de Bourbon, Prince de, *Advis donné au roy en son conseil par Monsieur le Prince*, n.p., n.d.

Condé, Henri II de Bourbon, Prince de, *Dernière lettre escrite à la royne par Monseigneur le Prince*, n.p., 1614.

Condé, Henri II de Bourbon, Prince de, *Double de la lettre escrite par Monseigneur le Prince de Condé suivant le vray original. A la royne régente mère du roy, le 19 février mil six cens quatorze*, Paris, n.d.

Condé, Henri II de Bourbon, Prince de, *Lettre de Monseigneur le Prince à MM. de la cour de Parlement*, n.p., 1614.

Condé, Henri II de Bourbon, Prince de, *Le Manifeste de M. le Prince envoyé à M. le Cardinal de Joyeuse*, n.p., 1614.

Conjouissance de Jacques Bonne Homme paysan de Beauvoisis avec Messeigneurs les Princes reconcilées, Paris, 1614.

Le conseiler fidèle à son roy, n.p., n.d.

Copie de la harangue fait en la presence du roy à l'entrée des Estats, par les députéz de la Rochelle, pour les églises réformées au raport de Mathoult, n.p., 1615.

Copie d'une lettre d'un prélat deputé du clergé à l'assemblée des Estats sur ce qui s'est passé touchant l'article contentieux employé pour le premier au cayer du Tiers Estat, n.p., 1615.

Le décret du concile de Constance . . . , n.p., n.d.

Discours à messieurs les députéz aux Estats généraux de France, n.p., n.d.

Discours de ce qui s'est passé à Mézières, n.p., n.d.

Discours de ce qui s'est passé en la presentation des remonstrances par escrit, que le Parlement alla faire en corps au Roy le mardy 22 mai 1615, n.p., n.d.

Discours de Maistre Jean Joufflu sur les débats et divisions de ce temps, n.p., 1614.

Discours de M. Guillaume et Jacques Bonhomme sur le deffaicte de trente cinq poulles . . . , Paris, 1614.

Discours d'un genti-homme françois à la noblesse de France, sur l'ouverture de l'assemblée des Estats genéráux dans la ville de Paris en ceste anné 1614 . . . , n.p., n.d.

Discours pour la conservation de l'annuel des offices, n.p., n.d.

Discours rémarquable advenus à Paris, pendant des Estats, n.p., 1615.

Discours sur la lettre de Monsieur le Prince, n.p., n.d.

Discours sur l'alliance faicte par le roy très-chrétien, avec le roy catholique, n.p., 1615.

Discours sur la réception du Concile de Trente en France, n.p., 1615.

Discours sur l'droict annuel, n.p., n.d.

Discours sur les calomnies et medisances publiées contre M. les Princes, n.p., 1614.

Discours sur les mariages de France et d'Espagne contenant les raisons qui ont meu Monseigneur le Prince a demander la surséance, n.p., 1614.

Discours véritable de ce qui s'est passé au Parlement, en suitte de l'arrest de la cour du 28 mars dernier, et des remonstrances, n.p., n.d.

Discours véritable des propos tenus entre deux marchâdes du Palais estant aux estuves près S. Nicolas de Champs . . . , Paris, 1614.

Le dispositif . . . advis à messieurs les députéz . . . , n.p., 1588.

D.M.B., *Le Tombeau de la polette dédié aux jeunes advocats*, n.p., 1615.

Du Perron, Jacques Davy, Cardinal, *Harangue faicte de la parte de la chambre ecclésiastique en celle du tiers Estat, sur l'article du serment par Monseigneur le Cardinal du Perron*, Paris, 1615.

Du Perron, Jacques Davy, *Lettre de Monseigneur le Cardinal du Perron à Monsieur le Prince*, Paris, 1614.

Du Perron, Jacques Davy, *Lettre de Monseigneur le Cardinal du Perron envoyée au sieur Casaubon en Angleterre*, Paris, 1612.

Du Perron, Jacques Davy, *Reglemens faits par Monsieur le Cardinal du Perron . . . et messieurs les juges ordonnéz par le roy pour le générale réformation des hospitaux, maladeries et autres lieux pitoyables de ce royaume*, Paris, 1614.

[Edmondes, Thomas,] *Remonstrances faictes par l'ambassadeur de la Grande Bretagne au roy et à la royne sa mère, en juin 1615*, n.p., 1615.

Ennuis de paysans champestres, addresséz à la Royne Régente, n.p., 1614.

L'Espagnol françois, n.p., n.d.

Exhortation aux Parisiens et allegresse à tous bons françois, sur la déliberation et bonne volonté des princes envers nostre très-chrestien roy ... , Paris, 1614.

Extraict de l'inventaire que c'est trouvé dans le coffre de môsieur le Chevalier de Guise ... , n.p., 1615.

Extraict des registres de la cour touchant ce qu s'est passé en l'affaire de Monsieur d'Espernon, vingt-quatriesme novembre 1614, n.p., 1615.

Extraict des registres des Estats sur le réception du concile de Trente au royaume de France, n.p., n.d.

Le financier à messieurs des Estats, n.p., 1615.

Foucade aux Estats, n.p., 1615.

De France et de Espagne, n.p., 1614.

Fresneau, Jacques, *A messieurs des Estats en la chambre de la noblesse*, n.p., 1615.

Gazette des Estats et de ce temps du Sieg^r Gio servitour de Piera Grosa. Traduite d'Italien en François le premier janvier 1615., n.p., n.d.

[Gillot, Jacques,] *Le Caton françois au roy*, n.p., 1614.

La harangue de Achior l'Ammonite ... , n.p., 1614.

La harangue de Alexandre le Forgeron, prononcé au conclave des réformateurs, n.p., 1614.

Harangue de l'amateur de justice aux trois estats, n.p. 1615.

Henri III, *La harangue faicte par le roy ... le seizième jour d'octobre, 1588*, Paris, 1588.

Henri III, *Proposition faicte par le roy ... le vie décembre 1576*, Paris, 1576.

L'hermaphrodite de ce temps, n.p., n.d.

Humble suplication au roy pour le soulagement du tiers Estat, n.p., 1614.

L'image de la France représentée à messieurs des Estats avec la réfutation d'un libelle intitulé le Caton françois, faict contre ceux qui maintennent la religion et l'estat le tout devisé en trois parties, n.p., n.d.

I. [Jacques] B. [de Brouillart], *Discours d'Estat presenté au roy, sur les alliances de France et d'Espagne, tant vielles que nouvelles*, Paris, 1615.

James I, *Déclaration du serrenissime Roy Jacques I Roy de la Grand' Bretagne, etc. déffenseur de la foy. Pour le droict des rois et independance de leurs couronnes. Contre la harangue de l'illustrissime Cardinal du Perron* ... , n.p., 1615.

James I, *A Remonstrance of the Most Gratious King James I King of Great Britain, France and Ireland for the Right of Kings and the Independance of the Crownes against an Oration of the Most Illustrious Card. of Perron* ... , Cambridge, 1616.

299

J.L.P.S., *A Monseigneur le Prince*, n.p., n.d.

Jugement définitif donné par Mathault . . . , n.p., 1614.

Juvigny, Samson de Saint Germain, *sieur* de, *Quatre Propositions* . . . , Paris, 1618.

Lettre de Guillaume sans Peur envoyée aux desbandéz de la cour, n.p., 1615.

Lettre de Jacques Bonhomme paysan de Beauvais à Messeigneurs les Princes retirés de la cour, Paris, 1614.

Libre et salutaire discours des affaires de France . . . , Paris, 1615.

Libre discours et véritable jugement sur l'hérédité des offices insinuée en France, dans le doux venim du droict annuel, Paris, 1615.

Libre Harangue faicte par Mathault . . . , n.p., 1614.

Louis XIII, *Articles presentées au Roy par les députés de la chambre du Tiers Estat avec les responses de sa majesté*, Paris, 1615.

Louis XIII, *Lettre du Roy à Monseigneur le Prince*, n.p., 1615.

Louis XIII, *Response du Roy faicte au remonstrances . . . par le Sr. Edmondes* . . . , n.p., 1615.

Loyac, *L'eupheme*, n.p., n.d.

Manifeste de ce qui se passé dernièrement aux Estats généraux entre la clergé et le tiers Estat, n.p., 1615.

Marmiesse, Pierre, *Remonstrances sur l'exécution des délibérations prises en la chambre du tiers Estat pour le retranchement des tailles, communication des cahiers entre les trois chambres et pour la poursuite d'une Chambre de Justice contre les financiers* . . . , Paris, 1615.

Marquemont, Denis Simon de, *Harangue prononcée . . . a l'ouverture des Estats* . . . , n.p., 1615.

Médicis, Marie de, *Copie de la lettre escritte à Monsieur Desdiguie par la Royne*, n.p., 1614.

Médicis, Marie de, *Double de la response de la royne régente, mère du roy, à la lettre escritte à sa majesté, par le Prince de Condé, le 19 de février, 1614*, Paris, 1614.

Médicis, Marie de, *Lettre de la royne régente à messieurs du Parlement*, Paris, 1614.

Médicis, Marie de, *Lettre de la royne au Parlement de Bretagne*, Paris, 1614.

Mémoires adresséz à messieurs des Estats pour présenter à sa majesté contenants les fautes, abus, et malversations comises par les officiers de finance, partisans et payeurs des rentes en l'estendue de ce royaume, n.p., n.d.

A messieurs des Estats, n.p., n.d.

Miron, Robert, *Harangue prononcée devant le roy et la reyne . . . à la présentation du cahier du Tiers Estat* . . . , n.p., n.d.

Morgard, Noël Jean, *Le Manifeste de Noël Morgard* . . . , Paris, 1619.

Morgard, Noël Jean, *Prédiction de Morgard pour la présente année MDCXIV avec les centuries pour le mesme année*, n.p., n.d.

Morgard, Noël Jean, *Prophéties de maistre Noël Jean Morgard . . . en l'an 1600 . . .*, n.p., n.d.

La noblesse françoise au chancelier, n.p., n.d.

Noyer, François du, *Ce sont ici autres parties de plusiers autres moyens . . .*, Paris, 1614.

Noyer, François du, *Ce sont icy partie des moyens . . .*, Paris, 1614.

Noyer, François du, *Proposition, advis et moyens . . .*, Paris, 1614.

Orange, Prince of, *Lettre du Prince d'Orange en forme de remonstrance . . .* Paris, 1615.

Le pacifique pour la défence de Parlement, n.p., n.d.

[Pasquier, Nicolas,] *Remonstrances à la Royne mère . . .*, Paris, 1610.

Le patois Limousin, n.p., 1615.

Paul V, *Lettre de nostre S. père le Pape, escrite à messieurs de la noblesse députéz aux Estats généraux de ce royaume*, n.p., n.d.

Paul V, *Lettre de nostre S. père le Pape, escrite à messieurs du clergé députéz au Estats de ce royaume avec la réponce faicte par L.E.D.*, n.p., 1615.

[Pelletier,] *Apologie pour Monsieur le Prince de Condé sur son départ de la cour*, n.p., 1614.

Pelletier, *Lettre à Monseigneur le Prince de Condé*, n.p., n.d.

Première lettre de Messieurs de l'Assemblée de Grenoble . . . au Roy . . . et seconde au Roy et à la Royne, n.p., 1615.

Procèz verbal de tout de qui s'est passé en la chambre du Tiers Estat touchant le premier article de leur cahyer presenté au Roy, n.p., 1615.

Projet des principaux articles de la paix . . ., Paris, 1614.

Le protecteur des Princes . . ., n.p., 1615.

Du 14ᵉ jour de février 1614, Avis aux trois estats de ce royaume sur les bruits qui courlt à présent de la guerre civille, Blois, 1614.

Raisons pour l'opposition de messieurs du clergé et de la noblesse à l'article proposé par aucuns en la Chambre du Tiers Estat, n.p., 1615.

Le recontre du Caton et Diogne . . . sur le sujet des Estats tenus à Paris en l'année 1615, n.p., n.d.

Recueil d'un réponse du Tiers Estat rendue à la chambre de la noblesse . . ., Paris, 1615.

Réfutation du discours contre les mariages de France et d'Espagne, n.p., 1614.

Remerciements à la Royne . . ., Paris, 1614.

Remerciement de la France à Messieurs les députéz . . ., Paris, 1615.

Remerciement des Poules à Monsieur de Bouillon, n.p., n.d.

Remonstrances presentées au roi par nosseigneurs de Parlement le 21 mai 1615, n.p., 1615.

Le Réponse du crocheteur de la Samaritaine à Jacques Bonhomme . . ., Paris, 1614.

Requeste presentée au roy par les députés du Tiers Estat, n.p., 1615.

Les résolutions et arrestéz de la chambre du Tiers Estat touchant le premier article de leur cahier presenté au Roy, Paris, 1615.

Résultat de l'assemblée des Estats de Provence tenus à Aix du mois de Juin, n.p., 1615.

Résurrection et triomphe de la polette dédié à messieurs les officiers de France, Paris, n.d.

Le resjouissance de la France pour la réconciliation de messieurs les princes, Paris, 1614.

Le reseveil de Maistre Guillaume aux bruits de ce temps . . . , n.p., 1614.

Résolution à la paix et au service du Roy, Paris, 1614.

Le reveil du soldat français au Roy, Paris, 1614.

Ribbier, Guillaume, *Apologie de l'article premier du Tiers Estat,* n.p., 1615.

Richelieu, Armand Jean du Plessis de, *Harangue prononcée en la salle du Petit Bourbon, le xxiii février . . . ,* Paris, 1615.

Savaron, Jean, *Advis donnéz au roy par le président Savaron député du Tiers Estat d'Auvergne aux Estats généraux tenus à Paris l'an 1615 pour la réformation du royaume,* n.p., n.d.

Savaron, Jean, *Discours abrégé avec l'ordonnance entière du roy sainct Loys contre les duels . . . ,* Paris, 1614.

Savaron, Jean, *Les erreurs et impostures de l'Examen du traicté de M. Jean Savaron de la souveraineté du roy . . . ,* Paris, 1616.

Savaron, Jean, *Second traicté de la souveraineté du Roy . . . ,* Paris, 1615.

Savaron, Jean, *Traicté contre les duels, avec les ordonnances et arrests du roy sainct Loys . . . ,* Paris, 1614.

Savaron, Jean, *Traicté de l'annuel et venalité des offices . . . ,* Paris, 1615.

Savaron, Jean, *Traicté de la souvernaineté du Roy et de son royaume à messieurs les députéz de la noblesse . . . ,* Paris, 1615.

S.B.S., *Considérations sur l'estat de la France,* Paris, 1614.

Seianus françois au roy, n.p., n.d.

Senecey, Baron de, *Remerciement fait au nom de la noblesse . . . ,* Paris, 1588.

Senecey, Claude de Bauffremont, Baron de, *Proposition de la Noblesse,* Paris, 1577.

Sentence arbitrale de M. Guillaume . . . , n.p., 1614.

Servin, Louis, *Action des gens du roy sur la déclaration de Louys XIII roy de France et de Navarre séant en son lict de justice en sa cour de Parlement au jour de sa majorité,* Paris, 1615.

Sourdis, François, Cardinal de, *Response de Monsieur le Cardinal de Sourdis à la lettre de Monseigneur le Prince,* Paris, 1614.

Sully, Maximilien de Bethune, duc de, *Paralleles de César et de Henri le Grand,* Paris, 1615.

Les terreurs panniques de ceux qui pensent que l'alliance d'Espagne doive mettre la guerre en France, Paris, 1615.

Très humbles remonstrances faictes au roy par les thrésoriers de France … sur la continuation du droict annuel, Paris, 1615.

Très humbles réqueste au Roy sur la disposition de la Chambre de Justice par un officier des finances, n.p., 1615.

Le Triomphe de la Fleur de Lys …, Paris, 1614.

Vendôme, Duc de, *Lettre de Monsieur de Vendôme à la Royne*, Paris, 1614.

Vias, Balthazar de, *Harangue faicte au roy et la royne par Monsieur Balthazar de Vias, assesseur et député de la ville de Marseille aux Estats généraux de France*, Paris, 1615.

C. SECONDARY WORKS

A. BOOKS

Anquez, Léonce, *Henry IV et l'Allemagne d'après les mémoires et la correspondance de Jacques Bongars*, Paris, 1887.

Anquez, Léonce, *Histoire des assemblées politiques des réformés de France, 1573–1622*, Paris, 1859.

Artonne, A. et al., *Répertoire des statuts synodaux des diocèses de l'ancienne France du XIIIᵉ à la fin du XVIIIᵉ siècle*, Paris, 1963.

Ascoli, Georges, *La Grande Bretagne devant l'opinion française au XVIIᵉ siècle*, 2 vols. Paris, 1930.

Ashton, Robert, *The Crown and the Money Market, 1603–1640*, Oxford, 1960.

Aumale, Henri, duc d', *Histoire des Princes de Condé pendant les XVIᵉ et XVIIᵉ siècles*, vols. II–III, Paris, 1885.

Baasch, Ernst, *Hollandische wirtschaftsgeschichte*, Jena, 1927.

Baehrel, René, *Une croissance: la Basse Provence rurale*, Paris, 1961.

Balteau, J., et al., *Dictionnaire de Biographie Français*, Vols. I–XII, Paris, 1932–.

Baschet, Armand, *Le Roi chez la Reine ou histoire secrète du mariage de Louis XIII et d'Anne d'Autriche*, 2nd ed., Paris, 1866.

Battifol, Louis, *Marie de Médicis, and Her Court*, trans. Mary King, London, 1908.

Baudson, Emile, *Charles de Gonzaque, duc de Nevers de Rethel et de Mantoue, 1580–1637*, Paris, 1888.

Bitton, Davis, *The French Nobility in Crisis, 1540–1640*, Stanford, Calif., 1969.

Blaizot, P., *Jacques Germain*, Poitiers, 1906.

Blet, Pierre, S. J., *Le clergé de France et la monarchie*, 2 vols., Rome, 1959.

Bluche, François, and Durye, Pierre, *L'Anoblissement par charges avant 1789*, 2 vols., n.p., 1962.

Bluche, François and Durye, Pierre, *Les Honneurs de la Cour*, 2 vols., Paris, 1957.

Bondois, M., *Le Maréchal de Bassompierre, 1579–1646*, Paris, 1925.

Bouchitté, M., ed., *Négociations, lettres et pièces relatives à la conférence de Loudun*, Paris, 1862.

Boullée, Auguste, *Histoire complète des Etats généraux et autres assemblées représentatives de la France depuis 1302 jusqu'en 1626*, 2 vols., Paris, 1845.

Boutriche, *et al.*, *Histoire de Bordeaux de 1453 à 1715*, Bordeaux, 1966.

Broutin, Pierre, *La réforme pastorale en France au XVIIᵉ siècle*, 2 vols. Brussels, 1956.

Buisseret, David, *Sully and the Growth of Centralized Government in France, 1598–1610*, London, 1968.

Cadart, Jacques, *Le régime electoral des Etats généraux de 1789 et ses origines*, Paris, 1952.

Caraccioli, L. A., *Notice intéressante et curieuse des ouvrages satyriques que parurens à l'époque des Etats généraux tenus en 1614 . . .* , Paris, 1789.

Catalogue raisonné des ouvrages qui parurent en 1614 et 1615 à l'occasion des Etats, n.p., 1789.

De la Chenaye-Desbois and Badier, *Dictionnaire de la noblesse*, 3rd ed., 19 vols., Paris, 1863–1876.

Chudoba, Bhodan, *Spain and the Empire, 1519–1643*, Chicago, 1952.

Church, W. F., *Constitutional Thought in Sixteenth Century France*, Oxford, 1941.

Clamageran, J. J., *Histoire de l'impôt en France*, Vol. II, Paris, 1867.

Clancy, Thomas H., S. J., *Papist Pamphleteers*, Chicago, 1964.

Clarke, J. H., *Huguenot Warrior: The Life and Times of Henri de Rohan, 1579–1638*, The Hague, 1966.

Clark, G. N., and Eysinga, W. van, *The Colonial Conference between England and the Netherlands, 1613–1615*, 2 vols. Leiden, 1940–1951.

Clément-Simon, Gustave. ed., *Archives historiques de la Corrèze*, 2 vols. Paris, 1903–1905.

Cozzi, Gaetano, *Il Doge Nicolo Contarini*, Venice, 1958.

Dangibeaud, Charles, *Le présidial de Saintes, Raimond de Montagne*, Paris, 1881.

De Landine, A., *Des États généraux ou histoire des assemblées nationales en France*, Paris, 1788.

Delmas, André, *Le Pays de Terrasson*, n.p., 1963.

Desalles, Madame Bellaud, *Les évêques Italiens de l'ancien diocèse de Béziers, 1547–1669*, Paris, 1901.

Devic, Dom Claude and Vaissete, Dom Jean, *Histoire générale de Languedoc*, Vols. XI–XII, Paris, 1889.

Deyon, Pierre, *Amiens, capitale provinciale*, Paris, 1967.

Dickerman, Edmond H., *Bellièvre and Villeroy: Power in France under Henry III and Henry IV*, Providence R. I., 1971.

Dickerman, Edmund H., 'The Kings' Men: The Ministers of Henry III and Henry IV, 1574–1610', unpublished doctoral dissertation, Brown University, 1965.

Dietz, Frederick, *English Public Finance, 1415–1641*, Vol. II, 2nd ed., London, 1964.

Dollinger, Heinz, *Studien zur Finanzreform Maximilians I von Bayern in den Jahren 1598–1618*, Göttingen, 1968.

Doucet, Roger, *Les institutions de la France au XVIᵉ siècle*, 2 vols., Paris, 1948.

Dourmel, Jules, *Histoire général de Péronne*, Paris, 1879.

Elliott, J. H., *Imperial Spain, 1469–1716*, New York, 1964.

Encyclopédie, ou dictionnaire raisonné des sciences, des arts et des métiers, Vols. VI, XIV, XVI, XVII, Paris, 1751–1765.

Extrait du Journal de l'instruction publique no. 2, January 5, 1850.

Faure, Henri, *Histoire de Moulins*, Vol. I, n.p., 1900.

Félibien, Dom Michel, *Histoire de la ville de Paris*, ed. D. Guy-Alexis, Vol. II, Paris, 1725.

Feret, Pierre, *Le Cardinal Du Perron*, Paris, 1877.

Fouqueray, Henri, S.J., *Histoire de la Compagnie de Jésus en France, 1582–1763*, Vol. III, Paris, 1922.

Frondeville, Henri de, *Les conseillers du Parlement de Normandie*, 2 vols., Paris, 1960–1964.

Frondeville, Henri de, *Les présidents du Parlement de Normandie*, Rouen, 1953.

Gallia Christiana, 16 vols, Paris, 1715–1865.

Garreau, Albert, *Jean Pierre Camus*, Paris, 1968.

Gauchat, P., *Hierarchia Catholica Medii et Recentoris Aevi*, Vol. IV, Munster, 1935.

Godefroy, Theodore, *Le cérémonial françois*, ed. Denis Godefroy, Paris, 1649.

Goubert, Pierre, *Beauvais et le Beauvaisis de 1600 à 1730*, Paris, 1958.

Griselle, E., *Etat de la maison du roi Louis XIII et de celle de sa mère, Marie de Médicis*, Paris, 1912.

Griselle, E., *Supplement à la maison du roi Louis XIII*, Paris, 1912.

Gulik, G. van, *Hierarchia Catholica Medii et Recentoris Aevi*, Vol. III, Munster, 1923.

Haag, Emile and Eugène, *La France Protestante*, 10 vols., Paris, 1846–1859.

Hamilton, Earl, *American Treasure and The Price Revolution in Spain, 1501–1650*, Cambridge, Mass., 1934.

Harsin, Paul, *Crédit publique et banque d'état en France du XVIᵉ au XVIIᵉ siècle*, Paris, 1933.

Hayem, Fernand, *Le Maréchal d'Ancre et Leonora Galigai*, Paris, 1910.

Jourdain, Charles, *Histoire de la Université de Paris au XVIIᵉ siècle*, Paris, 1862.

Kierstead, Raymond F., *Pomponne de Bellièvre*, Evanston, 1968.

Labrousse, Ernest *et al.*, *Histoire économique et sociale de la France*, Vol. II, Paris, 1970.

Lacroix, Paul, *XVIIᵉ siècle: Institutions, usages et coutumes*, Paris, 1880.

Ladurie, Emmanuel Le Roy, *Histoire du climat depuis l'an mil*, Paris, 1967.

Ladurie, Emmanuel Le Roy, *Les paysans de Languedoc*, 2 vols., Paris, 1966.

La Rochefoucauld, G. de, *Le Cardinal François de la Rochefoucauld*, Paris, 1926.

Laugel, Auguste, *Henry de Rohan, son rôle politique et militaire sous Louis XIII*, Paris, 1889.

Lebel, Germaine, *La France et les Principautés Danubiennes du XVIᵉ siècle à la chute de Napoléon*, Paris, 1955.

Lee, Maurice, Jr., *James I and Henri IV*, Urbana, Ill., 1970.

Lekai, Louis, *The Rise of the Cistercian Strict Observance in Seventeenth Century France*, Washington, 1968.

Lemaire, André, *Les lois fondamentales de la monarchie française d'après les théoriciens de l'Ancien Régime*, Paris, 1907.

Le Sourd, A., *Essai sur les Etats du Vivarais, 1601–1789*, Paris, 1926.

Le Sourd, A., *Le personnel des Etats du Vivarais, 1601–1789*, Lyon, 1923.

Lewy, Guenter, *Constitutionalism and Statecraft during the Golden Age of Spain*, Geneva, 1960.

Lot, Ferdinand and Fawtier, Robert, *Histoire des institutions françaises au moyen âge*, Vols. I–II, Paris, 1957–1958.

Lousse, Emile, *La société de l'Ancien Régime*, Louvain, 1943.

Lublinskaya, A. D., *Frantsiya v nachale XVII veka 1610–1620*, Leningrad, 1959.

Lublinskaya, A. D., *French Absolutism: The Crucial Phase, 1620–1629*, trans. B. Pierce, Cambridge, 1968.

Luttin, D., *Recherches historiques sur la ville d'Orléans*, Orléans, 1837.

Lynch, John, *Spain under the Habsburgs*, Vol. II, Oxford, 1969.

Macki, J. D., *Negotiations between James VI and Ferdinand I, Grand Duke of Tuscany*, London, 1927.

Major, J. Russell, *The Deputies to the Estates General of Renaissance France*, Madison, 1960.

Major, J. Russell, *Representative Institutions in Renaissance France, 1421–1559*, Madison, 1960.

Mariéjol, J. H., *Henri IV et Louis XIII*, Vol. VI, Part 2 of *Histoire de France*, ed. E. Lavisse, Paris, 1905.

Mariéjol, Jean, *La vie de Marguerite de Valois*, Paris, 1928.

Marongiu, Antonio, *Medieval Parliaments: a Comparative Study*, trans. S. J. Woolf, London, 1968.

Martin, Victor, *Le gallicanisme et la réforme catholique*, Paris, 1919.

Martin, Victor, *Le gallicanisme politique et le clergé de France*, Paris, 1928.

Mastellone, S., *La Reggenza di Maria de' Medici*, Florence, 1962.

Maugis, E., *Histoire du Parlement de Paris*, Vols. II–III, Paris, 1916.

Mesnard, Pierre, *L'essor de la philosophie politique du XVIᵉ siècle*, Paris, 1936.

Meyniel, Joseph, *Le Président Jean Savaron, ses théories, ses ouvrages*, Paris, 1906.

Miron de l'Espinay, A., *François Miron et l'administration municipale de Paris sous Henri IV de 1604 à 1606*, Paris, 1885.

Miron de l'Espinay, A., *Robert Miron et l'administration municipale de Paris de 1614 à 1616*, Paris, 1922.

Morenas, Henri Jougla de, *Grand Armorial de France*, 7 vols., Paris, 1934–1952.

Mousnier, Roland, *La plume, la faucille et le marteau*, Paris, 1970.

Mousnier, Roland, *L'Assassinat de Henri IV*, Paris, 1966.

Mousnier, Roland, *La venalité des offices sous Henri IV et Louis XIII*, Rouen, n.d.

Mousnier, Roland, *et al.*, *Le conseil du roi de Louis XII à la Révolution*, Paris, 1970.

Mousnier, Roland, Labatut J.-P. and Durand, Y. *Problèmes de stratification sociale: Deux cahiers de la noblesse, 1649–1651*, Paris, 1965.

Mouton, L., *Le Duc et le Roi*, Paris, 1924.

Nouaillac, J., *Villeroy, Sécretaire d'état de ministre de Charles IX, Henri III et Henri IV*, Paris, 1909.

Olivier-Martin, François, *Histoire du droit français des origines à la révolution*, 2nd ed., Paris, 1951.

Ouvré, Henri, *Aubéry du Maurier, étude sur l'histoire de la France et de la Hollande, 1566–1636*, Paris, 1853.

Pagès, Georges, *Les institutions monarchiques sous Louis XIII et Louis XIV*, Paris, 1933.

Pagès, Georges, and Tapié, V. L., *Naissance du grand siècle, la France de Henri IV à Louis XIV, 1598–1661*, Paris, 1948.

Pansey, Henrion de, *Des Assemblées Nationales en France depuis l'établissement de la monarchie jusqu'en 1614*, Paris, 1829.

Perrens, François T., *L'église et l'état sous Henri IV et Marie de Médici*, 2 vols., Paris, 1862.

Perrens, François T., *Les mariages espagnols sous le règne de Henri IV et la régence de Marie de Médicis*, Paris, 1869.

Petit, Jeanne, *L'assemblée des notables de 1626–1627*, Paris, 1937.

Picot, Georges, *Histoire des Etats généraux considérés au point de leur influence sur le gouvernement de la France de 1355 à 1614*. 5 vols. 2nd ed., Paris, 1888.

Popkin, R. H., *The History of Scepticism from Erasmus to Descartes*, New York, 1968.

Posthumus, N. W., *Inquiry into the History of Prices in Holland*, 2 vols., Leiden, 1946, 1964.

Pouy, Ferdinand, *Concini, Maréchal d'Ancre, son gouvernement en Picardie*, Amiens, 1855.

Prat, Jean-Marie, S.J., *Recherches historiques et critiques sur la Compagnie de Jésus en France au temps du P. Coton*, Vols. III, V, Lyon, 1876–1878.

Prunel, Louis, *Sébastien Zamet*, Paris, 1912.

Rathery, E. J. B., *Histoire des Etats généraux de France*, Paris, 1845.

Raunie, Emile, *Epitaphier du vieux Paris, Histoire générale de Paris*, Vol. I, Paris, 1890.

Ravenez, L. W., *Histoire du Cardinal de Sourdis*, Bordeaux, 1867.

Roncière, G. de la, *Histoire de la marine française*, Vol. IV, Paris, 1923.

Rothkrug, Lionel, *Opposition to Louis XIV: the Political and Social Origins of the Enlightenment*, New York, 1965.

Rothrock, George, 'The French Crown and the Estates General of 1614', (unpublished doctoral dissertation, University of Minnesota, 1958).

Rott, E., *Henry IV, les suisses et la haute Italie*, Paris, 1882.

Rott, E., *Histoire de la représentation de la France auprès des cantons suisses, de leur alliés et de leurs confédérés, 1559–1619*, Vol. II, Berne, 1902.

Roupnel, Gaston, *La ville et la campagne au XVIIᵉ siècle*, Paris, 1955.

Serbat, Louis, *Les assemblées du clergé de France*, Paris, 1906.

Shennan, J., *The Parlement of Paris*, London, 1968.

Sipple, Cornelius, 'The Noblesse de la Robe in Early Seventeenth Century France: A Study in Social Mobility', unpublished Ph.D. dissertation, University of Michigan, 1962.

Sihula de la Vielleuze, Francisco, *Matrimonios de España y Francia en 1615*, Madrid, 1901.

Smith, L. P., *The Life and Letters of Sir Henry Wotton*, 2 vols., Oxford, 1907.

Soule, Claude, *Les Etats généraux de France, 1302–1789*, Heule, 1968.

Spooner, Frank, *L'Economie mondiale et les frappes monetaires en France, 1493–1680*, Paris, 1956.

Sutherland, N. M., *The French Secretaries of State in the Age of Catherine de Médici*, London, 1962.

Swart, K. W., *The Sale of Offices in the Seventeenth Century*, 's-Gravenhage, 1949.

Tapié, Victor-Lucien, *Politique étrangère de la France et le début de la Guerre de Trente Ans, 1616–1621*, Paris, 1934.

Thibaudeau, Antoine C., *Histoire des Etats-généraux et des institutions représentatives en France depuis l'origine de la monarchie jusqu'à 1789*, 2 vols, Paris, 1843.

Thierry, Augustin, *Essai sur l'origine et des progrès du tiers état*, Vol. III, Paris, 1863.

Tyrell, Joseph, *The History of the Estates of Poitou*, the Hague, 1968.

Vallette, Regis, *Catalogue de la Noblesse Française contemporaine*, Paris, 1959.

Veillet, Réné, *Recherches sur la ville et sur l'église de Bayonne*, Bayonne, 1910.

Viénot, J., *Histoire de la Réforme française*, Vol. II, Paris, 1934.

Vignes, J. B. Maurice, *Histoire des doctrines sur l'impôt en France*, 2nd ed., Padua, 1961.

Whitmore, P. J. S., *The Order of Minims in Seventeenth Century France*, The Hague, 1967.

Wolfe, Martin, *The Fiscal System of Renaissance France*, New Haven, 1972.

Zeller, Berthold, *Louis XIII, Marie de Médicis chef du conseil*, Paris, 1898.

Zeller, Berthold, *La minorité de Louis XIII, Marie de Médicis et Sully*, Paris, 1892.

Zeller, Berthold, *La minorité de Louis XIII, Marie de Médicis et Villeroy*, 1897.

C. ARTICLES

Alzon, Claude, 'Quelque observations sur les Etats Généraux de 1614', *Journées Internationales Paris, 1957*, Louvain, 1959, pp. 35–42.

Ashton, Robert, 'Deficit Finance in the Reign of James I', *Economic History Review*, series 2, X, 1957, 15–29.

Barbiche, Bernard, 'Une tentative de réforme monétaire à la fin de règne de Henri IV: l'édit d'août 1609', *XVIIᵉ siècle*, no. 61, 1963, 3–17.

Battifol, Louis, 'Le trésor de la Bastille de 1605 à 1611', *Revue Henri IV*, III, 1909, 200–209.

Baulant, Micheline, 'Le prix de grains à Paris de 1431 à 1788', *Annales, Economies, Sociétés, Civilisations*, XXIII, 1968, 520–540.

Baulant, Micheline, 'Le salaire des ouvriers du batiment à Paris de 1400 à 1726', *Annales: Economies, Sociétés, Civilisations*, XXVI, 1971, 463–483.

Bitton, Davis, 'History and Politics: The Controversy over the Sale of Offices in Early Seventeenth-Century France' in *Action and Conviction in Early Modern Europe*, ed. T. K. Rabb and J. E. Seigel, Princeton, 1969, pp. 390–403.

Blet, Pierre, 'L'article du Tiers aux Etats généraux de 1614', *Revue d'histoire moderne et contemporaine*, II, 1955, 81–106.

Boiteux, L. A., 'Un économiste méconnu du Noyer de Saint Martin et ses projects, 1608–1639', *Revue d'histoire des colonies*, XLIV, 1957, 5–68.

Braudel, F. P., and Spooner F., 'Prices in Europe from 1540 to 1750', *Cambridge Economic History*, IV., ed. E. E. Rich and C. H. Wilson, Cambridge, 1967, 378–486.

Chamberland, Albert, 'Le Budget de l'Epargne en 1607 d'après des documents inédits', *Revue Henri IV*, II, 1907–1908, 312–326.

Chamberland, Albert, 'La compatibilité imaginaire des deniers des coffres du roi et les dettes Suisses', *Revue Henri IV*, II, 1908, 50–64.

Charnay, Jean-Paul, 'Naissance et développement de la vérification des pouvoirs dans les anciennes assemblées françaises', *Revue historique du droit français et étranger*, series 4, XL, 1962, 556–589, XLI, 1963, 20–56.

Dangibaud, Charles, 'Louis de Bassompierre, évêque de Saintes', *Revue de Saintogne et d'Aunis*, XLV, 1933–1935, 76–86.

Deyon, Pierre, 'A propos des rapports entre la noblesse française et la monarchie absolue pendant la première moitié du XVIIᵉ siècle', *Revue Historique*, CCXXI, 1964, 341–356.

Doucet, Roger, 'Les finances de la France en 1614 d'après le Traicté du revenue et dépense des finances', *Revue d'histoire économique et sociale*, XVIII, 1930, 133–163.

Dubois, Jacques, O.S.B., 'La carte des diocèses de France avant la Révolution', *Annales: Economies, Sociétés, Civilisations*, XX, 1965, 680–691 and map.

Dumont, François, 'Recherches sur les ordres dans l'opinion française sous l'Ancien Régime', *Album Helen Maud Cam* (Louvain, 1960), I, 187–202.

Dumont, François, 'La représentation de l'ordre du clergé aux états francais', in *Journées internationales, Paris, 1957*, Louvain, 1957, pp. 43–49.

Dupré, A., 'Notice sur Guillaume Ribier, magistrat blésois', *Mémoires de la Société des sciences et lettres de Loire-et-Cher*, IX, 1874–1875.

Fagniez, G., *Une banque de France en 1608*, extracted from *Bulletin de la Société de l'histoire de Paris et de l'Ile de France*, 1896, pp. 1–8.

Forman, Marcelle, 'Henri-Louis Chasteigner de le Rocheposay, évêque de Poitiers (1612–1651)', *Bulletin de la Société des Antiquaires de l'Ouest et des Musées de Poitiers*, 1955, pp. 165–231.

François, Michel, 'La réception du Concile en France sous Henri III', *Il Concilio di Trento e la Riforme Tridentina*, Rome, 1965.

Gadille, Jacques, Julia, Dominque and Venard, Marc, 'Pour un répertoire des visites pastorales', *Annales: Economies, Sociétés, Civilisations*, XXV, 1970, 561–566.

Gallouedec-Genuys, Françoise, 'Fénelon et les Etats', *Album Helen Maud Cam*, Louvain, 1960, I, 277–290.

Halkin, L. E., 'Les statuts synodaux de l'ancienne France', *Revue d'Histoire Ecclésiastique*, LXII, 1967, 429–436.

Hauser, Henri, 'Les questions industrielles et commerciales de la ville et des communautés de Paris aux Etats Généraux de 1614', *Vierteljahrschrift für Sozial- und Wirtschaftgeschichte*, I, 1903, 372–396.

Hayden, J. Michael, 'Continuity in the France of Henry IV and Louis XIII; French Foreign Policy, 1598–1615', *Journal of Modern History*, XLV, 1973, 1–23.

Hayden, J. Michael, 'Deputies et *Qualités*: The Estates General of 1614', *French Historical Studies*, III, 4, 1964, 507–524.

Heumann, P., 'Un traitant sous Louis XIII, Antoine Feydeau' in *Etudes sur l'histoire administrative et sociale de l'Ancien Régime*, Paris, 1938, pp. 183–223.

Hickey, Daniel, 'Politics and Commerce in Renaissance France, the Evolution of Trade along the Routes of Dauphiné', in *Canadian Journal of History/ Annales canadiennes d'Histoire*, VI, 1971, 133–151.

Horniker, L., 'Anglo-French Rivalry in the Levant from 1583 to 1612', *Journal of Modern History*, XVIII, 1946, 289–305.

Kermaingant, Laffleur de, 'Sommes dues par Henri IV à l'Angleterre', *Revue Henri IV*, I, 2nd ed., 1912, 66–68.

Labouchère, G., 'Guillaume Ancel envoyé résident en Allemagne (1576–1613) d'après sa correspondance,' *Revue d'historie diplomatique*, XXVII, 1923, 160–188, 348–367.

Lassaigne, Jean-Dominique, 'Les revendications de la noblesse de France pendant la Fronde', *Album Helen Maude Cam*, Louvain, 1960, I, 267–275.

LeRoy, Gabriel, Note in *Revue des Sociétés savantes des Départements*, series 5, II, 1870.

Lublinskaya, A. D., 'Les Etats Généraux de 1614–1615 en France', *Album Helen Maude Cam*, Louvain, 1960, I, 229–245.

Magen, A., 'De l'intervention de la municipalité Parisienne en matière monetaire pendant le premier tiers du XVIIe siècle', *Revue Historique du droit français et étranger*, series 4, vol. XXXVIII, 1960, 43–448, 549–557.

Major, J. Russell, 'Henry IV and Guyenne: A Study concerning the Origin of Royal Absolutism', *French Historical Studies*, IV, 1966, 363–383.

Major, J. Russell, 'The Loss of Royal Initiative and the Decay of the Estates General in France, 1421–1615', *Album Helen Maude Cam*, Louvain, 1961, II, 245–259.

Major, J. Russell, 'The Payment of the Deputies to the French National Assemblies, 1484–1627', *Journal of Modern History*, XXVIII, 1955, 217–229.

Maurice-Amour, L., 'Les poésies de Malherbe et les musiciens de son temps', *XVIIe Siècle*, no. 31, 1956, 296–331.

Meuvret, Jean, 'Comment les Français voyaient l'impôt au XVIIᵉ siècle', *XVIIᵉ Siècle*, IV, 1955, 59–82.

Meuvret, Jean, 'Les oscillations des prix des céréales aux XVIIᵉ et XVIIIᵉ siècles en Angleterre et dans les pays du Bassin Parisien', *Revue d'histoire moderne et contemporaine*, XVI, 1969, 540–554.

Morineau, Michel, 'D'Amsterdam à Seville: de quelle réalité l'histoire des prix est-elle le mirroir', *Annales: Economies, Sociétés, Civilisations*, XXIII, 1968, 178–205.

Mousnier, Roland, 'Le conseil du roi de la mort de Henri IV au gouvernment personnel de Louis XIV', *Etudes publiés par la Société d'histoire moderne*, I, 1947, 29–67.

Mousnier, Roland, 'Les règlements du conseil du roi sous Louis XIII', *Annuaire-Bulletin de la Société de l'histoire de France*, 1946, 92–211.

Parker, David, 'The Social Foundation of French Absolutism, 1610–1630', *Past and Present*, no. 53, 1971, 67–89.

Pérouas, Louis, 'La réforme Catholique au diocèse du Maillezais dans le premier quart de XVII siècle', *La Revue de Bas-Poitou* LXIX, 1958, 340–346.

Poulbrière, J. B., 'Les députés du Limousin et de la Marche aux divers Etats généraux de France', *Bulletin de la Société scientifique, historique et archéologique de la Corrèze*, 1890, pp. 293–321.

Richet, Denis, 'Croissance et blocages en France du XVᵉ au XVIIIᵉ siècle', *Annales: Economies, Sociétés, Civilisations*, XXIII, 1968, 759–787.

Rivière, Benjamin, 'Le tiers aux Etats généraux de 1614', *Mémoires de la Société d'agriculture, sciences et arts du Département du Nord*, series 3, V, 1893–1894, 227–339.

Rothrock, George, 'The French Crown and the Estates General of 1614', *French Historical Studies*, I, 1960, 295–318.

Schürr, Alexandre, 'La politique de Henri IV en Suède et en Pologne, 1602–1610', *Revue Henri IV*, II, 1908, 25–33.

Stocker, Christopher, 'Office as Maintenance in Renaissance France', *Canadian Journal of History/Annales Canadiennes d'Histoire*, VI, 1, 1971, 21–43.

Thomas-Lacroix, P., 'Les Bretons aux Etats généraux de 1614', *Mémoires de la Société d'histoire et de archéologie de Bretagne*, XV, 1934, 1–14.

Trevor-Roper, H. R., 'Spain and Europe, 1598–1621', in *New Cambridge Modern History*, Cambridge, 1970, IV, 260–282.

Veyrassat-Herren, Beatrice and Ladurie, E. Le Roy, 'Le rente foncière autour de Paris au XVIIᵉ siècle', *Annales: Economies, Sociétés, Civilisations*, XXIII, 1968, 541–555.

INDEX

absolutism, development of, 1–2, 130 n.,
    131–135, 139–146, 168, 197, 216–218
Achard, Antoine, deputy Third Estate, 278
Addled Parliament, 1
advisers of Marie de Médicis, definition of,
    10 n.
Aerssen, François van (1572–1641),
    ambassador of the Netherlands to France,
    49 n., 55 n.
Agenois, *sénéchaussée* of: deputies, 241, 256,
    272; *cahiers*, 205 n.
aides, 61, 180, 183, 193, 212, 221 n.
Aix-en-Provence, prices in, 226, 227, 228,
    229
Albert, Archduke of Austria (1559–1621),
    ruler of Spanish Netherlands, 40, 43, 46,
    170 n.
Albert, *sénéchaussée* of, deputies, 242, 257,
    273
Alençon, *bailliage* of, deputies, 240, 255, 271
Alexandre, Nicolas, deputy Third Estate, 272
ambassadors of France, *see* Ancel, Boderie,
    Boissise, Brèves, Brûlart, Buisseaux,
    Coeuvres, Rambouillet, Sainte
    Catherine, Vaucelas, Villiers-Saint
    Georges
ambassadors to France, *see* Aerssen, Asini,
    Bartolini, Botti, Cardenas, Carew,
    Contarini, Edmondes, Ubaldini; relative
    worth of correspondence, 45 n., 56 n.,
    135 n., 149 n.
Amboise, *bailliage* of, deputies, 249,
    264, 281
Amboise, Charles d', deputy Second Estate,
    95 n., 259
Amiens, *bailliage* of: elections, 73 n.; deputies,
    246, 260, 277
Ancel, Guillaume (d. 1615), French diplomat
    in Germany, 1576–1612, 49 n., 57–58
Ancre, Maréchal d', *see* Concini
Andrault de Langeron, Jean, deputy Second
    Estate, 266
Angennes, Charles d', deputy Second Estate,
    96, 112, 265
Angennes, Charles d', *see* Rambouillet

Angennes, Jacques d' (1574–1647), deputy
    First Estate, 93, 96, 239
Angenoust, Bernard, deputy Third Estate,
    275
Angers, city of, *cahier*, 201 n.
Angers, diocese of, *cahier*, 199 n., 201, 202,
    208
Anglebermer, Emanuel d', deputy Second
    Estate, 259
Anglicans, 133, 135 n., 143
Angoulême, *sénéchausseée* of, deputies, 249,
    264, 281
Anjou, *sénéchaussée* of: elections, 75 n.;
    deputies, 249, 264, 280; *cahiers*, 205 n.
Anne of Austria (1601–1666), wife of Louis
    XIII, 21, 41, 58 n., 171
Anquetil, Henri, deputy Second Estate, 255
Anzeray, François, deputy Second Estate,
    255
Apchier, Jean d', deputy First Estate,
    248
Apchon, Jacques d', deputy Second Estate,
    96 n., 263
Apchon, Jean d' (d. c. 1620), deputy Second
    Estate, 96 n., 263
Aquaviva, Claudio (1543–1615), general of
    the Jesuits, 133
Argy, René d', deputy Second Estate, 264
Arles, city of, deputies, 247, 262, 278
Armagnac, *sénéchaussée* of, deputies, 242,
    257, 273
Armuet, François (d. 1649?), deputy First
    Estate, 247
Arnauld, Antoine (1560–1619), member of
    Parlement of Paris, 136, 156
Arnauld, Isaac (1567–1617), intendant of
    finances, 13
Arnauld d'Andilly, Robert (1588–1674),
    author of memoirs, 105 n.
Arnaut, Coste, deputy Third Estate, 280
Artois, Estates of, 1
Asini, Luca degli, representative in France of
    Dowager Grand Duchess of Tuscany:
    letters from, 142 n., 145 n., 149 n.;
    value of letters, 45 n.

313

Fresneau, Jacques, and sea trade, 195 n.
Frottier, Gaspart, deputy Second Estate, 263

gabelles, 19, 27, 29, 30, 119, 128, 180, 181, 183, 187, 193, 197, 205, 209, 212
Galigai, Léonora (1568–1617), 13, 15, 32 n., 55 n., 172
Galigai, Sébastien Dori, 32 n.
Galilei, Galileo (1564–1642), 218
Gallicanism, 93, 99, 111, 130, 132, 133, 134, 135, 136, 149, 156, 157, 168, 175, 177, 183
Gallière, Daniel de, deputy Third Estate, 79, 276
Ganay, Claude de (d. 1633), deputy Third Estate, 270
Gascoing, Etienne, deputy Third Estate, 280
Gassot, Jules, secretary of the king, 119 n., 193 n.
Gaucher, Julien, deputy Third Estate, 281
Gautier, Jacques, deputy Third Estate, 280
Gaymaduc, Tomas de, deputy Second Estate, 258
Gegado, Jean de, deputy Second Estate, 258
Gélas, Claude (1564–1630), deputy First Estate, 111, 153, 241
General Agents of the Clergy, 82, 89, 251
general crisis theory, 70
Genest, Jean, deputy First Estate, 251
Genouillac (de Vaillac), Jean de (1575?–1652), deputy First Estate, 243
Gérard, François, deputy First Estate, 251
Germain, Jacques (1568–1620), deputy Third Estate, 271
Gervais, René, deputy Third Estate, 269
Gex, bailliage of: deputies, 239, 254, 270; cahier, 199 n.
Gien, bailliage of, deputies, 250, 265, 283
Gilbert, Etienne (de), deputy Third Estate, 277
Gilbertès, Antoine de (d. 1639), deputy First Estate, 247–248
Gisors, bailliage of, deputies, 240, 255, 271
Gissey, François de, deputy Third Estate, 269
Glandèsves, Toussaint de (1579–1647?), deputy First Estate, 96, 111, 247
Glandèves, Théocrenes de, deputy Second Estate, 96, 262
Gondi, Henri de (d. 1622), deputy First

Estate, 88, 147 n., 234
Gondin, Louis de, deputy Third Estate, 276
Gondomar, Diego Sarmiento de Acuña (1567–1626), count of, Spanish ambassador to England, 48 n., 71 n., 118 n.
Goualt, Claude de, deputy First Estate, 96, 243
Goualt, Guy, deputy Third Estate, 274; relationship, 96; president Breton delegation, 111 n.; letters on Estates General, 101 n., 120 n., 134 n., 207 n.; description of opening of Estates General, 105 n.; copy of First Article of the Third Estate, 132 n.; description of closing of Estates General, 159 n.
Goujon, Jean, deputy Third Estate, 278
Goujon, Raimond de, deputy Third Estate, 273
Gramont, Antoine de (d. 1644), deputy Second Estate, 96 n., 257
Grand Design (of Sully), 34, 39, 148
Grand, François de, deputy Third Estate, 275
grands, les, 11, 17, 34, 54, 56, 94, 98, 124, 167 n.; see also Condé, Bouillon
Greysolon, Claude, deputy Third Estate, 279
Grillet, Albert de, deputy First Estate, 239
Grollier, Charles, deputy Third Estate, 278
Guemadeue, Tomas de, see Gaymaduc
Guérin, Jean, deputy Third Estate, 79, 272
Guise, Charles de Lorraine (1571–1640), duke of, 55, 59, n., 171
Gustavus II Adolphus, king of Sweden (1611–1632), 6
Guyenne, gouvernement of: elections, 73, 79, 81, 86; deputies, 82–85, 89–91, 95, 97 n., 240–243, 256–258, 271–274; cahiers, 199, 201 n., 202, 203, 207; action in First Estate, 129; action in Second Estate, 129, 130; action in Third Estate, 111 n., 119, 129, 134, 138, 145, 146
Guyenne, sénéchaussée of: deputies, 240–241, 256, 271; cahiers, 199 n., 200, 201 n., 202, 203

Habert, Pierre (d. 1636), deputy First Estate, 236
Habsburgs, 1, 2, 34, 35, 37, 38, 41, 42, 44, 47, 48, 52
Hallé, Jacques (d. 1632), deputy Third Estate,